COLORADO GUIDE FLIES

COLORADO GUIDE FLIES

Patterns, Rigs, and Advice from the State's Best Anglers and Guides

PAT DORSEY

HEADWATER BOOKS

STACKPOLE BOOKS

Published by
HEADWATER BOOKS
PO Box 202
Boiling Springs, PA 17007
www.headwaterbooks.com

STACKPOLE BOOKS
4501 Forbes Boulevard, Suite 200
Lanham, Maryland 20706
www.stackpolebooks.com

Distributed by NATIONAL BOOK NETWORK

First edition

Cover design by Wendy A. Reynolds
Cover image by Mark Adams
Photos by the author except where noted

ISBN 978-1-934753-33-0

Library of Congress Control Number: 2015940063

Printed in India

To Jonathan Keisling, Charlie Meyers, Kevin Gregory, and Tom Whitley—
I am forever grateful for your support and streamside companionship.
The angling community misses each one of you.

CONTENTS

ACKNOWLEDGMENTS

I would like to thank all the fly shop owners, fly manufacturers, fly tiers, and professional guides that have submitted flies for this book. Without your dedication to detail and hard work, this endeavor would not have been possible. I would especially like to thank Brian Schmidt, Fly Production Specialist at Umpqua Feather Merchants, for his continued support of and commitment to this project. Brian submitted dozens of his company's top-selling flies for Colorado and shared valuable information on fly-tying materials, recipes, and the histories and originators of many of these patterns. I would like to also thank Ray Chang from Solitude Fly Company for providing his company's top-selling patterns and recipes for Colorado. I am confident that these time-tested patterns and their corresponding recipes will be greatly appreciated by readers.

Thank you to all the professional guides who spent their precious days off with me and Mark Adams, allowing us to capture the images seen on these pages. We greatly appreciate your willingness to work with us, and we are especially thankful for all the fishing knowledge you have shared with us. Thank you to Robert "The Bug Guy" Younghanz for lending his expertise on aquatic entomology. It's comforting to know that the information in this book is accurate and up to date.

Thank you to Jay Nichols for having the vision to produce this book. Nichols' fly photography is the backbone of this book, allowing fly tiers to re-create these works of art. I appreciate all the other supporting images you have contributed too. Your photography is an inspiration to me. I know editing the text was no easy task; thanks for your expertise and your hard work at making this book clear and concise. I also would like to thank Tim Gahr, editorial assistant at Stackpole Books, for his hard work.

I want to express my deepest gratitude to Mark Adams for capturing the stunning images you'll find throughout this book. Mark, you are in a league of your own when it comes to flash photography! Thanks for your photo-coaching, your post-processing tips, and the guidance along the way. You're a mentor in the truest form of the word, and I appreciate your willingness to share your photography knowledge with me. Our mini-vacations through Trout Country have been special to me; thanks for all the memories!

Finally, none of this would have been possible without the support of my family. Kim, Forrest, Zach, Hunter, Nicole, and Michael, I appreciate your patience and understanding while I traveled throughout Colorado, gathering all the information I needed for this book. Thanks for allowing me to spend hours behind my computer, editing photos, writing text, and answering emails and phone calls as I brought this project together.

INTRODUCTION

Colorado Guide Flies: Rigs, Patterns, and Advice from the State's Best Anglers and Guides is a project that is long overdue. For quite some time, I've wanted to compile a fly-pattern book that would help anglers match Colorado's hatches. My objectives were greater than simply collecting the latest and greatest trout flies and providing tying recipes; I wanted to take it a step further and focus on presentation and matching the hatch from a fly designer's perspective. It didn't take me long to figure out that this was going to be a huge undertaking and that I was going to need some help.

For over twenty-five years, I have had the opportunity to work with some with the best anglers and fly-fishing guides in Colorado. It made complete sense to involve these individuals in my new project. For three years, I traveled throughout Colorado, spending time with these experts and learning their tricks of the trade. Each member of this fly-fishing fraternity has contributed valuable information; they shared their proven, time-tested flies, along with tying tips, fishing methods, and expertise on how to best match Colorado's hatches. My traveling companion Mark Adams and I captured images along the way to help tell the story.

I began this endeavor by collecting over six hundred flies—a combination of new, cutting-edge guide flies, mixed and matched with some of the more classic patterns. Due to space constraints, I do not include many of the tried-and-true patterns such as the Royal Wulff, but that does not mean that they are not "guide" flies or are any less effective. In fact, many of the old standards are often neglected by anglers and

Fly tiers like Charlie Craven have changed the fly-fishing industry by producing realistic-looking patterns that have been tested rigorously on Colorado's best trout streams and stillwater impoundments. "My biggest innovation driver is improvement," says Craven. "Tying a fly that sinks quicker, floats better, is more durable to tie and fish, looks more like the real thing, maybe quicker to tie than existing patterns . . . all of these things spur my pattern development." JAY NICHOLS

therefore tend to work very well on pressured waters. Over two years, I amassed an impressive variety of patterns, comprising everything from tiny dry flies to large streamers and all the flies in between. Master fly tiers and renowned guides statewide have contributed their favorite patterns, some of which have been "secret weapons" until now. It is important to note that these patterns are the pros' picks, and they are time-tested patterns that have been plucked from the jaws of countless trout. Every pattern has been cataloged with a picture and tying recipe.

Colorado is known for its innovative fly designers. Many of these creative tiers are Signature Fly Designers for Umpqua Feather Merchants in Louisville, Colorado. The company currently has in excess of 150 Signature Fly Designers, with approximately forty of them residing in Colorado. I am proud to be part of that team of professionals. Fly manufacturers Solitude Fly Company, Pacific Fly Group, and Montana Fly Company also have several tiers who reside in Colorado. These companies (or some of their fly designers) have submitted patterns for this book.

Anglers across Colorado reap the benefits of these tiers' creativity. Their unique patterns have been field-tested rigorously in many of the state's well-known tailwaters and freestones, including the Frying Pan, Roaring Fork, Taylor, Gunnison, Blue, Colorado, Williams Fork, Cache La Poudre, and Arkansas Rivers, and along the South Platte in Cheesman Canyon, Elevenmile Canyon, and the Charlie Meyers State Wildlife Area. Patterns like the Copper John, Barr Emerger, Jujubaetis, Black Beauty, Rojo Midge, RS 2, Brassie, and Buckskin were designed by Colorado tiers to fool some of the most selective trout in the United States.

I have had the good fortune to spend time with some of the country's best fly designers including Charlie Craven, John Barr, Rick Takahashi, Greg Garcia, Dr. Eric Pettine, Steve Parrott, and Jim Cannon, to name only a few, trying to gain a better understanding of how they use their innovation to create super-effective patterns. I found it interesting to learn about what goes through their minds when they're designing new patterns to fool selective trout.

Oddly enough, none of the tiers that I talked to set out to invent something—new patterns are instead created through experimentation, time on the water, and the desire to improve existing patterns. Most of their designs are works in progress until they come up with the final fly that meets all their criteria.

One of the biggest breakthroughs for today's tier is the assortment of new synthetic fly-tying materials that are available. "Some of my patterns evolved from patterns I tied more than forty years ago," Pettine says. "The Tungsten Pyrite Caddis was first tied for the [Cache la] Poudre in 1969, though beads were added later. My stonefly nymph is also about forty years old. Like most of our flies they continue to evolve with newer materials and more modern ideas."

With these modern-day advancements, designing flies now entails more than tying with natural furs and feathers; creativity is fostered through the wealth of available synthetics, experimentation, and the observing the way these materials perform in and on the water. The main goal is to come up with something that looks natural to the fish, matches the hatch, breathes life, is durable, and most of all, catches fish.

"I like to tinker with things. Having had the chance to tie as many different types and styles of flies as I have, it has given me a pretty large toolbox and goody bag to work from," Craven says. "Taking techniques from steelhead and salmon flies and adding them to trout and saltwater patterns, using common materials in uncommon ways (such as Super Hair for the Jujubee Midge and Jujubaetis) and just being on the lookout for a better way to do things, is what really keeps me hot on the vise. Once I get an idea for a pattern with a new technique or material, I seem to endlessly tweak it here and there. One of the hardest things about a new fly is knowing when to call it finished. As far as I am concerned, they're never finished. There's always something out there, or soon to be out there, that can be added or substituted to make it better. I do know that when I come up with something that pleases my eye, catches fish, holds together, and makes people happy, it makes me happy too!"

Creative fly tiers like Chris Johnson are producing realistic patterns from a wide array of materials including natural furs, feathers, and a full spectrum of synthetic options.

John Barr has a similar philosophy: "I am a results-oriented fly tier. All of my patterns start with an idea that pops into my mind while I am fishing. A new pattern goes through hook and material changes and extensive field-testing before I am happy with it. There are more failures than successes but when I introduce a new fly it is already a proven pattern."

Rick Takahashi, coauthor of *Modern Midges* and *Modern Terrestrials*, takes a slightly different approach. "When designing and tying flies, I follow a Japanese philosophy called *shibui*, [which] when translated refers to an aesthetic approach to design that incorporates simple, subtle, and unobtrusive beauty," Takahashi explains. "Being an artist, I have come to appreciate the minimalist approach of Japanese art; I try to incorporate the same sense of design into tying flies. Some of the patterns I tie may incorporate many tying steps and may be more intricate in design, but I always try to reduce the steps and materials to make a functional pattern."

For Takahashi, a functional fly is one that is crafted well. "Craftsmanship is a very important element in the production of my flies. I've always taught that poor craftsmanship can ruin a good design and vice versa," Takahashi says. "I try to tie each fly and succeeding fly better than the last. I try to give respect to each fly I tie by tying it well . . . if not, I cut all materials off and start over. I'm an impressionist type of fly tier in that I try to give the fish an impression of a live, moving insect rather than an exact replica. I try to incorporate movement whenever possible and will try to establish features that might catch the trout's interest."

This book is broken down into chapters addressing midges, mayflies, caddisflies, stoneflies, as well as chapters on terrestrials and another category that includes egg patterns, aquatic worms, scuds, *Mysis* shrimp. Anglers should keep the same hatch-matching objectives in mind when they're trying to imitate these important trout foods. While you're not technically "matching the hatch," you are matching a predominant food organism based on the prevailing conditions.

My intention for each chapter is to provide readers with a refresher course on aquatic entomology and to pass along tips for matching Colorado hatches. To get the maximum benefit from this book, you should be able to decipher the difference between different life cycle stages of a given insect and most importantly, be competent enough to choose the appropriate fly to match the specific stage of development during a hatch. Tying tips and other recommendations are included in each chapter to help you improve your skills, organize your fly boxes, and compile the ultimate Colorado fly selection. The fly plates and tying recipes conclude each corresponding chapter.

The next phase of compiling the book was spending time on the river with Colorado's best fishing guides. My goal was to fish with a veteran guide in several of the state's watersheds. For instance, I fished with Steve Henderson on the Yampa, Bob Dye on the upper Colorado, Chris Wells on the Williams Fork, Will Sands on the Frying Pan, Matt Thomas on the Roaring Fork and lower Colorado, Greg Blessing in Elevenmile Canyon, John Perizzolo on Spinney Reservoir, Landon Mayer at Spinney Mountain Ranch in Charlie Meyers State Wildlife Area, Jason Booth on the Gunnison, Josh Cranson in the Gunnison Gorge, Greg Felt on the Arkansas, and Aaron Carithers on the San Juan. This all-star lineup was willing to share valuable information, knowledge that only comes from decades of hard fishing and guiding. Their tricks, tips, and techniques are interspersed throughout the book.

Colorado guides are faced with the challenge of getting their paying customers to catch fish 365 days a year. As you might imagine, this is not always an easy task! Many variables can affect a fishing day: changing flows, water clarity, unpredictable weather, fishing pressure, a lack of hatches, temperature fluctuations, and the angler's ability to execute the proper fish-catching techniques. The stakes are high for a guide when a customer pays for a good day on the water.

Exceptional guides are few and far between. A passion for fly fishing and the outdoors is one of the key ingredients to becoming a good guide. You cannot fake passion, or your love for the outdoors—you either have it or you don't. Some guides have an innate "fishiness" about them that quickly becomes evident when you spend time on the water with them. The best guides do their homework before each trip (research flows, hatches, and current conditions), know their rivers intimately, love to teach, and work hard all day. After a long, tough day on the stream, many guides tie flies in the evening to prepare for the next day.

A seasoned guide will stack the odds in his or her customer's favor, trying to match the angler's abilities with the prevailing conditions. Bob Dye, a colleague of mine at the Blue Quill Angler, sums it up best: "No matter what happens at the end of the day, good or bad, you're still the guide! You can make up all the excuses you want, but at the day's end, [you] have to be accountable." So then, what do guides do when fishing is tough or slow? What do they do when nothing discernible is hatching? What are their go-to guide flies? How do they handle intense fishing pressure? How do they rig their rods for nymphing, dry flies, dry-and-droppers, and streamers?

I think you get my point. Part of my game plan for this book is to reveal the answers to these questions, providing readers sophisticated information on how the best guides in Colorado rig their rods for a variety of fishing situations. Choosing the right fly doesn't always guarantee you'll catch fish. It is important to understand that the presentation, or how the fly is fished, is often the underlying factor for success. For instance, if trout are keying on emerging *Baetis*, dead-drifted nymphs may not be the best approach. Allowing your nymphs to swing in the current may be a better tactic, and swinging a soft hackle might be your best option. Fishing an adult caddis on the dead drift will certainly fool a few trout, but oftentimes, skating or skittering a caddis will produce better results.

I'm sure you've fished near a guide or a seasoned angler that is hooking and landing a lot of fish. There is nothing more frustrating than watching someone catch fish after fish, especially when you are struggling. I bet you've wondered what pattern they were using. Or better yet, you've probably speculated how they were rigged (fly spacing, weight, indicator depth) and exactly what they were doing to consistently catch fish. More times than not, it's the nuances that make the

Anglers can shorten their learning curve by spending a day or two on the river with a veteran guide like Jason Booth. A seasoned guide will teach you basic entomology, fly selection, and most importantly, the tactics and techniques required to catch fish on his or her favorite watersheds. MARK ADAMS

biggest difference in fooling trout. I've included helpful tidbits from the state's best anglers and guides in the hope that you will reduce this frustration and improve your thought processes and your productivity.

Reading the water is another essential skill that cannot be overemphasized. You can have the best gear and flies available, but if you are not fishing the correct water, your success diminishes quickly. Trout are not randomly spread out in the stream; they position themselves in strategic places called lies, or in areas that provide the fish with the greatest amount of food while expending the least amount of energy. It is important to understand that not all lies are feeding lies, and these strategic locations change with the season, hatches, water temperatures, and flows. My goal is to put you in the right place with the right flies when a hatch becomes evident, and for you to be able execute the correct tactics and techniques to consistently catch fish.

The chapter on rigs and fishing strategies covers a wide range of nymphing, dry-fly, and streamer tactics. In spending time on the water with nearly two dozen guides, I was exposed to numerous techniques and terminal tackle preferences in tandem rigs, leaders, tippets, strike indicators, weights (split shot versus putty alternatives), dry-fly setups, floatant options, streamer rigs, and many more. These tactics and strategies varied greatly depending on the watershed.

Aaron Carithers, owner of Anasazi Anglers in Durango, is a master when it comes to midge fishing. I have picked his brain for his tactics for fishing midge pupae on the San Juan River. Matt Miles is one of the best dry-fly fishermen I know. He has been gracious enough to lend his expertise on dry-fly fishing. Guides like Steve Henderson and Chris Wells shared their extensive knowledge on streamer fishing, while Matt Thomas and Jason Booth shared tips for success on a freestone stream like the Roaring Fork. Landon Mayer and Greg Blessing provided excellent information for improving your skills on tailwaters. These tips and dozens more are included.

I conclude with a contributor's section featuring the numerous guides that participated in this book. Included are their bios and contact information. Each angler has been extremely helpful, unselfishly providing information that will no doubt help thousands of anglers. Please patronize their businesses and let them know how much you appreciate the time and effort they expended on this project.

My goals for *Colorado Guide Flies: Rigs, Patterns, and Advice from the State's Best Anglers and Guides* will have been met if you somehow benefit from this information. I hope you will learn a wealth of knowledge pertaining to fly selection, matching the hatch, rigging, and presentation, and that you get hours of enjoyment from tying flies while using the fly plates and tying recipes as a handy benchside reference.

CHAPTER 1

Seasonal Strategies

For as long as I can remember, I've been mesmerized by moving water, trout fishing, and tying flies. I was fortunate enough to be born and raised in Colorado, which had its fair share of perks. I caught and landed my first trout with my father, Jim Dorsey, in the Gunnison Valley when I was ten years old. That first trout ignited an undying love for the outdoors and a passion for fly fishing that ultimately led me to a career in the fly-fishing industry.

My grandfather, dad, and uncle were all passionate anglers. My grandfather taught me to be patient and methodical on a trout stream. My uncle Jim Cantrall taught me how to tie my first fly, which further spiked my interest in fly fishing. I came to believe early on that catching a fish on a fly you tied was the pinnacle of the sport. As I was growing up, my dad and grandpa always made it a point to let me tag along on their annual pilgrimages to the Gunnison Valley, where they fished

Colorado is known for its world-class tailwaters. Fishing the South Platte River in Elevenmile Canyon should be on everyone's bucket list.

The fabled Mother's Day Caddis Hatch on the Arkansas begins during the latter part of April and continues through the first part of May. If Mother Nature and spring runoff are willing to cooperate, this hatch can produce some of the best dry-fly fishing of the year.

the Taylor, East, and Gunnison Rivers as well as many of the smaller creeks in the area.

By the time I was sixteen, my dad had exposed me to a number of Colorado's best trout streams. Colorado has a wide array of angling possibilities from small creeks to large, untamed freestones. The stillwater (lake) fishing in Colorado is not shabby either: the Black Lakes, on the top of Vail Pass, were among our favorites, and Spinney, Elevenmile, Antero, and Delaney Butte continue to be among the favorite destinations for stillwater enthusiasts. Dad and I fished a lot of lakes and beaver ponds and we caught fish consistently with Uncle Jim's Gray Hackle Yellow and Swayback Ant.

Colorado is especially known for its deep, bottom-release tailwaters that support a rich and diversified aquatic life. Tailwaters are best defined as those rivers that flow from beneath manmade impoundments called dams. They provide anglers with a four-season fishery that affords consistent flows, clear water, large populations of trout, and dependable hatches. A phenomenon referred to by aquatic biologists as "winter warm and summer cool" results in warmer releases (in comparison to a freestone stream) in the winter and cooler outflows during the summer.

Freestone, or unregulated, trout streams (those unimpeded by dams) offer excellent fishing during certain times of the year too, but they are consistently inconsistent—clarity, water temperature, flows, and hatches all vary. That's not to mention they can be jammed with ice for several weeks, if not months, during the winter. Freestones do provide adequate fishing in the winter during warm-weather trends and dependable fishing during the spring and fall shoulder seasons. Anglers will find reliable hatches and good dry-fly fishing during the post-runoff season. Bouncing back and forth between Colorado's best tailwaters and freestones, based on the prevailing conditions, will typically yield the best results.

Dry-fly enthusiasts will find reliable hatches year-round on most of Colorado's tailwaters. Midges hatch day in and day out, therefore anglers should familiarize themselves with all stages of their life cycle. Matching the hatch often involves imitating a specific stage in the midge's development, which can be challenging at times.

Mayfly hatches begin as early as mid-March in some watersheds with the emergence of Blue-Winged Olives (BWOs). The *Baetis* mayflies, which encompass Blue-Winged Olives, Blue Duns, and Blue Quills, are the first mayflies to hatch in the spring and the last to hatch during the autumn. There are always exceptions to the rule, however: for instance, the Arkansas River below Pueblo Reservoir has reliable Blue-Winged Olive hatches that occur during the winter.

While this is not the norm, savvy dry-fly anglers target this hatch when most of the other Blue-Winged Olive activity has finished for the season.

Anglers will find dependable Blue-Winged Olive hatches statewide on both tailwaters and freestones. My favorite rivers to fish "Olives" are the South Platte in Cheesman Canyon, the Colorado near Parshall, the Frying Pan below Ruedi, and the Arkansas River near Salida. All of these areas provide excellent dry-fly opportunities. The Arkansas River's Blue-Winged Olive emergence is a hidden gem that is overshadowed by the caddis hatch that occurs a few weeks later. Ignoring the BWO hatch can be a huge oversight, as it can be every bit as impressive as the caddis emergence—not to mention the crowds are light in comparison.

The most dependable Blue-Winged Olive hatches occur during nasty weather, as inclement conditions delay the emerging process and keep the duns sitting on the water longer. If Mother Nature is kind enough to drizzle all day, anglers can experience a blanket hatch where literally thousands of duns can be on the water at one time. Conversely, bright, sunny conditions accelerate the mayflies' development and the duns leave the water quickly. Don't let bluebird days fool you however—fishing can still be excellent with *Baetis* nymphs. Swinging soft hackles is a reliable tactic during springtime Blue-Winged Olive emergences.

During the latter part of April and early May, anglers will experience caddis hatches on many of the state's freestone streams. Noted freestones to keep in mind are the Animas, Arkansas, Rio Grande, Gunnison, Eagle, and Roaring Fork. Caddis hatches can be hit or miss depending on spring runoff. A warm-weather trend can discolor the water and shut down the hatch. More times than not, a cold snap will follow and the river will clear up again. As a general rule, the first week of May is prime time for caddis hatches. Colorado anglers tend to gravitate toward the Arkansas River between Cañon City and Buena Vista to fish this epic hatch.

Spring runoff typically begins by the middle part of May and lasts four to six weeks depending on the snowpack. As a general rule, high flows typically peak by Father's Day; then the river's edges begin to clear and fishing improves. Freestones are more challenging than tailwaters during runoff. Don't let the off-colored water fool you—the trout still have to eat, and fishing can be better than you think! If the water is stained from spring runoff, add Chamois Leeches, pink San Juan Worms, chartreuse egg patterns, large stonefly nymphs, and dark streamers to your bag of tricks.

Tailwaters are your best option during higher spates because releases remain clear, even during peak runoff. Flow fluctuations might temporarily discolor the water, but the river will clear up in a couple of hours after a discharge of water. Some of the best nymph fishing of the year can occur during higher flow regimes because larger food organisms like aquatic worms, craneflies, stoneflies, and scuds get dislodged from the substrate in huge numbers, producing a feeding frenzy.

During higher flows (spring runoff or during releases to meet downstream irrigation demand), aquatic worms, scuds, and *Mysis* shrimp all become factors in catching trout, especially on tailwaters. I have caught numerous brown trout that were stuffed with aquatic worms—I mean the worms were literally hanging out of their mouths—yet the trout somehow could not resist grabbing my San Juan Worm. I have experienced similar scenarios with *Mysis* shrimp on the Frying Pan, Taylor, and Blue Rivers during higher flows.

By the first week of June, dry-fly enthusiasts come out of the woodwork to target the Salmonfly hatch. Anglers will find reliable hatches on the Gunnison River in the Gunnison Gorge and on the Colorado River between State Bridge and Parshall. Nymphing along the edges of the stream is as good as it gets as the stoneflies migrate to the river's edge to emerge into adults. If you hit the hatch dead-on, it can be one of the most incredible fishing experiences of your life.

Golden Stonefly hatches follow, once again providing anglers explosive dry-fly action with large dry flies like Amy's Ants. Anglers will find Golden Stoneflies throughout Colorado, but my favorite place to fish this hatch is in Cheesman Canyon or on the Gunnison River. Huge rainbows will rise with confidence to eat Golden Stonefly imitations.

Yellow Sallies begin hatching in late June and provide anglers excellent dry-fly action statewide. The Yellow Sally hatch may be one of the most overlooked hatches in Colorado. Evidence of splashy rises along the streambank is a good sign the fish are eating Yellow Sally adults. Sporadic Yellow Sally hatches often last into the first part of August.

Midsummer (late June through July) brings both Pale Morning Duns and Green Drakes. Dry-fly fanatics can expect to find consistent Pale Morning Dun hatches on most of Colorado's trout streams. My favorite places to target the Pale Morning Dun hatch are on the Colorado, South Platte

The Gunnison River is known for its robust population of stoneflies. This Gunnison River brown was fooled with a Pat's Rubber Legs during the annual stonefly migration in July. Pat's Rubber Legs has become a guide favorite on both the upper Gunnison and in the Gunnison Gorge.

Anglers will find dependable Blue-Winged Olive hatches during the autumn months. This thick-bodied rainbow trout was caught on a Mathews' Sparkle Dun on the Frying Pan River below Ruedi Reservoir. MARK ADAMS

(Cheesman Canyon and Spinney Mountain Ranch), Taylor, and Frying Pan Rivers.

Green Drake hatches will provide excellent dry-fly fishing on the Taylor, Blue, Yampa, Roaring Fork, Frying Pan, and North Fork of the South Platte. These big mayflies produce epic dry-fly fishing each afternoon between 1:00 p.m. and 3:00 p.m. On average, Green Drake hatches typically last for about a month, but on certain drainages like the North Fork of the South Platte they may last clear into the first part of September.

Mid-to-late summer brings my favorite hatch in Colorado: the Trico spinnerfall. The Trico hatch will bring out the best in any serious dry-fly angler. Anglers will be forced into fishing with long leaders (9 to 12 feet) and tiny #22-26 spent-wing mayflies. This will be the most technically challenging dry-fly fishing you'll encounter in Colorado. (There's a reason why this hatch is often referred to as "the white-winged curse.") Fisherman will find dependable Trico hatches starting in late July and lasting through the latter part of September. It is not uncommon to see sporadic Tricos into late October or early November on some watersheds. You'll experience sporadic Trico hatches on the Arkansas below Pueblo Dam into the latter part of November and sometimes they'll continue hatching through the first week of December.

The most reliable Trico hatches occur on the South Platte at Spinney Mountain Ranch, Elevenmile Canyon, Deckers, Cheesman Canyon, on the Yampa, and on the Colorado below its confluence with the Williams Fork. At these spots, scores of rising fish feast on spent-wing mayflies for several weeks.

Red Quill mayflies make their appearance in August, oftentimes overlapping with Blue-Winged Olives. The Red Quill hatch typically lasts until mid-September on most Colorado watersheds. My favorite rivers to fish the Red Quill hatch include the Frying Pan, Blue, Williams Fork, and the Arkansas River near Salida. There have been numerous days when nymphing was not even a consideration on the Arkansas River because the dry-fly fishing was so exceptional. I can reflect on days when I stood in the same run and hooked twenty-five trout on dry flies during a Red Quill and Blue-Winged Olive hatch.

Autumn brings excellent dry-fly fishing with Blue-Winged Olives. With diminishing irrigation demand, the flows are the most consistent of the year. This alone creates optimum conditions for dependable dry-fly fishing. The fall Blue-Winged Olive is known as the *Pseudocloeon*, or the Tiny Blue-Winged Olive. I recommend cramming your fly boxes with Blue-Winged Olive patterns in size 22 to 26 to match this hatch, as the autumn Blue-Winged Olive is one to two sizes smaller than those found in the spring. Anglers will also find dense midge hatches in September and October, requiring them to dead drift pupa imitations in the upper part of the water column. Blue-Winged Olive hatches remain consistent until mid-November, when falling water temperatures bring the hatch to a screeching halt.

Sporadic midge hatches comprise the bulk of the trout's food throughout the winter. Anglers need to think simple, sparse, and most importantly, small. Colorado fly fishers need to carry a thorough assortment of larvae, pupae, and adults to match the hatch. Anglers will find intermittent dry-fly fishing with adults in the slower pools and tailouts throughout the winter.

CHAPTER 2

Midges and Their Imitations

As you begin your quest to match Colorado's hatches, I strongly recommend starting with a fly box that is jammed with midge imitations. Whether you're fishing one of Colorado's legendary tailwaters, untamed freestones, large stillwaters, or pristine alpine lakes, fishing midges is one of the most effective strategies for consistently fooling trout.

One of your hatch-matching objectives should be selecting patterns that imitate the various stages of a midge's development. For instance, you should tie or purchase a variety of larvae, pupae, adults, clusters, cripples, and stillborns. Each pattern will have a time and place, but make no mistake about it: a serious midge junkie who's loaded with hundreds of midge imitations will stack the odds in his favor when it comes to fooling selective, hard-fished Colorado trout.

Midges are members of a large insect order called true flies or Diptera. As their scientific name implies (*di* meaning "two," and *ptera* meaning "wings"), the adults have only two wings, a feature that distinguishes them from other flying insects. Entomologists estimate that there are more than 3,500 aquatic species of Diptera in North America. Diptera collectively outnumber all species of mayflies, caddisflies, and stoneflies combined.

Several factors increase Diptera's importance to both the angler and the trout. Diptera pass through what is referred to as complete metamorphosis, meaning their life cycle contains four stages of development. The interval between each stage of their life cycle—egg, larva, pupa, and adult—varies greatly depending on the species and their environment. Diptera live in almost every imaginable type of habitat, many of which are not conducive to thriving populations of mayflies, stoneflies, and caddisflies.

Unlike caddisflies (which also undergo complete metamorphosis), many species of aquatic Diptera are multibrooded, meaning that they produce two to five broods per year. Many species of Diptera can undergo a complete life cycle—egg to adult—in just a few weeks. This substantially increases the need for anglers to imitate various stages of the insect's life cycle on a continual basis. A unique quality of midges is that they can complete an entire life cycle during the coldest months of the year.

Bob Dye fooled this Arkansas River rainbow below Pueblo Reservoir with a tiny midge imitation. In many tailwaters midges make up a significant part of the trout's diet.

The most widespread group of midges are chironomids, or members of the Chironomidae family. There are an estimated 2,000 species of Chironomidae in North America. In nutrient-rich lakes larvae and pupae can exceed three-quarters of an inch in length. Most chironomids are small—but don't let their size fool you. What midges lack in size, they offset by their massive populations, making them a viable year-round food source for trout. In some watersheds, midges can make up as much as 50 percent of a trout's diet.

Trout feeding on midges will eat both opportunistically and selectively depending on the density of the hatch. Opportunistic trout will feed on larvae, pupae, and an occasional adult, as well as other food organisms that are readily available, at any given time of the day or night. These types of feeding behaviors tend to occur during intermittent midge hatches.

Trout may also feed selectively, meaning they key or focus on one particular food organism and ignore the rest. This can be extremely frustrating until you figure out exactly what size and stage of the life cycle the trout are keying on. Selective feeding phases tend to occur during moderate to dense midge hatches whereby anglers will need exact imitations to fool trout.

A stomach pump is a valuable tool that can help you decipher which phase of the midges' life cycle the fish are keying on. For instance, if you analyze the contents of a trout's stomach and you notice that size 22 brown midge pupae are most prevalent, it quickly narrows down your fly selection.

For decades, the size-shape-color formula has been a foolproof method for choosing an artificial imitation to match the hatch. Simply open up your fly box and choose a pattern that is close in size, has a similar silhouette, and is approximately the same color as the original. This is where having a thorough selection of midges (larvae, pupae, adults, cripples, and clusters) in a variety of sizes and colors will pay off. Another important consideration is that as a midge passes through each stage of development, it decreases in size. For example, if a midge is a size 18 as a larva, the pupa will become a size 20, the adult will become a size 22, and so on.

LARVAE

Midge larvae are characterized by their wormlike appearance. Larvae are slender and slightly curved with distinct segmentation. Their head is visible, but noticeably smaller than the nearby thorax segments. Larvae have a pair of prolegs just behind the head and on the tip of the last abdominal segment.

Most larvae that you'll encounter will range between one-eighth and one-half inch in length. Fly tiers can easily imitate larvae with hooks ranging from size 16 to 22. I personally tie the bulk of my larvae in size 18 and 20.

Midge larvae are commonly found in cream, tan, gray, pale olive, and red. Their populations are astonishing in some of our rivers and streams. Leonard C. Ferrington Jr., a professor in the Department of Entomology at the University of Minnesota points out, "Midge larval densities depend on month of year, productivity of stream, and kinds of stream-bottom substrate. Typical densities however may range from 800 to 2,000 larvae per square meter."

Larvae that reside in areas of a stream or lake with low oxygen levels are referred to as bloodworms. They contain hemoglobin, which makes them bright red in color. Hemoglobin allows midges to store oxygen within their bodies and enables them to survive in muddy or silty environments with little or no oxygen.

Many anglers mistakenly refer to bloodworms and pale-olive larvae as annelids. Although there are some obvious similarities, this is not technically correct. According to Rick Takahashi and Jerry Hubka's *Modern Midges*, "Due to physical similarities, some fly fishers mistakenly refer to midge larvae as an annelid (aquatic worm), but on closer examination, you will see the absence of the clitellum, a swelling found on earthworms, and the presence of prolegs, which are small appendages."

Larva imitations are effective year-round because they have a tendency to drift continuously in the current, a phenomenon referred to as constant drift. A steady supply of drifting midge larvae is especially important to opportunistic trout when other aquatic insects are inactive. My periodic stomach samples generally contain a few midge larvae, which leads me to believe larvae are in fact an important food source for trout.

From a fly tier's perspective, midge larvae are easy to imitate. Most tiers simply wrap tying thread, wire, Hareline Micro Tubing, Midge Braid, Pearl Quill Body, or something similar around a hook shank to create their segmented larvae. Red or pale olive Hareline Micro Tubing produces the most realistic imitations. Most tiers prefer using Tiemco 2487, 2488, or 200R hooks when tying larvae. These hooks have longer shanks (2X and 3X), which produce realistic imitations of the wormlike larvae. Midge larvae have a small head, which is easily imitated with a few wraps of tying thread.

There are some important considerations to think about before you begin tying larvae. Micro Tubing is transparent, therefore the tying thread wound around the hook shank ultimately affects the color of the finished fly. On my pale olive larvae, I use Light Cahill 8/0 Uni-Thread (underbody) and wrap light olive Hareline Micro Tubing over it. This produces a lifelike, segmented pale olive larva that resembles those found in stomach samples. For similar reasons, I use red 70-denier Ultra Thread on my red larvae patterns to achieve a rich, blood-red abdomen. Some fly tiers swear by the Daiichi 1273 (red hook) for their red larvae because it increases the vibrancy of the Micro Tubing, producing a brilliant body. Adding extra-small red glass beads on my red larvae has proven to be effective too.

Randy Gorby's Gorbinator is a nice option that offers ease of tying and durability, making it one of the most effective midge larvae that I've fished. Gorby prefers the Tiemco 200R for his larvae because it provides the correct profile. He uses primrose 14/0 Gordon Griffiths thread for the underbody, then overlays it with cream Hareline Micro Tubing. "The key to tying midge larvae is tying them thin and sparse," Gorby says. "The beauty of this fly is the simplicity of tying it. You can whip out a couple dozen in an hour. I have fooled trout on almost every tailwater in Colorado with this fly. Don't let the simplicity of this fly fool you—it really catches fish!"

Stock your fly boxes with an ample supply of red midge larvae in size 18-22. I have found a red larva to be an excellent attractor in my tandem nymphing rigs, especially on tailwaters like the Blue, Arkansas, Yampa, South Platte, San Juan, Taylor, and Frying Pan Rivers.

John Barr's Pure Midge Larva is another one of my favorite patterns. Barr uses clear Hareline Micro Tubing wrapped over a colored 70-denier Ultra Thread body. This strategy allows for several color possibilities when tying larvae. Barr ties in a length of the Micro Tubing behind the eye of the hook, stretches it slightly, and then wraps thread over the Micro Tubing towards the hook bend. He then returns the thread to the eye of the hook, keeping the thread wraps as smooth and symmetrical as possible. The final step is to wrap the Micro Tubing forward over the thread base, tie it off behind the eye, and clip off the excess. A few wraps of additional tying thread will build a smooth head. Complete the fly by applying a coat of Sally Hansen Hard As Nails on the head. Barr ties his Pure Midge Larva in fluorescent green, chartreuse, tan, olive, hot orange, red, blue, black, and white.

PUPAE

After larvae reach maturity they develop into pupae. Pupae are identified by their shorter, segmented abdomen and robust thorax, which distinguishes them from the slender, tubelike larvae. The swollen or bulbous thorax contains the wing pads, legs, and gills of the emerging adult. During this phase of the midge's development it is protected in a cocoon called a puparium.

The size of pupae varies greatly depending on the fishery and the time of year. Stillwater enthusiasts tend to fish with larger pupae imitations (up to a size 12) than those anglers who concentrate their efforts on rivers and streams. The largest midges of the year typically emerge in the spring on both freestone and tailwater fisheries. Savvy anglers will notice the spring midge is much larger that most of the midges you'll encounter throughout the remainder of the season. My recommendation is to tie a few Mercury Black Beauties, Top Secret Midges, Medallion Midges, Jujubee Midges, and Minute Midges in size 18 to match the midge hatches that occur in March and April (I cannot even begin to tell you how many fish I have fooled on Medallion Midges and Top Secret Midges). During the remainder of the season, you'll find that pupae will range between one-eighth and one-sixteenth inch in length. Most tiers use a size 20-26 Tiemco 2487, 2488, or 101 for most of their pupae imitations.

Tiers can easily imitate pupae by dubbing (twisting fur onto thread and wrapping it around the hook) an oval-shaped ball of fur in the thorax. The football-shaped thorax should represent about 25 percent of the completed fly. Other tiers with the same goal in mind opt to use an extra-small glass or tungsten bead to replicate the enlarged thorax area. Tungsten bead-head patterns are realistic imitations that are excellent for use in dry-and-dropper rigs.

Many innovative tiers use Hareline's Medallion Sheeting or Betts' Zing to create realistic wing buds. Dubbed bodies, in comparison, are more impressionistic. Furthermore, tiers can use Z-Lon, Darlon, McFlylon, or frizzed-out Oral-B Ultra Floss to simulate the gills. Greg Garcia's Rojo Midge is a good example of incorporating dental floss into a midge pupae design: "I tried many materials before I selected Oral-B Floss," Garcia explains. "First I used Z-Lon, Antron, and Darlon. All of these materials were hard to work with, especially when it came to consistency. If I put too much material on the hook, I could not get the bead over the gill bundle. Also, I found these materials were too stiff in the water and provided very little movement! Next I tried CDC. Again it was hard to get the right amount of stripped fibers without the stem on the hook. Most of the time they ended up on the floor. Then one day I came across Oral-B dental floss. When I cut the blue binder off and teased the material with a bodkin I knew this was the look I wanted. The size was perfect. The bead would slide over the gill bundle easily, and every fly looked the same. What I did not expect was that when fishing the Oral-B floss, it would move in the current, which is very important in the design. I also noticed that the floss would remain white and not take on other colors from dirt and moss. It remained opaque."

I recommend tying pupae in a variety of colors—black, brown, gray, and dark olive. To date, brown pupae have been my best producers.

Prior to emerging, pupae become restless and fidgety, repeatedly twitching and moving up and down in the water column before the adult finally breaks free from the pupal sheath and pushes its way through the meniscus. During this stage of development, a reflective layer of trapped gases produces a mirrorlike bubble in the thorax. Tiers use silver-lined glass beads, Flashabou, Mylar tinsel, and other flashy materials to simulate this stage of emergence. I routinely incorporate an extra-small Spirit River Hi-Lite Glass Bead (the bead is silver-lined) into my midge designs because it mimics this reflective trapped gas. I believe the flash acts as a trigger and

Forrest Dorsey caught this impressive 24-inch brown trout on the Taylor River with his Manhattan Midge. Dorsey's Manhattan Midge incorporates an extra-small silver-lined glass bead into its design to imitate the gas bubble trapped in the thorax prior to emergence. MARK ADAMS

attracts fish from several inches (sometimes feet) away when they are suspended and feeding on pupae.

Mike Mercer, one of the country's leaders in fly innovation and an Umpqua Signature Fly Designer, has carefully studied the life cycle of midges and has come to several conclusions. "When the pupae wiggle their way to the surface to emerge they are encased in an outer sheath of skin, beneath which is a highly reflective layer of trapped air," Mercer says. "In many cases, particularly when suspended in or near the surface film, they appear to be almost chrome-plated. Also, their anal and forward gills often hold air bubbles, increasing the refracted effect."

Based on these observations, Mercer developed a realistic midge imitation that he calls the Midgeling. I have fooled numerous trout on a root beer–colored size 20 Midgeling. Mercer explains the design process: "I designed the Midgeling with a layer of Krystal Flash beneath clear Midge Tubing to achieve both translucency and some reflection, visible segmentation from the tightly wound Micro Tubing, a glass bead to enhance the 'juicy morsel' effect, and a collar of ostrich herl to provide the always-needed material motion."

Mercer also likes to take a dark waterproof marker and create a stripe down the top of the abdomen. "Midges that I have seined in the substrate level of the streams often would be more translucent than reflective—nearly transparent in appearance. The abdominal segmentation of the pupa was always fairly pronounced, and was commonly darker on the dorsal side than the ventral," Mercer adds.

Pupae patterns are most effective during the height of a midge hatch, when the naturals are ascending to the water's surface. The emerging process is slow, giving trout ample opportunities to capitalize on an effortless meal when the pupae are hanging in a C-shape just below the surface film. Heavy concentrations of rising pupae will draw the attention of nearby trout, creating a steady feeding rhythm and producing good nymph fishing for the angler.

ADULTS

Adult midges emerge by pulling themselves out of their pupal sheath and breaking through the surface film. For a short period of time, the emerging midge appears to be twice as long as the pupa because the trailing shuck is hanging on to the adult's body. As the adult's wings struggle to free themselves from the pupal sheath, the trailing shuck can trigger the attention of nearby trout.

Jim Cannon's Snowshoe Suspender Midge is one of my favorite emerger patterns. "The Snowshoe Suspender Midge is a true emerger in my mind," Cannon says. "It closely resembles the stage when the adult is using its legs to push itself out of the pupal sheath. The wing is tied from snowshoe rabbit, which has some unique properties. I have carefully studied snowshoe rabbit fibers underneath a microscope. There are between four and twelve kinks in each fiber. These kinked-up snowshoe fibers trap air remarkably well and work excellent for tying wings on small dry flies."

Some adults never complete the emerging process because they get trapped in their pupal sheath. Stuck-in-the-shuck or trailing-shuck midges are excellent imposters for these ill-fated cripples. Most stuck-in-the-shuck or trailing-shuck imitations are tied with a few orange or amber Z-Lon or Darlon fibers extending one shank length beyond the hook. According to Mike Lawson in his book *Spring Creeks*, "Cripples are deadly imitations of these doomed midges. You can tie cripples on standard-size hooks, leaving some fibers of Z-Lon to represent the trailing husk, or you can tie them on longer-shank hooks with the shanks tied two-tone, the bottom third the color of the pupal husk and the upper two-thirds to represent the trapped adult. The second method offers the advantage of a larger hook when very small midges are emerging." Don't rule out adding a few strands of Z-Lon, Darlon, or McFlylon to your favorite midge adults like a Matt's Midge or a Griffith's Gnat. You'll be pleasantly surprised with their effectiveness.

Once the adult frees itself from the pupal sheath, it remains on the water momentarily as it dries its wings before of flight. I have found that down-wing imitations like Matt's Midge work best when midges are resting on the surface drying their wings. On numerous occasions, I have had refusals to anything other than down-wing imitations when trying to imitate newly hatched midges.

According to Matt Miles, the designer of Matt's Midge, "I designed Matt's Midge twenty years ago because there was a shortage of adult midge imitations. Like many anglers, I fished tiny Griffith's Gnats and Parachute Adams with success, but I felt like I needed a more realistic imitation. I designed Matt's Midge to mimic a single newly hatched midge, concentrating on the silhouette of the abdomen and the wing. I wanted a fly that was easy to see and the laid-back, semi-upright wing helps you find the fly on the water and closely resembles the natural."

It is common to see groups of midges clinging to one another or in clusters during the winter and spring. Trout feed on these clusters with confidence, as they provide an increased food opportunity compared to keying on a single midge. Large Griffith's Gnats (size 16-18) or a Dubas' Midge (size 15 or 17) will imitate these clusters effectively.

Greg Blessing's Purple Haze is tied with flashy synthetic materials to emulate the gases trapped in a midge's abdomen and thorax prior to emergence. The Purple Haze is one of Blessing's go-to midge patterns in Elevenmile Canyon.

Matt Miles fishes with a Matt's Midge to a pod of rising fish that are eating adult midges in Cheesman Canyon. Matt's Midge has become a local favorite among South Platte regulars.

MIDGE-FISHING STRATEGIES

Larvae

Fishing larvae imitations requires no special tactics or techniques. Like most anglers, I tend to fish larvae patterns when there are no obvious hatches. Many anglers feel that larvae are not as important as the pupae or adults because they are hidden in aquatic vegetation or buried in the mud and muck. This "out of sight, out of mind" philosophy can be a huge oversight.

Ed Engle, a Colorado guide, author, and a true authority when it comes to fishing tailwaters, believes midge larvae can be effective under the right conditions. In his book *Fly Fishing the Tailwaters*, Engle says, "I consider any disturbance in water flows as a good reason to put on a larva imitation. A change in discharge rates from the reservoir will sometimes knock midge larvae into the drift, and since populations of midge larvae can be astronomical in some tailwaters, this can mean a real feeding orgy will occur."

I have experienced similar situations in Cheesman Canyon when the Denver Water Board has increased the streamflow to meet downstream irrigation demand. My occasional stomach samples (procured with a stomach pump) lead me to believe that fish do eat a considerable amount of midge larvae, especially during a small flow increase of 50 to 100 cfs.

John Barr also believes midge larvae are an important food source for trout. In *Barr Flies*, he states, "Midge larvae drift at all hours of the day, and because they are so prolific, there can be massive numbers drifting in the currents at one time, providing an important, consistent food source for trout."

I fish my larvae patterns as the lead fly (closest to the weight) in my tandem nymphing rigs to ensure they drift closer to the substrate. I have found a red larva to be an excellent attractor in tandem nymphing rigs, especially in the spring and fall when the trout are preparing to spawn. Prespawn trout become easily agitated by bright colors like red, pink, and orange, which often trigger aggressive strikes. During the height of the spawning season, I have found red larvae to be more effective as attractors than egg patterns. Hordes of anglers fish with egg patterns during the spawn and the patterns lose some of their effectiveness because the trout see too many of them. Off the larvae, I typically drop a *Baetis* nymph or midge pupa depending on the most prevalent hatches at the time.

John Barr takes a similar approach: "I fish my larva as the bottom fly in a two- or three-nymph setup in both rivers and lakes. In flowing waters, I like to dead-drift the larva with an occasional twitch. The natural larvae will squirm and move around a little bit as they are drifting."

Other anglers like Bob Dye prefer fishing their larvae imitations dropped off an egg pattern. "I'm a big fan of egg-midge combos," Dye says. "I fish egg patterns year-round because there are always a few trout spawning in our streams. Egg patterns are excellent attractors and draw attention to your smaller midge imitations." Dye admits that while most of the time he fools trout on his midge patterns, there are times, especially during heavier spawning activity in the spring and fall, when egg patterns can be very effective. This fly combination has proven itself to be a reliable strategy most of the year.

Pupae

As soon as a midge hatch becomes evident, I recommend clipping off your midge larva and replacing it with two or three pupae. Signs of a midge hatch would include fish suspended in the water column (as opposed to fish hugging the bottom) and adult midges taking flight into the air. A noticeable increase in feeding behavior, such as flashes, fish lifting in the water column, or trout sweeping back and forth to intercept pupae, would be a good indication a midge hatch is in progress. Switching flies is a response to the trout changing from opportunistic to selective feeding as it keys on pupae.

Anglers should concentrate their efforts in the transitional zones—midchannel shelves and point gravel bars—during a midge hatch. These areas can be identified by a distinct color change in the substrate, which indicates a depth change that offers both food and protection for suspended trout that are feeding on pupae.

Aaron Carithers, owner of Anasazi Angler in Durango, Colorado, is a true expert when it comes to fishing with midge pupae. Carithers routinely guides customers on the fabled San Juan River below Navajo Dam. The San Juan tailwater is a popular destination for Colorado fishermen because of its exceptional year-round midge fishing. "I fish midge pupae a variety of ways," Carithers says. "Sometimes I fish heavy and deep, 6 or 7 feet from the indicator with a number 4 split shot, keeping my pupae midway in the water column. As the hatch intensifies, I fish my pupae 3 to 4 feet from the indicator with number 6s and 7s, or 2 to 3 feet from the indicator with number 8s and 9s. Fish feed on midges nearly everywhere in the system. A successful angler will need to adjust for speed of the current and depth of the feeding fish."

Another effective strategy that many anglers use when fishing midge pupae is a dry-and-dropper rig. This enables you to drift midge pupae just below the surface film without spooking suspended trout with a strike indicator splashing on the water. Heavily pressured trout become suspicious of conventional nymphing rigs floating over their heads. Carithers taught me an interesting method for fishing pupa in the surface film: "If the fish are feeding in the surface

Most anglers dredge their midge larvae imitations on the dead drift, using a two- or three-fly tandem nymphing rig near the substrate where the largest concentrations of naturals are found. I have had my best success with pale olive and red larvae imitations in size 18-20. MARK ADAMS

Fishing with midge pupae requires more finesse and skill than fishing with larvae because you'll need to keep your flies in the correct feeding zone to consistently fool trout. Adjusting your weight and strike indicator depth can make or break your success. Typically midge-feeders will be suspended in the mid to upper part of the water column.

tension I fish a pupa about 12 inches below a large dry. In order to get the midge just below the surface, I clip the 12 inches of tippet in the middle, tie a surgeon's knot, add a number 9 split above the knot, and tie the pupa on the end of the remaining 5 to 6 inches of tippet, creating a dry-dropper rig for midging fish."

I am a big fan of dry-and-dropper rigs for suspending a midge pupa in the upper part of the water column. I routinely fish heavily hackled Griffith's Gnats or Dubas' Midges in size 16-18 to suspend my pupa. The setup is straightforward—simply drop a pupa like a Dorsey's Tungsten Flashback Black Beauty or Craven's Poison Tung from the bend of your dry fly with 12 to 18 inches of 6X tippet. Look for any visible flashes or movement below your dry fly or for the dry fly abruptly sinking—these are indications that a trout has eaten your pupa.

The greased-leader technique is another method that works well when trying to fool trout that are keying on pupae just below the surface. Apply silicone floatant to the entire leader with the exception of the final 6 to 12 inches closest to the fly. The untreated section of the leader will allow the pupa to sit just below the surface, precisely where you would expect to find a lot of emerging pupae. Watch your greased portion of the leader closely; look for any movement or twitches, as this indicates that a trout has grabbed your suspended pupa.

Adults

The best midge hatches occur during subdued light. I've experienced the most reliable hatches at dawn or dusk before the overhead light becomes harsh. Once the sunlight hits the water, midge hatches lose their intensity and rising fish become few and far between. Sporadic midge hatches occur all day, but not in enough numbers to find trout that will to rise to the adults. It's a risky proposition for a trout to rise to the surface and eat the occasional single midge. If inclement weather or overcast conditions are present, midday midge hatches can range from good to excellent. Evening midge hatches are typically the best fishing of the day once the light softens and the trout become comfortable feeding on the surface.

During the initial stages of the hatch, trout will often feed on both pupae and adults. A dry-and-dropper rig is effective when trout are randomly feeding on both stages of the midge's life cycle. When trout are showing signs of opportunistic feeding (feeding on both pupae and adults) I apply the same dry-and-dropper tactics that were discussed in the pupae section.

My observations and experiences lead me to believe that once a trout commits to the adults, the pupae become less important, and they quit feeding on them. When this occurs, I cut off my dropper and focus on trying to fool the surface feeders that are keying on the adults. I typically fish with two dry flies to increase my odds.

Midge fishing requires a lot of patience and finesse. Fish feeding on adult midges tend to suspend themselves just below the surface, requiring accurate casting on behalf of the dry-fly angler. The feeding window is narrow; a cast that is a foot to the right or left of the rising fish is not sufficient enough to fool it. Toss in cruising trout and things become extremely challenging.

My recommendation is to get as close to the rising fish as possible without spooking them. Keep your false casting to a minimum and target specific fish rather than randomly casting. Remain stealthy and keep a low profile to avoid spooking fish. Most anglers fish their adult midge imitations on the dead drift. Some anglers like Matt Miles twitch their fly occasionally if there are a lot of skittering midges on the water's surface. "On occasion if there are a lot of midges dancing around on the surface I will give the fly a slight twitch. I think it helps with getting the trout's attention," Miles advises.

Midge adults can be difficult to see under the best conditions, let alone when there is severe surface glare. If you're having difficulty seeing your fly, apply Frog's Fanny (a dry-fly desiccant) to the topside of your adult midge because it will turn it white and make it easy to see. This strategy has worked well for me over the years, and even smaller flies like a size 26 Parachute Adams become visible after dousing them with Frog's Fanny.

If you still cannot locate your fly, try to at least have a reasonably good idea of where the end of your leader is. If there are any surface disturbances in that general area, assume a trout has eaten your fly, and set the hook. Another option would be to fish with a high-visibility pattern (flies with bright orange or pink wings) like Matt's Midge or a Griffith's Gnat. I carry both variations of these patterns and prefer the hi-viz version when I am fishing in high glare or having difficulty seeing my fly in foam or bubble lines.

"A year or so after I developed Matt's Midge, I found the need for a brighter wing (hi-viz) so that I could see it in foam and scum lines," Matt Miles says. "Back eddies trap huge concentrations of adult midges that get stuck in the foam and trout have a field day eating them. There was only one problem: you couldn't see Matt's Midge with the white wing so I headed back to the vise to create a Hi-Viz Matt's Midge." It was an easy fix: Miles swapped the white Z-Lon wing for a bright orange McFlylon wing and the problem was solved.

Fishing cripples or stuck-in-the-shuck imitations is similar to fishing adults. These imitations display the trapped adult extending partially out of the pupal sheath. Stuck-in-the-shuck imitations should be fished on the surface, and cripples should be fished half in and half out of the surface film.

Hi-viz midge imitations are easier to see on the water, especially in high glare situations or when you're struggling to see your fly in foam or bubble lines. Many fly tiers use cerise or bright orange McFlylon for their parachute patterns (or wings) because it makes them easier to see.

MIDGE PATTERNS

M & M (Midges and Mayflies) (Black)

Originator: Steve Henderson
Tier: Steve Henderson

Hook: #18-22 Tiemco 200R
Thread: Black 8/0 Uni-Thread
Abdomen: Black turkey biot
Thorax: Peacock herl
Wing: Light dun Darlon
Wing Case: Light dun Darlon

Note: Effective color variations include red, green, and olive.

Tungsten Zebra Midge (Black)

Originator: Ted Welling
Tier: Steve Henderson

Hook: #16-22 Tiemco 2488H
Bead: Spirit River silver brass or tungsten
Thread: Black 140-denier Ultra Thread
Abdomen: Black 140-denier Ultra Thread
Rib: Silver Ultra Wire (Brassie)

Note: Another effective color variation is red. Use a $^{3}/_{32}$" bead for sizes 16-18 and $^{5}/_{64}$" for sizes 20-22.

Rhinestone Midge

Originator: Bob Dye
Tier: Bob Dye

Hook: #18-24 Tiemco 2487
Bead: Gunmetal Killer Caddis glass (extra small)
Thread: Black 8/0 Uni-Thread
Abdomen: Black 8/0 Uni-Thread
Rib: Silver Ultra Wire (small)

Cobalt Blue Midge

Originator: Bob Dye
Tier: Bob Dye

Hook: #18-24 Tiemco 2487
Bead: Cobalt blue glass (extra small)
Thread: Black 8/0 Uni-Thread
Abdomen: Green rainbow MFC Midge Body Thread
Thorax: Black UV Ice Dub

Note: Cobalt blue bead purchased at a craft store.

Cinnamon Midge Emerger

Originator: Bob Dye
Tier: Bob Dye

Hook: #18-24 Tiemco 2487
Thread: Cinnamon 14/0 MFC
Abdomen: Tying thread
Rib: Tying thread colored black with Sharpie
Wing: Purple Krystal Flash
Thorax: Black Superfine

Dr. Love Emerger

Originator: Bob Dye
Tier: Bob Dye

Hook: #20-26 Tiemco 2488
Thread: Olive dun 8/0 Uni-Thread
Abdomen: Tying thread
Rib: Tying thread colored black with Sharpie
Wing: White Razor Foam, clipped
Thorax: Black Superfine

Colorock Midge

Originator: Bob Dye
Tier: Bob Dye

Hook: #20-26 Tiemco 2488
Thread: Yellow 14/0 Gordon Griffiths
Abdomen: Tying thread
Rib: Tying thread colored black with Sharpie
Thorax: Brown UTC Midge Braid
Head: Tying thread colored black with Sharpie

Rootbeer Midge

Originator: Bob Dye
Tier: Bob Dye

Hook: #18-24 Tiemco 2487
Bead: Black Killer Caddis (extra small)
Thread: Black 8/0 Uni-Thread
Abdomen: Copper MFC Midge Body Thread
Rib: Yellow Gordon Griffiths 14/0 colored black with Sharpie

Pabst Blue Ribbon (PBR)

Originator: Bob Dye
Tier: Bob Dye

Hook: #20-24 Tiemco 2488
Bead: Clear silver-lined Killer Caddis (extra small)
Thread: Red 8/0 Uni-Thread
Abdomen: Chartreuse Flashabou
Thorax: Olive UV Ice Dub

Periwinkle

Originator: Adrian Keeler
Tier: Bob Dye

Hook: #20-24 Tiemco 2487
Bead: Cherry Cola glass (extra small)
Thread: Olive 70-denier Ultra Thread
Abdomen: Olive 70-denier Ultra Thread
Rib: Black Ultra Wire (Brassie)
Thorax: Olive UV Ice Dub

Two-Tone Larva

Originator: Bob Dye
Tier: Bob Dye

Hook: #16-20 Tiemco 2457
Thread: Olive 70-denier Ultra Thread
Abdomen: Clear Hareline Micro Tubing

Note: Color the top of the abdomen with a black Sharpie.

Atta Boy Midge

Originator: Bob Dye
Tier: Bob Dye

Hook: #18-24 Tiemco 2487
Thread: Red 70-denier Ultra Thread
Abdomen: Pearl tinsel (medium)
Thorax: Black Ice Dub

D Midge (Red)

Originator: Dennis Miller
Tier: Dennis Miller

Hook: #18-20 Tiemco 2488
Bead: Red size 17 or 1.5 glass lined
Thread: Red 70-denier Ultra Thread
Tail: White Fluoro Fibre
Abdomen: Red 70-denier Ultra Thread
Rib: Silver Lagartun Wire (fine)
Thorax: Red 70-denier Ultra Thread
Wings: White Fluoro Fibre

Note: Color variations include black, olive, purple, and blue dun. Use thread and beads to match color of abdomen.

J's Midge Pupa

Originator: J Core
Tier: J Core

Hook: #20-24 Dai-Riki 310
Bead: Black glass (extra small)
Thread: Black 8/0 Uni-Thread
Abdomen: Dark brown Midge Diamond Braid
Wing: Glamour Madeira
Thorax: Black Superfine

Coffee Time

Originator: John Keefover
Tier: John Keefover

Hook: #18-22 Tiemco 2488
Bead: Coffee MFC tungsten Lucent (1.5mm)
Abdomen: Camel 8/0 Uni-Thread
Rib: Copper Ultra Wire (small)

Green Machine

Originator: John Keefover
Tier: John Keefover

Hook: #18-22 Tiemco 101
Bead: Deep emerald MFC tungsten Lucent (1.5mm)
Abdomen: Chartreuse 8/0 Uni-Thread
Rib: Black Ultra Wire (small)
Thorax: Olive dun Hareline Dubbin

Blood Midge

Originator: John Keefover
Tier: John Keefover

Hook: #18-22 Tiemco 101
Bead: Red Spirit River glass (extra small)
Thread: Red 8/0 Uni-Thread
Abdomen: Red 8/0 Uni-Thread
Rib: Silver Ultra Wire (fine)

Orange Sherbert

Originator: John Keefover
Tier: John Keefover

Hook: #18-22 Tiemco 2488H
Bead: Peacock Spirit River glass (extra small)
Thread: Fire orange 6/0 Uni-Thread
Underbody: Fire orange 6/0 Uni-Thread
Abdomen: Danville pearl Mylar tinsel (small)
Rib: Silver Danville wire (fine)
Thorax: Fire orange 6/0 Uni-Thread

UV Midge Larva

Originator: Chris Karl
Tier: Rick Takahashi

Hook: #18-22 Tiemco 200R or Daiichi 1270
Thread: White 70-denier Ultra Thread
Underbody: White 70-denier Ultra Thread and Ice Blue Tinsel
Abdomen: Clear Stretch Magic (.5mm)
Head: Tying thread colored with tan permanent marker

Note: Cover entire fly with thin head cement.

Tak's Thread Midge Larva

Originator: Rick Takahashi
Tier: Rick Takahashi

Hook: #18-22 Tiemco 200R or Daiichi 1270
Thread: Red 8/0 Uni-Thread
Underbody: Red 8/0 Uni-Thread
Abdomen: Clear Stretch Magic (.5mm)
Head: Tying thread

Note: Cover entire fly with thin head cement.

Tak's Holo Blue Chironomid

Originator: Rick Takahashi
Tier: Rick Takahashi

Hook: #12-18 Tiemco 2302 or Daiichi 1260
Thread: Black 70-denier Ultra Thread
Abdomen: Black 70-denier Ultra Thread
Rib 1: Blue Holographic Tinsel
Rib 2: Silver Lagartun (fine)
Wing Pads: White goose biot
Wing Case: UV Pearl Tinsel
Gills: Oral B Ultra Floss

Note: Cover entire fly except the gills with Hydro Clear Cure Goo.

Tak's Crystal Chironomid

Originator: Rick Takahashi
Tier: Rick Takahashi

Hook: #12-18 Tiemco 2302
Thread: Olive brown 70-denier Ultra Thread
Abdomen: Clear or chartreuse Stretch Magic (.5mm)
Wing Pads: Orange goose biot
Wing Case: UV Pearl Tinsel
Gills: Oral B Ultra Floss

Note: Cover entire fly except the gills with Hydro Clear Cure Goo.

Tak's Mini Bow Tie Buzzer

Originator: Rick Takahashi
Tier: Rick Takahashi

Hook: #16-22 Tiemco 2488 or Daiichi 1140
Thread: Black 70-denier Ultra Thread
Tail: Oral B Ultra Floss
Rib: Silver Lagartun wire (fine)
Abdomen: Black 70-denier Ultra Thread
Wing Case: Natural latex colored with black permanent marker
Thorax: Peacock Ice Dub
Gills: Oral B Ultra Floss

Note: Cover wing case with Hydro Clear Cure Goo.

Tak's Gilled Pupa

Originator: Rick Takahashi
Tier: Rick Takahashi

Hook: #18-24 Tiemco 100
Abdomen: Summer brown Coats and Clark Sewing Thread (54A)
Gills: Oral B Ultra Floss
Head: Black 8/0 Uni-Thread

Tak's C-Thru Midge Pupa

Originator: Rick Takahashi
Tier: Rick Takahashi

Hook: #16-26 Dai-Riki 060
Thread: White 12/0 Veevus
Abdomen: Clear Stretch Magic Lace colored with tan permanent marker
Flash: Pearl Krystal Flash
Head: Black 12/0 Veevus

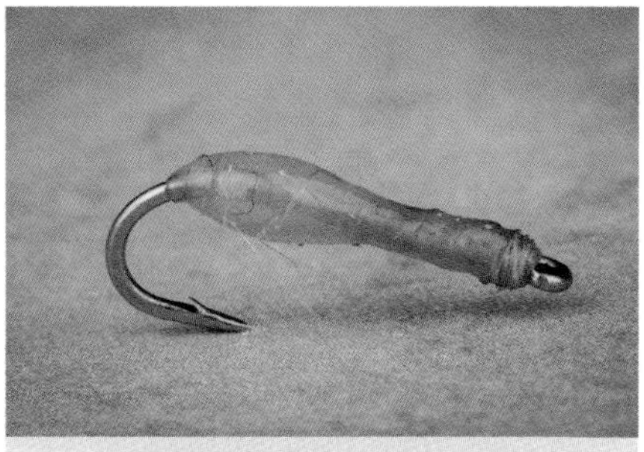

Yamauchi's Black Fly Larva

Originator: Brian Yamauchi
Tier: Rick Takahashi

Hook: #18-22 Daiichi 1180
Thread: White 16/0 Veevus
Underbody: White 16/0 Veevus
Abdomen: Natural latex strip
Head: White 16/0 Veevus colored with tan permanent marker

Note: Cover entire body with Hydro Clear Cure Goo.

Keisling's Glass Midge (Black)

Originator: Jonathan Keisling
Tier: Jonathan Keisling

Hook: #16-20 Tiemco 2488 or Dai-Riki 125
Thread: Black 14/0 Gordon Griffiths
Abdomen: Black and silver Ultra Wire (small)
Thorax: Pearl Flashabou covered with Clear Cure Goo Hydro

Note: Abdomen variations include chartreuse, blue, copper, red, and green.

Cream Cheese

Originator: Greg Blessing
Tier: Greg Blessing

Hook: #18-24 Tiemco 2487
Bead: Gold tungsten
Thread: Yellow 70-denier Ultra Thread
Shuck: Yellow Krystal Flash
Abdomen: Yellow 70-denier Ultra Thread
Thorax: UV yellow Ice Dub
Wing: Pearl poly yarn Metallica

Note: Pearl poly yarn Metallica can be purchased from Hobby Lobby. Use a 3/32" bead for size 18 and 5/64" for size 20-24.

Cheesman Emerger

Originator: Chris Ramos
Tier: Greg Blessing

Hook: #20-24 Tiemco 2487
Bead: Olive tungsten
Thread: Olive brown 70-denier Ultra Thread
Tail: Yellow Krystal Flash, one strand
Abdomen: Olive brown 70-denier Ultra Thread
Wing: White Antron
Thorax: Olive Spirit River Spectrablend

Note: Use a 5/64" bead for size 20-24.

Lip Smacker Emerger

Originator: John Keefover
Tier: John Keefover

Hook: 18-24 Tiemco 2488
Bead: Red glass (extra small)
Thread: Brown 8/0 Uni-Thread
Tail: Pheasant tail fibers
Abdomen: Pheasant tail fibers
Rib: Brown 8/0 Uni-Thread
Wing: White Razor Foam
Thorax: Buffalo fur

Black Rubber Midge

Originator: Greg Blessing
Tier: Greg Blessing

Hook: #18-22 Tiemco 2487
Thread: Light cahill 8/0 Uni-Thread
Shuck: Black Spirit River rubber leg (small)
Rib: Light cahill 8/0 Uni-Thread
Wing: White poly yarn
Head: Black 70-denier Ultra Thread

Soap Creek Midge

Originator: Greg Blessing
Tier: Greg Blessing

Hook: #18-22 Tiemco 2487
Thread: Peacock blue 70-denier Ultra Thread
Shuck: Root beer Krystal Flash
Abdomen: Peacock blue and black 70-denier Ultra Thread
Thorax: Black UV Ice Dub
Hackle: Black Whiting Farms Hebert Miner

Crystal Midge

Originator: Jeremy Hyatt
Tier: Jeremy Hyatt

Hook: #18-22 Tiemco 2487
Bead: Killer Caddis Diamond Glass (extra small)
Thread: Black 8/0 Uni-Thread
Abdomen: Black 8/0 Uni-Thread
Rib: Copper Uni-Wire (small)
Wing: Pearl Krystal Flash
Thorax: Black Superfine

Pure Midge Larva

Originator: John Barr
Tier: Jeremy Hyatt

Hook: #18-22 Tiemco 2488
Thread: White 8/0 Uni-Thread
Abdomen: Clear Micro Tubing
Head: Black 8/0 Uni-Thread

Hershey Emerger

Originator: Joel Hubscher
Tier: Joel Hubscher

Hook: #18-22 Tiemco 2487
Thread: Black 8/0 Uni-Thread
Abdomen: Brown goose biot
Thorax: Brown Hareline Dubbin
Wing: White poly yarn

Ginny Midge

Originator: Eric Atha
Tier: Eric Atha

Hook: #18-24 Tiemco 2488
Bead: Spirit River clear silver lined glass (extra small)
Thread: Black 14/0 Gordon Griffiths
Abdomen: Pearl Flashabou
Wing: Pearl Flashabou (loop wing style)
Thorax: Peacock herl

Mr. Midge (Copper)

Originator: Eric Atha
Tier: Eric Atha

Hook: #20-24 Tiemco 2488
Bead: MFC dirty olive Lucent
Thread: Brown 14/0 Gordon Griffiths
Abdomen: Spirit River Copper Midge Bodi
Collar: Brown 14/0 Gordon Griffiths

Note: Color variations include dark olive and red. Use a 2.0 bead for size 20 and 1.5 for size 22-24.

Jelly Bean Midge

Originator: Eric Atha
Tier: Eric Atha

Hook: #16-22 Tiemco 2488
Thread: Black 14/0 Gordon Griffiths
Abdomen: Blue Ultra Wire (small)
Wing: Wapsi Razor Foam

Chan's Stillwater Chironomid Bomber

Originator: Brian Chan
Tier: Richard Pilatzke

Hook: #12 Dai-Riki 135
Bead: White glass
Thread: Black 6/0 Uni-Thread
Abdomen: Double layer of black 6/0 Uni-Thread
Rib: Hot orange Ultra Wire (Brassie)
Thorax: Peacock herl
Overcoat: Sally Hansen Hard As Nails

Pearly Gates

Originator: Richard Pilatzke
Tier: Richard Pilatzke

Hook: #12 Dai-Riki 135
Bead: White glass
Thread: Black 6/0 Uni-Thread
Abdomen: Black 6/0 Uni-Thread and UTC flat pearl tinsel (medium)
Rib: Hot orange Ultra Wire (Brassie)

Note: Cover abdomen with Sally Hansen Hard As Nails.

Poison Tung

Originator: Charlie Craven
Tier: Charlie Craven

Hook: #16-20 Tiemco 2488
Bead: Silver tungsten
Thread: Gray 8/0 Uni-Thread
Body: Gray 8/0 Uni-Thread
Rib: Peacock blue Lagartun wire or blue Ultra Wire (extra small)
Head: UV gray Ice Dub

Note: Color variations include brown, purple, black, olive-black, and red. Use a 3/32" bead for sizes 16-18 and 5/64" for size 20.

Jujubee Midge (Brown)

Originator: Charlie Craven
Tier: Charlie Craven

Hook: #18-22 Tiemco 2488
Thread: White 16/0 Tiemco and Camel 8/0 Uni-Thread
Abdomen: Two strands brown and one strand white Super Hair
Wing Case: White Flouro Fibre
Thorax: Camel 8/0 Uni-Thread
Wingbuds: White Flouro Fibre

Note: Color variations include olive, zebra, red, chartreuse, and blue.

Jumbo Juju Chironomid (Red)

Originator: Charlie Craven
Tier: Charlie Craven

Hook: #10-16 Tiemco 2302 or Daiichi 1760
Bead: White Hot Bead
Thread: Fluorescent white 70-denier Ultra Thread and black 8/0 Uni-Thread
Butt: Fluorescent white 70-denier Ultra Thread colored with red marker
Abdomen: Three strands brown and two strands orange Super Hair
Flashback: Opal Mirage Tinsel (medium)
Wing Case: Black Thin Skin
Thorax: Black Superfine
Body Coating: Clear Cure Goo, brushable

Note: Color variations include olive, blue, zebra, and red. Use a 5/32" bead for size 10, 1/8" for sizes 12-14 and 3/32" for size 16.

Nationwide Chironomid Bomber

Originator: Rich Pilatzke
Tier: Rich Pilatzke

Hook: #12 Dai-Riki 135
Bead: White glass
Thread: Black 6/0 Uni-Thread
Body: Black 6/0 Uni-Thread
Rib: Hot orange Ultra Wire (Brassie)
Overbody: Strip of anti-static bag wrapped over black thread
Thorax: Peacock herl
Coating: Sally Hansen Diamond Strength Nail Polish

Tungsten Tube Midge (Black)

Originator: Landon Mayer
Tier: Umpqua Feather Merchants

Hook: #18-22 Tiemco 2488
Bead: Black tungsten
Thread: Black 8/0 Uni-Thread
Abdomen: Black Ultra Wire inserted into clear Micro Tubing
Head: Black 8/0 Uni-Thread

Note: Color variations include red. Use a 3/32" bead for size 18 and 5/64" for sizes 20-22.

Tungsten Rainbow Warrior

Originator: Lance Egan
Tier: Umpqua Feather Merchants

Hook: #16-22 Tiemco 2457 or 2487
Bead: Silver tungsten
Thread: Red 6/0 Danville
Tail: Natural pheasant tail fibers
Abdomen: Pearl tinsel
Thorax: Rainbow Sow Scud Dubbing
Wing Case: Pearl tinsel

Note: Use a 3/32" bead for sizes 16-18 and 5/64" for sizes 20-22.

ICU Midge (Red)

Originator: Norm Maktima
Tier: Umpqua Feather Merchants

Hook: #14-18 Tiemco 2499SPBL
Bead: Copper tungsten
Thread: Red 6/0 Danville
Abdomen: Red 6/0 Danville coated with head cement
Rib: Red 6/0 Danville colored with black Sharpie
Thorax: Natural rabbit dubbing
Cheeks: Pearl tinsel (medium)

Note: Color variations include light olive and chartreuse. Use a 1/8" bead for size 14 and 3/32" for sizes 16-18.

Bling Midge Larva

Originator: Mike Kruise
Tier: Mike Kruise

Hook: #18-22 Tiemco 2488
Thread: Black 14/0 Gordon Griffiths
Abdomen: Mallard flank
Rib: Copper Ultra Wire (extra small)
Thorax: Ice blue pearl UTC tinsel (small)

Olive Bling Midge Pupa

Originator: Mike Kruise
Tier: Mike Kruise

Hook: #18-22 Tiemco 200R
Bead: Olive glass (extra small)
Thread: Black 14/0 Gordon Griffiths
Abdomen: Light olive Hareline Micro Tubing
Thorax: Ice blue pearl UTC tinsel (small)
Collar: Black 14/0 Gordon Griffiths
Tuft: White Hareline Antron

Note: Cover entire fly except the tuft with Hard as Hull Head Cement.

Primrose and Pearl

Originator: Mike Kruise
Tier: Mike Kruise

Hook: #16-22 Tiemco 2488
Bead: Copper
Thread: Hot yellow 70-denier Ultra Thread
Abdomen: Yellow Krystal Flash
Rib: Hot yellow Ultra Wire (small)
Collar: Hot yellow Ice Dub

Note: Use a 3/32" bead for sizes 16-18 and 5/64" for sizes 20-22.

Bomber Chironomid

Originator: Mike Kruise
Tier: Mike Kruise

Hook: #12-18 Tiemco 2487
Bead: White brass or tungsten
Thread: Black 70-denier Ultra Thread
Abdomen: Black Hareline Midge Tubing
Rib: Red Ultra Wire (small or extra small)

Note: Use a 1/8" bead for sizes 12-14 and 3/32" for sizes 16-18.

Black RK Midge Pupa

Originator: Mike Kruise
Tier: Mike Kruise

Hook: #18-22 Tiemco 2487
Bead: Silver brass or tungsten
Thread: Black 16/0 Veevus
Abdomen: Black Hareline Micro Tubing
Rib: Silver Ultra Wire (extra small)
Tuft: White Antron

Mercury Zebra Midge

Originator: Dick Shinton
Tier: Dick Shinton

Hook: #18-22 Dai-Riki 270
Bead: Clear silver-lined glass (extra small)
Thread: Black 70-denier Ultra Thread
Abdomen: Black 70-denier Ultra Thread
Rib: Silver Ultra Wire (extra small)
Collar: UV black Ice Dub

Silver Streak Midge Pupa

Originator: Dick Shinton
Tier: Dick Shinton

Hook: #18-22 Dai-Riki 270
Bead: Clear silver-lined glass (extra small)
Thread: White 14/0 Gordon Griffiths
Abdomen: Pearl UTC Mirage Tinsel (medium)
Rib: Black Ultra Wire (extra small)
Collar: UV gray Ice Dub
Gills: Oral B Super Floss

Bulletproof Midge

Originator: Unknown
Tier: Dick Shinton

Hook: #18-22 Dai-Riki 270
Thread: Cream 70-denier Ultra Thread
Abdomen: Ecru Hobby Lobby crochet thread (medium)
Collar: Light blue Krystal Flash
Head: Tying thread colored with a black Sharpie

Duracell Midge

Originator: Jim Neiberger
Tier: Jim Neiberger

Hook: #18-22 Tiemco 2487
Bead: Black glass (extra small)
Thread: Trico 17/0 Uni-Thread
Abdomen: Brown, wine, and amber Ultra Wire (small)
Wing: Oral B Dental Floss

Spanish Ruby

Originator: Jim Neiberger
Tier: Jim Neiberger

Hook: #18-22 Tiemco 2487
Bead: Red glass (extra small)
Thread: Trico 17/0 Uni-Thread
Abdomen: Silver and wine Ultra Wire (small)
Wing: Oral B Dental Floss

UPS Midge

Originator: Jim Neiberger
Tier: Jim Neiberger

Hook: #18-22 Tiemco 2487
Bead: Gunmetal glass (extra small)
Thread: Trico 17/0 Uni-Thread
Abdomen: Brown and yellow Ultra Wire (small)
Wing: Oral B Dental Floss

Sage Flashback Midge

Originator: Jim Neiberger
Tier: Jim Neiberger

Hook: #18-22 Tiemco 2487
Thread: Trico 17/0 Uni-Thread
Abdomen: Black and golden olive Ultra Wire (small)
Wing Case: White Razor Foam (.05mm) overlaid by Flashabou
Thorax: Peacock herl

Olive Lace Midge

Originator: Jim Neiberger
Tier: Jim Neiberger

Hook: #18-22 Tiemco 2487
Bead: Black glass (extra small)
Thread: Trico 17/0 Uni-Thread
Abdomen: Black and golden olive Ultra Wire (small)
Wing: Pearl Krystal Flash

Ghost Midge

Originator: Herman deGala
Tier: Herman deGala

Hook: #16-14 Tiemco 2302
Thread: Trico 17/0 Uni-Thread
Tag: Wapsi Red Tinsel (small)
Abdomen: Clear D-Rib (small)
Lateral Line: Gold Lagartun Wire (extra fine)
Wing Case: Mottled brown Medallion Sheeting and UV Knot Sense
Thorax: Tan ostrich herl
Gills: White Flouro Fibre
Wingpads: Natural goose biots

Note: Color thread with an AD tan permanent marker to match body color.

Swimming Black Midge

Originator: Herman deGala
Tier: Herman deGala

Hook: #16-18 Daiichi 1222 or Daiichi 1521
Thread: Trico 17/0 Uni-Thread
Tag: Wapsi Red Tinsel (small)
Underbody: Black thread
Abdomen: Clear D-Rib (small)
Wing Case: Mottled brown Medallion Sheeting and UV Knot Sense
Thorax: Peacock herl
Wingpads: Natural goose biots

Note: Color thread with a permanent marker to match body color.

Okole Midge (Red)

Originator: Herman deGala
Tier: Herman deGala

Hook: #16-20 Tiemco 206BL
Thread: Trico 17/0 Uni-Thread
Tag: Wapsi Red Tinsel (small)
Abdomen: Natural peacock, stripped
Wing Case: Mottled brown Medallion Sheeting and UV Knot Sense
Thorax: Tan ostrich herl
Wingpads: Natural goose biots

Note: Color thread with an AD tan permanent marker to match body color. Color variations include olive and black.

Mamba Midge Pupa

Originator: Duane Redford
Tier: Duane Redford

Hook: #20-24 Tiemco 2488
Thread: Black 8/0 Uni-Thread
Abdomen: Black 8/0 Uni-Thread
Rib: Gold Ultra Wire, reversed ribbed (small)
Wing: Pearl Flashabou
Head: Black 8/0 Uni-Thread

South Platte Shimmer Midge

Originator: Tom Uba
Tier: Duane Redford

Hook: #20-22 Tiemco 2488
Thread: Black 70-denier Ultra Thread
Abdomen: Black 70-denier Ultra Thread
Rib: Metallic blue Sulky
Wing: Johnson and Johnson unwaxed dental floss
Head: Black Superfine

Note: Cover abdomen with RIO UV Knot Sealer.

Thin Blue Midge

Originator: Josef Shafer
Tier: Josef Shafer

Hook: #18-22 Tiemco 200R
Thread: Iron gray 8/0 Uni-Thread
Abdomen: Iron gray 8/0 Uni-Thread
Rib: Metallic Sulky Holoshimmer Thread
Thorax: Hareline muskrat dubbing

Tricky Bug

Originator: Josef Shafer
Tier: Josef Shafer

Hook: #22-24 Tiemco 2488
Thread: Black 8/0 Uni-Thread
Abdomen: Spirit River black turkey biot and Metallic Sulky Holoshimmer Thread
Wing: White Larva Lace Dry Foam
Thorax: Black Superfine

Shafermid

Originator: Josef Shafer
Tier: Josef Shafer

Hook: #16-18 Tiemco 200R
Bead: Pearl tungsten (2mm)
Thread: Light tan 6/0 Danville
Rib: Brown Danville waxed Monocord
Thorax: Tan Ice Dub

Red H. Midge

Originator: Tom Whitley
Tier: Tom Whitley

Hook: #16-20 Tiemco 2487
Bead: Red Spirit River glass (extra small)
Thread: Black 14/0 Veevus
Abdomen: Black 14/0 Veevus
Rib: Gold Ultra Wire (fine)
Tuft: White Antron
Thorax: Pheasant tail Ice Dub

Beavis

Originator: Tom Whitley
Tier: Tom Whitley

Hook: #16-20 Tiemco 2487
Thread: Black 6/0 Uni-Thread
Abdomen: Black Superfine
Rib 1: Blue Flashabou
Rib 2: Copper Ultra Wire (small)
Thorax: Tan Awesome Possum

Flashback Brassie

Originator: Tom Whitley
Tier: Tom Whitley

Hook: #16-20 Mustad 3906
Bead: Gold Spirit River glass (extra small)
Thread: Gray 14/0 Veevus
Tail: Pearl Flashabou
Flashback: Pearl Flashabou
Abdomen: Copper Ultra Wire
Rib: Copper Ultra Wire
Thorax: Peacock Ice Dub

Flash

Originator: Tom Whitley
Tier: Tom Whitley

Hook: #16-20 Mustad 3906
Thread: Black 8/0 Uni-Thread
Abdomen: Black 8/0 Uni-Thread
Rib: Pearl Flashabou
Head: Black Superfine

Crystal Serendipity

Originator: Tom Whitley variation of original
Tier: Tom Whitley

Hook: #16-22 Tiemco 100
Thread: Gray 14/0 Veevus
Abdomen: Red, blue, pearl, gold, and copper Krystal Flash
Wing: Trimmed natural deer hair

Midge Pupa

Originator: Tom Whitley
Tier: Tom Whitley

Hook: #18-20 Mustad 3906
Bead: Purple glass (extra small)
Thread: Olive 14/0 Veevus
Tail: Brown Betts' Tailing Fibers
Abdomen: Olive Hareline Micro Tubing
Thorax: Peacock Ice Dub

Gunmetal Midge

Originator: Tom Whitley
Tier: Tom Whitley

Hook: #16-24 Tiemco 2487
Bead: Spirit River gunmetal glass (extra small)
Thread: Gray 14/0 Veevus
Abdomen: Pearl Flashabou
Wing: White Antron
Thorax: Peacock Ice Dub

Chironoflash

Originator: Steve Parrott
Tier: Umpqua Feather Merchants

Hook: #18-22 Tiemco 2488
Thread: Rusty dun 8/0 Uni-Thread
Abdomen: Olive brown Hareline Micro Tubing
Collar: Pearl Micro Flashabou
Wing Case: Dark dun Medallion Sheeting
Thorax: Gray Superfine

Zombie Bomber Pupa

Originator: John Perizzolo
Tier: John Perizzolo

Hook: #12-18 Tiemco 2487
Thread: Olive dun 8/0 Uni-Thread
Abdomen: Gray D-Rib
Thorax: Olive black Hareline STS Trilobal Leech Dubbing
Tuft: White Uni-Floss

Note: Coat abdomen with Loon UV Clear Fly Finish.

Tube Midge

Originator: Landon Mayer
Tier: Umpqua Feather Merchants

Hook: #18-22 Tiemco 2488
Thread: Red 8/0 Uni-Thread
Abdomen: Clear Midge Tubing with red Ultra Wire (small) inserted into tubing
Head: Black 8/0 Uni-Thread

Note: Black is also effective.

Black Beauty

Originator: Pat Dorsey
Tier: Pat Dorsey

Hook: #18-24 Tiemco 101
Thread: Black 8/0 Uni-Thread
Rib: Copper Ultra Wire (extra small)
Abdomen: Black 8/0 Uni-Thread
Thorax: Black Superfine

Mercury Flashback Black Beauty

Originator: Pat Dorsey
Tier: Pat Dorsey

Hook: #18-24 Tiemco 2488
Bead: Clear silver-lined glass (extra small)
Thread: Black 8/0 Uni-Thread
Flashback: Pearl Mylar tinsel (small)
Rib: Copper Ultra Wire (extra small)
Abdomen: Black 8/0 Uni-Thread
Collar: Black Superfine

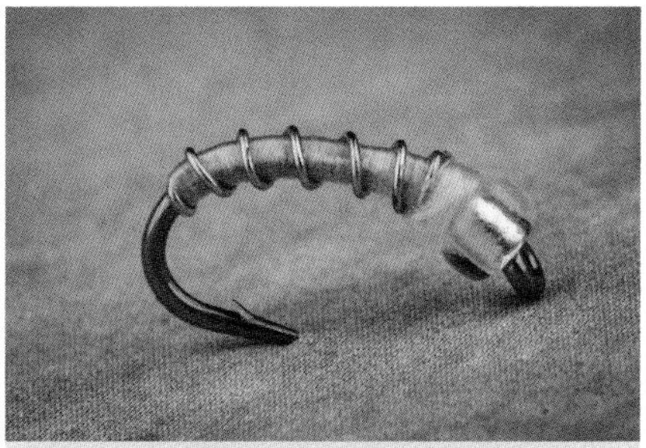

Mercury Midge (White)

Originator: Pat Dorsey
Tier: Pat Dorsey

Hook: #18-22 Tiemco 2487
Bead: Clear silver-lined glass (extra small)
Thread: White 6/0 Danville
Rib: Copper Ultra Wire (extra small)
Abdomen: White 6/0 Danville
Collar: White 6/0 Danville

Note: Color variations include black, brown, olive, and gray.

Medallion Midge Pupa

Originator: Pat Dorsey
Tier: Pat Dorsey

Hook: #18-24 Tiemco 101
Thread: Dark brown 8/0 Uni-Thread
Abdomen: Dark brown 8/0 Uni-Thread
Rib: White 6/0 Uni-Thread
Thorax: Rust brown Superfine
Wingbuds: Medium-dun Medallion Sheeting

Pale Olive Midge Larva

Originator: Pat Dorsey
Tier: Pat Dorsey

Hook: #16-20 Tiemco 2487
Thread: Light cahill 8/0 Uni-Thread
Underbody: Light cahill 8/0 Uni-Thread
Body: Clear Micro Tubing
Head: Light cahill 8/0 Uni-Thread

Beadhead Red Larva

Originator: Unknown
Tier: Pat Dorsey

Hook: #18-22 200R
Bead: Red glass (extra small)
Thread: Red 8/0 Uni-Thread
Underbody: Red 8/0 Uni-Thread
Body: Red Micro Tubing

Mercury Brassie (Copper)

Originator: Pat Dorsey variation of Gene Lynch, Tug Davenport, and Ken Chandler original
Tier: Pat Dorsey

Hook: #18-22 Tiemco 2487
Bead: Clear silver-lined glass (extra small)
Thread: Black 8/0 Uni-Thread
Abdomen: Copper Ultra Wire (small)
Thorax: Peacock herl

Note: Color variations include blue, black, chartreuse, red, and green.

Mercury Blood Midge

Originator: Pat Dorsey
Tier: Pat Dorsey

Hook: #18-22 Tiemco 200R
Bead: Clear silver-lined glass (extra small)
Thread: Red 8/0 Uni-Thread
Rib: Gold Ultra Wire (extra small)
Abdomen: Red 8/0 Uni-Thread
Thorax: Peacock herl

Top Secret Midge

Originator: Pat Dorsey
Tier: Pat Dorsey

Hook: #18-26 Tiemco 2488
Thread: Dark brown 8/0 Uni-Thread
Rib: White 6/0 Uni-Thread
Wing: Glamour Madeira
Thorax: Rust brown Superfine

Black Fly Larva

Originator: Steve Parrott
Tier: Umpqua Feather Merchants

Hook: #16-22 Tiemco 100
Thread: Gray 8/0 Uni-Thread
Abdomen: Olive-brown Micro Tubing
Feelers: White CDC puff

Note: Shape body like a bowling pin.

Little Purple Bug

Originator: Steve Parrott
Tier: Umpqua Feather Merchants

Hook: #18-22 Tiemco 2488
Thread: Gray 8/0 Uni-Thread
Abdomen: UV purple Krystal Flash
Wing: White Razor Foam (1mm)
Thorax: Adams gray Superfine

San Juan Emerger

Originator: Chuck Rizuto
Tier: Pat Dorsey

Hook: #18-24 Tiemco 100
Thread: Black 8/0 Uni-Thread
Abdomen: Pheasant tail fibers
Rib: Copper Ultra Wire (small)
Wing: White Z-Lon

Minute Midge (Olive)

Originator: Vince Wilcox
Tier: Umpqua Feather Merchants

Hook: #12-22 Tiemco 2488
Bead: Peacock glass (extra small)
Thread: Black 8/0 Uni-Thread
Abdomen: Olive Midge Braid
Thorax: Olive brown Ice Dub
Flashback: Fuchsia Holographic Tinsel

Note: Color variations include black, copper, red, and brown.

Rojo Midge (Red)

Originator: Greg Garcia
Tier: Greg Garcia

Hook: #18-22 Tiemco 200R
Bead: Silver lined ruby glass (extra small)
Thread: Red 70-denier Ultra Thread
Abdomen: Red 70-denier Ultra Thread
Rib: Silver Lagartun (fine)
Thorax: Dyed bright green peacock herl
Gills: Oral B Ultra Floss

Note: Color variations include green and black.

Tungsten Flashback Black Beauty

Originator: Pat Dorsey
Tier: Pat Dorsey

Hook: #18-24 Tiemco 2488
Bead: Black tungsten (1.5mm)
Thread: Black 8/0 Uni-Thread
Flashback: Pearl Mylar tinsel (small)
Rib: Copper Ultra Wire (extra small)
Abdomen: Black 8/0 Uni-Thread

Flashback Mono Midge (Gray)

Originator: Unknown
Tier: Aaron Carithers

Hook: #20-26 Tiemco 2488
Thread: Gray 8/0 Uni-Thread
Rib: 5X monofiliament
Abdomen: Gray 8/0 Uni-Thread
Wing Case: UV pearl Krystal Flash (2 strands)
Thorax: Gray Fine and Dry

Note: Color variations include black and olive.

Big Mac Midge Pupa

Originator: John Tavenner
Tier: Aaron Carithers

Hook: #20-22 Tiemco 200R
Thread: Gray 8/0 Uni-Thread
Abdomen: Clear Hareline Midge Tubing
Rib: Red 6/0 Uni-Thread
Thorax: Black Fine and Dry

Trojin Midge

Originator: Jin Choi
Tier: Jin Choi

Hook: #16-18 Tiemco 2457
Thread: Black 12/0 Benecchi
Abdomen: Black 12/0 Benecchi
Rib: Copper Ultra Wire (extra small)
Thorax: Peacock herl and styrofoam ball (small) wrapped in latex

Trojin Bloodworm

Originator: Jin Choi
Tier: Jin Choi

Hook: #14-18 Tiemco 2457
Thread: Red 12/0 Benecchi
Abdomen: Red Spanflex (small)
Thorax: Peacock herl and styrofoam ball (small) wrapped in latex

Curmidgeon

Originator: Jin Choi
Tier: Jin Choi

Hook: #18-22 Tiemco 101
Bead: Silver tungsten
Thread: Red 12/0 Benecchi
Abdomen: Black Superfine, copper French tinsel (extra small), and clear Micro Tubing
Thorax: Gray UV Ice Dub and white CDL with chickabou

Note: Use a 5/64" bead for sizes 18-20 and 1/16" for size 22.

Cupcake Midge

Originator: Joe Johnson
Tier: Joe Johnson

Hook: #18-24 Tiemco 2487
Bead: Clear silver-lined glass (extra small)
Thread: Brown 8/0 Uni-Thread
Abdomen: Brown 8/0 Uni-Thread
Rib: Copper Ultra Wire (small)
Thorax: Fluorescent hot pink Hareline UV Ice Dub

Orange Crush

Originator: Aaron Carithers
Tier: Aaron Carithers

Hook: #18-24 Tiemco 2488
Thread: Fire orange 8/0 Uni-Thread
Rib: UV pearl Krystal Flash
Abdomen: Clear Midge Tubing
Head: Fire orange 8/0 Uni-Thread

Sorry Charlie Pearl Legs

Originator: Bubba Smith
Tier: Bubba Smith

Hook: #18-24 Tiemco 200R
Thread: Brown Bennechi #14
Rib: Black Krystal Flash
Abdomen: Brown Bennechi #14
Thorax: Black 8/0 Uni-Thread
Wing Case: White Fluoro Fibre
Legs: White Fluoro Fibre
Head: Tying thread colored with a black Sharpie

Note: Color variations include light brown, black, pale yellow, tan, gray, and olive.

Flash Collar Midge Larva (Brown)

Originator: Bubba Smith
Tier: Bubba Smith

Hook: #18-24 Tiemco 200R
Thread: Brown 70-denier Ultra Thread
Abdomen: Brown 70-denier Ultra Thread
Collar: Pearl midge Krystal Flash
Thorax: Black Bennechi #14

Note: Coat fly with Hard As Nails. Color variations include gray, watery olive, black, and white.

Foam Back Midge (Black)

Originator: Bubba Smith
Tier: Bubba Smith

Hook: #18-24 Tiemco 2487
Thread: Black 70-denier Ultra Thread
Abdomen: Black 70-denier Ultra Thread
Rib: Black Midge Tubing
Wing Case: Foam off the outside of a to-go cup from a coffee shop
Thorax: Black 70-denier Ultra Thread

Note: Color variations include olive and gray.

Wellsey's Skinny Midge

Originator: Chris Wells
Tier: Chris Wells

Hook: #18-24 Tiemco 2488
Bead: Clear silver lined Killer Caddis glass (extra small)
Thread: Olive dun 8/0 Uni-Thread
Rib: White 8/0 Uni-Thread
Thorax: Peacock herl

Wellsey's Flash Midge

Originator: Chris Wells
Tier: Chris Wells

Hook: #18-24 Tiemco 2488
Bead: Clear silver lined Killer Caddis glass (extra small)
Thread: Black 8/0 Uni-Thread
Abdomen: Black 8/0 Uni-Thread
Rib: Pearl Krystal Flash (single strand)
Wing: Pearl Krystal Flash
Thorax: Peacock herl

Bling Midge (Gray)

Originator: Ray Johnston
Tier: Solitude Fly Company

Hook: #18-24 Daiichi 1110
Thread: Black 8/0 Uni-Thread
Abdomen: Charcoal Gudebrod rod wrapping thread
Thorax: Pearl Krystal Flash
Head: Black 8/0 Uni-Thread

Note: Color variations include brown and black.

Tubing Midge Emerger

Originator: Ray Johnson
Tier: Solitude Fly Company

Hook: #18-24 Tiemco 2487
Thread: Brown 8/0 Uni-Thread
Tail: Tan Stalcup's Trailing Shuck
Abdomen: Brown Micro Tubing
Wing: Poly yarn
Thorax: Chocolate rabbit dubbing

Olive Glass Bead Midge

Originator: Brad Befus
Tier: Brad Befus

Hook: #16-24 Tiemco 2488
Bead: Clear pearl glass (extra small)
Thread: Gray 70-denier Ultra Thread
Abdomen: Olive goose biot
Rib: Gold Ultra Wire (extra small)
Thorax: Light gray UV Ice Dub

Note: Color variations include red, gray, and black.

Flux Capacitor

Originator: Juan Ramirez
Tier: Juan Ramirez

Hook: #18-24 Tiemco 2488
Thread: Red 8/0 MFC
Body: Red 8/0 MFC
Rib: Black Ultra Wire (extra small)
Thorax: Red 8/0 MFC
Wing Case: Lagartun Pearl Micro Flat Sparkle Braid
Overcoat: Epoxy

Note: Color variations include black, purple, and fire orange.

Twisted Sister Midge

Originator: Juan Ramirez
Tier: Juan Ramirez

Hook: #18-24 Tiemco 101
Thread: Black 8/0 MFC
Abdomen: Summer brown (54A) Coats and Clark sewing thread, twisted
Wing: Glamour Madeira
Head: Black 8/0 MFC

Note: For the cream variation use cream (116) Coats and Clark sewing thread for abdomen.

Hub's Gray Reefer

Originator: Jerry Hubka
Tier: Jerry Hubka

Hook: #18-22 Tiemco 2488BL
Bead: Rainbow black glass (extra small)
Thread: Blue dun 70-denier Ultra Thread
Rib: Silver Ultra Wire (extra small)
Wing: UV Pearl Krystal Flash

Note: Color variations include fluorescent fire orange.

Hub's Red Honey Dip Chironomid

Originator: Jerry Hubka
Tier: Jerry Hubka

Hook: 18-12 Daiichi 1273
Thread: Red 70-denier Ultra Thread
Body: Yellow UTC Vinyl Rib Midge (MDG size)
Thorax: Peacock black Ice Dub
Wing Case: Opaque Red Wapsi Razor Foam (.5mm) under Ice Blue Pearl UTC Tinsel (large)
Gills: Oral B Ultra Floss Dental Floss

Note: Coat wing case foam, tinsel and vinyl rib with Clear Cure Goo Hydro. Color variations include blue and chartreuse.

Kleis' Midge

Originator: Jon Kleis
Tier: Jon Kleis

Hook: #20-24 Tiemco 2488
Bead: Clear silver lined glass (extra small)
Thread: Olive dun 8/0 Uni-Thread
Underbody: Olive dun 8/0 Uni-Thread
Abdomen: Light olive Hareline Micro Tubing
Wing Bud: Peacock Krystal Flash
Thorax: BWO Superfine

Note: Color variations include purple, blue, black brown, and chocolate.

Manhattan Midge

Originator: Forrest Dorsey
Tier: Forrest Dorsey

Hook: #18-22 Tiemco 2487
Bead: Clear silver-lined glass (extra small)
Thread: Black 8/0 Uni-Thread
Abdomen: Black 8/0 Uni-Thread
Rib: Copper Lagartun wire (small)
Wing: Glamour Madeira
Thorax: Peacock herl

Note: This fly can be tied in a flashback version by adding a strip of Mylar tinsel underneath the rib.

Zombie Midge (Cream)

Originator: John Perizzolo
Tier: John Perizzolo

Hook: #18-22 Tiemco 2487
Bead: Gunmetal glass (extra small)
Thread: White 8/0 Uni-Thread
Abdomen: Pearl glow Flashabou

Note: Color variations include red, brown, and black. Coat fly with Loon UV Clear Fly Finish.

Griffith's Gnat

Originator: George Griffith
Tier: Steve Henderson

Hook: #16-22 Tiemco 100
Thread: Black 8/0 Uni-Thread
Abdomen: Peacock herl
Hackle: Grizzly Whiting Farms rooster
Rib: Copper Ultra Wire (extra small)

Matt's Midge

Originator: Matt Miles
Tier: Matt Miles

Hook: #20-24 Tiemco 101
Thread: Black 8/0 Uni-Thread
Abdomen: Black 8/0 Uni-Thread
Wing: White Z-Lon or McFlylon
Hackle: Grizzly rooster

Matt's Hi-Viz Midge

Originator: Matt Miles
Tier: Matt Miles

Hook: #20-24 Tiemco 101
Thread: Black 8/0 Uni-Thread
Abdomen: Black 8/0 Uni-Thread
Wing: Cerise Z-Lon or McFlylon
Hackle: Grizzly rooster

Tak's Hovering Midge

Originator: Rick Takahashi
Tier: Rick Takahashi

Hook: #18-22 Daiichi 1180
Thread: Black 12/0 Veevus
Abdomen: Black 12/0 Veevus
Thorax: Black 12/0 Veevus
Wing: Dun MFC Widow's Web
Hackle: Whiting Farms grizzly saddle

Note: Trim bottom of hackle.

Tak's High Post Midge

Originator: Rick Takahashi
Tier: Rick Takahashi

Hook: #18-22 Daiichi 1180
Thread: Black 12/0 Veevus
Abdomen: Black 12/0 Veevus
Hackle: Whiting Farms black midge saddle
Wing: Black Antron fibers

Purple Haze

Originator: Greg Blessing
Tier: Greg Blessing

Hook: #16-24 Tiemco 2487
Thread: Black 8/0 Uni-Thread
Shuck: Root beer Krystal Flash (two strands knotted at end)
Abdomen: Black, purple, and dark blue Flashabou (one strand each)
Thorax: UV purple Ice Dub
Soft Hackle: Whiting Farms Hebert Miner Wet Fly Hackle (two or three wraps)

Note: Pearl poly yarn Metallica can be purchased from Hobby Lobby.

Para Midge

Originator: Greg Blessing
Tier: Greg Blessing

Hook: #18-24 Tiemco 2487
Thread: Black 70-denier Ultra Thread
Shuck: Root beer Krystal Flash, two strands
Abdomen: Hareline gray muskrat
Wing: Gray CDC
Post: White closed-cell foam
Hackle: Grizzly rooster hackle

Midge Cluster

Originator: Greg Blessing
Tier: Greg Blessing

Hook: #18-24 Tiemco 100
Thread: Purple 70-denier Ultra Thread
Post: Purple Antron
Hackle: Grizzly Whiting Farms rooster and brown hackle

Spider Midge

Originator: Fred Gender
Tier: Umpqua Feather Merchants

Hook: #18-22 Tiemco 206BL
Thread: Black 8/0 Uni-Thread
Abdomen: Black 8/0 Uni-Thread
Rib: White 8/0 Uni-Thread
Thorax: Black beaver dubbing
Hackle: Starling
Wing Case: Natural CDC
Wing: CDC tips from wing case

Hi-Viz Midge

Originator: Dr. Eric Pettine
Tier: Dr. Eric Pettine

Hook: #18-24 Tiemco 101
Thread: Medium dun 14/0 Veevus
Tail: Medium dun Antron
Abdomen: Palmered medium dun midge hackle
Overbody: Black closed-cell foam
Indicator: Burnt orange Antron

Low Rider Midge

Originator: Larry Kingrey
Tier: Larry Kingrey

Hook: #18-24 Tiemco 100
Thread: Black 8/0 Uni-Thread
Abdomen: Black foam strip (.5mm)
Rib: White flat waxed nylon
Wing: UV Minnow Belly
Hackle: Grizzly rooster, clipped on bottom

Midge Cluster

Originator: Paul Dubas
Tier: Pat Dorsey

Hook: #15-17 Tiemco 102Y
Thread: Black 8/0 Uni-Thread
Underbody: Black 8/0 Uni-Thread
Hackle: Brown and grizzly rooster
Post: Black Z-Lon
Head: Black 8/0 Uni-Thread

Hi-Viz Griffith's Gnat

Originator: Variation of George Griffith original
Tier: Pat Dorsey

Hook: #18-26 Tiemco 101
Thread: Black 8/0 Uni-Thread
Abdomen: Peacock herl
Post: Cerise McFlylon
Hackle: Grizzly rooster

Snowshoe Midge Emerger (Black)

Originator: Jim Cannon
Tier: Jim Cannon

Hook: #18-24 Tiemco 2488
Thread: Black 8/0 Uni-Thread
Abdomen: Black Micro Tubing
Thorax: Black Fine and Dry
Wing: Black and natural snowshoe rabbit hind foot dubbing mixed with white Ice Dub

Note: Color variations include brown and olive.

Snowshoe Suspender Midge

Originator: Jim Cannon
Tier: Jim Cannon

Hook: #16-26 Tiemco 2488
Thread: Black 8/0 Uni-Thread
Abdomen: Natural goose biot
Thorax: Black Fine and Dry
Wing: Black snowshoe rabbit hind foot dubbing mixed with white Ice Dub

Hi-Viz Midge

Originator: Pat Dorsey
Tier: Pat Dorsey

Hook: #18-24 Tiemco 2487
Thread: Tan 8/0 Uni-Thread
Abdomen: Tan Superfine
Wing: Fluorescent orange McFlylon
Thorax: Tan Superfine
Hackle: Grizzly rooster

Brooks' Sprout Midge

Originator: Bob Brooks
Tier: Solitude Fly Company

Hook: #18-22 Tiemco 2487
Thread: Black 8/0 Uni-Thread
Abdomen: Black 8/0 Uni-Thread
Post: White Round Rainy's Foam (small)
Hackle: Black rooster

Zing Wing Midge

Originator: John Betts
Tier: Randy Smith

Hook: #18-22 Tiemco 101
Thread: Black 8/0 Uni-Thread
Abdomen: Black 8/0 Uni-Thread
Wing: Metz Betts' Zing (clear)
Legs: Black Z-Lon
Thorax: Black Superfine

Midge Cluster

Originator: Bubba Smith
Tier: Bubba Smith

Hook: #15-17 Tiemco 102Y
Thread: Black 8/0 Uni-Thread
Abdomen: Black CDC in dubbing loop

Cranefly Larva (Olive)

Originator: John Barr
Tier: Umpqua Feather Merchants

Hook: #6-10 Tiemco 200R
Weight: .020" lead wire
Thread: Olive 70-denier Ultra Thread
Tail: Pale olive-gray marabou
Rib: 3X monofilament
Shell Back: Tan Thin Skin
Abdomen: Gray-olive Arizona Synthetic Dubbing.

Note: Tan is also effective for the abdomen.

Driftless Cranefly Adult

Originator: Jon Uhlenhop
Tier: Jon Uhlenhop

Hook: #11-15 Tiemco 112Y
Thread: Tan 14/0 Veevus
Abdomen: Tan craft foam (2mm) and tan Z-Lon
Wing: White Z-Lon
Legs: Tan Betts' Tailing Fibers
Thorax: Tan Superfine
Hackle: Cree or ginger rooster

Note: Color variations include amber, brown, and tan.

Furled Cranefly Adult

Originator: Jon Uhlenhop
Tier: Jon Uhlenhop

Hook: #11-15 Tiemco 112Y
Thread: Tan 14/0 Veevus
Abdomen: Tan craft foam (2mm)
Legs: Pheasant tail fibers (knotted)
Wing: Light dun or white hen hackle tips
Thorax: Tan Superfine
Hackle: Silver badger or ginger rooster

Note: Color variations include amber, brown, and tan.

CHAPTER 3

Mayflies and Their Imitations

Mayflies and their imitations have fueled more fly-fishing addictions than any other group of aquatic insects. The three stages of a mayfly's life cycle—nymph, dun, and spinner—are among the foundations of fly fishing. Angling history is filled with inspiring literature that showcases mayflies' importance to both the angler and the trout. Their dense population, unique behavior, and abundance make them one of the most important trout foods to have ever been imitated by an artificial fly.

Entomologists believe there are more than 700 species of North American mayflies. They are members of the Ephemeroptera insect order, which translates to "short-lived winged insect." Mayflies pass through incomplete metamorphosis, meaning their life cycle consists of an egg, a nymph, and two phases of the adult known as the subimago (dun) and the imago (spinner). Most mayflies have a one-year life cycle. The average duration for the egg phase is one to three months. Mayflies spend most of their life (eight to eleven months) in

A Green Drake dun from the Frying Pan River. Réne Harrop sums up mayflies best in his book Trout Hunter*: "Mayflies are the aristocrats of aquatic insects. They are fragile and graceful creatures, considered synonymous with clear streams, delicate dry flies, and rising trout. The adults resemble a miniature sailboat and are a familiar sight to most fishermen."* JAY NICHOLS

The size-shape-color formula is helpful when trying to select the appropriate fly. Anglers like Bob Dye believe that the behavior of the fly should be included in this time-tested recipe for success. Oftentimes it's the action or behavior of the nymph that can make the biggest difference in fooling selective trout.

their immature stage, known as the nymph. The dun and spinner stages, like the order's scientific name implies, are seldom longer than forty-eight hours.

Mature nymphs and adults can range in length from one-eighth inch to nearly an inch. The smallest mayflies are fall Blue-Winged Olives (previously called *Pseudocloeon*) and *Tricorythodes*, which are commonly tied on size 22-24 hooks. The largest mayflies are Green Drakes, Gray Drakes, and *Callibaetis*, which range between three-quarters and one inch long. *Callibaetis* mayflies are found on lakes and ponds or slow-moving, weedy streams. Rich Pilatzke says, "*Callibaetis* hatches in Colorado occur from late May to early September. The *Callibaetis* life cycle is approximately six weeks, so some waters in Colorado will get three generations of *Callibaetis* in a year. Like many mayflies, each succeeding generation is smaller. They start as size 12 and end the end the season as a size 18. The best months for the *Callibaetis* hatch in Colorado are June and July, when the hatches are thick and can last for hours."

All mayfly duns look similar in appearance, with a slender, slightly curved body, a pair of upright wings, a pair of hindwings (absent in some species), and two or three delicate tails depending on the species.

Understanding the mayfly life cycle will greatly improve your odds of catching fish. Matching the hatch involves understanding both the physical appearance and behavior of the nymphs, duns, and spinners. Trout recognize these differences and so should anglers who tie and fish their various imitations. The nymphs are easy to identify because they live underwater and do not have wings. The dun is a winged version that hatches from the nymph. The dun is not a true adult because it is not sexually mature and cannot mate in this stage of its life. Distinguishing mayfly duns from spinners is more complex. Careful observation will help you decipher the difference between each stage. The biggest difference is the dun has a smoky-colored, opaque wing in comparison to the spinner, which has a clear, glasslike wing. The spinner is the final, or true adult, stage of development, where mating and egg laying occurs.

NYMPHS

Mayfly nymphs have several distinguishing features that aid in their identification: two or three tails (depending on the species), platelike gills on the sides of their segmented abdomen, and a single tarsal claw on the end of each leg. Mayfly nymphs are found in a variety of sizes, shapes, and colors. Mayflies spend most of their life in the nymphal stage. They exhibit a wide range of behaviors and the different species thrive in varied habitats.

Entomologists have divided mayflies into four groups—swimmers, crawlers, clingers, and burrowers—based on the behavior of the nymph. In *An Angler's Guide to Aquatic Insects and Their Imitations*, Rick Hafele notes, "Insect behavior is of major importance to fly fishers. By dividing all mayflies into four groups, not only is their identification greatly simplified, but much of the difficulty of pattern selection and presentation is eliminated." Anglers who study and become familiar with these groups of mayflies will be able choose the appropriate patterns and tactics to imitate the naturals.

Swimmers are among the most important mayfly nymphs to imitate because their active behavior routinely causes them to drift in the current, especially prior to emergence. Swimmers are recognized by their slender, tapered bodies, thin legs, and three tails. There are more than 200 species of mayflies that are considered swimmers. Some of the most prevalent swimmers are members of the Baetidae family, which includes more than 150 species. This large group of mayflies is more commonly known as Blue-Winged Olives, and they provide excellent dry-fly fishing during the spring and fall.

Crawlers also play a significant role in Colorado. Members of the Ephemerellidae and Leptohyphidae families belong in this group, part of the approximately 220 species of mayflies that are considered crawlers. Pale Morning Duns,

Western Green Drakes, and Tricos are the common names that most anglers recognize. Crawlers can be distinguished from other mayflies because they have a squared-off head, a boxy rectangular body, noticeable forked gills, and three tails. Crawlers spend most of their time crawling along the substrate, feeding on algae and decaying vegetation. Their behavior and abundance increases their availability to trout. Crawlers typically live in faster currents where they often get knocked loose from the substrate. Crawlers are feeble swimmers; therefore, it takes them longer to get back to the stream bottom in comparison to swimmers. This makes them an important food source for opportunistic trout.

Clinger mayflies thrive in swifter streams with medium to fast riffles and runs. The nymphs are poor swimmers, but as their name implies, they cling to the stream bottom extremely well and are rarely found drifting in the current. Clingers belong to the Heptageniidae family, which includes more than 130 species. One prominent identifying feature is a broad flat head that is wider than the thorax and abdomen. Other distinguishing characteristics include large platelike gills and three tails. The nymphs' flat shape allows them to withstand heavy currents and avoid getting knocked loose from the substrate. The small Western Red Quill is the most important crawler found in Colorado waters.

Burrowers are routinely identified by their size: They are the largest mayflies found in North America. The nymphs dig cavities in the substrate where they hide during the day and come out to feed during the low-light hours. The nymphs can live for two or three years before they reach maturity. The nymphs have noticeable tusklike mandibles, stout digging legs, large, fluffy gills, and three tails fringed heavily with hairlike follicles. This group of mayflies is of the least importance to Colorado anglers, as there are only approximately three families, four genera, and six species throughout the United States. The Western Brown Drake (*Ephemera simulans*) and the Western Gray Drake (*Siphlonurus occidentalis*) are the only two burrowers that Colorado anglers need to familiarize themselves with.

Throughout a mayfly's one-year development, nymphs may molt 20 to 30 times before reaching maturity. As the nymph grows, it sheds its exoskeleton and replaces it with a slightly larger one. The stage between each molt is known as the instar. Warmer water temperatures accelerate the nymphs' development. The best growth rates occur when the water temperatures exceed 45 degrees, which only occurs about eight months of the year. When the nymph reaches maturity, it develops darkened wing pads and becomes unusually active before emergence.

Most mayflies emerge in the surface film or on the surface of the water. A few species, however, emerge underwater and some crawl to the edge of the streambank to emerge. Prior to emergence, the nymph's body cavities begin to fill with gases, forming air bubbles that cling to the exoskeleton. The trapped gases assist with the emerging process by providing buoyancy that forces the emerging nymph to the surface.

Joe Mitchell's Split Case series of mayfly nymphs has become popular in Colorado. I am especially fond of the tungsten version because it allows anglers to fish it as a dropper off an Elk Hair Caddis or other medium-size dry fly. Shallow riffles become prime areas to target during mayfly emergences. Conventional nymphing rigs will often spook trout or get hung up, spoiling your chances of fooling actively feeding fish in shallow riffles.

Similar to caddis and midges, trapped air produces a highly reflective area or brightness in the thorax area of the nymph. This becomes a trigger that helps trout differentiate live nymphs from empty shucks. Mike Mercer's Trigger Nymph imitates this reflective stage of a mayfly's emergence better than any pattern I've fished. "The Trigger Nymph style of tying—and it is a style, more than a specific pattern or patterns—came about as an attempt to imitate that stage of emergence where aquatic insects are making their final ascent to the surface," Mercer says. "Even underwater, many are already actively emerging from their nymphal shucks and have a distinctly different look than they had even just hours earlier, when they were crawling around on the bottom. A few species even emerge fully before swimming to the surface. So my challenge when sitting down to try and emulate this stage was to ask myself, "What were the trout seeing?" Flashbacks of various styles were already very popular when I came up with the Trigger Nymphs, and I knew one reason was that they were imitating this point of emergence. I designed my Trigger Nymphs to imitate specific insects (PMDs, BWOs, Green Drakes, etc.), with the hallmark feature of bursting wing buds created from Ice Dub. These emerging wings were rounder, more three-dimensional than a flat application of Flashabou, and exhibited the illusion of escaping gases that many bugs experience as their wing cases split open."

EMERGERS

Emergence occurs when the thorax area or wing case splits or cracks open lengthwise, allowing the adult to pull itself from the nymphal shuck. The wing buds appear first, followed by the thorax, head, and legs. Using the surface tension of the water, the partially emerged dun pulls the remaining parts of its abdomen and tail out of the nymphal shuck. Trout key on emergers because they are vulnerable and provide an easy meal that requires minimal effort.

Soft-hackle imitations are excellent patterns that represent emerging mayflies. Fly tiers simply incorporate a few turns of hen hackle or partridge into their design to simulate the wings and legs of the emerger. These emergers can be fished in the surface film or swung with traditional wet-fly tactics. The swinging or uplifting action closely resembles the emerging process.

Charlie Craven's Soft-Hackle Emerger has become a Colorado favorite. "I developed the Soft-Hackle Emerger back in my guiding days as an alternative to the South Platte River favorite, the RS 2," Craven explains. "My reasoning back then was that I wanted something that presented a similar silhouette but was just different enough to stand out from what all the other guides' clients were throwing." The sparse soft-hackle collar imitates the mayfly's legs and the white Fluoro Fibre imitates the emerging wing. Tied in a variety of colors—

J's Soft Hackle is an excellent imitation of a Blue-Winged Olive emerger. This Cheesman Canyon rainbow could not resist J's Soft Hackle during a spring Blue-Winged Olive hatch in the upper canyon. MARK ADAMS

gray, olive-black, pale yellow, and rust—this pattern will work well for imitating Blue-Winged Olives, Pale Morning Duns, Green Drakes, Tricos, and Red Quills. "The Soft-Hackle Emerger is really a simple little pattern. It requires little in the way of sophisticated tying skills, and perhaps its most important feature is its slimness," Craven adds.

J's Soft Hackle is another good option to consider when you are fishing emergers. "Several years ago when I was on the stream, I noticed a pod of fish feeding just under the surface. The fish were leaving a ring on the surface of the water but there were no visible signs that would indicate they were feeding on adults. After seining the upper water column, I found numerous mayfly nymphs that were just about ready to break the surface. I developed my Soft Hackle to simulate the emerger stage of Blue-Winged Olives. I fish this pattern in a similar fashion as you would fish a dry fly. Most of the time I make my cast up and across the current, letting it dead drift until it starts to swing. The swing is the most productive part of the drift, especially as it reaches the surface film."

Many mayfly duns never complete the emerging process and get trapped in their nymphal skin, ultimately causing them to perish. Cripples, stillborns, impaired duns, and captive duns are terms that anglers frequently use to describe mayflies that cannot complete the emerging process. Several conditions can prove to be detrimental during the emerging process; these include intense sunshine, low humidity, and wind, all of which can dehydrate the duns quickly and cause them to die.

Craig Mathews' Sparkle Dun has become one of my favorite flies. I can honestly say that I have fooled more trout with this pattern than any other mayfly imitation. "The evolution of this Sparkle Dun is interesting. Myself and my fishing friend and coworker at Blue Ribbon Flies, John Juracek, had used patterns as first tied by Swisher and Richards with limited success," Mathews says. "One morning while observing emerging Pale Morning Duns on the Railroad Ranch section of the Henry's Fork we noted a great number of stillborn or impaired duns coming down in the drift. Most of these impaired duns were trapped or attached to the nymphal shuck, which sparkled and shimmered in the light. We felt that this sparkle-shimmering feature of the still-attached shuck may have been the trigger to the rise for these stillborn/impaired duns."

Patterns like Bob Quigley's Cripple are also excellent imposters when trout are keying on cripples or stillborns. Quigley's design displays part of the mayfly's body below the surface film while a protruding wing above the surface simulates a mayfly dun trying to pull itself free from the nymphal skin. Industry professionals like Mike Lawson, who wrote the book *Spring Creeks*, believe that emergers and cripples drift considerable distances as they struggle to push their way through the surface film. Many of them never escape, providing an effortless meal as they enter the trout's window of vision.

DUNS

While the description of a mayfly dun as a miniature sailboat has been used over and over again for generations, the cliché still best defines the insect's shape and appearance. The dun can be identified by its slim body, large upright opaque wings, a pair of smaller wings called hindwings (absent in some species), and two or three tails. Once the dun has emerged from the nymphal shuck it floats on the surface until its wings dry. The duns are defenseless as they drift long distances before their wings dry. If you closely analyze the behavior of the newly hatched duns, you'll notice them trying to skip or skitter off the surface water, a positive indication that their wings are almost dry and they are ready to take flight. This behavior often becomes a trigger and entices a fish to eat the newly hatched duns. Once the wings of the dun are dry, they fly from the water's surface to seek protection from predators.

Bright and sunny days accelerate this process, enabling the duns to leave the water quickly. Overcast or inclement weather produces the best hatches because the high humidity stalls the emerging process and duns remain on the water longer. These conditions force the wings to unfold and dry slowly, making the duns extremely vulnerable until they take flight. If conditions are right, mayfly duns can cover the water, resulting in a blanket hatch. I have observed cases where there were several dozen mayflies within a square foot of surface area.

Too many or not enough mayflies can present problems for the dry-fly angler. The fishing becomes more challenging as the number of mayfly duns sitting on the water increases. In a dense hatch, your artificial imitation is one of many to choose from, which naturally diminishes your success. A shortfall of duns is problematic too. Fish that let a dozen sporadic naturals float overhead are tough to attract with a fly. Toss in cruising trout, and things become really challenging. The ideal situation is when a trout eats a dun every three to five seconds. During this type of consistent feeding rhythm the trout become much easier to fool.

The dun stage of a mayfly's life cycle has probably motivated more fly tiers than any other form of aquatic insect. The dun's graceful nature represents a pure form of fly fishing that has inspired innovation for decades. Tiers have developed several unique styles to imitate the beautiful dun—Catskill dry flies, thorax duns, no-hackles, Compara-duns, and parachute varieties—all of which have fooled selective trout on Colorado waters. Each variety or style has its advantages and disadvantages with regard to visibility, durability, and the way it sits in the surface film. All of these factors must be considered when choosing or tying dun patterns.

Most fly tiers would agree that the single most important element in tying the dun is creating a realistic silhouette of the wing. Many authors and guides prefer no-hackles or Compara-duns because they sit flush in the surface film. Mike Lawson believes that patterns tied with little or no hackle will not detract from the silhouette of the wing. In *Spring Creeks*, Lawson states, "I believe the Duck Quill No-Hackle, first described by Doug Swisher and Carl Richards in *Selective Trout*, will outperform all other patterns on glassy smooth water. I have heard anglers put them down because they say they are not durable. It is a fact that the duck quill fibers start to split after only a few casts and after a fish or two become totally shredded. Their fibers, however, hold the impressionistic shape of the wing better than any other material, and the wing is truer after the quill fibers separate."

My favorite dun pattern is the hair-wing variation of the no-hackle called Mathews' Sparkle Dun. Invented by Craig Mathews of Blue Ribbon Flies, it meets all the criteria of the ultimate guide fly: It has a simple design, floats well, is easy to see, is extremely durable, and it fools some of the most selective trout during a mayfly hatch. "Combining a wing of deer hair for durability, a dubbed body, and a sparkling-shimmering shuck of Z-Lon we created a pattern which is easy to tie, floats well, is visible, and produces better than other no-hackle designs or impaired or stillborn duns we have tried," Mathews says. "The sparkling Z-Lon shuck seems to be the key to this fly's effectiveness; it imitates the shuck better than any other material we have tried."

I have found the Sparkle Dun to fish well under a wide range of conditions and life cycle stages, from cripples or impaired duns to full-blown, completely emerged duns. Bar none, this is my go-to mayfly dun. Available in a wide range of colors, Mathews' Sparkle Dun can imitate anything from Green Drakes to Red Quills and everything in between. I am especially fond of the Blue-Winged Olive Sparkle Dun because in Colorado success in both the spring and fall hinges on a good Blue-Winged Olive dun imitation.

Barr's Vis-A-Dun is another great option for dry-fly fanatics. The fly incorporates both durability and visibility. In *Barr Flies*, Barr writes, "I developed the original Vis-A Dun twenty-five years ago, but back then it was called the Bulletproof Dun, inspired by my search for a fly that was not only visible, but also durable. In subsequent years, I started calling it the Vis-A-Dun because the named flowed off my tongue with less effort. Finding a dry-fly pattern that held up to several fish was a preoccupation of mine since all of the patterns I was using, especially the small ones, came apart after a few trout."

Like many anglers, Barr found that small dry flies (size 18 and smaller) fell apart easily because a trout's teeth would nick the fragile hackle stems and cause them to unravel. Barr came up with an easy fix: "I resolved this issue by cutting the hackle fibers off under the body flush with the dubbing and then laid a bead of vinyl cement over the exposed hackle stem, cementing the stem to the dubbed body."

For increased durability and visibility, Barr uses a light dun-colored polypropylene wing tied in the Compara-dun style. Barr fans out the wing and then adds a drop of cement to help the wing keep its shape. By changing the color of the dubbing, you can easily tie Blue-Winged Olives, Pale Morning Duns, Red Quills, and Tricos, which constitute a large percentage of the mayfly hatches in Colorado.

Jim Cannon's Snowshoe Dun is yet another no-hackle variation that is extremely durable and easy to see. The tail is

Jim Cannon fights a powerful Cheesman Canyon rainbow that he fooled with a Snowshoe Dun. Cannon's Snowshoe Dun series has become a guide favorite in Colorado during Blue-Winged Olive, PMD, and Trico hatches.

composed of split Microfibetts, the body is tied from a wrapped goose biot, and the wing is constructed from hind-foot snowshoe rabbit dubbing. Cannon's pattern represents a delicate blend of simplicity, visibility, and durability without any compromise.

Parachute patterns and high-visibility variations can provide a distinct advantage amid foam lines and harsh glare. A parachute-style fly has the hackle wrapped horizontally around the wing (oftentimes referred to as the post) rather than wound vertically around the shank of the hook. Parachute patterns have the same goal in mind as a no-hackle in that they allow the body to sit lower in the surface film, imparting a more realistic impression to the fish. The upright wing not only produces the important silhouette that dun imitations require, but also makes the fly much easier to see and follow on the water. By swapping the traditional white calf hair post with McFlylon for the wing, tiers can reduce the bulk in the thorax area, which produces a thin and sparse abdomen—a common characteristic of newly hatched duns.

White and gray wings provide the most realistic imitations, but these colors are not always the easiest to see. Tying parachute patterns with a brightly colored post will allow anglers to see the fly even under extreme conditions. Orange, cerise, and chartreuse McFlylon wings can be used to create hi-viz variations that provide optimal visibility in foam or bubble lines or extreme surface glare.

SPINNERS

Mayflies are not sexually mature until they pass through the final stage of their development, known as the spinner. Should the dun escape predation from hungry trout and birds, it will fly to nearby foliage to seek shelter and rest. In a process that takes anywhere from one hour to two days, the dun molts by shedding its exoskeleton and transforms into a spinner. Spinners are what entomologists consider true adults, as this is the stage when mating occurs, followed by the females' egg-laying phase. The spinnerfall occurs after the females release their eggs on the surface film and fall to the water to die.

Many anglers have difficulty distinguishing between duns and spinners. While the stages share many similarities, the differences are quite noticeable. The most obvious characteristic is the spinner's transparent, glasslike wing, as compared to the dun's opaque wing. Further analysis reveals that the spinner's tail is noticeably longer, the abdomen is thinner, the eyes are bigger, and the legs are elongated in comparison to the dun. The color of the abdomen is frequently different than that of the dun. Complicating things is the fact that males and females of the same species are sometimes a different color: Males tend to be darker with shiny abdomens and the females are lighter because the eggs inside produce a translucent abdomen.

Mating flights generally occur in the early morning and evening hours. Males take flight first, followed by the females. Males select a mate as the females join the mating flight.

The Trico spinnerfall is one of the premier hatches in Elevenmile Canyon. Greg Blessing was able to persuade this outstanding brown trout to the net after it took one of his beautifully tied Trico spinners.

You'll know you're experiencing a mating flight if you see mayflies dancing up and down along the streambank or observe huge swarms of mayflies flying back and forth over the water's surface. Some mating flights are so thick they resemble a tuft of smoke. The good news is that the spinnerfall is about to take place when you see pods of mayflies hovering over the stream.

Many anglers fail to capitalize on the spinnerfall because they arrive to the water too late or leave the river prematurely. A prime example of this is the Trico spinner hatch, which typically occurs shortly after dawn. The duns begin hatching an hour or two after sun-up and the spinnerfall starts as early as 9:00 a.m. If you show up to the stream midmorning, chances are pretty good that you have missed the best part of the hatch. Another example is the Red Quill hatch, which typically occurs between 4:30 p.m. and 6:30 p.m. If you decide to quit fishing by 4:00 p.m., you'll miss some excellent dry-fly fishing opportunities with Red Quill spinners.

Several factors can influence the density of the hatch or delay the spinnerfall. These include flow irregularities, cool nights or mornings, precipitation, and wind; all of them can have adverse effects on the hatch. On numerous occasions, I have experienced a flow increase at the Dream Stream or in Cheesman Canyon that has spoiled the morning Trico hatch. If the flows remain stable for twenty-four hours, the hatch comes off the next day like nothing ever happened. Cool summer nights can stall the morning mating flights and spinnerfall for an hour or two. This is no big deal, as the hatch still comes off, just a little later in the day. This is a common occurrence during the autumn season, especially with Tricos. Wind can be problematic when heavy gusts can blow around mating flights, which results in fewer spinners hitting the water.

Spent-wing mayflies have a distinct silhouette that differentiates them from the duns. Spinners lie on the water spread-eagle, with the tail, abdomen, and wings sitting flush on the surface. Anglers who fail to switch from upright-wing dun imitations to spent-wing patterns will most likely become frustrated by their inability to catch fish. Unlike duns that leave the water quickly, dying spinners remain on the water for long periods of time. Trout recognize this and feed on them with a vengeance.

Spinner imitations should have a long tail that is between one and one and a half shank lengths. Most tiers use three Microfibetts for their tails because they are easy to split and provide additional support and floatation on the back end of the fly. A slender, segmented abdomen is mandatory when tying realistic spinner imitations. Choosing the materials for a spinner's abdomen is a matter of personal preference. The most common options are thread, dubbing, or goose biots. My favorite spinner imitations incorporate goose biots into their abdomen design. Biots allow tiers to create beautiful, durable, segmented abdomens with little difficulty. Goose biots are

MAYFLY SPINNERS: INSIGHTS ON TYING AND FISHING

Rick Yancik

Spinners represent the final stage of the life of an adult mayfly. In some ways, spinners are an often overlooked and underrated stage. This has to do with occurrence, environmental conditions, and recognition.

The importance of mayfly spinners to trout is not equal across all species of mayflies. For example, PMD, Trico, and Gray Drake spinners usually occur in great abundance and contribute significantly to a trout's diet, whereas spinners of other mayfly species are not as significant. To the angler who notices and understands the spinner stage, fly fishing during a spinnerfall can be rewarding in many ways, and not just in catching trout. It's one of nature's great phenomena to witness.

In general, tying spinner imitations requires attention to a few simple details that are relatively easy to mimic. First, spinners upon falling to the water lie flat and exhibit little movement. After all, they are in the final stage of life as they deposit their eggs before dying. Spinners of a few species sit up on the water surface similar to adult duns, but even then it is only for a very brief time. Second, the bodies of spinners are typically thinner than those of the adult duns. This is the result of the dun shedding its skin as it transitions to the spinner stage. Third, spinner bodies tend to exhibit pronounced segmentation and often vary in color from adult duns. Fourth, tails are much more elongated than that of the adult dun, and upon falling onto the water are noticeably spent. And fifth, spinner wings are transparent or translucent, and are spent (lie flat) on the water; for some species of mayflies such as Brown Drakes and *Callibaetis*, the wings may be upright for a considerable amount of time. The combination of all these details translates into a "silhouette" on the surface in the eyes of trout below the surface. Thus, wings and tails should be tied with sparseness in mind. Use only enough material to allow the spinner to lie flat in the film and not sink. Avoid bulkier wings, tails, and bodies except in cases of fast water or in the presence of larger mayfly spinners such as Gray and Brown Drakes. Because spinners lie flat and their spent wings are transparent, they often appear invisible to the angler.

The Biot Paraspinner pattern created by Bonnie Harrop is an excellent imitation of a spinner that also provides enhanced visibility through the use of a CDC post. The use of grizzly hackle that's v-notched in front provides a transparent appearance that is characteristic of the spent wings of natural spinners. This allows the fly to ride in the surface film flat and enhance its visibility. The use of goose biot (which aids buoyancy) to represent the thin and segmented body and the Coq de Leon fibers of the elongated tails offer a realistic imitation of the naturals. When visibility is not critical, CDC, Z-Lon, and hackle clipped on top and bottom are also excellent materials for imitating spent wings. When used sparsely, these wing materials offer excellent transparency and are aerodynamic, reducing the likelihood of the fly spinning and generating twists in the tippet. Having a mixture of spinner imitations made from these wing materials offers the angler a "changeup" feature that might be just what is needed to entice the most selective trout.

In fly fishing the spinner stage, it's important to understand the environmental conditions under which mating and spinnerfalls occur. Wind speed, air temperature, and precipitation play significant roles and affect the occurrence and intensity of a spinnerfall. In many cases, the spinnerfall is delayed as a result of weather conditions, postponed until later in the evening or to the following day. Wind and rain are spinnerfall "showstoppers." Depending on the species, spinnerfalls often occur under low-light conditions typically observed later in the evening or in early morning; conditions are optimal when air temperatures are cooler, winds are calmer, and precipitation is nonexistent or very light at best. Spinnerfalls can also occur

dyed in a variety of colors, which helps simplify matching the hatch.

Biots are the leading edge of the primary flight feather in a goose wing. The first feather on each wing will provide the best biots. In *Charlie Craven's Basic Fly Tying*, the author discusses a foolproof method of properly tying and wrapping a goose biot to form a smooth, segmented abdomen. "To form a smooth biot body, I tie the biot in with the notch at its base facing down," Craven writes. "Tying the feather in this way allows me to wrap the feather with the stand-up edge leading the way down the hook, and to overlap it with the smooth back edge of the biot to create a smooth segmented body. Another way of looking at it is that a stand-up edge that leads will be covered by the backside of the next turn, creating a smooth body. A stand-up edge that follows will create a fuzzy rib."

The spent wing is the most important part of the spinner's profile. Wing materials vary from tier to tier, but the most popular options are white CDC, snowshoe rabbit, light dun hen wingtips, and white or light dun Z-Lon, Darlon, or McFlylon. In riffled water you can get away with a heavier wing, but in

Mayfly Spinners: Insights on Tying and Fishing

during the dun emergence stage. Trout often will switch from feeding on duns to spinners, which are not going to leave the water. Hence the importance of observing the feeding behavior of trout under such conditions.

So, what are signs of an impending spinnerfall and how can you determine the potential intensity of that fall? The intensity of the dun emergence earlier in the day can indicate both the potential for a spinnerfall and its intensity. If the emergence of duns was sporadic and light, then the subsequent spinnerfall likely will be light or perhaps nonexistent that day. Several factors are important to observe, as mating happens only under the right wind, temperature, and precipitation conditions. Note any grasses, bushes, and trees (especially willows) in close proximity to streambanks, as they provide ideal habitat for mating. As favorable conditions unfold, swarms of mating spinners can be observed dancing above the vegetation and along the edges of the water. The intensity of such behavior will increase until these swarms of spinners move over the water, slowly lowering their flight before beginning to fall. The falling of spinners can be intense over a very short time period under optimal conditions. The fall can be of short duration or last several hours depending on both the abundance of duns and the environmental conditions—hence the importance of observing the degree of dun emergence earlier in the day or observing the previous day's spinner activity.

In general, spinnerfalls are not equally distributed along a river or stream or among water types such as riffles, runs, pools. The presence and abundance of spinners is influenced by dun emergence characteristics and habitat, which can vary significantly over very short distances along a river or stream. The heaviest spinnerfalls tend to be located where vegetation conditions are ideal (tall grass, bushes, willows) and at the heads of riffles or similar moving water, as opposed to slower water. Spinners of some mayfly species tend to fall closer along the edges of the water whereas others tend to be more concentrated over midstream. Trout often will move into riffles during the early stages of the spinnerfall knowing an abundance of food is to come. All of a sudden, large numbers of trout are congregated in a relatively small area readily sipping spinners. What was once only the sound of moving water is now coupled with the sound of trout eagerly sipping spinners as the water becomes alive.

The position and feeding behavior of trout varies according to water type. Trout in riffles and faster-moving water tend to hold their positions and feed rhythmically, sipping spinners with little effort. Trout in slower-moving water tend to cruise around seeking out spinners in a "gulping" manner and often do not move in a straight line. Hence the importance of timing and feeding distance in slower-moving waters, and of letting a trout come to you rather than chasing it and spooking other trout. As water slows, trout have a greater amount to time to be selective. Trout are typically less selective during the intense stages of a spinnerfall and become more selective as the spinnerfall decreases. Amid diminishing light conditions, trout tend to feel safer from predators and actively feed in areas other than along the banks. These are the times when the largest trout hog the prime feeding lanes where they can effortlessly consume large quantities of spinners.

Approach and presentation are very important in fishing spinners. Four things are critical to fishing spinners: your ability to see the fly, mimicking a dead (drag-free) drift, the fly reaching the trout before the tippet does, and selecting a trout to which to target your cast. Select a trout first and then decide which approach (upstream or downstream) optimizes the other three factors. As mentioned earlier, low-light conditions are common when fishing spinners. Seeing your spinner imitation becomes more challenging as light decreases and/or the water becomes faster and more broken or abrupt. Sometimes you make compromises in your position in order to cast or see the fly. Recall that spinners upon landing on water exhibit little movement, especially when compared to the dun emergence stage. A dead-drift (drag-free) float is critical and can be the difference between having an opportunity for acceptance or clear refusal and possibly spooking the trout. A dead drift within three feet of the target trout is all that is warranted because of the trout's rhythmic feeding behavior and the angler's ability to see the fly. Of equal

slow-moving, glassy currents where trout have longer to inspect your flies, I recommend sparse wings.

Z-Lon, Darlon, and McFlylon do a nice job of imitating the spinner's transparent wing. When light reflects off these synthetic materials, they resemble the spinner's see-through wing. Air bubbles also get trapped between the fibers, which helps simulate the spinner's pleated wings. Z-Lon, Darlon, and McFlylon are extremely durable, which makes them a tier's favorite. CDC and hen wings also provide a realistic profile. One downfall to those natural materials is that they are not quite as durable as synthetics and they require more on-stream maintenance with floatants and desiccants. Snowshoe rabbit, on the other hand, is extremely durable and floats well.

BLUE-WINGED OLIVE FISHING STRATEGIES

Blue-Winged Olives, otherwise known as *Baetis*, are the first mayflies to hatch in the spring and the last to hatch in the fall. Unlike the other species of mayflies, Blue-Winged Olives are multibrooded, meaning they produce two or three generations each year. *Baetis* are known for their ability to hatch in cold

Mayfly Spinners: Insights on Tying and Fishing

importance is the fly reaching the trout before the tippet or leader does; this is even more critical when fishing slow-flowing waters such as spring creeks. In instances of very slow-moving water where trout are feeding in a "gulper-like" fashion, the trout move in search of spinners and their movement is usually not in a straight line or easily predictable. The angler should take note of the time and distance between "gulps" and make his or her presentation accordingly, keeping in mind the trout cannot be seen under the low-light conditions. Select the closest trout first, and then work your way to the others to avoid casting over pods of fish and potentially spooking the wiser ones, or, worse yet, spooking the entire pod of trout. In summary, the approach one takes in fishing spinners is situational and each fish warrants understanding and respect.

I prefer a downstream approach, casting across and down at an angle from 30 from 45 degrees, the exception being situations where visibility is more impaired or the backcast impeded. I tend to have more options for managing the length of the fly's dead drift and the fly always reaches the trout before the tippet and leader. I throw slack in the line as the fly falls to the water by making a gentle lift of the rod tip and then lowering the rod with little or no mending. I cast so the fly gently lands on the water like the natural would, about three feet ahead of the trout I'm targeting. Upon a take (and the trout's take is delicate), I gently lift the rod tip, which is enough to set the hook. Keep in mind that if you planned for a three-foot dead drift, then there's not significant slack in the leader. The challenging part is landing the trout, as the fish already have the advantage of being downstream of you. However, remember that these waters tend to be slower-moving and "coursing" the trout is not difficult as long as the trout is not over-pressured. I prefer leaders 12 to 14 feet in length, of which the tippet is 3 to 4 feet long. I rarely make casts in excess of 40 feet; most are less than 25 feet. Lengthy dead drifts are more difficult to achieve, and when coupled with greater difficulty in seeing the fly, result in a decreased probability of even setting the hook. Remember, you may need to make lots of casts to very selective trout before your spinner is accepted. If you suffer what seems to be endless denials, consider changing to flies tied with a different wing material and you'll likely be rewarded.

In terms of equipment, fast-loading, slow-action fly rods in the 3- to 5-weight range and 8 to 9 feet in length are preferred. The ability to quickly load the rod and cast to trout feeding readily on spinners is facilitated by these types of rods. In addition, when held properly the soft tips of these rods complement light tippets by taking pressure off the tippet and absorbing more of the "shock." Leaders in the 12 to 14 foot range with 3- to 4-foot tippets are desired. Lighter tippets, 6X to 8X, are also preferred, especially on spring creek–type conditions. The combination of longer leaders and longer and lighter tippets is important for a couple of reasons. First, the longer and lighter tippet facilitates a dead drift and the natural movement of a spinner as it floats downstream. Second, this combination of leader and tippet helps in absorbing the initial shock when setting the hook. And third, a longer tippet is more elastic, aiding the angler in being able to hold onto larger fish with lighter tippets than one might think. While such tackle takes a bit more skill to cast, the rewards are worth it. With that said, as spinner size and the speed of moving water increase, tippet size decreases in particular to avoid tippet "twisting." As noted earlier, denser spinner wings are less aerodynamic and will cause the fly to spin more, resulting in twists in lighter tippets—a showstopper to trout and a real pain for the angler. Lastly, sunglasses equipped with polarized, low-light-enhancing lenses are a must-have piece of equipment, especially when fishing spinners in late evenings and early mornings.

In closing, one of the most important things in fly-fishing is to watch the fish—they tell you most everything you need to know. Take time to observe and use this hindsight as foresight, and adjust accordingly. Think simplicity in both tying and presentation, and introduce complexity as warranted. And finally, enjoy the gift of life and the opportunity to experience its little treasures, such as a spinnerfall, to create memories that last forever. It's about the journey; catching a fish is a bonus, but it does not define the journey in and of itself. ■

water temperatures where other mayflies cannot exist. Spring hatches begin mid to late March and continue through the second or third week of May. Blue-Winged Olives reappear again in late August or September and continue hatching until the latter part of November. During the warm summer months, Blue-Winged Olive hatches are sporadic at best. You'll occasionally experience a few Blue-Winged Olives on overcast days during cool summer weather trends.

Baetis nymphs can be identified by their three tails, their slender, dark-olive abdomen, and their prominent wing pads. Their wing pads become darkened prior to emergence, a distinguishing feature that fly tiers should be concerned with when tying their imitations. Black Z-Lon, Tyvek colored with a black Sharpie, dark brown Medallion Sheeting, and black Thin Skin are all good options for constructing wing cases.

Baetis nymphs thrive in both tailwaters and freestones. Their densest populations are found on streams with weed-rich substrates. *Baetis* nymphs are excellent swimmers, especially prior to emergence when they become unusually active. Their energetic behavior draws the attention of nearby trout as they

Blue-Winged Olives, often referred to as Baetis, *produce reliable hatches during the spring and autumn months.* JAY NICHOLS

ascend to the surface to emerge into a dun. My favorite *Baetis* nymphs are Shane Stalcup's Baetis Nymph and Charlie Craven's Jujubaetis. I cannot live without these two patterns, especially when I'm guiding in Cheesman Canyon. Craven believes the effectiveness of his fly stems from its slim silhouette and tapered profile. The Mirage Tinsel and Fluoro Fibre legs add a dash of flash to the pattern that fools even the most selective trout. Stalcup's Baetis is another one of the most realistic *Baetis* nymphs that I've found. Once again, the effectiveness of this fly is a result of its thin and sparse design.

I typically fish my *Baetis* nymphs on the dead drift with a conventional two- or three-fly tandem rig. I have found the Jujubaetis to be an excellent attractor in a multifly nymphing rig. During the spring and fall, I routinely drop a Stalcup's Baetis off the Jujubaetis when I know the fish are keying heavily on *Baetis* nymphs. During the initial phases of the hatch, you should dredge your nymphs close to the bottom, but as the hatch intensifies, you'll need to back off on the weight and fish the nymphs higher in the water column.

Choosing the right water can make or break your success during a Blue-Winged Olive hatch. The most aggressive feeding takes place in shallow riffles, narrow slots, and transitional zones (point bars and midchannel shelves). My streamside observation leads me to believe that fish can eat 15 to 25 *Baetis* nymphs per minute during the height of a heavy Blue-Winged Olive hatch.

During the initial phases of a Blue-Winged Olive hatch, trout will key heavily on Baetis *nymphs. Having the right size, shape, and color is critical for success when choosing the appropriate fly to match the hatch.* MARK ADAMS

Matt Miles offers this helpful piece of advice: "I try and pay attention to the fish as much as possible. If I can visually see fish rise in the water column eating ascending nymphs, I assume they're feeding on *Baetis* nymphs. I like to be in the

Freestones like the Gunnison River are known for their excellent Blue-Winged Olive hatches. During the initial phases of the hatch, guides like John Keefover use a Stalcup's Baetis or Jujubaetis to imitate emerging nymphs. MARK ADAMS

head of the run or at the drop-off of a gravel bar. The fish will slide up in the shallow riffles or sit on the drop-off of the gravel bar to eat nymphs before they make their final ascent to the surface. Adjusting your strike indicator and weight is key to keeping your *Baetis* nymph in the right part of the water column."

During a heavy hatch, I am especially fond of using a Churchill's Sparkle Wing RS 2, a Mercury Flashback RS 2, Whitley's Flashback RS 2, or a Chocolate Foam Wing Emerger. As I mentioned before, Charlie Craven's and J's Soft-Hackle Emergers also perform well during heavy Blue-Winged Olive emergences. As far as nymphs are concerned, I fish them with a conventional nymphing rig, but reduce my weight to allow the flies to drift more naturally and higher in the water column.

Blue-Winged Olive duns have a sleek, olive-brown body with slate-gray wings. They typically hatch during the afternoon between 1 p.m. and 3 p.m. As noted, the best hatches typically occur amid overcast conditions or inclement weather. High humidity stalls the emerging process and keeps the duns on the water longer, which produces excellent dry-fly fishing.

Bright and sunny conditions accelerate the hatches and the duns leave the water quickly. Don't be disappointed by bluebird conditions though, because nymphing with *Baetis* nymphs can be just as exciting as dry-fly fishing. Trout will move as far as 18 inches to intercept an emerging *Baetis*, especially in slower to moderate-paced currents, glassy pools, and transitional zones (point bars and midchannel shelves) that funnel into deeper runs and pools.

Trout often key on the behavior of the swimming or emerging nymph and ignore perfectly dead-drifted imposters. This is where allowing your flies to swing in the current or swinging soft hackles can produce a distinct advantage. Special lifting techniques like the Leisenring Lift will entice trout that are keying on emerging *Baetis* nymphs.

Bob Dye and I believe that the Chocolate Foam Wing Emerger imitates the *Baetis* nymph's swimming behavior better than any other emerger because the squared-off foam wing, constructed from 2mm white craft foam, forces the fly to sway back and forth on the swing. This action simulates the swimming behavior of a *Baetis* nymph as the fly tightens and lifts in the water column. This lifelike swimming behavior becomes a trigger and entices trout to eat the fly.

Spring Blue-Winged Olives are much larger than those you'll find during the autumn months, so you'll need to adjust your fly selection accordingly. Dry-fly fanatics can get away with size 20 dun imitations in the spring, but the fall requires patterns that are one to two sizes smaller. My favorite Blue-Winged Olive dun imitations include size 20-22 Mathews' Sparkle Duns, size 20-24 Hi-Viz Baetis, size 20-22 Cannon's Snowshoe Duns, and size 20-22 Barr's Vis-A-Duns.

Successfully matching a hatch during the dun phase of a Blue-Winged Olive hatch is one of the most rewarding parts of fly fishing. Watching a trout gently slurp your dry fly is as good as it gets! Should you be unsuccessful, walking away empty-handed after seeing and hearing trout rise all around you during a heavy hatch can be one of the most frustrating parts of fly fishing. Many anglers outthink themselves or stray away from a few simple guidelines, mistakes that ultimately affect their productivity.

The best advice I can give you is to get as close to the rising fish as possible without spooking them. Cast to a specific fish as opposed to casting randomly. Make accurate deliveries and concentrate on getting a dead drift. If the fly drags at all, you'll get a refusal. I typically try to cast my fly about 18 inches above my desired target, reducing the chance of drag. Most anglers lead the fish with too much line, resulting in drag caused by conflicting cross-stream currents. A reach mend or S-cast can apply some slack into your leader, allowing the fly to drift helpless in the current and helping you make a good presentation.

Ed Engle encourages anglers to be observant at all times: "All rising trout are not the same," Engle says. "Sometimes it may appear they are taking mayfly duns from the surface when most of the feeding is taking place on emerging duns. If you're not sure what's going on, pick a mayfly dun on the water's surface and watch it float downstream until a trout eats it or it flies off the water. At the beginning of the hatch you'll often see that a trout may occasionally take a dun that 'gets in the way,' but is most interested in vacuuming up easy-to-catch emergers in the surface film or cripples. Choose your fly imitation accordingly and be aware that the hatch is a dynamic event. You may have to change imitations several times as the hatch progresses."

Anglers can fish their Blue-Winged Olive imitations upstream, up and across, down and across, or downstream. A down-and-across or downstream delivery is my preference because the first thing the trout sees is your fly—not the tippet, leader, or fly line, all of which can make the fish suspicious and lead to a refusal.

Aaron Carithers understands the importance of a good dry-fly presentation, as he routinely has to fool some of the most selective surface feeders in the West when he guides out of Durango. "Most of the fish that rise on the San Juan are in slow to intermediate currents, which really complicates things," Carithers says. "Trying to fool rising fish on slow, glassy currents provides the ultimate challenge because the trout have a lot of time to scrutinize your pattern and presentation. Under these conditions an angler should position themselves upstream at an angle that will allow the fly to reach the fish before the tippet. Another way to achieve this goal is to make a reach cast, pushing the rod tip to the left or to the right on the forward stroke, allowing the fly line and leader to land above the fly."

Casting accuracy cannot be overemphasized with small dry flies. Trout will not move more than a few inches to eat small offerings because the calories gained will not compensate for the amount of energy expended to grab the insect. "For consistent dry-fly success, your casting skills are as important as fly selection," Carithers says. "Learn to cast accurately, make a few false casts to measure the distance of the rising fish, and place the fly in the fish's feeding lane within inches of where the fish is feeding. Trout feeding on small insects will not move more than a few inches out of their feeding lane. One common mistake anglers make is leading the fish with more fly line than is necessary. Too much of a lead will allow the current to push or pull the fly away from the fish. Cast to the fish, leading the riser by inches, not feet. If the fish does not 'take,' let the fly pass and pull the fly out of the water with a slow and smooth stroke."

Grace Smith landed this large rainbow on the Blue River with a Sparkle Wing RS 2 during a heavy Blue-Winged Olive emergence. Midchannel shelves are prime areas to target during the height of a Blue-Winged Olive hatch. MARK ADAMS

Once the duns fly off the water, they seek shelter and rest. After molting into a spinner, they mate and then the females oviposit their eggs, which is done by diving under the water surface. After the females deposit their eggs, they drift in the surface film or mid-column, offering trout an effortless meal.

Charlie Craven believes his gray Soft-Hackle Emerger doubles for a drowned spinner: "It was while I was working with John Barr on *Barr Flies* that he related to me the phenomenon of the drowned spinner. When I hear about something like this, my mind immediately sets about trying to design a pattern to imitate it, but in this case, I already had." In the case of the Soft-Hackle Emerger, the fly's Fluoro Fibre wing produces flash that mimics the spinner's folded wings, and the sparse soft-hackle collar imitates the spinner's legs.

Drowned spinners can be fished mid-column with a traditional nymph rig or dry-and-dropper setup, or fished with conventional dry-fly tactics in the surface film. When I nymph drowned spinners, I shorten my yarn strike indicator and place

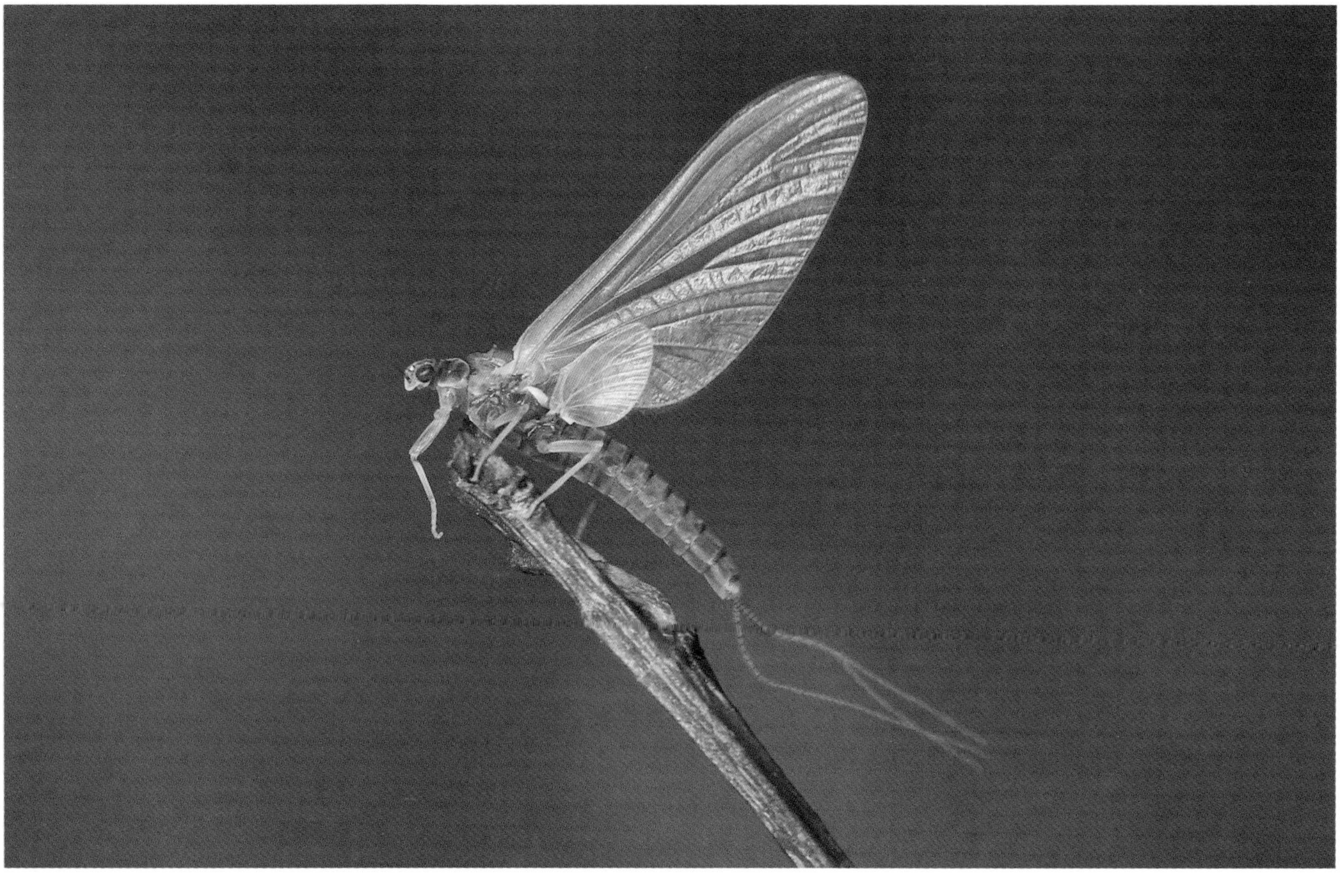

Pale Morning Duns, or PMDs, emerge midsummer. Hatches last a few weeks to several months, depending on water conditions. JAY NICHOLS

a micro shot 12 inches above my drowned spinner. Craven prefers to fish it dry or damp behind a more visible dry fly like a Parachute Adams. "The Soft-Hackle Emerger sits flush in the surface film, sometimes on its side, which can replicate the position of the naturals quite well," Craven says. "I do not apply dry-fly floatant to the fly, as I prefer to let it hang ever so slightly below the surface."

PALE MORNING DUN FISHING STRATEGIES

Pale Morning Duns, or PMDs, provide anglers with reliable dry-fly fishing during the summer months. Their widespread population, convenient hatching times, and willingness to hatch in beautiful weather makes them one of the most popular aquatic insects. Daily emergences can last for a few weeks to several months depending on the drainage, water temperatures, and stream flows. Hatches typically begin in mid-June and continue through September. Western Pale Morning Duns include two species that are especially worth noting by Colorado anglers: *Ephemerella dorothea infrequens* and *Ephemerella excrucians*.

"Starting as early as the latter part of June and extending well into October, the Pale Morning Dun hatches on the Frying Pan provide anglers exceptional daily dry-fly fishing," says Will Sands, manager of Taylor Creek Fly Shop in Basalt. "The epicenter of this hatch is truly mid-July through mid-September, where anglers should expect to find several species of PMDs hatching daily between noon and 4 p.m. Of the several species of Pale Morning Duns that occur on the Pan, the two most prominent species are *Ephemerella infrequens* and *Ephemerella excrucians*."

Like many other species of mayflies, PMDs become smaller as the season progresses and they try to preserve body moisture. According to Fred Arbona Jr. in his book *Mayflies, the Angler, and the Trout*, "Not only do the species move to earlier and later times of the day for the preservation of moisture, they will also get smaller in size and lighter in color. Both of these physical body changes will ensure low heat absorption which will help the mayflies remain internally cooler during the summer months." In June, anglers will typically fish with a size 16 Pale Morning Dun imitation, but later in the season (August and September), anglers will need to use a size 18 to match the naturals.

Anglers will find excellent PMD hatches on both tailwaters and freestones throughout Colorado. Tailwaters tend to produce more reliable hatches because of their ideal water conditions. Stable water temperatures and uniform flows promote consistent hatches that last for several months. Hatches on freestones can be excellent too, but they are shorter in duration because of temperature and flow variations.

Anglers will find good PMD hatches on many of the freestone streams on both the east and west sides of Rocky Mountain National Park. According to Dick Shinton, "My favorite streams for PMDs are the Big Thompson from the Fern Lake trailhead and into Forest Canyon, just about anywhere on Glacier Creek from its confluence with the Big Thompson to Mills Lake, a side channel of the Big Thompson on the south side of Moraine Park (often called Cub Creek), and the North St. Vrain and its tributaries in the Wild Basin area. My top flies for this hatch are my Parachute Park PMD trailed by a PMD Mini-Merger. This rig will fool trout that are sipping on or just below the surface during a Pale Morning Dun hatch."

PMD nymphs are crawlers and thrive in a wide range of habitats from small gravel to large cobble substrates. PMDs prefer streams with slow- to moderate-paced currents with plenty of rooted aquatic vegetation. In some streams the PMD populations are mind-boggling, with several hundred nymphs per square meter. The nymphs vary in color from a yellow-brown to dark brown with their underside being a noticeable shade lighter than their top.

Unlike *Baetis* nymphs, which have streamlined bodies, Pale Morning Dun nymphs are thick-bodied and robust. They are poor swimmers and spend most of their lives crawling along the stream bottom feeding on algae, decomposed plants, and other decaying matter. Their inability to swim increases their odds of being susceptible to catastrophic drift, making them an important food source because it takes them longer to get back to the bottom in comparison to swimmer nymphs.

It is important to carry a thorough selection of PMD nymphs in June and July. Landon Mayer fooled this fish with a size 18 Barr's Flashback PMD Emerger.

Pheasant Tail Nymphs are excellent PMD imitations when tied in size 16-18. I tie them with natural pheasant tail fibers and a fluffy thorax of peacock herl to imitate the natural's rectangular shape, short and stout legs, and fringed tails. Steve Henderson's variation of a Flashback Pheasant Tail has proven itself to be a consistent producer during the midsummer months. Henderson uses a combination of pheasant tail fibers and Mylar tinsel for the thorax of his pheasant tail. This bulks up the thorax ever so slightly, which produces the perfect silhouette for PMD nymphs. "My Pheasant Tail is a variation of a classic nymph," Henderson says. "It fishes well for a PMD nymph throughout the summer months. I tie my Pheasant Tails without beads or any other external form of weight, which allows them to drift more naturally as a point fly behind a weighted nymph."

Prior to emergence, the nymphs become restless and begin moving about the stream, climbing on top of cobble that they would normally hide under. As they prepare for emergence, they let go of the substrate and swim to the surface film where they escape their nymphal shuck. According to Robert Younghanz, a Colorado Springs guide and aquatic entomologist, "The PMD is an abundant food source that occurs in most of our major river drainages in Colorado. As a nymph it is robust in stature, a feeble swimmer and most often dark brown in color. When it emerges, its large size makes it easy to identity as it gracefully makes it way upriver during its nuptial flight. This is why it is one of the most exciting mayflies for an angler who is looking to match the hatch."

John Barr's PMD Emerger and Joe Mitchell's Split Case PMD are two of my favorite emerger patterns. I have fooled hundreds of selective trout with these patterns. During the height of the hatch you can nymph them, fish them in the surface film, or suspend them off a dry fly. John Barr fishes the flashback variation because he has the most confidence in it. I have enjoyed a tremendous amount of success with bead-head variations of both of these patterns fished off an Elk Hair Caddis. In *Barr Flies*, Barr admits that, "Some pressured trout don't like the flash or beads, so the plain version still has a spot in my fly box." In some cases, the duns emerge underwater and swim up to the surface. When this occurs, J's PMD Soft Hackle is effective when fished down and across with a traditional wet-fly presentation.

The duns vary in color from a yellow-olive to rusty-yellow color. The females are yellow olive and the males tend to be more of a rusty color. On some streams, Pale Morning Duns emerge in the mornings from 10 a.m. to noon, while other drainages produce hatches between noon and 2 p.m. As the summer season progresses and the days get hotter, the duns will hatch earlier in the day to preserve body moisture. Overcast and humid conditions produce the best hatches.

Captive duns and cripples are a common sight during hot, dry summer days. Many duns perish from dehydration before they can escape their nymphal shuck. Bob Quigley's Cripple and Craig Mathews' Sparkle Dun are two of my favorite imitations, as their Z-Lon fibers represent the trailing shuck with the trapped adult still attached. Barr's Vis-A-Dun, Stalcup's

CDC PMD Compara-dun, Cannon's PMD Snowshoe Dun, and Parachute PMDs are effective dun imitations.

Some anglers believe the spinnerfall is as important as the hatch itself. According to Younghanz, "PMD spinnerfalls can take place from midmorning to late afternoon, sometimes into the evening. The males mate and hit the water first, then gravid females dip their eggs into the water shortly after copulation. The different spinnerfall times are often a result of air temperatures. The cooler the weather, the later the spinnerfall takes place."

Will Sands believes that evening spinnerfalls are an underappreciated aspect of the Frying Pan River's Pale Morning Dun hatches, as these spinnerfalls can provide epic dry-fly fishing. "Daily hatches of PMDs yield evening spinnerfalls that many anglers miss out on," Sands explains. "Anglers visiting the valley may have evening obligations that preclude their inclusion during this hatch or they simply may not be aware that it exists. Others get so caught up fishing the banker's hour hatches that they are content to forgo fishing until dark. Thus an often-overlooked derivative of daily PMD hatches is the epic rusty spinnerfall that ensues during the last couple hours before dark. One scenario to note is that windy, rainy evenings will shut spinnerfalls down. Warm dry nights are when this occurrence really goes off. Spinnerfalls can start two hours before dusk or fifteen minutes before dusk and last well into the darkness. Either way, anglers that encounter an epic fall will see hundreds of rising fish and literally have the fishing experience of a lifetime."

The male spinners are darker than the females. The males take on a rusty-brown appearance while the females keep their yellow-olive color. "I carry a number of PMD spinner patterns," Younghanz says. "Rusty spinners are one of my

Barr's PMD Vis-A-Dun is one of Landon Mayer's favorite flies when the fish are keying on Pale Morning Duns. MARK ADAMS

Jason Booth and Pat Dorsey team up during the famous Green Drake hatch on the Gunnison River. The Green Drake hatch can provide epic dry-fly fishing for almost a month. MARK ADAMS

favorites, but any yellowish, goldish, or pinkish sulphur spinner will do. Their colors can vary somewhat depending on the drainage and how long they have been on the water. Pay close attention to the color of the abdomen and choose the appropriate pattern to match the hatch."

You'll want to have an ample supply of size 16-18 Rusty Spinners for the Frying Pan spinnerfall. "The spinners on 'the Pan' have rust-colored bodies, hence the name Rusty Spinner. The spinners are typically a size 16. Note that the naturals will have tails much longer than any commercial shop pattern; tail length seems to be of little importance to your imitation, but many anglers are often caught off-guard when they witness the tails of the natural and believe they are seeing another species altogether," Sands says.

PMD spinners are considerably more difficult to see on the water in comparison to duns. My recommendation is to get as close to the rising fish as possible without spooking them. Make short, accurate presentations, and keep your false casting to a minimum. It is also important to have a reasonably good idea where your fly landed. Set the hook to any surface disturbance close to the end of your leader. Make sure you lift the rod gently, otherwise you may spook several trout.

WESTERN GREEN DRAKE FISHING STRATEGIES

Every summer anglers anxiously await the arrival of the fabled Western Green Drake hatch. Emergence begins in late June and continues through the latter part of August. In some drainages like the Frying Pan and North Fork of the South Platte, Green Drakes hatch well into September. "The North Fork of the South Platte River has a little secret that many anglers are unaware of . . . the Green Drake Hatch," says Chris Wells, owner of Mile High Angler. "Every year beginning in July, these giant mayflies begin their annual mating ritual. The nymphs become active in the morning and the fish can be seen feeding on them. Sight-fishing with big dark nymphs is the most productive method during the early phases of this hatch. Usually by noon the adults begin to hatch and for two or three hours the fish feed almost exclusively on the surface. Hatches typically last through mid-September."

The Western Green Drake hatch comprises two different species—*Drunella grandis* and *Drunella doddsii*. Most anglers lump these two species into one hatch because they share so many similarities. It's not uncommon to find both species in the same stream or even under the same rock. The duns look alike, with the exception that the *Drunella doddsii* is slightly smaller. Carry several sizes of duns (sizes 10-14) and choose the appropriate pattern as you see fit.

Green Drakes thrive in large cobbled substrates with moderate- to fast-paced currents. Colorado's widespread population of Green Drakes means anglers will find reliable hatches on both tailwaters and freestones. Some of the most popular fishing destinations include the Roaring Fork, Frying Pan,

Yampa, Taylor, Blue, and Gunnison Rivers and the North Fork of the South Platte. Savvy dry-fly anglers mark the Green Drake Hatch in their calendar because it often produces some of the most exciting dry-fly fishing of the season. "The Green Drake is the largest Western mayfly. When it hatches, most of the fish in the river key on them," says Jason Booth, co-owner of Gunnison River Guides. "The best time to fish drakes on the Gunnison River is from June 15 to July 10."

Anglers from all over the West come to Colorado to fish the Green Drake hatch. "The Frying Pan has a world-famous Green Drake hatch," Sands says. Those making the trip should heed Sands' advice: "Frying Pan fish can be extremely selective, especially when the large dominant Green Drake is out. Complex hatches [multiple insect species hatching at the same time] often confuse anglers. Having a basic understanding of complex hatches is of the utmost importance when fishing the Frying Pan. Due to the longevity of many hatches on 'the Pan,' anglers will often encounter Blue-Winged Olives, caddis, and Green Drakes all hatching at the same time. These overlapping hatches often get the better of anglers because it's much easier lobbing size 10 Green Drakes to rising fish. However if PMDs are occurring at the same time, trout may eat half a dozen PMDs to every drake that passes overhead. This is extremely true late in the hatch when fish have been stung too many times by Green Drake imitations."

Green Drake nymphs can be identified by their robust stature. Prominent features include three tails, wide abdomens, stout legs, a boxlike thorax, and a squared-off head with highly visible eyes. Their large size differentiates them from most other mayflies found in Colorado, as mature nymphs often reach three-quarters of an inch in length (excluding the tails). *Drunella grandis* have a pronounced spine that runs along the topside of their head, thorax, and abdomen, which helps with their identification.

Being in the right place at the right time is critical for success during a Green Drake hatch. Contact a local fly shop or guide service for up-to-date hatch information before you head to the stream.

The *Drunella doddsii* do not have a spine, but instead they have a patch of fine dense hairs that covers the underside of their abdomens. These hairs are sometimes referred to by entomologists as a "friction disc." According to Rick Hafele in *Nymph-Fishing Rivers and Streams*, "These hairs function like one side of a Velcro strip, providing a tenacious grip on the bottom rocks." While Green Drake nymphs are well equipped to handle fast water, don't rule out them becoming victims of catastrophic drift from time to time. Opportunistic trout will rarely resist the opportunity to capitalize on a large, beefy Green Drake nymph tumbling helplessly in the current.

Booth's favorite Green Drake nymphs include size 8-10 Green Drake Epoxy Back Nymphs, Green Drake Emergers, Baby 20-Inchers, large Pheasant Tails, and soft hackles. "Emergers and soft hackles work well in June and July," Booth says. "I like to fish them behind a drake nymph and swing them to imitate the emergers."

I would also recommend carrying a few each of John Barr's Jumbo John, Mike Mercer's Poxyback Green Drake, and Shane Stalcup's Green Drake Nymph in sizes 10 and 12. These flies have proven themselves extremely effective imitations of Green Drake nymphs.

The biggest concentration of Green Drake nymphs is not readily available to trout until they are close to emergence. Prior to emergence, mature nymphs migrate to slower riffles and runs. Their availability to trout increases dramatically during this migratory period because they are poor swimmers and often drift long distances before they attempt to feebly swim towards the water's surface. Emergence occurs underwater or just below the surface film. Soft hackles and wet flies are excellent imposters for the emerging duns.

Green Drake hatches slowly progress upstream each day. Pinpointing the heaviest part of the hatch is often one of the greatest challenges of this hatch. It's not a bad idea to check with a local fly shop or guide service to get up-to-date information, otherwise your success may be limited. "The speed of the hatch is dictated by the amount of runoff, weather conditions, and water temperatures," Booth explains. "Overcast, windless days are optimum conditions and the hatch lasts for hours and moves slowly up the river. Hot days and sunshine, the hatch is short and moves upstream very fast. The hatch usually enters the Taylor River the first week of July. Here it slows because of the cool, consistent water temperature of Taylor Canyon. There's reliable drake fishing the whole month of July." Booth's favorite dry flies include size 8-10 Green Drake Cripples, CDC Green Drake Parachutes, Furimski Foam Green Drakes, Colorado Green Drakes, and CDC Flavilinea Duns.

The duns typically hatch between 1 p.m. and 3 p.m. each afternoon. The spinnerfall occurs at dark. In certain watersheds like the Frying Pan, the spinnerfall is an important part of the hatch. Once the duns break through the water's surface,

nymph does have some importance. While the nymphing period is usually short and sweet, it should not be overlooked.

In *Fishing Small Flies*, Ed Engle writes, "Unlike most other small-fly fishers, I do carry a Trico nymph imitation. I've read reports that the nymph imitation has no importance because the hatch occurs too early in the morning. I have found it useful when the trout become selective to the dun imitations later in the season. I simply trail the nymph 15 inches behind the dun imitation."

Trico nymphs have a robust thorax because of their large triangular gills. Trico nymphs vary in color from a tan to dark brown. Their lidlike operculate gills protect them from silt and other debris, allowing them to survive these silty areas.

Trico imitations should be tied slightly chunky to imitate their boxy silhouette. I have found it's hard to go wrong with a size 22 Pheasant Tail Nymph tied with a fluffy peacock herl thorax when trout are taking Trico nymphs. John Barr's Trico Barr Emerger is another good option for a Trico nymph. I also carry a Mercury Trico tied in tan, brown, and black.

Once you see duns on the water, snip off your nymph and begin fishing a dun imitation. The females have an olive abdomen and black thorax. Some anglers feel compelled to fish exact imitations while others couldn't care less. I personally have never run across a Trico feeder that wouldn't eat a solid black dun imitation. My favorite dun pattern is Shane Stalcup's CDC Trico Compara-dun, but I have also had good success with a Mathews' Sparkle Dun in olive and black.

The males, which hatch the night before, are solid black. You'll find them resting on streamside foliage when you arrive at the stream in the morning. Careful inspection of these mayflies will confirm these as duns, as their wings are opaque. They rest until the morning temperatures warm up a bit, and then they molt into spinners. The female's transformation from dun to spinner occurs much quicker; in fact, the duns change into spinners within a couple minutes of emergence. This most often occurs between 7 a.m. and 8:30 a.m.

Both the males and females will have molted by 9 a.m. and the mating swarm begins to form. The fish will continue to feed on a sporadic dun or two until the spinners finally hit the water. Once the female spinners start hitting the water, fish switch from duns to spinners. The riseform will become unmistakable—it will change from a classic head-to-tail rise in which the fish grabs a single dun to a gulping rise in which the trout sweeps back and forth in the current, eating several spinners at a time.

Spent-wing Tricos have a distinct silhouette that distinguishes their appearance from the duns. Spinners lie on the water spread-eagle, with the tail, abdomen, and wings sitting flush on the water. Anglers who fail to switch from upright-wing dun imitations to spent-wing patterns will often become frustrated by their inability to catch fish. Unlike duns that leave the water quickly, dying spinners remain on the water for long periods of time. Trout recognize this opportunity and feed on them with a vengeance. Once again, my favorite Trico imitation is Shane Stalcup's CDC Trico Compara-dun. It fishes well as both a Trico dun and a spinner, not to mention it's easy to see and it can be fished as a drowned spinner by simply adding a number 6 split shot and fishing it mid-column.

This South Platte brown trout was fooled with a Stalcup's CDC Trico Compara-dun during a Trico spinnerfall at Deckers. Stalcup's CDC Trico Compara-dun is a must-have if you plan on fishing during a Trico spinnerfall. MARK ADAMS

Towards the latter part of September, the Trico hatch takes on a new twist as the males no longer hatch in the evening due to cooler air temperatures. Cool mornings have the same effect on the females, which delays the hatch by an hour or two. The two hatches (the males normally hatch in the evening and the females hatch in the morning) evolve into one, with the male duns hatching first, followed by the females. Spinnerfalls typically occur around noon and last for an hour or so. Later in the season, I have found the dun fishing to be spectacular.

The Trico hatch has been dubbed the "white-winged curse" by many fly fishers. If you have fished a Trico hatch before, you understand why—the Trico hatch is the most technically challenging mayfly hatch in the West. Many anglers are fooled into believing this hatch is easy because of the number of rising trout, but think again: the odds are pretty good that you'll become frustrated quickly.

Trico hatches will typically bring even the wariest and most selective trout to the surface. They stack up in the prime feeding lies and gorge themselves on spinners. If you have not experienced a Trico hatch, this is one of the most impressive sights you'll ever see on a trout stream. You'll need 9- to 12-foot leaders terminating in 7X tippet. I recommend using size 22-24 duns and a size 24 spinner, although using such small tackle further complicates things—it's hard enough to fool a Trico feeder, let alone land a fish on a size 24 dry fly with cobweb-thin tippet.

It is important to get as close to the rising fish as possible without spooking them. Seasoned dry-fly veterans know the

Grace Smith caught this brown trout during a Trico spinnerfall on the South Platte River near Deckers. Anglers will find reliable Trico hatches around the Deckers area during August and September. MARK ADAMS

importance of making several repeated casts to a Trico feeder until it eventually takes your fly. It's critical to have a dead drift! It may take dozens of casts before you finally get the timing right. Ed Engle offers this tip in *Fishing Small Flies*: "Forget about cleverly timing your cast. The key to the Tricos is to simply make as many accurate casts as you can and hope that one of them coincides with the trout's feeding cycle. Put the fly 8 inches to a foot above the trout, again, and again, and again. You will risk putting the fish down, but if you do, it will probably come back in a matter of minutes. If it doesn't, you won't have any trouble finding another one to cast to."

Another trick is to find a fly you can see in the foam and bubble lines. Trico spinners are difficult to see even under the best conditions. That's why I like Stalcup's CDC Trico Compara-dun, Jim Cannon's Snowshoe Dun, and John Betts' Z-Lon Dun, because they all have a white wing that is easy to see. While their names imply they are dun imitations, from the bottom (the orientation in which the trout sees the fly) the fanned-out wing looks like a spent-wing spinner. The trout feeding on Trico spinners are sitting just below the surface, therefore their feeding window is very narrow and they cannot see any silhouette of an upright wing. It is important to keep these flies properly dressed with Frog's Fanny to ensure they float high. If the fly becomes waterlogged, it tends to lose its effectiveness and you will not get as many strikes. This problem is easily fixed by re-dressing the fly frequently, especially after each fish you catch.

The Poor Witch (designed by the late Jim Poor) is another longtime Colorado favorite. I first learned about the Poor Witch from Bob Saile, the former outdoor editor for the *Denver Post*. I quickly learned how effective the Poor Witch could be during the Trico hatches on the South Platte below Spinney Mountain Reservoir and below Deckers. The Poor Witch is a modified Adams, using blue dun hen's wings (instead of grizzly) with a split moose body hair tail.

As the hatch begins to wind down, observant anglers will notice a lot of feeding activity below the surface of the water. That's because the trout have switched their focus to sunken or drowned spinners. This voracious feeding behavior can last for thirty minutes to an hour after the last Trico spinners have hit the water. This is often one of the most overlooked parts of the Trico hatch. For years, fishing a drowned Trico has been a guide secret, but more and more anglers are beginning to figure it out. "In a pinch, a drowned Trico can be fished as the point fly on a dead-drift nymphing rig, but it's more fun fished either as a single fly or as a trailer behind a dry fly," Engle says. I hate to admit it, but I often find myself fishing drowned Tricos during the hatch because it is so effective. I routinely fish two Stalcup's CDC Trico Compara-duns below a yarn strike indicator. Shorten the distance between your strike indicator and the weight to allow your flies to drift in the upper two or three feet of the water column. I use a number 4-6 split shot to keep the sunken Tricos in the correct part of the feeding zone.

RED QUILL FISHING STRATEGIES

Small Western Red Quills (commonly referred to as Red Quills) hatch during the latter part of the summer and into the autumn season. *Rhithrogena undulata* is the most common species, and the one that anglers should concentrate their efforts on. Red Quills begin hatching mid-August, filling an important void between the midsummer mayflies (Pale Morning Duns and Green Drakes) and the fall Blue-Winged Olives. Hatches of Red Quills add some excitement to the dog days of summer when fishing traditionally becomes challenging due to lower

Greenback cutthroats will waste no time eating Mike Kruise's Spent-Wing Biot Red Quill on many of the streams in Rocky Mountain National Park.

flows and warmer water temperatures. In *Mayflies, the Angler, and the Trout*, Fred Arbona states, "The hatches of the Small Western Red Quills are frequent, predictable, and dense. In my personal experience, they rank above those of any other mayfly that thrives in faster water sections of western trout streams."

Anglers will find reliable Red Quill hatches on the Arkansas, Roaring Fork, Colorado, Gunnison, Frying Pan, Blue, Yampa, Williams Fork, and several streams in Rocky Mountain National Park. "The Red Quill hatch on the Williams Fork and Colorado River is an angler's chance to participate in some of the best dry-fly fishing in Colorado," says Chris Wells, owner of Mile High Angler. Red Quills emerge in the afternoon or early evening between 4 p.m. and 6 p.m. Hatching times vary from drainage to drainage; therefore it's best to check with a local fly shop for specifics.

"The Red Quills are one of my favorite hatches," says Mike Kruise, co-owner of the Laughing Grizzly Fly Shop. "In the Rocky Mountain National Park area, Red Quills begin hatching towards the latter part of July. The hatch varies from stream to stream depending on elevation and temperature. The Red Quills will continue hatching into the latter part of August."

Kruise enjoys the Red Quill hatch because it's a nice way to end a great day of fishing: "Many fisherman miss the hatch because they are off the water before it starts. When I fish the Red Quill hatch, I generally start around 6 p.m. and fish it until dark. Moraine Park is an excellent Red Quill area, but it sees a lot of daytime traffic so it will test your skills. Presentation is paramount because the fish are wary and very selective. But when you present your dry fly well the rewards are high." Kruise's favorite patterns are Gordon's Red Quill and his Spent-Wing Biot Red Quill in size 16-18.

Western Red Quills are clingers and favor moderate- to fast-paced currents. The tan to dark-brown nymphs have three tails, a flat, rugged abdomen with prominent gills, six sturdy legs, and a robust thorax—a body that allows them to handle quicker currents. A size 16 Pheasant Tail will imitate the nymphs as well as any pattern available.

Prior to emergence, the nymphs become increasingly active and swim halfheartedly to the surface film. The nymphs emerge underwater within inches of the surface film. Soft-Hackle Pheasant Tails in size 14-16, fished down and across, are excellent imitations of the emerging duns. Greg Felt recommends using reddish nymphs like the red Two-Bit Hooker, red Copper John, or a red Pheasant Tail for the Arkansas River. "When I do take fish off the surface, it is often with a traditional Red Quill dry-fished along the shady edges late in the day," Felt says. "This is a big mayfly, size 14-16, and is identifiable by its rusty color and very long tails. The red

Anglers will find reliable Red Quill hatches on the Williams Fork River during the middle part of August and in early September. Chris Wells is all smiles after catching this brown trout on a Red Quill Mathews' Sparkle Dun.

Mike Kruise's Spent-Wing Biot Red Quill in size 16-18 is an excellent choice for Rocky Mountain National Park during late July and August. Anglers will find dependable Red Quill hatches on the upper Big Thompson, lower Chaos Creek, Cony Creek, Fall River, Roaring River, Glacier Creek, Fern Creek, Fish Creek, Ouzel Creek, Sand Beach Creek, and the upper St. Vrain.

quills have been indicative of the proliferation of mayflies and stoneflies that have resulted from improvements to water quality in the Arkansas River."

In September, afternoon Blue-Winged Olive hatches may overlap with the beginning of the Red Quill hatch. Closer inspection of the newly hatched duns will help decipher which dun the fish are keying on. The Red Quill mayflies are noticeably larger than the Blue-Winged Olives. In addition to their size, the Red Quills can be identified by their mahogany-colored body versus the pale olive color of the Blue-Winged Olive. I find it beneficial to fish two dry flies under these circumstances—one Red Quill imitation trailed by a Blue-Winged Olive. This way, you have both hatches covered!

My favorite Red Quill imitation is A. K. Best's Parachute Red Quill. A. K.'s Red Quill has many advantages over Catskill-style Red Quill imitations. First and most importantly, because it's a parachute, it sits flush in the film and provides a realistic silhouette that fools the most discerning surface feeders. Another feature I have come to appreciate is how easy the fly is to see in harsh afternoon and evening glare. A. K.'s Red Quill is extremely durable, which is an important attribute when selecting a good dry fly.

Wells' favorite pattern is a size 16 Red Quill Sparkle Dun. "I typically fish a Mathews' Sparkle Dun (Red Quill) during this hatch as the slender profile helps fool the picky trout," Wells says. "You'll find fish rising in all the likely spots and classic runs, but I like to target the bank-sippers adjacent to deep-cut banks. This is where some of the Williams Fork's biggest fish hide."

The Red Quill spinnerfall typically begins between 6 p.m. and 7 p.m. The mating flight will be completely obvious as the mayflies are moving elegantly up and down in a three- to-four-foot vertical motion. If you observe fish rising, but cannot see what they are eating, chances are pretty good they are sipping Red Quill spinners.

MAYFLY PATTERNS

Tungsten Beadhead Hare's Ear (Natural)

Originator: Variation of James Ogden original
Tier: Steve Henderson

Hook: #12-18 Tiemco 3761
Bead: Spirit River copper tungsten
Thread: Dark brown 140-denier Ultra Thread
Tail: Natural hare's mask guard hairs (from forehead)
Abdomen: Natural hare's mask
Rib: Copper Ultra Wire (Brassie)
Wing Case: Turkey tail (one hook gap wide)
Thorax: Natural hare's mask with a lot of guard hairs

Note: Effective color variations include olive and dark brown. Use a 1/8" bead for sizes 12-14 and 3/32" for sizes 16-18.

Tungsten Beadhead Flashback Hare's Ear (Olive)

Originator: Variation of James Ogden original
Tier: Steve Henderson

Hook: #12-16 Tiemco 3761
Bead: Spirit River copper tungsten
Thread: Dark brown 140-denier Ultra Thread
Tail: Brown hare's mask guard hairs (from forehead)
Abdomen: Brown hare's mask
Rib: Copper Ultra Wire (Brassie)
Wing Case: Turkey tail (one hook gap wide) and Pearl Mylar tinsel (medium)
Thorax: Brown hare's mask with a lot of guard hairs

Note: Effective color variations include natural and olive. Use a 1/8" bead for sizes 12-14 and 3/32" for sizes 16-18.

Flashback Pheasant Tail

Originator: Variation of Frank Sawyer original
Tier: Steve Henderson

Hook: #14-18 Tiemco 3761
Thread: Camel 8/0 Uni-Thread
Tail: 6 to 8 pheasant tail fibers
Abdomen: Pheasant tail fibers
Rib: Copper Ultra Wire (Brassie)
Wing Case: 8 pheasant tail fibers and Wapsi Pearl Tinsel (medium)
Thorax: 2 to 3 wraps of pheasant tail fibers
Legs: Pheasant tail fibers

Copper John (Copper)

Originator: John Barr
Tier: Umpqua Feather Merchants

Hook: #10-18 Tiemco 5262
Bead: Metz brass or tungsten
Thread: Black 70-denier Ultra Thread
Tail: Golden brown goose biots
Abdomen: Copper Ultra Wire (Brassie)
Wing Case: Black Thin Skin and pearl Flashabou covered with epoxy
Thorax: Peacock herl
Legs: Mottled brown hen back

Note: Effective color variations include red, black, blue, and chartreuse. Use a 5/32" bead for size 10, 1/8" for sizes 12-14, and 3/32" for sizes 16-18.

Baedye Nymph

Originator: Bob Dye
Tier: Bob Dye

Hook: #16-20 Tiemco 2488
Thread: Brown 8/0 Uni-Thread
Tail: Gold Krystal Flash
Underbody: Peacock herl
Abdomen: Gold Krystal Flash
Thorax: Peacock herl
Wing Case: Gold Krystal Flash
Legs: Gold Krystal Flash

Dirty Bird

Originator: Ken Morrish
Tier: Idylwilde Flies

Hook: #8-14 Tiemco 3761
Bead: Black tungsten
Thread: Black 140-denier Ultra Thread
Tail: Partridge fibers
Rib: Copper Ultra Wire (Brassie)
Abdomen: Rust and olive Hareline Dubbin
Collar: Pearl Krystal Flash
Hackle: Partridge
Beard: Black Superfine

Note: Use a 5/32" bead for sizes 8-10, 1/8" for sizes 12-14, and 3/32" for sizes 16-18.

Matt's Baetis

Originator: Matt Miles
Tier: Matt Miles

Hook: #18-22 Tiemco 200R
Bead: Gold Spirit River glass (small)
Thread: Camel 8/0 Uni-Thread
Tail: Pheasant tail fibers
Abdomen: Camel 8/0 Uni-Thread
Rib: Copper Ultra Wire (small)
Thorax: Brown Superfine
Wing Case: Black Krystal Flash
Legs: Black Krystal Flash

Matt's Gold Digger

Originator: Matt Miles
Tier: Matt Miles

Hook: #12-18 Tiemco 2488H
Bead: Gold Spirit River tungsten
Thread: Camel 8/0 Uni-Thread
Tail: Pheasant tail fibers
Abdomen: Brown and yellow Ultra Wire (small)
Thorax: Golden brown Ice Dub
Wing Case: Pheasant tail fibers
Legs: Pheasant tail fibers

Note: Use a 1/8" bead for sizes 12-14 and 3/32" for sizes 16-18.

J's Electric Bug

Originator: J Core
Tier: J Core

Hook: #14-18 Dai-Riki 135
Bead: Rainbow tungsten
Thread: Black 8/0 Uni-Thread
Tail: Pheasant tail fibers
Abdomen: Opal Mirage Tinsel
Rib: Black Ultra Wire (Brassie)
Thorax: Peacock Ice Dub

Note: Use a 1/8" bead for size 14 and 3/32" for sizes 16-18.

Tak's Sparkle Olive P.T. Nymph

Originator: Rick Takahashi
Tier: Rick Takahashi

Hook: #16-22 Tiemco 3761 or Daiichi 1220 or 1222
Thread: Olive gray 16/0 Veevus
Tail: Olive pheasant tail fibers
Abdomen: Olive pheasant tail fibers
Rib: Olive Ultra Wire (small)
Thorax: Light olive hare's ear Ice Dub
Wing Case: Pearl Flashabou

Tak's Bop Nymph

Originator: Rick Takahashi
Tier: Rick Takahashi

Hook: #16-20 Dai-Riki 060
Thread: Olive 70-denier Ultra Thread
Tail: Dun colored tapered paint brush fibers
Abdomen: Olive 70-denier Ultra Thread
Rib: Olive Ultra Wire (small)
Thorax: Light olive hare's ear Ice Dub
Wing Case: Pearl Flashabou
Legs: Olive hen fibers

Note: Wing Case covered with Hydro Clear Cure Goo colored with olive Chartpak marker.

Tak's Baetis Nymph

Originator: Rick Takahashi
Tier: Rick Takahashi

Hook: #16-20 Tiemco 2302
Thread: Olive dun 16/0 Veevus
Tail: Wood duck fibers
Abdomen: Dyed BWO stripped Nature's Spirit peacock herl
Thorax: Muskrat dubbing
Wing Case: Black Larva Lace Foam
Legs: Dark dun TroutHunter CDC fibers

Tak's BWO Nymph

Originator: Rick Takahashi
Tier: Rick Takahashi

Hook: #16-20 Dai-Riki 060
Thread: Olive dun 16/0 Veevus
Tail: Olive Antron fibers
Abdomen: Dark olive D-Rib (fine)
Thorax: Olive brown hare's ear Ice Dub
Wing Case: Brown mottled Medallion Sheeting
Legs: Dark TroutHunter CDC fibers

Tak's Go 2 Prince

Originator: Rick Takahashi
Tier: Rick Takahashi

Hook: #14-16 Dai-Riki 060
Bead: Brass or tungsten
Thread: Black 94-denier Lagartun
Tail: Brown hen hackle
Abdomen: Peacock herl
Rib: Pearl Krystal Flash
Wing Post: White poly yarn
Hackle: Brown midge saddle hackle
Collar: Peacock Ice Dub

Note: Use a $^{1}/_{8}$" bead for size 14 and $^{3}/_{32}$" for size 16.

Tak's Go 2 Copper Top

Originator: Rick Takahashi
Tier: Rick Takahashi

Hook: #14-16 Dai-Riki 060
Bead: Brass or tungsten
Thread: Black 94-denier Lagartun
Tail: Brown hen hackle
Abdomen: Copper Krystal Flash
Rib: Copper Ultra Wire (small)
Wing Post: White poly yarn
Hackle: Brown midge saddle hackle
Collar: Copper Ice Dub

Note: Use a $^{1}/_{8}$" bead for sizes 14 and $^{3}/_{32}$" for size 16.

Chud (Black)

Originator: Cody Scott
Tier: Cody Scott

Hook: #16-22 Tiemco 2487 or Dai-Riki 125
Bead: Black tungsten
Thread: Gray 14/0 Gordon Griffiths
Tail: Black pheasant tail fibers
Abdomen: Black pheasant tail fibers
Rib: Black Ultra Wire (extra small)
Wing Case: Black pheasant tail fibers
Thorax: Adams gray Superfine
Legs: Black pheasant tail fibers
Head: Tying thread colored with black Sharpie

Note: Color variations include red, olive, natural, and blue. Flashback optional by swapping pheasant fibers for Mylar tinsel. Use a 3/32" bead for sizes 16-18 and 5/64" for sizes 20-22.

Tungsten Hare's Ear Jig Nymph

Originator: Variation of Umpqua Feather Merchants pattern
Tier: Cody Scott

Hook: #8-16 Tiemco 403BLJ or Umpqua C400BL
Bead: Black tungsten slotted faceted, oversized
Weight: .010" lead wire
Thread: Fluorescent orange 8/0 Uni-Thread
Tail: Guard hairs from hare's ear mask
Abdomen: Natural Wapsi Rabbit Dubbing (tied with dubbing loop)
Rib: Fluorescent orange Ultra Wire (small)
Wing Case: Opal Mirage Tinsel (large)
Collar: Fluorescent orange 8/0 Uni-Thread

Note: Use a 5/32" bead for sizes 8-10, 1/8" for sizes 12-14, and 3/32" for size 16.

Tungsten Micro Mayfly

Originator: Mike Mercer
Tier: Umpqua Feather Merchants

Hook: #16-20 Tiemco 921
Bead: Copper tungsten, oversized
Thread: Olive 8/0 Uni-Thread
Tail: Olive pheasant tail fibers
Abdomen: Stripped peacock herl (quill)
Rib: Gold Ultra Wire (extra small)
Wing Case: Mottled turkey feather, two strands
Thorax: Mercer's olive Buggy Nymph Dubbing
Legs: Olive pheasant tail fibers

Note: Use a 3/32" bead for sizes 16-18 and 5/64" for size 20.

Tungsten Skinny Nelson

Originator: Tracy Peterson
Tier: Cody Scott

Hook: #18-22 Tiemco 3761 or Dai-Riki 060
Bead: Black tungsten
Thread: Black 70-denier Ultra Thread
Tail: Natural pheasant tail fibers
Abdomen: Black 70-denier Ultra Thread
Rib: Gold Ultra Wire (small)
Wing Case: Pearl Flashabou, 2 strands
Thorax: Peacock herl

Note: Use a 3/32" bead for size 18 and 5/64" for sizes 20-22.

Fall Special

Originator: Mathew Thomas
Tier: Mathew Thomas

Hook: #16-18 Tiemco 3761
Bead: Spirit River copper brass
Thread: Wine 6/0 Flymaster
Tail: Natural pheasant tail fibers
Abdomen: Natural pheasant tail fibers
Rib: Red Ultra Wire (small)
Hackle: Brown Whiting Farms hen, tied collar style

Note: Use a 3/32" bead for sizes 16-18.

Colorado River Special

Originator: Mathew Thomas
Tier: Mathew Thomas

Hook: #12-16 Tiemco 3761
Bead: Spirit River copper
Thread: Wine 6/0 Flymaster
Tail: Orange marabou
Abdomen: Peacock
Rib: Red Copper Ultra Wire (small)
Hackle: Brown Whiting Farms hen

Note: Use a 1/8" bead for sizes 12-14 and 3/32" for size 16.

Red Prince Nymph

Originator: Mathew Thomas
variation of original
Tier: Mathew Thomas

Hook: #12-16 Tiemco 3761
Bead: Spirit River copper brass
Thread: Brown 6/0 Flymaster
Tail: Brown goose biots
Abdomen: Red V Rib
Wings: White goose biots
Thorax: Peacock herl
Hackle: Brown Whiting Farms hen

Note: Use a 1/8" bead for sizes 12-14 and 3/32" for size 16.

Green Drake Nymph

Originator: Mathew Thomas
Tier: Mathew Thomas

Hook: #10-14 Tiemco 3761
Bead: Spirit River black brass
Thread: Black 70-denier Ultra Thread
Tail: Black pheasant tail fibers
Abdomen: Black Ultra Wire (Brassie)
Thorax: Peacock herl
Hackle: Olive grizzly Whiting Farms hen

Note: Use a 5/32" bead for size 10 and 1/8" for sizes 12-14.

PMD Spinner Nymph

Originator: Mathew Thomas
Tier: Mathew Thomas

Hook: #16-18 Tiemco 5262
Bead: Spirit River gold brass
Thread: Light cahill 8/0 Uni-Thread
Tail: Dun rooster hackle fibers
Abdomen: Amber Ultra Wire (Brassie)
Hackle: Dun Whiting Farms hen

Note: Use a 3/32" bead for sizes 16-18.

Old Yeller

Originator: Eric Atha
Tier: Eric Atha

Hook: #16-22 Tiemco 101
Thread: Brown 14/0 Gordon Griffiths
Tail: Yellow pheasant tail fibers
Abdomen: Yellow pheasant tail fibers
Rib: Gold Ultra Wire (small)
Thorax: Golden brown Ice Dub
Wing Case: Yellow Pheasant Tail Fibers, butt ends

Tungsten Split Case PMD

Originator: Joe Mitchell
Tier: Joe Mitchell

Hook: #14-20 Tiemco 3716
Bead: Black tungsten
Thread: Dark brown 8/0 Uni-Thread
Tail: Wood duck flank
Abdomen: Chocolate brown Fine and Dry
Rib: 5X monofilament
Legs: Wood duck flank
Wing Case: Yellow closed-cell foam and two black turkey biots

Note: Use a 1/8" bead for sizes 12-14, 3/32" for sizes 16-18, and 5/64" for size 20.

Tungsten Split Case BWO

Originator: Joe Mitchell
Tier: Joe Mitchell

Hook: #16-20 Tiemco 3716
Bead: Black tungsten
Thread: Olive dun 8/0 Uni-Thread
Tail: Olive wood duck flank
Abdomen: Olive Fine and Dry
Rib: 5X monofilament
Legs: Olive wood duck flank
Wing Case: Light gray closed cell foam and two black turkey biots

Note: Use a 3/32" bead for sizes 16-18 and 5/64" for size 20.

Split Case Green Drake

Originator: Joe Mitchell
Tier: Joe Mitchell

Hook: #10-12 Tiemco 3716
Bead: Black tungsten
Thread: Dark brown 6/0 Uni-Thread
Tail: Wood duck flank
Abdomen: Chocolate brown Fine and Dry
Abdomen backstrap: Turkey tail
Rib: 5X monofilament
Legs: Wood duck flank
Wing Case: Lime green closed-cell foam and two black turkey biots

Note: Use a 5/32" bead for size 10 and 1/8" for size 12.

Flashback Gilled Callibaetis Nymph

Originator: Richard Pilatzke
Tier: Richard Pilatzke

Hook: #14 Dai-Riki 070
Thread: Olive 8/0 Uni-Thread
Tail: Olive ostrich herl
Abdomen: Olive ostrich herl
Rib: Copper Ultra Wire (extra small)
Wing Case: Pearl flat Mylar tinsel
Thorax: Olive Superfine
Legs: Pheasant tail fibers

Silverback Callibaetis Nymph

Originator: Richard Pilatzke
Tier: Richard Pilatzke

Hook: #14-16 Dai-Riki 070
Thread: Olive 8/0 Uni-Thread
Tail: Pheasant tail fibers
Abdomen: Tan 4235 Targus dubbing or equivalent
Rib: Copper Ultra Wire (extra small)
Thorax: Medium olive brown 1850 Targus dubbing or equivalent
Wing Case: Silver braided tinsel
Legs: Three pheasant tail fibers on each side

Jujubaetis

Originator: Charlie Craven
Tier: Charlie Craven

Hook: #18-22 Tiemco 2488
Thread: White 16/0 Tiemco and black 8/0 Uni-Thread
Tail: Mottled brown India hen saddle fibers
Abdomen: Two strands brown and one strand black Superhair
Flash: Opal Mirage Tinsel (medium)
Wing Case: Gray Flouro Fibre
Thorax: Black 8/0 Uni Thread
Legs: Gray Flouro Fibre
Body Coating: Clear Cure Goo, brushable

Beadhead Jujubaetis

Originator: Charlie Craven
Tier: Charlie Craven

Hook: #18-22 Tiemco 2488
Bead: Copper tungsten
Thread: White 16/0 Tiemco and black 8/0 Uni-Thread
Tail: Mottled brown India hen saddle fibers
Abdomen: Two strands red and one strand brown Super Hair
Flash: Opal Mirage Tinsel (medium)
Wing Case: Gray Flouro Fibre
Thorax: Black 8/0 Uni Thread
Legs: Gray Flouro Fibre
Body Coating: Clear Cure Goo, brushable

Note: Use a 3/32" bead for size 18 and 5/64" for sizes 20-22.

Two Bit Hooker (Red)

Originator: Charlie Craven
Tier: Charlie Craven

Hook: #14-18 Tiemco 3769
Thread: Red 70-denier Ultra Thread and black 16/0 Tiemco
Tail: Mottled brown India hen saddle fibers
Abdomen: Red 70-denier Ultra Thread
Rib: Black 16/0 Tiemco
Wing Case: Opal Mirage Tinsel (medium)
Thorax: Rusty brown Superfine
Legs: Mottled brown India hen saddle fibers
Body Coating: Clear Cure Goo, brushable

Note: Color variations include black, brown, light olive, and dark olive.

Beadhead CDC Pheasant Tail

Originator: Umpqua Feather Merchants
Tier: Umpqua Feather Merchants

Hook: #12-16 Tiemco 5262
Bead: Copper
Thread: Brown 8/0 Uni-Thread
Tail: Pheasant tail fibers
Abdomen: Pheasant tail fibers
Thorax: Peacock herl
Flashback: Pearl Flashabou
Collar/Legs: Dun CDC

Note: Use a 1/8" bead for sizes 12-14 and 3/32" for size 16.

Jigged Tungsten Pheasant Tail

Originator: Umpqua Feather Merchants
Tier: Umpqua Feather Merchants

Hook: #12-18 Tiemco 403BLJ
Bead: Tungsten slotted copper
Thread: Tobacco brown 6/0 Danville
Tail: Pheasant tail
Abdomen: Pheasant tail
Rib: Copper Ultra Wire (small)
Thorax: Lead wire, peacock herl
Wing Case: Opal saltwater Mirage Flashabou
Hackle: Rusty brown CDC

Note: Use a 1/8" bead for sizes 12-14 and 3/32" for sizes 16-18.

Jigged Tungsten Hare's Ear

Originator: Umpqua Feather Merchants
Tier: Umpqua Feather Merchants

Hook: #12-18 Tiemco 403BLJ
Bead: Tungsten slotted
Thread: Tobacco brown 6/0 Danville
Tail: Natural hare's mask
Abdomen: Hare's ear blend
Rib: Gold French oval tinsel (small)
Thorax: Lead wire, hare's ear blend
Wing Case: Opal saltwater Mirage Flashabou
Collar: Fluorescent fire orange 70-denier Ultra Thread

Note: Use a 1/8" bead for sizes 12-14 and 3/32" for sizes 16-18.

Jigged Tungsten Prince Nymph

Originator: Umpqua Feather Merchants
Tier: Umpqua Feather Merchants

Hook: #12-18 Tiemco 403BLJ
Bead: Gold tungsten slotted
Thread: Tobacco brown 6/0 Danville
Tail: Brown goose biot
Abdomen: Peacock herl
Rib: Copper Ultra Wire (small)
Thorax: Lead wire, peacock herl
Wing: White goose biots
Collar: Red 70-denier Ultra Thread

Note: Use a 1/8" bead for sizes 12-14 and 3/32" for sizes 16-18.

Guide's Choice Hare's Ear (Natural)

Originator: Chad Olson
Tier: Umpqua Feather Merchants

Hook: #12-18 Tiemco 3761
Bead: Gold brass or tungsten
Thread: Brown Danville 6/0
Tail: Natural hare's mask
Abdomen: SLF Squirrel dubbing
Rib: Gold tinsel (small)
Thorax: Peacock herl
Wing Case: Pearl saltwater Mirage Flashabou
Hackle: Partridge

Note: Olive is another effective variation. Use a 1/8" bead for sizes 12-14 and 3/32" for sizes 16-18.

Opal Belly Glint Nymph

Originator: Mike Mercer
Tier: Umpqua Feather Merchants

Hook: #12-18 Tiemco 3716
Bead: Black tungsten
Thread: Camel 8/0 Uni-Thread
Tail: 3 pheasant tail fibers
Abdomen: Opal Flashabou
Abdomen Backstrap: Black Holographic Flashabou
Rib: Gold Ultra Wire (extra small)
Thorax: Natural gray ostrich herl
Wing Case: Black Thin Skin, pearl Flashabou
Legs: Partridge

Note: Color variations include red, yellow, orange. Use a 1/8" bead for sizes 12-14 and 3/32" for sizes 16-18.

Gold Bead Poxyback PMD Nymph

Originator: Mike Mercer
Tier: Umpqua Feather Merchants

Hook: #14-18 Tiemco 2302
Bead: Gold brass or tungsten
Thread: Camel 8/0 Uni-Thread
Underbody: .015" lead wire
Tail: 3 dyed yellow ringneck pheasant tail fibers
Rib: Pearl Flashabou
Carapace: Slip of dark mottled turkey tail
Abdomen: PMD Mercer's Select Buggy Nymph Dubbing
Thorax: PMD Mercer's Select Buggy Nymph Dubbing
Gills: Cream/gray marabou clumps
Wing Case: Slip of dark mottled turkey tail, coated with 5-minute epoxy
Legs: 3 dyed olive ringneck pheasant tail fibers per side
Head: PMD Mercer's Select Buggy Nymph Dubbing

Note: Use a 1/8" bead for size 14 and 3/32" for sizes 16-18.

Poxyback Green Drake Nymph

Originator: Mike Mercer
Tier: Umpqua Feather Merchants

Hook: #10-12 Tiemco 2302
Thread: Olive 8/0 Uni-Thread
Underbody: .020" lead wire
Tail: 3 natural ringneck pheasant tail fibers
Rib: Copper Ultra Wire (small)
Carapace: Golden brown mottled turkey tail
Gills: Olive dyed ringneck aftershaft feathers
Abdomen: Zing-Wing Mercer's Buggy Nymph Dubbing
Wing Case: Golden brown mottled turkey tail coated with 5-minute epoxy
Thorax: Zing-Wing Mercer's Buggy Nymph Dubbing
Legs: Golden brown mottled hen back feather
Head: Zing-Wing Mercer's Buggy Nymph Dubbing

Gold Bead Poxyback Green Drake Nymph

Originator: Mike Mercer
Tier: Umpqua Feather Merchants

Hook: #10-12 Tiemco 2302
Bead: Gold brass
Thread: Olive 8/0 Uni-Thread
Tail: 3 natural ringneck pheasant tail fibers
Rib: Copper Ultra Wire (small)
Carapace: Golden brown mottled turkey tail
Gills: Olive dyed ringneck aftershaft feathers
Abdomen: Z-Wing Mercer's Select Buggy Nymph Dubbing
Wing Case: Z-Wing Mercer's Select Buggy Nymph Dubbing coated with 5-minute epoxy
Thorax: Z-Wing Mercer's Select Buggy Nymph Dubbing
Legs: Golden brown mottled hen back feather
Head: Z-Wing Mercer's Select Buggy Nymph Dubbing

Note: Use a 5/32" bead for size 10 and 1/8" for size 12.

Quasimodo Pheasant Tail

Originator: Umpqua Feather Merchants
Tier: Umpqua Feather Merchants

Hook: #12-22 Tiemco 2488H or 2488
Bead: Copper tungsten
Thread: Brown 6/0 Danville
Tail: Pheasant tail fibers
Abdomen: Pheasant tail fibers
Rib: Copper Ultra Wire (extra small)
Thorax: Peacock herl
Wing Case: Pheasant tail fibers and pearl Flashabou
Legs: Pheasant tail fibers

Note: Use a $^{1}/_{8}$" bead for sizes 12-14, $^{3}/_{32}$" for sizes 16-18, and $^{5}/_{64}$" for sizes 20-22.

Psycho Prince

Originator: Mike Mercer
Tier: Umpqua Feather Merchants

Hook: #12-18 Tiemco 3769
Bead: Gold or tungsten
Lead: 6 to 8 wraps of lead wire (.010" or .020")
Thread: Tan 6/0 Danville
Tail: Dark brown turkey biot
Abdomen: Orange Ice Dub
Rib: Copper Ultra Wire (extra small)
Back: Golden brown mottled turkey
Wing Sprout: Yellow Angel Hair
Wings: March Brown turkey biots
Head: Brown Ice Dub

Note: Use a $^{1}/_{8}$" bead for sizes 12-14 and $^{3}/_{32}$" for sizes 16-18.

PT Prince Nymph

Originator: Mike Mercer
Tier: Umpqua Feather Merchants

Hook: #14-18 Tiemco 3761
Bead: Black tungsten
Thread: Camel 8/0 Uni-Thread
Tail: Mahogany brown goose biots
Abdomen: Pheasant tail Hareline Midge Tubing
Rib: Copper wire
Thorax: Peacock herl
Wings: Gold goose biots
Legs: Brown partridge fibers
Head: PMD Mercer's Buggy Nymph Flash Dubbing

Note: Use a $^{1}/_{8}$" bead for sizes 12-14 and $^{3}/_{32}$" for sizes 16-18.

Jumpin Jack Flash

Originator: Dick Shinton
Tier: Dick Shinton

Hook: #14-20 Umpqua U202
Bead: Silver Canadian Llama tungsten
Thread: Black 70-denier Ultra Thread
Tail: Lagartun Midge Braid
Underbody: Black UTC Holographic Tinsel (medium)
Shell Back: Ice blue pearl UTC Flashback Tinsel
Rib: Silver Ultra Wire
Wing Case: Ice blue pearl UTC Flashback Tinsel (medium)
Thorax: UV black Ice Dub
Legs: Lagartun Midge Braid

Note: Use medium Flashback Tinsel and small Ultra Wire for #14-16 and small Flashback Tinsel and extra small Ultra Wire for #18-20. Use a $^{1}/_{8}$" bead for size 14 and $^{3}/_{32}$" for sizes 16-18 and $^{5}/_{64}$" for size 20.

Extended Body Baetis Nymph

Originator: Herman deGala
Tier: Herman deGala

Hook: #20-22 Tiemco 2488H
Thread: Trico 17/0 Uni Thread
Abdomen/Tail: Hareline Midge Tubing and Coq de Leon
Thorax: Black rhea tail
Legs: Partridge
Wing Case: Mottled brown Medallion Sheeting and UV Knot Sense

Note: You can also tie this with a 1.5mm black tungsten bead. Color thread with an AD permanent marker to match body color. To create the rib, heat hemostats and crimp the tubing.

CDC Callibaetis (Tan)

Originator: Herman deGala
Tier: Herman deGala

Hook: #14-16 Tiemco 2302
Bead: Gold brass or tungsten (1.5mm)
Thread: Trico 17/0 Uni-Thread
Tail: Tan ostrich herl
Abdomen: Tan D-Rib (small)
Legs: CDC and UV tan Ice Dub
Wing Case: Mottled brown Medallion Sheeting

Note: Chartreuse is also effective. Color thread with an AD permanent marker to match body color.

Beadhead Soft Hackle Pheasant Tail

Originator: Soft hackle variation of Frank Sawyer original
Tier: Duane Redford

Hook: #16-18 Mustad 3906
Bead: Gold brass or tungsten
Thread: Black 8/0 Uni-Thread
Tail: Pheasant tail fibers
Abdomen: Pheasant tail fibers
Rib: Gold Ultra Wire, reversed ribbed (small)
Collar: Partridge
Thorax: Peacock herl

Note: Use a 3/32" bead for sizes 16-18.

Girl Scout

Originator: Duane Redford
Tier: Duane Redford

Hook: #18-22 Tiemco 2487
Thread: Dark brown 8/0 Uni-Thread
Tail: Two pheasant tail fibers
Abdomen: Dark brown and olive 8/0 Uni-Thread
Rib: Gold Ultra Wire (small)
Wing: Pearl Flashabou
Head: Tying thread

Beadhead PT

Originator: Tom Whitley variation of original
Tier: Tom Whitley

Hook: #14-20 Tiemco 2487
Bead: Spirit River gold glass (extra small)
Thread: Olive 6/0 Uni-Thread
Tail: Natural pheasant tail fibers
Rib: Copper Ultra Wire (fine)
Abdomen: Pheasant tail fibers
Thorax: Peacock Ice Dub
Wing: White Antron

Bi-color Pheasant Tail

Originator: Dr. Eric Pettine
Tier: Dr. Eric Pettine

Hook: #14-18 Tiemco 3762
Bead: Orange and gold brass
Thread: Brown 70-denier Ultra Thread
Tail: Natural pheasant tail fibers
Rib: Lagartun oval tinsel (fine)
Thorax: Peacock herl
Wing Case: Natural pheasant tail fibers
Hackle: Brown India hen back

Note: Use a 1/8" bead for size 14 and 3/32" for sizes 16-18.

The Green Hornet

Originator: Dr. Eric Pettine
Tier: Dr. Eric Pettine

Hook: #14-18 Tiemco 3762
Thread: Olive 70-denier Ultra Thread
Tail: Yellow-gold Sulky Holoshimmer (one strand)
Overbody: Green Thin Skin
Thorax: Olive Prism Dubbing
Wing Case: Black and green Aero Dry Wing
Legs: Black and green Aero Dry Wing
Head: Tying thread

Orange Asher Variant

Originator: Dr. Eric Pettine
Tier: Dr. Eric Pettine

Hook: #14-18 Tiemco 2488
Bead: White and gold brass
Thread: Burnt orange 70-denier Ultra Thread
Tail: White hackle
Abdomen: Orange Ice Dub
Overbody: White Aero Dry Wing
Rib: Copper Ultra Wire (fine)
Legs: White Aero Dry Wing
Thorax: Cream Prism Dubbing

Note: Use a 1/8" bead for size 14 and 3/32" for sizes 16-18.

Tungsten and Orange Soft Hackle

Originator: Dr. Eric Pettine
Tier: Dr. Eric Pettine

Hook: #14-18 Tiemco 3761
Bead: Gold tungsten
Thread: Burnt orange 70-denier Ultra Thread
Abdomen: Burnt orange 70-denier Ultra Thread
Thorax: Hare's ear Ice Dub
Hackle: Speckled brown India hen back

Note: Use a 1/8" bead for size 14 and 3/32" for sizes 16-18.

Big Bear's Baetis

Originator: Bear Goode
Tier: Solitude Fly Company

Hook: #18-22 Tiemco 200R
Thread: Light cahill 8/0 Uni-Thread
Tail: Natural pheasant tail fibers
Backstrap: Natural pheasant tail fibers
Wing Case: Black Antron
Legs: Black Antron
Head: Color thread with brown Sharpie

Poxyback Callibaetis

Originator: Mike Mercer
Tier: Umpqua Feather Merchants

Hook: #14-18 Tiemco 200R
Weight: 4 to 6 wraps of .015" lead wire
Thread: Olive 8/0 Uni-Thread
Tail: Natural gray ostrich herl
Rib: Pearl Flashabou
Abdomen: Tan Damsel Buggy Nymph Dubbing
Gills: Natural gray marabou clumps
Thorax: Tan Damsel Buggy Nymph Dubbing
Legs: Wooduck flank
Wing Case: Dark mottled turkey tail feather coated with 5-minute epoxy
Head: Tan Damsel Buggy Nymph Dubbing

Crystal Hunchback Baetis

Originator: Andy Burk
Tier: Umpqua Feather Merchants

Hook: #18-22 Tiemco 2488
Bead: Copper tungsten
Thread: Olive 70-denier Ultra-Thread
Tail: Mallard flank dyed wood duck
Rib: Olive Midge Krystal Flash
Abdomen: BWO Superfine
Thorax: BWO Superfine
Wing Case: Mirage Tinsel
Legs: Mallard flank dyed wood duck and olive Midge Krystal Flash

Note: Use a 3/32" bead for size 18 and 5/64" for sizes 20-22.

Tyvek Baetis

Originator: Randy Smith
Tier: Pat Dorsey

Hook: #18-24 Tiemco 101
Thread: Brown 8/0 Uni-Thread
Tail: Wood duck fibers
Abdomen: Olive beaver dubbing
Wing Case: Tyvek colored with a black Sharpie
Legs: Wood duck fibers

Baetis Nymph

Originator: Shane Stalcup
Tier: Solitude Fly Company

Hook: #18-22 Tiemco 200R
Thread: Olive 6/0 Uni-Thread
Tail: Partridge
Abdomen: Olive-brown D-Rib (small)
Thorax: Olive-brown Superfine
Legs: Partridge
Wing Case: Olive-brown Medallion Sheeting

Flash Fox Nymph

Originator: Steve Parrott
Tier: Steve Parrott

Hook: #14-16 Umpqua C200BL
Bead: Copper tungsten
Thread: Cream 70-denier Ultra Thread
Tail: Dark Coq de Leon feathers
Abdomen: Whitlock Red Fox Squirrel Dubbing (Thorax)
Rib: Ice blue UTC Pearl Tinsel (small)
Wing Case: Brown Thin Skin
Thorax: Whitlock Red Fox Squirrel Dubbing (Abdomen)
Hot Spot: Fluorescent hot orange Datum Glo Brite Floss (#5)

Note: Use a $^{1}/_{8}$" bead for size 14 and $^{3}/_{32}$" for size 16.

Bling Nymph

Originator: Steve Parrott
Tier: Steve Parrott

Hook: #12-14 Umpqua Competition C500BL
Bead: Brown tungsten
Thread: Cream 70-denier Ultra Thread
Tail: Wood duck fibers
Abdomen: Brown Micro Tubing
Flash: UTC Opal Mirage Tinsel (small)
Wing Case: Brown Jan Siman Magic Shrimp Foil
Thorax: PMD Mercer's Buggy Nymph Dubbing
Hot Spot: Fluorescent orange Datum Glo Brite Floss (#4)

Note: Use a $^{1}/_{8}$" bead for sizes 12-14.

Good and Plenty Micro Mayfly

Originator: Steve Parrott
Tier: Steve Parrott

Hook: #14-16 Umpqua Competition C260BL
Weight: Round lead wire (.010") flattened
Thread: Black 70-denier Ultra Thread
Tail: Dark Coq de Leon
Abdomen: Yellow olive 70-denier Ultra Thread
Rib: Green Jan Siman Pearl Body Quill
Head: Black 8/0 Uni-Thread

Note: Coat entire fly with Clear Cure Goo Hydro.

Mercury Baetis

Originator: Pat Dorsey
Tier: Pat Dorsey

Hook: #20-22 Tiemco 200R
Bead: Clear silver-lined glass (extra small)
Thread: Light cahill 8/0 Uni-Thread
Tail: Black hackle fibers
Abdomen: Blue-Winged Olive Superfine
Thorax: Blue-Winged Olive Superfine
Wing Case: Black Z-Lon
Legs: Black Z-Lon

Note: Color thread with a black Sharpie prior to whip-finishing.

Mercury PMD

Originator: Pat Dorsey
Tier: Pat Dorsey

Hook: #18-22 Tiemco 200R
Bead: Clear silver-lined glass (extra small)
Thread: Light cahill 8/0 Uni-Thread
Tail: Brown hackle fibers
Abdomen: Pale Morning Dun Superfine
Thorax: Pale Morning Dun Superfine
Wing Case: Brown Z-Lon
Legs: Brown Z-Lon

Note: Color thread with a brown Sharpie prior to whip-finishing.

Mercury Trico Nymph

Originator: Pat Dorsey
Tier: Pat Dorsey

Hook: #18-24 Tiemco 101
Bead: Clear silver-lined glass (extra small)
Thread: Brown 8/0 Uni-Thread
Tail: Brown hackle fibers
Abdomen: Rusty brown Superfine
Thorax: Rusty brown Superfine
Wing Case: Black Z-Lon
Legs: Black Z-Lon

Note: Color thread with a black Sharpie prior to whip-finishing.

Green Drake Nymph

Originator: Shane Stalcup
Tier: Solitude Fly Company

Hook: #18-22 Tiemco 5263
Bead: Black nickel
Thread: Brown 8/0 Uni-Thread
Tail: Olive and brown marabou
Abdomen: Olive and brown marabou
Rib: Copper Ultra Wire (extra small)
Thorax: Green Drake Mercer's Buggy Nymph Dubbing
Legs: Partridge
Wing Case: Brown Medallion Sheeting

Fold Over Baetis

Originator: Greg Garcia
Tier: Greg Garcia

Hook: #18-22 Tiemco 101
Thread: Dark dun 70-denier Ultra Thread
Tail: Dark Pardo (dun) Coq de Leon
Abdomen: Dark Pardo (dun) Coq de Leon
Rib: Silver Lagartun (fine)
Thorax: Gray Superfine
Wing Case: Black Spanflex
Flash: Black Krinkle Mirror

Note: Cover abdomen and wing case with Clear Cure Goo Hydro.

Darth Baetis

Originator: Greg Garcia
Tier: Greg Garcia

Hook: #16-22 Tiemco 2488
Thread: Purple 70-denier Ultra Thread
Tail: Black Nature's Spirit Tailing Fibers
Abdomen: Purple 70-denier Ultra Thread
Rib: Silver Lagartun (fine)
Thorax: Light gray Prism SLF dubbing
Wing Case: Black Flashabou
Legs: Dark gray MFC Midge Body Thread

Hot-Wired Prince (Red/Yellow)

Originator: Umpqua Feather Merchants variation of Doug Prince original
Tier: Umpqua Feather Merchants

Hook: #12-16 Tiemco 5262
Bead: Gold brass or tungsten
Thread: Black 140-denier Ultra Thread
Tail: Brown goose biots
Abdomen: Yellow and red Ultra Wire (Brassie)
Thorax: Peacock herl
Collar: Brown hen
Horns: White goose biots

Note: Color variations include olive/copper, green/yellow, and blue/red. Use a 1/8" bead for sizes 12-14 and 3/32" for size 16.

Purple Prince

Originator: Umpqua Feather Merchants variation of Doug Prince original
Tier: Umpqua Feather Merchants

Hook: #12-16 Tiemco 5262
Bead: Black nickel or tungsten
Thread: Black 140-denier Ultra Thread
Tail: Black goose biots
Abdomen: Purple Ice Dub
Rib: Red Ultra Wire (small)
Collar: Black hen
Horns: Black goose biots

Note: Use a 1/8" bead for sizes 12-14 and 3/32" for size 16.

Tung Teaser

Originator: John Barr
Tier: Umpqua Feather Merchants

Hook: #8-18 Tiemco 5262
Bead: Gold tungsten
Weight: .020" lead wire (#12), .015" lead wire (#14-16), .010" lead wire (#18)
Thread: Black 140-denier Ultra Thread
Tail: White goose biots
Rib: Gold Ultra Wire (small)
Abdomen: Bronze Arizona synthetic peacock dubbing
Wing Case: Mottled bustard Thin Skin with pearl Flashabou covered with epoxy
Thorax: Bronze Arizona synthetic peacock dubbing
Legs: Mottled brown hen back fibers

Note: Use a 5/32" bead for sizes 8-10, 1/8" for sizes 12-14, and 3/32" for sizes 16-18. Cover wing case with Clear Cure Goo Hydro.

Pickpocket Nymph

Originator: Ken Morrish
Tier: Idylwilde Flies

Hook: #12-18 Tiemco 5262
Bead: Black nickel or tungsten
Thread: Brown 8/0 Uni-Thread
Tail: Natural pheasant tail fibers
Abdomen: Brown and gold Ultra Wire (Brassie)
Backstrap: Brown goose biot
Rib: Gold wire from abdomen
Thorax: Olive brown Ice Dub
Legs: Root beer Krystal Flash
Wing Case: Brown goose biot

Note: Use a 1/8" bead for sizes 12-14 and 3/32" for sizes 16-18.

Finn's PMD Nymph

Originator: Aaron Carithers
Tier: Aaron Carithers

Hook: #16-20 Tiemco 101
Thread: Rust brown 8/0 Uni-Thread
Tail: Pheasant tail fibers
Rib: Amber Ultra Wire (extra small)
Abdomen: Ginger Hare Tron Dubbin (50%) and orange Hareline Dubbin (50%)
Wing Case: Root beer Krystal Flash
Thorax: Ginger Hare Tron Dubbin (50%) and orange Hareline Dubbin (50%)
Legs: Pheasant tail fibers

Hover Tail

Originator: Jin Choi
Tier: Jin Choi

Hook: #16-20 Tiemco 101
Thread: Tan 70-denier Ultra Thread
Tail: Pheasant tail fibers
Abdomen: Black Krystal Flash, clear Micro Tubing, and white ostrich herl
Backstrap: Pheasant tail fibers
Thorax: Yellow foam cylinder (1/8")
Wing Case: Brown Razor Foam (.5mm) and black Krystal Flash
Legs: Partridge

Note: Use 3/32" yellow foam cylinder for size 20. Cover wing case with Clear Cure Goo Hydro.

Fuzzy Baetis (Gray)

Originator: Bubba Smith
Tier: Bubba Smith

Hook: #18-24 Tiemco 200R
Bead: Pearl glass (extra small)
Thread: Brown Bennechi #14
Tail: Pheasant tail fibers
Abdomen: Brown Bennechi #14
Backstrap: Pheasant tail fibers
Rib: Copper Ultra Wire (extra small)
Thorax: Natural CDC in dubbing loop
Wing Case: Foam off the outside of a to-go cup from a coffee shop

Note: Brown is also effective.

Pheasantly Delicious

Originator: Chris Wells
Tier: Chris Wells

Hook: #12-18 Tiemco 2488
Bead: Gold tungsten
Thread: Rust brown 8/0 Uni-Thread
Tail: Pheasant tail fibers
Abdomen: Pheasant tail fibers
Rib: Silver Ultra Wire (extra small)
Hackle: Brown Whiting Farms hen
Wing: Gold/silver Uni-Mylar (regular)

Note: Use a 1/8" bead for sizes 12-14 and 3/32" for sizes 16-18.

Prince of Pheasants

Originator: Chris Wells
Tier: Chris Wells

Hook: #12-18 Tiemco 2488
Bead: Gold tungsten
Thread: Fire orange 8/0 Uni-Thread
Tail: Pheasant tail fibers
Abdomen: Pheasant tail fibers
Rib: Copper Ultra Wire (extra small)
Thorax: Peacock herl
Hackle: Brown Whiting Farms hen
Wing: White goose biots

Note: Use a 1/8" bead for sizes 12-14 and 3/32" for sizes 16-18.

Tungsten Hide-A-Bead Baetis

Originator: Jake McKittrick
Tier: Solitude Fly Company

Hook: #16-20 Daiichi 1120
Bead: Nickle tungsten
Thread: Gray 8/0 Uni-Thread
Tail: Gray goose biot
Underbody: Gray 8/0 Uni-Thread
Abdomen: Gray and brown Ultra Wire (Brassie or small)
Thorax: Peacock herl
Wing Case: Silver Holographic Tinsel
Collar: Dark dun CDC

Note: Use a 3/32" bead for sizes 16-18, 5/64" for size 20.

Tungsten Redemption PMD

Originator: Tim Woodard
Tier: Solitude Fly Company

Hook: #14-18 Daiichi 1120
Bead: Gold tungsten
Thread: Brown 6/0 Uni-Thread
Tail: Dyed mallard flank
Abdomen: Brown goose biot
Rib: Gold Lagartun Wire (small)
Thorax: Dyed brown peacock herl
Legs: Partridge
Wing Case: Brown Scud Back

Note: Use a 1/8" bead for size 14 and 3/32" for sizes 16-18.

Tungsten Salvation Nymph

Originator: Devan Ence
Tier: Solitude Fly Company

Hook: #8-16 Daiichi 1120
Bead: Gold tungsten
Thread: Black 6/0 Uni-Thread
Tail: Pheasant tail fibers
Abdomen: Purple Ice Dub
Backstrap: Dark gray Medallion Sheeting
Rib: Copper Ultra Wire (small)
Thorax: Peacock Ice Dub
Wing Case: Black Scud Back and pearl Flashabou
Legs: Black Super Floss

Note: Use a 5/32" bead for sizes 8-10, 1/8" for sizes 12-14 and 3/32" for sizes 16-18. Cover wing case with five minute epoxy. Color variations include emerald and brown.

Tungsten Bruised Baetis

Originator: Devan Ence
Tier: Solitude Fly Company

Hook: #16-20 Daiichi 1120
Bead: Black tungsten
Thread: Purple 8/0 Uni-Thread
Tail: Purple pheasant tail fibers
Abdomen: Black Micro Tubing
Thorax: Purple UV Dubbing
Wing Case: Purple Sparkle Organza
Legs: Purple Sparkle Organza

Note: Use a 3/32" bead for sizes 16-18 and 5/64" for size 20.

KGB (Killer Green Bug) Nymph

Originator: Jeremy Stott
Tier: Solitude Fly Company

Hook: #8 Daiichi 1150
Thread: Egg shell 6/0 Danville
Tail: Olive pheasant tail fibers
Abdomen: Nature's Spirit Emergence Dubbing #82
Thorax: Tan Hare's Ear Plus
Wing Case: Olive pheasant tail fibers
Legs: Olive pheasant tail fibers

Fakey Nymph

Originator: Tyler Befus
Tier: Tyler Befus

Hook: #10-18 Tiemco 2457
Bead: Brass or tungsten
Thread: Dark olive 70-denier Ultra Thread
Tail: Pheasant tail fibers
Rib: Ultra copper wire (fine)
Abdomen: Pheasant tail fibers wrapped
Flashback: Pearl Mirage Tinsel over the top of the abdomen
Legs: Olive/black barred round rubber (extra small)
Thorax: Peacock Ice Dub
Collar: Brown hen neck

Note: Use a 1/8" bead for sizes 12-14 and 3/32" for sizes 16-18.

Slim Shady Baetis

Originator: Juan Ramirez
Tier: Juan Ramirez

Hook: #18-22 Tiemco 200R
Thread: Purple 8/0 MFC
Tail: Hareline black India hen back
Abdomen: MFC Purple Holographic High Voltage Tinsel
Backstrap: Hareline black India hen back
Rib: Black Hareline Ice Thread
Thorax: Purple 8/0 MFC
Wing Case: MFC Purple Holographic High Voltage Tinsel
Overcoat: Deer Creek Diamond Fine Resin
Legs: Black Spirit River Fluoro Fibre (6 strands on each side)

Note: For the cream variation, use MFC cream thread, brown India hen back for the tail, and tan Fluoro Fibre for the wing case and legs.

Sniper Baetis

Originator: Juan Ramirez
Tier: Juan Ramirez

Hook: #18-24 Tiemco 2488
Thread: Rusty brown 8/0 MFC
Tail: Mottled brown hen hackle
Rib: Black Ultra Wire (extra small)
Thorax: Rusty brown Superfine
Wing Case: Brown Fluoro Fibre
Legs: Brown Fluoro Fibre

Tungsten Hot Shot Nymph

Originator: Juan Ramirez
Tier: Juan Ramirez

Hook: #14-18 Tiemco 2457
Bead: MFC Christmas red Lucent tungsten
Thread: Brown 8/0 MFC
Tail: Pheasant tail fibers
Abdomen: Cinnamon caddis Hareline Dubbin
Rib: Copper Ultra Wire (small)
Shell Back: Pheasant tail fibers
Thorax: Olive brown UV Ice Dub
Legs: Brown hen back

Note: Use a 7/64" bead for size 14 and 3/32" for size 16-18.

Baetis Nymph

Originator: Chris Steinbeck
Tier: Chris Steinbeck

Hook: #18-24 Tiemco 2488
Bead: Purple glass (extra small)
Thread: Iron gray 8/0 Uni-Thread
Tail: Black Fluoro Fibre (3 strands)
Abdomen: Olive brown Hareline Micro Tubing
Thorax: UV purple Ice Dub
Legs: Brown hen soft hackle

Note: Color thread black prior to whip-finishing.

Soft Hackle Hare's Ear

Originator: Variation of traditional pattern
Tier: Steve Henderson

Hook: #12-18 Tiemco 3761
Thread: Dark brown 70-denier Ultra Thread
Tag: Red 70-denier Ultra Thread
Abdomen: Natural hare's mask
Rib: Copper Ultra Wire (small)
Hackle: Partridge

Pseudo Emerger

Originator: Bob Dye
Tier: Bob Dye

Hook: #20-24 Tiemco 2488
Thread: Dark brown 8/0 Uni-Thread
Tail: Brown hackle
Abdomen: Dark brown 8/0 Uni-Thread
Wing: White Razor Foam

J's Blue-Winged Olive Soft Hackle

Originator: J Core
Tier: J Core

Hook: #16-20 Dai-Riki 075
Thread: Gray 8/0 Uni-Thread
Abdomen: Dark brown Midge Diamond Braid
Rib: Gold Ultra Wire (small)
Thorax: Adams gray Superfine
Hackle: Dun Whiting Farms hen

Tak's Baetis Emerger

Originator: Rick Takahashi
Tier: Rick Takahashi

Hook: #18-22 Dai-Riki 280
Thread: Olive brown 16/0 Veevus
Tail: Olive Z-Lon fibers
Abdomen: Dyed BWO stripped Nature's Spirit peacock herl
Thorax: BWO Superfine
Wing: Dun poly yarn
Legs 1: Natural CDC fibers
Legs 2: Dun polyester fibers colored with olive permanent marker

Tak's GRHE Emerger

Originator: Rick Takahashi
Tier: Rick Takahashi

Hook: #18-22 Tiemco 3761 or 3769
Thread: Black 16/0 Veevus
Tail: Guard hairs from hare mask
Abdomen: Light hare's ear dubbing
Rib: Lagartun gold wire (small)
Thorax: Light hare's ear dubbing
Wing: White poly yarn

Beadhead Soft Hackle Pheasant Tail

Originator: Greg Blessing
Tier: Greg Blessing

Hook: #14-20 Dai-Riki 060
Bead: Silver brass
Thread: Black 70-denier Ultra Thread
Tail: Olive partridge fibers
Abdomen: Pheasant tail fibers
Rib: Copper Ultra Wire (small)
Thorax: Hareline Caddis Dubbing (80%) mixed with Hareline Chartreuse UV Dubbing (20%)
Legs: Whiting Farms Hebert Miner black hen hackle, two wraps
Wing Case: Pearl Mylar tinsel

Note: Use a 1/8" bead for size 14, 3/32" for sizes 16-18, and 5/64" for size 20.

J's Pale Morning Dun Soft Hackle

Originator: J Core
Tier: J Core

Hook: #16-20 Dai-Riki 075
Thread: Light cahill 8/0 Uni-Thread
Abdomen: Dark brown Midge Diamond Braid
Rib: Gold Ultra Wire (small)
Thorax: Pale Morning Dun Superfine
Hackle: Dun Whiting Farms hen

Soft Hackle Emerger

Originator: Charlie Craven
Tier: Charlie Craven

Hook: #16-22 Tiemco 100
Thread: Gray 8/0 Uni-Thread
Tail: Three strands white Flouro Fibre
Abdomen: Gray muskrat or beaver dubbing
Wing: White Flouro Fibre
Hackle: Medium dun hen neck hackle
Head: Gray muskrat or beaver dubbing

BWO Barr Emerger

Originator: John Barr
Tier: Umpqua Feather Merchants

Hook: #16-24 Tiemco 2487
Thread: Iron gray 8/0 Uni-Thread
Tail: Brown hackle fibers
Abdomen: Blended olive and brown Superfine
Flashback: Mirage Tinsel (medium)
Wing Case/Legs: Blue dun hackle fibers
Thorax: Adams gray Superfine

Note: Color variations include Pale Morning Dun and Trico.

BWO Drymerger

Originator: Brian Schmidt
Tier: Umpqua Feather Merchants

Hook: #16-22 Tiemco 100
Thread: Rusty brown 8/0 Uni-Thread
Tail: Medium Pardo CDL tailing fiber
Abdomen: BWO Nature's Spirit Hand Spun Yarn
Thorax: BWO Superfine
Wing: Natural dun CDC
Legs: Hungarian partridge

Poxyback Green Drake Emerger

Originator: Mike Mercer
Tier: Umpqua Feather Merchants

Hook: #10-12 Tiemco 200R
Thread: Yellow 8/0 Uni-Thread
Tail: Sparse clump of pearl Angel Hair over sparse clump of brown Z-Lon over 3 natural gray ostrich herl tips over sparse clump of natural gray marabou
Abdomen: Olive turkey biot, mottled on dorsal surface with brown marking pen
Gills: Sparse clumps of natural gray marabou
Thorax: Micro Mayfly Mercer's Buggy Nymph Dubbing
Wing Case: Golden brown turkey tail slip, coated with 5 minute epoxy
Hackle: Grizzly dyed green dry-fly hackle, trimmed flat on bottom
Wing: Natural deer hair
Buoyancy Plug: Chartreuse foam

Red Baetis Emerger

Originator: Mike Kruise
Tier: Mike Kruise

Hook: #18-22 Daiichi 1273
Thread: Black 14/0 Gordon Griffiths
Abdomen: Red Hareline Micro Tubing
Thorax: Black Superfine
Wing Case: Brilliant white Hareline Sparkle Organza (colored with brown Sharpie)
Legs: Brilliant white Hareline Sparkle Organza

BWO Mini-Merger

Originator: Dick Shinton
Tier: Dick Shinton

Hook: #18-20 Tiemco 206BL
Thread: Brown olive 70-denier Ultra Thread
Tail: Amber Z-Lon
Abdomen: Stripped natural peacock herl
Wing Case/Legs: Gray Flouro Fibre, topped with UTC Mirage Tinsel
Thorax: Olive brown Ice Dub

Note: Use a $^{3}/_{32}$" bead for size 18 and $^{5}/_{64}$" for sizes 20.

PMD Mini-Merger

Originator: Dick Shinton
Tier: Dick Shinton

Hook: #18-20 Tiemco 206BL
Thread: Brown 70-denier Ultra Thread
Tail: Amber Z-Lon
Abdomen: PMD Nature's Spirit dyed peacock herl
Wing Case/Legs: Gray Flouro Fibre, topped with UTC Mirage Tinsel
Thorax: UV tan Ice Dub

South Platte Emerger

Originator: Tom Whitley
Tier: Tom Whitley

Hook: #18-20 Mustad 3906
Thread: Gray 14/0 Veevus
Tail: Olive Antron
Abdomen: Gray 14/0 Veevus
Rib: Olive Ultra Wire (extra small)
Tuft: Olive Antron

Iceberg Mayfly Emerger

Originator: Larry Kingrey
Tier: Larry Kingrey

Hook: #18-22 Tiemco 2487
Thread: Brown 8/0 Uni-Thread
Shuck: Dun Sparkle Yarn
Abdomen: Goose or turkey biot
Wing: Dun CDC, tied loop wing style
Thorax: Olive brown UV Ice Dub

CDC Loop Wing Emerger

Originator: Shane Stalcup
Tier: Umpqua Feather Merchants

Hook: #18-22 Tiemco 2487
Thread: Rusty dun 8/0 Uni-Thread
Tail: Dun hen saddle fibers
Abdomen: Olive goose biot
Thorax: Gray olive Superfine
Wing Case: Dun CDC fibers
Legs: Dun hen saddle

CDC Green Drake Emerger

Originator: Shane Stalcup
Tier: Umpqua Feather Merchants

Hook: #10-12 Tiemco 2302
Thread: Olive 6/0 Danville
Tail: Brown partridge
Abdomen: Olive turkey biot
Rib: Copper Ultra Wire (extra small)
Legs: Partridge
Thorax: Olive Superfine
Wing: Natural gray CDC
Overwing: Dun Z-Lon
Head: Tying thread

Mayhem PMD

Originator: Chris Walker
Tier: Solitude Fly Company

Hook: #16-20 Tiemco 3761
Tail: Steel gray Antron
Rib: Silver Ultra Wire (extra small)
Abdomen: Light olive 6/0 Danville
Thorax: Peacock herl
Legs: Dun rooster hackle
Wing Case: Tan Razor Foam (1mm)

Sparkle Wing RS 2 (Gray)

Originator: Bob Churchill variation of Rim Chung's original
Tier: Pat Dorsey

Hook: #16-24 Tiemco 101
Thread: Gray 8/0 Uni-Thread
Tail: Gray saddle hackle fibers
Abdomen: Gray Superfine
Wing: Pearl Braid
Thorax: Gray Superfine

Note: Color variations include olive, brown, black, and PMD.

Full Winged RS 2

Originator: Variation of Rim Chung original
Tier: Steve Henderson

Hook: #16-20 Tiemco 100
Thread: Olive 70-denier Ultra Thread
Tail: Two moose body hairs
Abdomen: Olive 70-denier Ultra Thread
Rib: Copper Ultra Wire (extra small)
Wing: Natural dun CDC puff

Note: Effective color variations include brown, black, and cream. Wing length should be as long as the hook shank.

RS 2

Originator: Variation of original RS 2
Tier: Greg Blessing

Hook: #18-24 Dai-Riki 305
Thread: Black 70-denier Ultra Thread
Tail: White Betts' Tailing Fibers
Abdomen: Hareline Dark Dun Hare-Tron Dubbin and gray Antron Dubbing
Abdomen Flashback: Pearl Flashabou
Wing: Pearl poly yarn Metallica

Note: Pearl poly yarn Metallica can be purchased from Hobby Lobby.

Trico RS 2

Originator: Ed Engle
Tier: Ed Engle

Hook: #18-22 Tiemco 2488
Thread: Black 10/0 Gudebrod
Tail: White Betts' Tailing Fibers (two)
Abdomen: Black 10/0 Gudebrod
Thorax: Black beaver fur
Wing: White Saap Wing Fiber

Flashback RS 2 (Gray)

Originator: Tom Whitley
Tier: Tom Whitley

Hook: #16-20 Mustad 3906
Thread: Gray 14/0 Veevus
Tail: Light dun Betts' Tailing Fibers (split)
Flashback: Danville pearl Mylar tinsel (medium)
Abdomen: Adams gray Superfine
Wing: Webbing from white saddle hackle

Note: Color variations include black and olive.

Ice Dub RS 2

Originator: Tom Whitley
Tier: Tom Whitley

Hook: #16-20 Mustad 3906
Thread: Gray 14/0 Veevus
Tail: Light Dun Betts' Tailing Fibers (split)
Abdomen: Gray Ice Dub
Tuft: Webbing from gray saddle hackle

Original RS 2

Originator: Rim Chung
Tier: Rim Chung

Hook: #18-22 Tiemco 101
Thread: Gray 8/0 Uni-Thread
Tail: Dun Betts' Tailing Fibers
Abdomen: Natural beaver fur
Wing: Gray saddle hackle webbing
Thorax: Natural beaver fur

Mercury Flashback RS 2 (Gray)

Originator: Pat Dorsey variation of Rim Chung's original
Tier: Pat Dorsey

Hook: #16-24 Tiemco 101
Bead: Clear silver-lined glass (extra small)
Thread: Gray 8/0 Uni-Thread
Tail: Gray saddle hackle fibers
Flashback: Pearl Mylar tinsel (small)
Abdomen: Gray Superfine
Wing: Glamour Madeira
Thorax: Gray Superfine

Note: Color variations include olive, brown, black, and PMD.

Zombie Mayfly Emerger

Originator: John Perizzolo
Tier: John Perizzolo

Hook: #16-22 Tiemco 2487
Thread: Olive dun 8/0 Uni-Thread
Tail: Medium dun Betts' Tailing Fibers
Abdomen: Olive dun 8/0 Uni-Thread
Wing: White Wapsi Thin Fly Foam

Note: Cover abdomen and head with Loon UV Clear Fly Finish.

Foam Wing Emerger (Chocolate)

Originator: John Tavenner
Tier: Aaron Carithers

Hook: #18-22 Tiemco 200R
Thread: Dark brown 8/0 Uni-Thread
Tail: Brown hackle fibers
Body: Dark brown 8/0 Uni-Thread
Wing: White closed-cell foam (2mm)
Thorax: Brown Fine and Dry

Note: Gray is also effective.

Chocolate CDC Loop Wing Emerger

Originator: Variation of Shane Stalcup original
Tier: Aaron Carithers

Hook: #20-22 Tiemco 200R
Thread: Dark brown 8/0 Uni-Thread
Tail: Brown hackle fibers
Abdomen: Dark brown 8/0 Uni-Thread
Wing: Brown CDC
Thorax: Brown Fine and Dry

Bear's Baetis

Originator: Bear Goode
Tier: Aaron Carithers

Hook: #18-24 Tiemco 2488
Thread: Camel 8/0 Uni-Thread
Tail: Brown hackle fibers
Abdomen: Camel 8/0 Uni-Thread
Rib: Copper Ultra Wire (extra small)
Wing: White closed-cell foam
Head: Camel 8/0 Uni-Thread

A-WAX-2 Nymph

Originator: Jin Choi
Tier: Jin Choi

Hook: #18-22 Tiemco 101
Thread: Light gray 12/0 Benecchi
Tail: Black Betts' Tailing Fibers
Abdomen: Gray Superfine
Rib: Copper Ultra Wire (extra small)
Thorax: Styrofoam ball (small) wrapped in latex
Legs: White Super Hair

KF Foam Wing BWO

Originator: Bubba Smith
Tier: Bubba Smith

Hook: #18-22 Dai-Riki 060
Thread: Gray 8/0 Uni-Thread
Tail: Pearl midge Krystal Flash
Abdomen: Gray 8/0 Uni-Thread
Wing: White Razor Foam (1mm)
Thorax: Gray Fine and Dry

Note: Color variations include olive and brown with a gray Razor Foam wing.

Beadhead Foam Emerger BWO

Originator: Bubba Smith
Tier: Bubba Smith

Hook: #18-22 Dai-Riki 060
Bead: Peacock glass
Thread: Olive 70-denier Ultra Thread
Tail: Olive Fluoro Fibre
Abdomen: Olive 70-denier Ultra Thread
Wing: Foam off the outside of a to-go cup from a coffee shop
Thorax: Olive Fine and Dry

Note: Color variations include black, brown, gray, and white.

BWO Foam Wing Baetis (Brown)

Originator: Bubba Smith
Tier: Bubba Smith

Hook: #18-24 Tiemco 200R
Thread: Brown 70-denier Ultra Thread
Tail: Brown Fluoro Fibre
Abdomen: Brown 70-denier Ultra Thread
Wing Case: White Razor Foam (.5mm)
Thorax: Brown Fine and Dry

Note: Color variations include gray and olive.

Winger Emerger (Gray)

Originator: Shane Stalcup
Tier: Solitude Fly Company

Hook: #16-22 Daiichi 1130
Thread: Gray 6/0 Danville
Tail: Gray Antron
Abdomen: Gray olive goose biot
Wing: Medium dun hen hackle
Thorax: Adams gray Superfine
Hackle: Medium dun rooster

Note: Color variations include BWO and PMD.

Parachute Emerger (BWO)

Originator: Brad Befus
Tier: Brad Befus

Hook: #16-24 Tiemco 2488
Thread: Olive 70-denier Ultra Thread
Shuck: Olive brown Z-Lon
Abdomen: Olive brown SLF dubbing
Post: Orange closed cell foam
Thorax: Olive Superfine
Hackle: Medium dun rooster

Note: PMD is also effective.

Floss Back Emerger

Originator: Juan Ramirez
Tier: Juan Ramirez

Hook: #18-24 Tiemco 2488
Thread: Gray 8/0 Uni-Thread
Tail: Grizzly hackle fibers
Body: Gray 8/0 Uni-Thread
Rib: Black Ultra Wire (extra small)
Wing: Oral B Ultra Floss
Thorax: Adams gray Superfine

Note: Color variations include olive, brown, and black.

Ice Emerger

Originator: Juan Ramirez
Tier: Juan Ramirez

Hook: #18-24 Tiemco 101
Thread: Rusty brown 8/0 Uni-Thread
Tail: Dun Microfibetts
Rib: Black Hareline Ice Thread
Abdomen: Rusty brown 8/0 Uni-Thread
Wing Bud: UV *Callibaetis* Ice Dub
Thorax: Rusty brown Superfine

Parachute Adams

Originator: Steve Henderson variation of original
Tier: Steve Henderson

Hook: #12-20 Tiemco 100
Thread: Gray 8/0 Uni-Thread
Tail: Moose body hair
Abdomen: Adams gray Superfine
Wing: Medium dun Z-Lon
Hackle: Grizzly and brown Whiting Farms rooster saddle

Tak's Thorax Baetis

Originator: Rick Takahashi
Tier: Rick Takahashi

Hook: #18-22 Tiemco 100 or Daiichi 1220
Thread: Olive brown 16/0 Veevus
Tail: Dun colored polyester tapered paint brush fibers
Abdomen: Dyed BWO Nature's Spirit stripped peacock herl
Thorax: BWO Superfine
Wing: Dun poly yarn
Hackle: Dun Whiting Farms Midge Saddle

Tak's Quill Bodied Compara-dun

Originator: Rick Takahashi
Tier: Rick Takahashi

Hook: #18-22 Tiemco 100 or Daiichi 1220
Thread: Olive brown 16/0 Veevus
Tail: Dun colored polyester tapered paint brush fibers
Abdomen: Dyed BWO Nature's Spirit stripped peacock herl
Thorax: BWO Superfine
Wing: Nature's Spirit Compara-dun Deer Hair

Tak's CDC Dun

Originator: Rick Takahashi
Tier: Rick Takahashi

Hook: #18-22 Tiemco 100 or Daiichi 1220
Thread: Olive brown 16/0 Veevus
Tail: Dun colored polyester tapered paint brush fibers
Abdomen: Dyed BWO Nature's Spirit stripped peacock herl
Thorax: BWO Superfine
Wing: 3 natural CDC feathers
Hackle: Dun Whiting Farms Midge Saddle

Coffman's Gray H&L Variant

Originator: Ralph Coffman
Tier: Rick Takahashi

Hook: #18-22 Tiemco 100SPBL or Daiichi 1220
Thread: Olive brown 16/0 Veevus
Tail: White deer hair
Abdomen: Dyed BWO Nature's Spirit stripped peacock herl
Thorax: BWO Superfine
Wing: White deer hair
Hackle: Dun Whiting Farms midge saddle

Poor Witch

Originator: Jim Poor
Tier: Rick Takahashi

Hook: #15-19 Tiemco 102Y
Thread: Dun 16/0 Veevus
Tail: Dun colored polyester tapered paint brush fibers
Abdomen: Adams gray Superfine
Wing: Light dun hen hackle tips
Hackle: Dun and brown Whiting Farms midge saddle, mixed

Mahogany Dun

Originator: Rick Takahashi
Tier: Rick Takahashi

Hook: #18-22 Tiemco 100 or Daiichi 1220
Thread: Rusty brown 8/0 Uni-Thread
Tail: Dun colored polyester tapered paint brush fibers
Abdomen: Rusty brown 8/0 Uni-Thread
Rib: Rusty brown 8/0 Uni-Thread colored with permanent brown marker
Wing: Dun poly yarn
Hackle: Dun Whiting Farms midge saddle

Neil's Blue-Winged Olive

Originator: Neil Luehring
Tier: Greg Blessing

Hook: #16-24 Tiemco 100
Thread: Olive brown 70-denier Ultra Thread
Tail: Dun rooster hackle fibers
Abdomen: Olive Superfine
Post: White Antron
Hackle: Medium dun rooster hackle (clipped on bottom)

South Platte Cripple

Originator: Greg Blessing
Tier: Greg Blessing

Hook: #20-24 Tiemco 100
Thread: Black Gordon Griffiths 14/0
Shuck: Olive Antron and black Z-Lon
Abdomen: Olive marabou
Rib: Gold Ultra Wire (extra small)
Thorax: Hareline Hare's Ear Dubbing
Wing: Stacked elk hair
Hackle: Grizzly Whiting Farms rooster

CDC Biot Baetis

Originator: Greg Blessing
Tier: Greg Blessing

Hook: #16-24 Tiemco 100
Thread: Brown olive 70-denier Ultra Thread
Tail: Dun Betts' Tailing Fibers
Abdomen: Olive goose biot
Thorax: Brown olive Life Cycle Nymph Dubbing
Wing: Natural CDC with white poly yarn

Foam Body PMD

Originator: Mathew Thomas
Tier: Mathew Thomas

Hook: #16-18 Tiemco 100
Thread: Light cahill 8/0 Uni-Thread
Tail: Dun rooster hackle fibers
Abdomen: Yellow Razor Foam (1mm)
Wings: Dun Whiting Farms hen hackle tips
Hackle: Medium dun Whiting Farms rooster

Pheasant Tail Floating Nymph

Originator: Ed Engle
Tier: Ed Engle

Hook: #16-20 Tiemco 100
Thread: Black 10/0 Gudebrod
Tail: Brown hackle fibers
Abdomen: Natural pheasant tail fibers
Rib: Copper Ultra Wire (small)
Thorax: Brown Superfine
Dubbing Ball: Sulphur orange Superfine
Hackle: Brown rooster

Quigley Cripple (Callibaetis)

Originator: Bob Quigley
Tier: Richard Pilatzke

Hook: #14-16 Cabela's Model 2
Thread: Rusty dun 6/0 Uni-Thread
Shuck: Gray Antron
Abdomen: Gray ostrich herl
Wing: Medium dun Nature's Spirit Compara-dun hair
Hackle: Dun Whiting Farms 100 pack rooster

Quigley Cripple (Green Drake)

Originator: Bob Quigley
Tier: Richard Pilatzke

Hook: #10-12 Tiemco 100
Thread: Olive 6/0 Uni-Thread
Shuck: Olive Antron
Abdomen: Olive ostrich herl
Wing: Olive deer hair
Hackle: Grizzly dyed olive

Quigley Cripple (Pale Morning Dun)

Originator: Bob Quigley
Tier: Richard Pilatzke

Hook: #16-18 Cabela's Model 2
Thread: Olive 8/0 Uni-Thread
Shuck: Olive Antron
Abdomen: PMD Fine and Dry
Rib: Copper Ultra Wire (extra small)
Wing: Medium dun Nature's Spirit Compara-dun hair
Hackle: Dun Whiting Farms rooster

Red Quill Quigley Cripple

Originator: Bob Quigley
Tier: Richard Pilatzke

Hook: #16-18 Cabela's Model 2
Thread: Camel 8/0 Uni-Thread
Shuck: Rust Antron
Abdomen: Red/orange Wapsi Crawdub Dubbing
Rib: Copper Ultra Wire (extra small)
Wing: Medium dun Nature's Spirit Compara-dun hair
Hackle: Brown Whiting Farms rooster

Last Chance Cripple Green Drake

Originator: Réne Harrop
Tier: Solitude Fly Company

Hook: #10 Tiemco 100BL
Thread: Tan 8/0 Uni-Thread
Tail: Brown Z-Lon and wood duck
Abdomen: Dark brown goose biot
Thorax: Brown-olive Réne Harrop Professional Dubbing
Wing: Paired dark dun CDC feathers
Hackle: Whiting grizzly dyed yellow

Mole Fly

Originator: Charlie Craven
Tier: Charlie Craven

Hook: #16-24 Tiemco 2487
Thread: Gray 8/0 Uni-Thread
Wing: Natural dun CDC
Body: Brown beaver dubbing

Brooks' Sprout Baetis

Originator: Bob Brooks
Tier: Solitude Fly Company

Hook: #16-26 Daichi 1120
Thread: Olive 8/0 Uni-Thread
Shuck: Olive brown Z-Lon
Abdomen: Olive turkey biot
Thorax: BWO Superfine
Post: White round Rainy's Foam (small)
Hackle: Blue dun rooster

Light Cahill

Originator: Dan Cahill
Tier: Umpqua Feather Merchants

Hook: #14-20 Tiemco 100
Thread: Tan 8/0 Uni-Thread
Tail: Ginger hackle fibers
Abdomen: Light cahill Superfine
Wing: Dyed mallard flank
Hackle: Ginger rooster

Para-Wulff Adams (Gray)

Originator: Jack Dennis
Tier: Umpqua Feather Merchants

Hook: #12-18 Tiemco 9300
Thread: Adams gray 8/0 Uni-Thread
Tail: Grizzly and brown hackle fibers
Abdomen: Adams gray Superfine
Thorax: Adams gray Superfine
Rib: Pearl Flashabou
Wings: White calf tail
Hackle: Grizzly and brown rooster

Note: Color variations include purple, Pale Morning Dun, Green Drake, royal, and Blue-Winged Olive.

Improved PMD Sparkle Dun

Originator: Craig Mathews
Tier: Umpqua Feather Merchants

Hook: #16-20 Tiemco 100
Thread: Light cahill 8/0 Uni-Thread
Tail/Shuck: Epeorus Z-Lon
Abdomen: Tan Superfine
Thorax: PMD Superfine
Wing: Natural deer, Epeorus Z-Lon

Parachute Park PMD

Originator: Dick Shinton
Tier: Dick Shinton

Hook: #14-18 Umpqua U003
Thread: Primrose 14/0 Gordon Griffiths Sheer
Tail: Moose body hair
Abdomen: PMD Superfine
Wing Post: Pale yellow Wapsi poly yarn
Thorax: PMD Superfine
Hackle: Whiting Farms medium dun rooster

Generic Mayfly (BWO)

Originator: Dick Shinton
Tier: Dick Shinton

Hook: #14-22 Umpqua U001
Thread: Brown 70-denier Ultra
Tail: Moose body hair
Abdomen: BWO Superfine
Wing: Dun Wapsi poly yarn tied upright and divided
Hackle: Whiting Farms dun rooster

Note: Color variations include Pale Morning Dun, Red Quill, and Green Drake.

The Heckle Dun (BWO)

Originator: Dr. Eric Pettine
Tier: Dr. Eric Pettine

Hook: #14-22 Tiemco 101
Thread: Medium dun 14/0 Veevus
Tail: Medium dun hackle
Abdomen: Olive turkey biot
Wing: Dun hackle
Thorax: Olive turkey biot
Hackle: Medium dun rooster

Note: Color variations include PMD, Red Quill, Green Drake, and Trico. Change the turkey biot to match the appropriate hatch.

Umpqua Green Drake

Originator: Brian Schmidt
Tier: Umpqua Feather Merchants

Hook: #10-12 Tiemco 100
Thread: Black 6/0 Danville
Tail: Moose body
Abdomen: Olive Superfine
Thorax: Olive Superfine
Rib: Chartreuse floss (one strand)
Hackle: Grizzly dyed olive rooster, hackle stacker style
Wings: Dun hen
Head: Black 6/0 Danville

Quill Compara-dun PMD

Originator: Larry Kingrey
Tier: Larry Kingrey

Hook: #16-18 Tiemco 100
Thread: Light cahill 8/0 Uni-Thread
Tail: Light yellow Hareline Mayfly Tails
Abdomen: PMD dyed hackle quill, stripped
Wing: Bleached cow elk
Thorax: Dubbing blend, $^{1}/_{3}$ each of Hareline cream Ice Dub, UV light yellow Ice Dub, and hot yellow Ice Dub

Silhouette Dun

Originator: Andy Burk
Tier: Umpqua Feather Merchants

Hook: #16-22 Tiemco 100
Thread: Olive 8/0 Uni-Thread
Tail: Dark dun Microfibetts
Abdomen: Olive hackle quill
Thorax: Olive Superfine
Wing: Light dun turkey flat
Hackle: Medium dun rooster

CDC Green Drake Parachute

Originator: Shane Stalcup
Tier: Umpqua Feather Merchants

Hook: #10-12 Tiemco 2312
Thread: Olive 6/0 Danville
Tail: Dun Betts' Tailing Fibers
Rib: Brown monofilament
Abdomen: Green Drake Superfine
Post: Dun poly yarn
Thorax: Green Drake Superfine
Hackle: Natural gray CDC

Colorado Green Drake

Originator: Umpqua Feather Merchants
Tier: Umpqua Feather Merchants

Hook: #10-12 Tiemco 100
Thread: Olive 6/0 Danville
Tail: Moose fibers
Rib: Brown floss
Abdomen: Green Drake Superfine
Wing: Dun hen hackle
Thorax: Green Drake Superfine
Hackle: Olive grizzly and brown mixed

Lucent Wing Green Drake

Originator: MFC
Tier: MFC

Hook: #10-12 MFC 7000
Thread: Olive Danville 6/0
Tail: Dun Betts' Tailing Fibers
Abdomen: Green Drake True Mayfly Body (medium)
Wing: Dark dun Organza
Thorax: Olive Frog's Hair Dubbing
Hackle: Olive grizzly dyed

Foam Green Drake

Originator: Ben Furimsky
Tier: MFC

Hook: #10-12 MFC 7000
Thread: Rusty brown 8/0 Uni-Thread
Tail: Moose fibers
Abdomen: Zote Foam colored with permanent marker
Rib: Rusty brown 8/0 Uni-Thread
Thorax: Peacock herl
Hackle: Grizzly dyed olive
Wing: Smoke Widow's Web

DOA Green Drake Cripple

Originator: Ben Furimsky
Tier: Rowan Nyman

Hook: #10-12 MFC 7000
Thread: Black 8/0 Uni-Thread
Tail: MFC Z Yarn
Rib: Yellow Nymo Thread
Abdomen: Light olive Frog's Hair Dubbing
Wing Case: Gray dun poly yarn
Wing: Gray dun poly yarn
Hackle: Grizzly dyed olive

Green Drake Sparkle Dun

Originator: Craig Mathews
Tier: Umpqua Feather Merchants

Hook: #10-12 Tiemco 100
Thread: Rusty dun 8/0 Uni-Thread
Tail: Olive Z-Lon
Abdomen: Green Drake Superfine
Rib: Olive floss
Wing: Deer hair

Extended Body Green Drake

Originator: Mike Lawson
Tier: Umpqua Feather Merchants

Hook: #10-12 Tiemco 100
Thread: Olive 6/0 Danville
Tail: Dyed dark olive mallard flank
Thorax: Olive Superfine
Hackle: Dyed chartreuse rooster saddle
Wings: Dark dun EP Fibers

Vis-A-Dun (PMD)

Originator: John Barr
Tier: Umpqua Feather Merchants

Hook: #16-24 Tiemco 100
Thread: Light cahill 8/0 Uni-Thread
Tail: Watery dun hackle fibers
Abdomen: PMD Superfine
Wing: Light gray poly yarn
Thorax: PMD Superfine
Hackle: Light dun rooster

Note: Color variations include Blue-Winged Olive, Trico, and Red Quill.

Hi-Viz Baetis

Originator: Pat Dorsey variation of a parachute BWO
Tier: Pat Dorsey

Hook: #16-24 Tiemco 101
Thread: Light cahill 8/0 Uni-Thread
Tail: Dun saddle hackle fibers
Abdomen: BWO Superfine
Post: Cerise McFlylon
Hackle: Dun rooster

Note: Color variations include PMD, Red Quill, and Trico.

Limeade

Originator: Pat Dorsey
Tier: Pat Dorsey

Hook: #10-20 Tiemco 100
Thread: Black 6/0 Uni-Thread
Tail: Moose body hair
Abdomen: Green Flashabou and peacock herl
Wing: Chartreuse calf tail
Hackle: Brown rooster

Note: Color variations include Cherry Limeade, which uses red Flashabou and pink calf tail for the wings.

H&L Variant

Originator: R. C. Coffman
Tier: Umpqua Feather Merchants

Hook: #10-20 Tiemco 100
Thread: Black 6/0 Uni-Thread
Tail: Calf body hair
Abdomen: Stripped peacock quill and peacock herl
Wing: Calf body hair
Hackle: Brown rooster

Renegade

Originator: Taylor "Bear Tracks" Williams
Tier: Umpqua Feather Merchants

Hook: #10-20 Tiemco 100
Thread: Black 6/0 Uni-Thread
Rear Hackle: Brown rooster
Abdomen: Peacock herl
Front Hackle: White rooster

Snowshoe Dun (BWO)

Originator: Jim Cannon
Tier: Jim Cannon

Hook: #18-26 Tiemco 101
Thread: Olive dun 8/0 Uni-Thread
Tail: Dark dun Microfibetts
Abdomen: Olive dun 8/0 Uni-Thread
Thorax: BWO Fine and Dry
Wing: Dun snowshoe rabbit hind foot dubbing mixed with Blue-Winged Olive Ice Dub

Snowshoe Dun (PMD)

Originator: Jim Cannon
Tier: Jim Cannon

Hook: #16-20 Tiemco 101
Thread: Light cahill 8/0 Uni-Thread or cream 70-denier Ultra Thread
Tail: Ginger Microfibetts
Abdomen: Light cahill 8/0 Uni-Thread
Thorax: PMD Fine and Dry
Wing: Light dun snowshoe rabbit hind foot dubbing mixed with PMD Ice Dub

Note: Tweak abdomen color to match PMDs on your local waters. Abdomen colors can vary greatly on different watersheds.

Black Male Trico Dun

Originator: Greg Blessing
Tier: Greg Blessing

Hook: #18-24 Tiemco 100
Thread: Black 70-denier Ultra Thread
Tail: White Betts' Tailing Fibers
Abdomen: Black Stalcup's Micro Fine Dubbing
Post: White poly yarn
Wing: Grizzly/brown rooster mixed

Male Snowshoe Trico Dun

Originator: Jim Cannon
Tier: Jim Cannon

Hook: #18-24 Tiemco 2488
Thread: Black 8/0 Uni-Thread
Tail: White Microfibetts
Abdomen: Black 8/0 Uni-Thread
Thorax: Black Fine and Dry
Wing: Natural snowshoe rabbit hind foot dubbing mixed with white Ice Dub

Note: Female Trico dun can be tied by swapping olive 8/0 Uni-Thread for black 8/0 Uni-Thread.

CDC Trico Compara-dun

Originator: Shane Stalcup
Tier: Solitude Fly Company

Hook: #18-24 Tiemco 100
Thread: Black 8/0 Uni-Thread
Tail: White Microfibetts
Abdomen: Black goose biot
Wing: White CDC
Thorax: Black Superfine

A. K.'s Red Quill

Originator: A. K. Best
Tier: Umpqua Feather Merchants

Hook: #14-18 Tiemco 100
Thread: Rusty brown 8/0 Uni-Thread
Tail: Brown hackle fibers
Abdomen: Stripped light brown dyed rooster stem
Wing: White turkey flat
Thorax: Tan Superfine
Hackle: Brown rooster

CDC Compara-dun (PMD)

Originator: Shane Stalcup
Tier: Solitude Fly Company

Hook: #14-18 Tiemco 100
Thread: Light cahill 8/0 Uni-Thread
Tail: PMD Betts' Tailing Fibers
Abdomen: PMD goose biot
Wing: Dun CDC and wood duck fibers
Thorax: PMD Superfine

Sparkle Dun (PMD)

Originator: Craig Mathews
Tier: Umpqua Feather Merchants

Hook: #16-20 Tiemco 100
Thread: Light cahill 8/0 Uni-Thread
Tail: Brown Z-Lon
Abdomen: PMD Superfine
Wing: Deer hair
Thorax: PMD Superfine

Note: Color variations include Blue Winged Olive, Trico, and Red Quill.

Hi-Viz Parachute Adams

Originator: Variation of original Parachute Adams
Tier: Umpqua Feather Merchants

Hook: #12-22 Tiemco 100
Thread: Gray 8/0 Uni-Thread
Tail: Brown and grizzly hackle fibers
Abdomen: Adams gray Superfine
Wing: Fluorescent orange calf hair
Thorax: Adams gray Superfine
Hackle: Brown and grizzly rooster

CDC Compara-dun (BWO)

Originator: Shane Stalcup
Tier: Solitude Fly Company

Hook: #18-20 Tiemco 100
Thread: Olive Danville 6/0
Tail: Dun Betts' Tailing Fibers
Abdomen: BWO goose biot
Wing: Dun CDC and wood duck fibers
Thorax: BWO Superfine

Antron Baetis

Originator: Unknown
Tier: Aaron Carithers

Hook: #18-22 Tiemco 101
Thread: Gray 8/0 Uni-Thread
Tail: Gray hackle fibers
Abdomen: Gray 8/0 Uni-Thread
Wing: Dark gray Anton yarn
Hackle: Dun rooster

Hover Drake

Originator: Jin Choi
Tier: Jin Choi

Hook: #10-12 Tiemco 100
Thread: Yellow 70-denier Ultra Thread
Tail: Black ostrich herl, three strands
Abdomen: Yellow Senyo's Laser Dub
Backstrap: Medium brown Krystal Flash and dark gray ostrich herl
Thorax: Yellow foam cylinder (3/16")
Wing Case: Brown Razor Foam (1mm), medium brown Krystal Flash, and dark gray ostrich herl
Legs: Brown and black MFC Sexi-Legs

Peemer

Originator: Jin Choi
Tier: Jin Choi

Hook: #16-18 Tiemco 100
Thread: Yellow 70-denier Ultra Thread
Tail: Lemon wood duck and dark gray Antron
Abdomen: PMD turkey biot
Thorax: PMD Superfine
Wing: Badger rooster hackle tips
Hackle: Light dun rooster

Tak's Poly Yarn Wing Humpy

Originator: Rick Takahashi
Tier: Rick Takahashi

Hook: #10-16 Tiemco 100
Thread: Black 8/0 Uni-Thread
Tail: Dark moose body
Underbody: Black 8/0 Uni-Thread
Overbody: White poly yarn
Wing: White poly yarn
Hackle: Black Whiting Farms saddle hackle

Para Ext Body (BWO)

Originator: Shane Stalcup/Ray Chang
Tier: Solitude Fly Company

Hook: #16-22 Daiichi 1310
Thread: Olive 6/0 Danville
Tail: Dun Betts' Tailing Fibers
Underbody: White Z-Lon and olive 6/0 Danville
Abdomen: Clear Betts' Zing wrapped over underbody
Post: White calf hair
Thorax: BWO Superfine
Hackle: Medium dun rooster

Note: Also effective in PMD.

Simple Drake

Originator: Chris Wells
Tier: Chris Wells

Hook: #10-14 Tiemco 100
Thread: Olive 6/0 Danville
Tail: Pheasant tail fibers
Abdomen: Olive Superfine
Rib: Rust brown 6/0 Uni-Thread
Hackle: Grizzly and olive-dyed grizzly rooster (oversized)

KGB Green Drake

Originator: Jeremy Stott
Tier: Solitude Fly Company

Hook: #12 Daiichi 1160
Thread: Olive 6/0 Uni-Thread
Tail: Moose hair
Abdomen: Olive deer body hair
Wing: Medium dun hen and elk hair
Thorax: Olive Superfine

Para Ext Body (PMD)

Originator: Shane Stalcup/Ray Chang
Tier: Solitude Fly Company

Hook: #16-22 Daiichi 1310
Thread: Light olive 6/0 Danville
Tail: Dun Betts' Tailing Fibers
Underbody: White Z-Lon and light olive 6/0 Danville
Abdomen: Clear Betts' Zing wrapped over underbody
Post: White calf hair
Thorax: PMD Superfine
Hackle: Light dun rooster

Note: This pattern is also effective in a BWO version.

Adams Superfly

Originator: Umpqua Feather Merchants
Tier: Umpqua Feather Merchants

Hook: #10-18 Tiemco 100
Thread: 8/0 gray Uni-Thread
Tail: Moose
Abdomen: Gray dyed deer body (extended body style)
Thorax: Adams gray Superfine
Wing: Grizzly hen tips
Hackle: Grizzly rooster

CDC Spun Dun

Originator: Juan Ramirez
Tier: Juan Ramirez

Hook: #18-24 Tiemco 101
Thread: Gray 8/0 MFC
Tail: Amber Z-Lon
Abdomen: Gray 8/0 MFC
Wing: Gray CDC spun

Note: Use Marc Petijean Magic Tool Clip to hold and insert CDC into a dubbing loop. Olive is another effective variation.

Red Quill Spinner

Originator: Variation Theodore Gordon original
Tier: Mike Kruise

Hook: #15-17 Tiemco 102Y
Thread: Rust brown 8/0 Uni-Thread
Tail: Dun Betts' Tailing Fibers
Abdomen: Brown hackle stem
Wings: Dun CDC
Thorax: Rusty brown Superfine

Red Quill Spinner

Originator: Mike Kruise
Tier: Mike Kruise

Hook: #15-17 Tiemco 102Y
Thread: Rust brown 8/0 Uni-Thread
Tail: Dun Betts' Tailing Fibers
Abdomen: Rusty brown Superfine
Hackle: Brown and grizzly rooster, trimmed on bottom

CDC Biot Rusty Spinner

Originator: Shane Stalcup
Tier: Umpqua Feather Merchants

Hook: #16-20 Tiemco 100
Thread: Rusty dun 8/0 Uni-Thread
Tail: Dun Betts' Tailing Fibers
Abdomen: Rust turkey biot
Underwing: Light dun CDC
Overwing: Medium dun Z-Lon
Thorax: Rusty brown Superfine

CDC Biot Trusty Rusty Paraspinner (PMD)

Originator: Bonnie Harrop
Tier: Rick Yancik

Hook: #16-20 Tiemco 100
Thread: Rust 8/0 Uni-Thread
Tail: Whiting Farms Coq de Leon fibers, light-speckled
Abdomen: TroutHunter rusty-colored stripped goose biot
Wing: TroutHunter paired white CDC
Thorax: Rusty spinner TroutHunter Professional Dubbing
Hackle: Whiting Farms grizzly

Note: Color variations include Pale Morning Dun and Blue-Winged Olive.

Z-Lon Biot Rusty Spinner (PMD)

Originator: Rick Yancik
Tier: Rick Yancik

Hook: #16-20 Tiemco 101
Thread: Rust 8/0 Uni-Thread
Tail: Whiting Farms Coq de Leon fibers
Abdomen: TroutHunter rusty-colored stripped goose biot
Wing: White Z-Lon
Thorax: Rusty spinner TroutHunter Professional Dubbing

Note: Color variations include Pale Morning Dun, Blue-Winged Olive, and Trico.

CDC Biot Rusty Spinner (PMD)

Originator: Rick Yancik
Tier: Rick Yancik

Hook: #16-20 Tiemco 101
Thread: Rust 8/0 Uni-Thread
Tail: Whiting Farms Coq de Leon fibers
Abdomen: TroutHunter rusty-colored stripped goose biot
Wing: White TroutHunter CDC
Thorax: Rusty spinner TroutHunter Professional Dubbing

Note: Pale Morning Dun is another effective variation.

Hackle Biot Rusty Spinner (PMD)

Originator: Rick Yancik
Tier: Rick Yancik

Hook: #16-20 Tiemco 100
Thread: Rust 8/0 Uni-Thread
Tail: Whiting Farms Coq de Leon fibers
Abdomen: TroutHunter rusty-colored stripped goose biot
Wing: Whiting Farms light dun hen hackle
Thorax: Rusty spinner TroutHunter dry-fly dubbing

Hackle Biot Olive Spinner (PMD)

Originator: Rick Yancik
Tier: Rick Yancik

Hook: #16-20 Tiemco 101
Thread: Light olive 8/0 Uni-Thread
Tail: PMD Betts' Tailing Fibers
Abdomen: TroutHunter PMD-colored stripped goose biot
Wing: Whiting Farms light dun
Thorax: PMD TroutHunter dry-fly dubbing

Note: Color variations include Blue-Winged Olive and Red Quill.

CDC Biot Spinner (BWO)

Originator: Rick Yancik
Tier: Rick Yancik

Hook: #18-22 Tiemco 100
Thread: Olive dun 8/0 Uni-Thread
Tail: Whiting Farms Coq de Leon fibers
Abdomen: TroutHunter BWO-colored stripped goose biot
Wing: Light dun TroutHunter CDC
Thorax: BWO TroutHunter dry-fly dubbing

Matt's Hi-Viz Trico

Originator: Matt Miles
Tier: Matt Miles

Hook: #20-24 Tiemco 101
Thread: Black 8/0 Uni-Thread
Tail: White Betts' Tailing Fibers
Abdomen: Black 8/0 Uni-Thread
Wing: White Z-Lon
Post: Cerise McFlylon
Thorax: Black Superfine

Trico Soft Tackle

Originator: John Keefover
Tier: John Keefover

Hook: #18-22 Tiemco 101
Thread: Black 14/0 Gordon Griffiths
Tail: White Betts' Tailing Fibers
Abdomen: Black 14/0 Gordon Griffiths
Hackle: Light dun Whiting hen hackle
Thorax: Black Superfine

Trico Spinner

Originator: Shane Stalcup
Tier: Umpqua Feather Merchants

Hook: #18-24 Tiemco 100
Thread: Black 8/0 Uni-Thread
Tail: Dun Betts' Tailing Fibers
Abdomen: Black goose biot
Wing: White Z-lon and white CDC
Thorax: Black Superfine

Trico Spinner

Originator: Rick Takahashi
Tier: Rick Takahashi

Hook: #18-22 Tiemco 100 or Daiichi 1220
Thread: Black 16/0 Veevus
Tail: Dun colored polyester tapered paint brush fibers
Abdomen: Black 16/0 Veevus
Wing: Dun poly yarn
Hackle: Dun Whiting Farms midge saddle

Sailboat Trico Spinner

Originator: Joe Johnson
Tier: Joe Johnson

Hook: #18-22 Tiemco 100
Thread: Black 70-denier Ultra Thread
Tail: Two stiff white hackle fibers
Abdomen: White hackle quill
Wings: Two large half stripped white neck hackles
Shell: Black closed-cell foam (1mm)
Thorax: Black Superfine

Sunken Trico

Originator: Ed Engle
Tier: Ed Engle

Hook: #20-22 Tiemco 100
Thread: Black 10/0 Gudebrod
Tail: White Betts' Tailing Fibers (two or three)
Abdomen: Black 10/0 Gudebrod
Thorax: Black beaver fur
Wing: Pearl Krystal Flash (three strands)

Drowned Trico

Originator: Ed Engle
Tier: Ed Engle

Hook: #20-22 Tiemco 2488
Thread: Black 10/0 Gudebrod
Tail: White Betts' Tailing Fibers (two or three)
Abdomen: Black Ultra Wire (extra small)
Thorax: Black beaver fur
Wing: White Saap Wing Fiber

Note: Use chartreuse Ultra Wire (small) for the males.

Drowned Trico

Originator: John Barr
Tier: Umpqua Feather Merchants

Hook: #14-22 Tiemco 2488H
Thread: Black 6/0 Danville
Tail: Pale watery dun hackle fibers
Abdomen: Black 6/0 Danville
Wings: White Antron
Thorax: Black Quick Descent Dubbing

CHAPTER 4

Stoneflies and Their Imitations

Stoneflies are members of the order Plecoptera, which means "folded wings" (*Pleco* means "folded" and *ptera* means "wings"). They rival mayflies in their diversity, boasting nearly 600 species throughout North America. Unlike mayflies, however, stoneflies don't require the same level of sophistication in tactics and patterns because they are available to trout in only two stages of their life cycle—the nymph and the egg-laying adult. Stoneflies range in size from a half inch to nearly two inches in length depending on the species. Their importance varies greatly depending on the watershed and the time of year.

Stoneflies pass through an incomplete metamorphosis, meaning their life cycle consists of an egg, a nymph, and an adult. The duration between each phase depends on the species and water temperatures. The smaller species (such as Winter Stoneflies and Yellow Sally stoneflies) typically live one year,

Golden Stonefly nymphs are an important year-round food source on the Arkansas River. Wise anglers like Eugene Rea know the importance of fishing Golden Stoneflies in the winter, especially during February and March when the insects are molting.

in comparison to the larger varieties such as Golden Stoneflies and *Pteronarcys*, which may live three to four years.

Many anglers underestimate the importance of stoneflies, because as their common name implies, the nymphs are usually hidden underneath stones, rocks, and other debris. Most stoneflies thrive in similar habitats because they have specialized gill structures that limit their living quarters to cold, highly oxygenated, unpolluted trout streams. Throughout Colorado, it's rare to flip over a rock or log and not find a stonefly or two crawling underneath it.

If you're still not convinced of the stonefly's prolific nature, try collecting a seine sample from fast riffle or run; it will be an eye-opening experience. My guess is that your seine sample will contain several stonefly nymphs of various sizes and species. "A fast-water seine sample or flipping over a rock in riffled water on the South Platte River near Deckers will reveal a healthy population of Golden Stoneflies," says Jeremy Hyatt, co-owner of Flies & Lies fly shop in Deckers. "The Golden Stoneflies are often overlooked because the South Platte below Cheesman Reservoir is notorious for small flies. This can be a huge oversight, however, as the Golden Stoneflies are an important part of the trout's diet."

Stonefly nymphs can be recognized by their forked tails, segmented abdomens, branched gills, three pairs of sturdy, double-clawed legs and wing pads, prominent eyes, and antennae. Stoneflies spend the bulk of their lives as aquatic nymphs, therefore anglers should be prepared to fish nymphs year-round—not just before emergence. One of the benefits of the larger stoneflies' multiyear life cycle is that there are several year-classes in the stream at any given time and the nymphs remain plentiful year-round, even after the adults have emerged for the season.

"Golden Stonefly nymphs are an important year-round food source along the Arkansas River corridor, especially during the spring months," said Larry Kingrey, a veteran guide for Royal Gorge Anglers. "By the latter part of February and during the first part of March, the Golden Stoneflies molt, passing through their final instar. Arkansas River trout key on these stoneflies because they are often knocked into [the] drift and become the first big meal of the year. The newly molted stoneflies are a pale buttery-yellow color, plus they are squishy and soft, which really draws attention to them."

Stonefly nymphs (Golden, left, and Pteronarcys, *right) are an important part of the trout's diet. They thrive in fast, oxygenated trout streams where they often become victims of catastrophic drift.*

Kingrey recommends modifying your stonefly tactics and techniques for the spring months: "You should fish a pale-yellow stonefly nymph in the faster riffles or the head of the run during the morning. Within hours the dorsal surface of the newly molted stoneflies darkens as the exoskeleton hardens. Later in the day, typically by noon, I suggest fishing with a darker Golden Stonefly towards the middle and back of the run." The stonefly molt typically lasts for two or three weeks. You'll find a similar stonefly molt occurring on several other rivers throughout Colorado in roughly the same time frame. The same tactics and techniques will fool trout there too.

Later in the season during emergence, stoneflies migrate towards the river's edge by crawling from the river to land, where they will hatch into an adult. Because the "hatch" occurs on dry land, the adults are not available to trout during the emerging process. They are a huge factor, however, during the migration period, and nymphing along the river's edge during this time can be extremely rewarding.

Prior to emergence, stoneflies crawl up on a rock, protruding log, bridge abutment, tree trunk, or other suitable structure to transform into an adult. Evidence of stonefly exoskeletons on the abovementioned structure will remove any doubt as to whether or not there are good populations of *Pteronarcys* or Golden Stoneflies nearby.

Adults look similar to the nymph, with the exception of their folded wings that lie straight back over their abdomen. Adult stoneflies are characterized by their two pairs of veined, glasslike wings—two forewings and two hindwings—with the latter being one-third longer than the former.

Stoneflies do not produce a typical mating swarm (like those of mayflies or caddisflies), but instead they mate on land, rocks, or streamside vegetation. The male and female stoneflies locate one another with a drumming sound created by tapping their abdomens on branches, tree trunks, or substrate. Males initiate a pattern, which is subsequently answered by a female. Each species has its own unique drumming pattern.

Adult stoneflies live between one and three weeks (providing they don't get gobbled up by an opportunistic trout or bird) because they are able to intake fluids as food. Adult stoneflies rarely fly from streamside vegetation, unless females are depositing their eggs. Stoneflies are clumsy fliers and often fall into the water during the egg-laying process, creating the perfect opportunity for a trout to get an easy meal.

WINTER STONEFLY FISHING STRATEGIES

Winter Stoneflies are little brown stoneflies from the Nemouridae, Taeniopterygidae, Capniidae, and Leuctridae families that emerge during the coldest months of the year.

Winter Stonefly imitations are effective on the lower Colorado and Roaring Fork Rivers between February and March. Matt Thomas caught this impressive Colorado River rainbow on one of his Winter Stonefly imitations during the last week of February.

The best hatches occur between January and March, which accounts for their common name of Winter Stoneflies. Even during a frigid day in February or March, Winter Stoneflies can be abundant enough that an angler can fool fish with their imitations.

According to Captain Matt Thomas, an Orvis-Endorsed Guide in the Roaring Fork Valley, "Winter Stoneflies are effective in February and March on the Roaring Fork and the Colorado and it's never a bad idea to tie one on. In the spring, I typically drop a Winter Stonefly imitation off an egg pattern, then drop a *Baetis* nymph of some sort off the stonefly to cover my bases."

Winter Stonefly nymphs thrive in streams with moderate flows and large cobbled substrates. In Colorado, you'll find Winter Stoneflies on just about any watershed you fish, from small creeks to larger rivers and everything in between. Like many other species of stoneflies, Winter Stoneflies require clean, oxygenated water, and they are among the first aquatic insects to disappear when the water becomes contaminated by heavy metals or other pollution. Finding Winter Stoneflies crawling on the snow and ice is a good indication that you're fishing a healthy trout stream.

Winter Stonefly nymphs hide under organic debris (piles of leaves, branches, twigs) until they mature. Their largest populations are found where detritus gets deposited behind rocks,

This Winter Stonefly was found crawling along the streambanks of the Yampa River. Winter Stoneflies are important to both the angler and the trout during the latter part of winter and early part of spring.

logs, and other current-blocking obstructions. Similar to other species of stoneflies, once they reach maturity they migrate to the river's edge where they emerge on land, crawling up on the snow and ice and undergo their final molt into an adult.

Dick Shinton, a guide at the Laughing Grizzly Fly Shop in Longmont, shares his expertise with Winter Stoneflies: "I see these little adult stoneflies as early as mid-February crawling around on the snow, even at relatively high altitudes—9,000 feet or higher. Hatches are sporadic in early February, but as the season progresses—late February through March—they become more common, although I'd never call them prolific. The adults are dark brown to black with clear wings speckled with black. They are about one to 1.3 centimeters long."

The adults are easily overlooked unless you are paying close attention and specifically looking for them. Observant anglers will notice small black stoneflies crawling on top of the snow along the river's edge, which would indicate the emergence is taking place. When I see the adults crawling on the snow, I typically tie on a thin and sparse size 18 black Pheasant Tail Nymph and fish it in the softer cushions along the streambank. I would highly recommend Captain Matt Thomas' and Dick Shinton's Winter Stonefly patterns as excellent options too.

The adults mate on the snow, ice, or nearby foliage. After a few days, the females oviposit their fertilized eggs, which quickly hatch into small nymphs. The adults do not produce large mating flights, but instead they oviposit their eggs intermittently throughout the day. My past experiences lead me to believe that Winter Stoneflies rarely produce good dry-fly fishing. Dick Shinton agrees: "I can't say that I have ever seen fish rising to these bugs, but I do have a couple of adult patterns that I catch fish with." Shinton's findings obviously suggest the fish are aware of the adult stoneflies' presence and will feed on them opportunistically when the females are ovipositing their eggs.

GIANT STONEFLY (SALMONFLY) FISHING STRATEGIES

The *Pteronarcys californica*, routinely referred to as Willow Flies or Salmonflies, begin hatching during the first or second week of June and continue for approximately two weeks. On some watersheds, like the lower Colorado River near State Bridge, Salmonflies begin hatching during the last week of May. If drought conditions exist, the hatch may begin a week or two earlier because of warmer water temperatures. If there is an unusually deep snowpack, the hatch will oftentimes be delayed for a week or two until the water temperature reaches the mid-50s.

When conditions are right, Salmonfly hatches can produce some of the best dry-fly fishing of the summer. According to Ben Olson, guide and director at Black Canyon Anglers, "Hitting a Salmonfly hatch is on every serious angler's bucket list. The Gunnison River has one of the largest Salmonfly hatches in the country. As an outfitter, we tend to book up six months to a year in advance for 'the hatch,' so if you are interested in hitting the Salmonflies, you better plan ahead. This hatch is the backbone of Black Canyon Anglers and has become known worldwide."

Fly-fishing aficionados know that Salmonfly hatches can be hit or miss. If you hit the hatch dead-on, it will be one of the most spectacular experiences in fly fishing; miss it, and it's one of the biggest disappointments of the year. The Salmonfly hatch progresses steadily upstream a few miles each day. Being at the right place at the right time is critical for success.

"The weather is the main factor in how quickly the hatch moves upstream. If the weather is cool and damp the hatch moves upstream slowly. If the weather is warm and dry the hatch moves upstream rapidly," Olson says. "On the main stem of the Gunnison the hatch starts in two places: the confluence of the North Fork and the Gunnison and Ute Park (eight or nine miles upstream). These sections of water are wider and have a more consistent depth so the substrate warms up quicker than other areas in the canyon. From these two places the hatch works its way upstream until the whole river is filled with adult Salmonflies. It typically takes three to five days for the Salmonfly adults to cover the fourteen-mile section of the Gunnison Gorge."

During heavy emergences, the streambanks and nearby foliage are littered with Salmonflies, producing a steady supply of egg-laying adults. Too many Salmonflies can actually be problematic, however: If the trout are crammed full with adults, they'll decline your offering, regardless of the number of fluttering adults that are on the water.

"Salmonfly hatches can be so thick on the Rio Grande the air will be littered with millions of insects migrating on an up-canyon breeze a few hundred feet above the river," says Will

The Gunnison Gorge in known for its world-class Salmonfly hatches. Anglers come from all over the United States to experience this incredible hatch. ANGUS DRUMMOND

The Gunnison River is known for one of the best Salmonfly hatches in the country. Veteran guides like Josh Cranson are booked a year in advance for this epic event.

Blanchard, owner of Animas Valley Anglers. "Meanwhile, down at the water the trout will be smacking and slashing adult insects that have awkwardly fallen into the river. At certain times during the hatch the fish will be so stuffed with the adults it is hard to get them to eat your fly."

I have found the least productive stretch to be where the heaviest concentration of stoneflies occurs. My preference is to be either on the leading edge of the hatch or lagging behind the hatch by two or three days. The nymphing can be excellent on the front end of the hatch, but the dry-fly fishing can suffer because oftentimes the trout are stuffed with nymphs before the adults begin to hit the water. The best dry-fly fishing is generally on the back end of the hatch because the trout will be hungry again and will continue to hit large dry flies for up to a week after the hatch.

Olson's favorite stonefly nymph is Pat's Rubber legs in a size 6 or 8 with a coffee/black body and brown Sili Legs. "It is the most reliable stonefly imitation we use. Size 6 or 8 Twenty-Inchers and Halfback Nymphs also work well," Olson says. Other options include size 6-8 Kaufmann's Stones, size 6-10 Dorsey's Paper Tigers, size 8 Halfback Nymphs, and size 6-10 Bitch Creeks.

Pat's Rubber Legs has become one of the most popular stonefly imitations in the history of our sport. "This pattern is effective because of its simplicity and realistic appearance. In a variety of sizes and colors, you can imitate both *Pteronarcys*

Pat's Rubber Legs has become a guide's favorite and a must-have in the Gunnison Gorge. I recommend carrying sizes 8-10 in brown/black and 10-12 in golden. You cannot live without this pattern when you're in Colorado! MARK ADAMS

Some of the Gunnison Gorge's biggest fish of the year are caught with stonefly imitations. Josh Cranson, head guide for Black Canyon Anglers, caught this chunky rainbow on a Pat's Rubber Legs.

and Golden Stones," says Pat Bennett, the fly's originator. "With stoneflies taking three or four years to mature, Pat's Rubber Legs is effective year-round, which is a distinct advantage to this fly. I primarily fish it as the lead fly in my two-fly nymphing rigs. Because Pat's Rubber Legs is heavily weighted, I rarely use any other weight because it gets down fast."

Stonefly hatches provide some of the best opportunities to fool large trout on dry flies. Big fish (trout over 20 inches) rarely rise to feed on tiny mayflies or caddis, but they will rise to eat a large Salmonfly. The caloric value of each Salmonfly outweighs the trout's risk of exposing itself to predators. There is nothing more exciting than watching a huge trout crush a size 4 or 6 dry fly. Olson's favorite dry flies are the Rogue Foam Giant Stone for moving water and the Bank Robber in a size 4 or 6 for slow or still water.

Olson offers this bit of advice for anglers visiting his area: "Dead drifting the adults works but you will catch more fish if you 'twitch' your fly just enough to make your bug look alive. Salmonflies will crawl out of the river onto cliff walls that overhang the river to hatch, [and] trout will hold in crevices next to the wall waiting for them to hit the water. Your chances of enticing a strike will double if your fly is within 6 inches of the cliff walls. Some days the fish just smash it as soon as it hits the water."

GOLDEN STONEFLY FISHING STRATEGIES

Golden Stoneflies, *Calineuria pacifica*, are the more prolific of the two larger stonefly species found in Colorado. Their dense populations exist in both freestones and below deep bottom-release tailwaters. Their emergences can last up to one month or more on many Colorado watersheds. Golden Stonefly nymphs range in color from a rich golden-brown to dark brown, with their underside being one shade lighter than their topside. Their active behavior frequently causes them to get dislodged from the rocky substrate, resulting in a hearty meal for opportunistic trout.

Golden Stonefly nymphs are productive year-round in many streams throughout Colorado because of their multiyear life cycle. Jeremy Hyatt advises anglers not to overlook Golden Stoneflies during the winter months: "Anchor ice will often dislodge Golden Stoneflies from the stream bottom into the drift, thus winter can be a productive time to fish their imitations."

Larry Kingrey admits that more times than not, he uses a Golden Stonefly for his lead fly in his tandem nymphing rigs on the Arkansas River. "Most of the time I use a Golden Stonefly nymph as a starting point for my attractor in my nymphing rigs," Kingrey says. "Later in the year, when the adults have emerged for the season, I fish smaller imitations, usually a size 14, then progress to a size 12 by the latter part of summer."

Jeremy Hyatt also recommends fishing Golden Stonefly patterns during a flow increase, as fluctuating water levels will often knock the naturals loose from the substrate. Opportunistic trout are always on the prowl for a Golden Stonefly drifting helplessly in the current. Hyatt's favorite Golden Stonefly patterns are size 8-10 Mercer's Epoxy Biot Golden Stoneflies, size 10-12 Pat's Rubber Legs, and size 8-10 Barr's Tungstones.

During the summer, Golden Stonefly strategies are similar to those used during the Salmonfly hatch. In the days preceding the hatch, anglers should focus their efforts on the fast riffled areas near the streambank. Hyatt agrees the best time of the year to fish Golden Stonefly imitations is prior to their emergence, when stoneflies are on the move towards the river's edge to emerge into adults: "Late spring and early summer is when the Golden Stoneflies start to migrate toward the stream's bank to emerge into adults. The nymphing can be excellent along the edges of the stream before their emergence."

One of my favorite Golden Stonefly patterns is a woven-body Golden Stonefly that I tie from Larva Lace. By weaving brown and yellow Larva Lace together, you can achieve a darker topside and a lighter underside that mimics the naturals. Pat's Rubber Legs in size 8-10 and Larry Kingrey's Golden Stone are also among my favorite stonefly imitations.

The Golden Stonefly emergence follows the giant Salmonfly hatch by approximately two weeks, occurring between early July and mid-August. There is often some overlap between the two hatches, which means both golden and *Pteronarcys* stoneflies can be emerging at the same time. When the salmonflies begin to thin out, you'll should employ the same tactics and techniques, but switch to smaller Golden Stonefly imitations in size 8-10.

Ben Olson recommends tweaking your Golden Stonefly tactics a bit to increase your odds of fooling more fish: "By the time the Golden Stones hatch the fish have seen a lot of artificial flies. You will start getting refusals. The same tactics you use for Salmonflies will work, but if you get a little more technical you will catch even more fish. I turn fishing into hunting fish. I like to spot the fish and then make downstream casts to them, making sure I do not spook them with the line. My first drift is lined up directly upstream of them, six to ten feet from them. Once my drift gets in their zone of sight (three to four feet from them), I start twitching the fly toward me, pausing in between twitches; during these pauses you must maintain your drift by letting out line."

Olson tries to get the fish to move off their feeding lies to grab your fly. "If you get the trout to a move a foot or so from

Golden Stonefly nymphs like John Barr's Tungstone are effective year-round because several year classes of Golden Stoneflies remain in the stream even after the adults have emerged for the season. MARK ADAMS

their feeding lie, they'll often commit, and eat your fly," Olson says. "If you get a refusal, change flies and make another cast. The water clears up significantly from the beginning of the Salmonfly hatch to the beginning of the Golden Stone hatch. You'll need to downsize your leaders and tippet from 1X and 2X to 3X or 4X during the Golden Stone hatch."

The best dry-fly fishing occurs in the afternoon when the adults come back to the water to deposit their eggs. According to Larry Kingrey, "The biggest tip on the Arkansas River is to fish your Golden Stones close to the streambank. I mean, within inches of the grass. This is where the fish are stacked up and looking for Golden Stonefly adults to fall into the water." Effective adult imitations include size 8-10 Rogue Foam Stoneflies (golden), Clark's Stoneflies, size 8-10 Yellow Stimulators, and size 8-10 Amy's Ants (olive).

YELLOW SALLY FISHING STRATEGIES

The most prolific stonefly to hatch on western waters is the Yellow Sally (*Isoperla* sp.). Yellow Sallies begin emerging mid-June and continue through the first part of August. Anglers will find significant populations of Yellow Sallies on both freestones and tailwaters but they must be willing to adapt to a variety of conditions. Tailwaters with clear, stable flows provide the most reliable hatches in June when unregulated trout streams are blown out from spring runoff. High water will no doubt have adverse effects on the dry-fly fishing, but don't let that fool you—the nymphing remains good to excellent despite the higher flows. Freestones become prime candidates for targeting Yellow Sally hatches after spring runoff subsides and flows stabilize, which usually occurs toward the first part of July.

Colorado anglers will find excellent Yellow Sally hatches statewide. Some of the most popular destinations include the South Platte, Colorado, Gunnison, Arkansas, Roaring Fork, Yampa, Williams Fork, and Blue Rivers. According to Greg Felt, co-owner of ArkAnglers in Salida, "The Yellow Sally hatch has become a significant part of our summer. I say 'become' since it wasn't a big part of the picture prior to the metals cleanup of the mid-nineties. Now in a more supportive environment, these bugs seem to be flourishing and are a key aspect of the summer trout diet on the Arkansas."

Yellow Sally nymphs are brown, tan, or light yellow with mottled abdomens and wing pads. They thrive in rocky substrates with moderate to fast flows and are frequently knocked loose from the substrate during spring runoff or fluctuating flows. My favorite Yellow Sally nymphs are size 12-14 Oliver Edwards Yellow Sallies, which have become some of my go-to attractors between mid-June and the end of July.

Similar to other species of stoneflies, once the nymphs mature they migrate to the river's edge and crawl out on rocks, logs, bushes, and trees to emerge into adults. The Yellow Sally's migration to the river's edge provides yet another

With improving water quality on the Arkansas River, Yellow Sally hatches are thriving. Yellow Sally adults can provide some excellent dry-fly fishing during the latter part of June through early August.

Kim Dorsey prepares to net a beautiful brown trout that she fooled with an Oliver Edwards Yellow Sally nymph. A Yellow Sally nymph is an excellent attractor in a tandem nymphing rig during July and August. MARK ADAMS

opportunity to fish a stonefly nymph. Felt adds a valuable piece of advice: "Fishing the 'hatch' is really about fishing a shoreline nymph since the fish do not have access to the adults at emergence. Fishing a dry-dropper or suspended nymph on a short tether beneath an indicator along the shoreline pocket water is a good way to imitate the nymphs that are making their way to the river's edge. Since the Yellow Sally hatch normally occurs from late June to early August, our typical midsummer flows still have many brown trout pinned up against the banks and out of the higher current velocities. There, the nymphs have to crawl through a gauntlet of hungry fish to reach the shore and this is why the short dropper technique works well. My favorite pattern for this bug is the Morrish Iron Sally in a size 16. A red-and-yellow Hot Wire Prince works well too."

The Yellow Sally adults exhibit a yellowish-green color, which separates them from other fluttering insects like caddis. It is not uncommon to see Yellow Sallies hatching with Pale Morning Duns and caddis, which can further complicate things in regard to fly selection. Don't be afraid to experience with multifly dry-fly rigs; for instance, fish with tandem rigs consisting of a Yellow Sally and a caddis, or a Yellow Sally and a Pale Morning Dun. Watch the riseform carefully and decipher which insect the trout are keying on. Evidence of splashy or aggressive rises along the streambank is a good sign the fish are eating fluttering insects like Yellow Sallies. Yellow Stimulators in size 16, yellow Crystal Stimulators, Puterbaugh's Foam Stone, and Headlight Sallies are among my favorites for imitating the adult.

"Yellow Sallies are best imitated during the ovipositing phase of their life cycle," Felt advises. "This is when the fertilized females return to the river to lay their eggs and are actually available to the fish. This is generally a mid-to-late afternoon phenomenon and it often coincides with the hatching of Pale Morning Dun mayflies. The color and size similarities of the two often confuse anglers as to what is going on; a tandem dry-fly rig combining adults of each species can cover both bases. For the adult, my favorite pattern is simply a size 16 yellow Stimulator. There are many elegant adult Yellow Sally patterns but few match the yellow Stimulator for realistic portrayal, durability, and buoyancy."

STONEFLY PATTERNS

Pat's Rubber Legs (Brown)

Originator: Pat Bennett
Tier: Steve Henderson

Hook: #6-10 Tiemco 5263
Thread: Brown 140-denier Ultra Thread
Weight: .025" lead wire
Tail: Light brown Flexi Floss
Abdomen: Brown chenille (medium)
Legs: Light brown Flexi Floss
Antennae: Light brown Flexi Floss

Note: Effective color variations include black and brown/black.

Twenty-Incher

Originator: Brad Tutor
Tier: Bob Dye

Hook: #8-14 Tiemco 5262
Bead: Brass or tungsten
Thread: Black 140-denier Ultra Thread
Tail: Brown goose biots
Abdomen: Peacock herl
Rib: Gold Lagartun oval tinsel (medium)
Legs: Hungarian partridge
Wing Case: Turkey

Note: Use a 5/32" bead for sizes 8-10 and 1/8" for sizes 12-14.

Tak's Masking Tape Stonefly Nymph

Originator: Rick Takahashi
Tier: Rick Takahashi

Hook: #8-10 Daiichi 1730
Thread: Yellow 3/0 Monocord or Hopper Yellow 140-denier Ultra Thread
Tail: Brown tan goose biots
Dorsal: Masking tape colored with brown permanent marker
Underbody: Golden stonefly dubbing
Rib: Brown Ultra Wire (Brassie)
Legs: Brown tan goose biots
Gills: Gray ostrich herl
Thorax: Golden stonefly dubbing
Wing Case: Masking tape colored with brown permanent marker

Adult Yellow Sally Nymph

Originator: Mathew Thomas
Tier: Mathew Thomas

Hook: #12-16 Tiemco 3761
Bead: Spirit River gold brass
Thread: Cream 6/0 Flymaster
Egg Sac: Red Ultra Wire (small)
Abdomen: Amber Ultra Wire (Brassie)
Wing: Cream Z-Lon
Hackle: Ginger Whiting Farms hen

Note: Use a 1/8" bead for sizes 12-14 and 3/32" for size 16.

Juvenile Stonefly

Originator: Mathew Thomas
Tier: Mathew Thomas

Hook: #12-16 Tiemco 200R
Thread: Dark brown 8/0 Uni-Thread
Tail: Brown pheasant tail fibers
Abdomen: Brown pheasant tail fibers
Rib: Gold Ultra Wire (extra small)
Thorax: Brown pheasant tail fibers
Wing Case: Brown pheasant tail fibers
Legs: Brown pheasant tail fibers

Winter Stonefly

Originator: Mathew Thomas
Tier: Mathew Thomas

Hook: #16-18 Tiemco 3761
Thread: Black 8/0 Uni-Thread
Tail: Black pheasant tail fibers
Abdomen: Black 8/0 Uni-Thread overlaid with black pheasant tail fibers
Thorax: Black pheasant tail fibers
Rib: Black 8/0 Uni-Thread
Wing Case: Black pheasant tail fibers
Legs: Black pheasant tail fibers

Little Black Stonefly Nymph

Originator: Dick Shinton
Tier: Dick Shinton

Hook: #18-20 Dai-Riki 300
Bead: Clear silver-lined glass (extra small)
Thread: Black 14/0 Gordon Griffiths
Tail: Black Krystal Flash
Abdomen: Black Hareline Dubbin
Rib: 4X mono
Thorax: Black Hareline Dubbin
Wing Case: Black Lateral Scale
Legs: India hen back

CDC Golden Stone

Originator: Charlie Craven
Tier: Charlie Craven

Hook: #10-14 Tiemco 5262
Bead: Gold tungsten
Weight: .020" lead wire
Thread: Yellow Danville 6/0
Tail: Yellow dyed pheasant tail fibers
Shell Back: Opal Mirage Tinsel (large)
Rib: Hot yellow Ultra Wire (Brassie)
Abdomen: Golden brown House of Harrop nymph dubbing
Thorax: Golden brown House of Harrop nymph dubbing
Collar: Natural tan CDC
Hackle: Grizzly saddle dyed gold

Note: Use a 5/32" bead for size 10, 1/8" for sizes 12-14.

Iron Sally

Originator: Ken Morrish
Tier: Idylwilde Flies

Hook: #14-16 Tiemco 5262
Bead: Gold brass
Thread: Tan 8/0 Uni-Thread
Tail: Yellow goose biots
Abdomen: Gold Ultra Wire (small) and black Krystal Flash
Rib: Gold Ultra Wire (small)
Wing Case: Turkey tail
Legs: Black Krystal Flash
Thorax: Wapsi Golden Stone Awesome Possum Dubbing

Note: Use a 1/8" bead for size 14 and 3/32" for size 16.

Gold Bead Biot Epoxy Golden Stone

Originator: Mike Mercer
Tier: Umpqua Feather Merchants

Hook: #8-12 Tiemco 2302
Bead: Gold brass or tungsten
Thread: Tan 8/0 Uni-Thread
Tail: Sulfur-orange turkey biot, mottled with brown marker
Underbody: .020" lead wire
Abdomen: Sulfur-orange turkey biot, mottled with brown marker
Wing Case: Golden brown turkey tail coated with epoxy
Thorax: Mercer's Golden Stone Select Buggy Nymph Dubbing
Legs: Mottled brown hen

Note: Use a 5/32" bead for sizes 8-10 and 1/8" for size 12.

Arkansas River Stonefly

Originator: Larry Friedrichs
Tier: Larry Friedrichs

Hook: #12-14 Tiemco 5262
Bead: Gold brass or tungsten
Thread: Brown 8/0 Uni-Thread
Tail: Amber goose biots
Abdomen: Hot yellow and brown Ultra Wire (medium)
Thorax: Peacock herl
Wing Case: Pheasant tail fibers
Legs: Brown hen saddle

Note: Use a 1/8" bead for sizes 12-14.

Golden Stonefly Nymph

Originator: Dr. Eric Pettine
Tier: Dr. Eric Pettine

Hook: #8-10 Tiemco 200R
Thread: Brown 140-denier Ultra Thread
Shape: Two strands of lead wire on each side of hook shaft
Butt: Golden brown Hare 'E Ice Dub
Tail: Brown goose biots
Abdomen: Golden brown Hare 'E Ice Dub
Overbody: Natural mottled bustard Thin Skin
Rib: Amber Vinyl Rib
Thorax: Golden brown Hare 'E Ice Dub
Legs: Brown hackle
Wing Case: Natural mottled bustard Thin Skin
Antennae: Stripped hackle stem

Golden Stonefly Nymph

Originator: Larry Kingrey
Tier: Larry Kingrey

Hook: #8-10 Tiemco 9395
Weight: .020" lead wire, flattened
Thread: Tan 6/0 Uni-Thread
Underbody: Dubbing blend
Tail: Tan goose biots
Dorsal stripe: 1/8" brown Scud Back
Rib: Brown Ultra Wire (small)
Abdomen: Hareline yellow tubing (standard)
Thorax: Dubbing blend
Wing Case: 1/4" brown Scud Back
Legs: Natural pheasant rump feather
Antennae: Tan goose biots

Paper Tiger

Originator: Pat Dorsey
Tier: Pat Dorsey

Hook: #4-10 Tiemco 300
Weight: .020" lead wire
Thread: Dark brown 6/0 Uni-Thread
Underbody: Brown yarn
Tail: Black goose biots
Abdomen: Tyvek strip
Legs: Natural pheasant tail fibers
Wing Case: Tyvek strip
Antennae: Black goose biots

Note: Color Tyvek with a permanent brown marker.

Woven-Body Golden Stonefly

Originator: Pat Dorsey's variation of Larry Walker's woven-body stonefly
Tier: Pat Dorsey

Hook: #4-10 Tiemco 5263
Weight: .020" lead wire, smashed flat
Thread: Dark brown 6/0 Uni-Thread
Tail: Amber goose biots
Abdomen: Yellow and brown Larva Lace
Thorax: Mercer's Golden Stone Buggy Nymph Dubbing
Legs: Yellow dyed grizzly rooster
Wing Case: Brown Swiss Straw
Antennae: Amber goose biots

Tungsten Goldie

Originator: Brian Schmidt
Tier: Umpqua Feather Merchants

Hook: #8-16 Tiemco 2457
Bead: Metz gold tungsten
Weight: .015" or .020" lead wire
Thread: Brown 6/0 Danville
Tail: Dyed ginger pheasant tail fibers
Abdomen: UV light yellow Ice Dub
Backstrap: Dyed ginger pheasant tail fibers
Flash: Gold Holo Flash
Rib: Amber Ultra Wire (small)
Thorax: UV light yellow Ice Dub
Wing Case: Dyed ginger pheasant tail fibers and gold Holo Flash
Hackle: Ginger barred hen

Note: Use a 5/32" bead for sizes 8-10, 1/8" for sizes 12-14, and 3/32" for size 16.

Stubby Stone

Originator: Mike Mercer
Tier: Umpqua Feather Merchants

Hook: #8-12 Tiemco 2499SPBL
Bead: Black tungsten
Thread: Dark brown 8/0 Uni-Thread
Tail: Rusty brown goose biots
Abdomen: Dark brown Mercer's Buggy Nymph Dubbing
Rib: Black Ultra Wire
Back: Black Thin Skin, pearl Flashabou
Thorax: Peacock herl
Wing Case: Black Thin Skin
Legs: Brown Centipede Legs (mini)
Antennae: Brown Centipede Legs (mini)

Note: Use a 5/32" bead for sizes 8-10 and 1/8" for size 12.

Flashback Tungstone

Originator: John Barr
Tier: Umpqua Feather Merchants

Hook: #8-12 Tiemco 5263
Weight: Lead wire
Thread: Yellow 6/0 Danville
Tail: Ginger goose biots
Abdomen: Tan Wapsi Sow Scud dubbing
Rib: 3X monofilament
Flashback: Pearl Lateral Scale
Thorax: Tan Wapsi Sow Scud Dubbing
Wing Case: Golden stone mottle oak Thin Skin
Legs: Gold-dyed grizzly hen saddle

Poxyback Little Yellow Stone

Originator: Mike Mercer
Tier: Umpqua Feather Merchants

Hook: #14-18 Tiemco 2302
Thread: Tan 8/0 Uni-Thread
Tail: Two splayed ringneck pheasant tail fibers
Rib: Copper Ultra Wire (small)
Abdomen: Light cahill Mercer's Buggy Nymph Dubbing
Carapace: Lemon wood duck flank fibers
Thorax: Light cahill Mercer's Buggy Nymph Dubbing
Wing Case: Golden mottled turkey tail segment, coated with 5-minute epoxy
Legs: Brown Hungarian partridge fibers
Antennae: Two splayed ringneck pheasant tail fibers
Collar: Light cahill Mercer's Buggy Nymph Dubbing

CDC Fox Squirrel

Originator: Chris Johnson variation of Dave Whitlock original
Tier: Chris Johnson

Hook: #10-16 Tiemco 200R
Bead: Gold tungsten
Thread: Iron gray 74-denier Lagartun
Tail: Stacked fox squirrel tail and barred pumpkin Silicone Legs (nymph)
Rib: Gold French Tinsel (small)
Abdomen: Red Squirrel Nymph Abdomen Whitlock SLF Dubbing
Collar: Spun CDC blend of Marc Petitjean Bistre and super select CDC dyed wood duck
Legs: Barred pumpkin Silicone Legs (nymph)
Thorax: Red Squirrel Nymph Thorax Whitlock SLF Dubbing

Note: Use a 5/32" bead for size 10, 1/8" for sizes 12-14, and 3/32" for size 16.

O.D.B. Stone

Originator: Steve Parrott
Tier: Steve Parrott

Hook: #8-12 Umpqua Competition C300BL
Bead: Black tungsten
Weight: Jan Siman heavy flat lead wire
Thread: Brown 70-denier Ultra Thread
Tail: Brown goose biots
Abdomen: Golden stone Kaufmann SLF Dubbing
Back Foil: Natural Thin Skin Mottled Bustard
Rib: .006" mono thread or 6X tippet
Thorax: Golden stone Kaufmann SLF Dubbing
Legs: India hen back
Wing Pads: Natural Thin Skin Mottled Bustard
Antennae: Brown goose biots

Note: Use a 5/32" bead for sizes 8-10 and 1/8" for size 12.

Steve's Stone

Originator: Steve Thomas
Tier: Steve Thomas

Hook: #6-12 Tiemco 300
Weight: .020" lead wire
Thread: Brown 6/0 Uni-Thread
Tail: Brown goose biots
Rib: Red Ultra Wire (small)
Abdomen: Dark brown hare's mask
Thorax: Dark brown hare's mask
Wing Case: Brown Swiss Straw
Legs: Natural pheasant tail fibers
Antennae: Brown goose biots

Yellow Sally Nymph

Originator: Oliver Edwards
Tier: The Orvis Company

Hook: #12-16 Tiemco 5262
Thread: Light cahill 8/0 Uni-Thread
Tail: Yellow Betts' Tailing Fibers
Abdomen: PMD Superfine
Rib: 5X tippet
Back: Clear Thin Skin colored with brown permanent marker
Thorax: Golden Stone Mercer's Buggy Nymph Dubbing
Legs: Yellow partridge
Wing Pads: Clear Thin Skin colored with brown permanent marker
Antennae: Two guard hairs for dubbing

Halfback Nymph

Originator: John Dexheimer
Tier: Umpqua Feather Merchants

Hook: #6-12 Tiemco 5263
Weight: .020" lead wire
Thread: Black 8/0 Uni-Thread
Tail: Pheasant tail fibers
Abdomen: Peacock herl
Backstrap: Pheasant tail fibers
Hackle: Brown rooster

Bitch Creek

Originator: Unknown
Tier: Umpqua Feather Merchants

Hook: #6-12 Tiemco 5263
Weight: .020" lead wire
Thread: Black 6/0 Uni-Thread
Tail: White rubber legs (medium)
Abdomen: Black and orange chenille (woven)
Hackle: Brown rooster
Antennae: White rubber legs (medium)

Conehead Rubber Legged Golden Stonefly

Originator: Larry Kingrey
Tier: Larry Kingrey

Hook: #8-10 Tiemco 300
Cone: Gold brass or tungsten
Thread: Tan 6/0 Uni-Thread
Underbody: .025" lead wire
Tail: Pumpkin/olive Crazy Legs
Body: Olive/orange Speckled Chenille (#2)
Legs: Pumpkin/olive Crazy Legs

Hover Legs

Originator: Jin Choi
Tier: Jin Choi

Hook: #6-8 Tiemco 5363
Thread: Black 140-denier Ultra Thread
Tail: Yellow and black MFC Sexi-Legs
Abdomen: Peacock herl and $^{1}/_{4}$" Lightning Strike Fluorescent Indicator
Legs: Yellow and black MFC Sexi-Legs
Backstrap: Black Razor Foam (1mm), tan ostrich plume, and black Krystal Flash
Antennae: Yellow and black MFC Sexi-Legs

Tungsten Pteronarcys

Originator: Joe Johnson
Tier: Joe Johnson

Hook: #8-10 Umpqua C300BL
Bead: Black tungsten to match hook size
Weight: .025" lead wire
Thread: Fire orange 8/0 Uni-Thread
Tail: Brown goose biots
Underbody: Brown Hareline Hare 'E Ice Dub
Abdomen: Brown Wapsi Thin Skin
Thorax: Brown ostrich herl
Legs: Brown MFC Sexi-Floss
Wing Case: Wapsi mottled black Thin Skin
Collar: Fire orange 8/0 Uni-Thread

Note: Use a $^{5}/_{32}$" bead for size 8-10.

Golden Wired Stone

Originator: Brad Befus
Tier: Brad Befus

Hook: #6-12 Tiemco 200R
Bead: Brass or tungsten
Thread: Olive brown 70-denier Ultra Thread
Tail: Ginger goose biots, split with golden stone SLF dubbing ball
Abdomen: Brown and yellow Ultra Wire wrapped together
Thorax: Peacock herl
Legs: Ginger goose biots
Wing Case: Mottled Brown Medallion Sheeting

Note: Use a $^{3}/_{16}$" bead for size 6 and $^{5}/_{32}$" for sizes 8-12.

Tungsten Golden iStone

Originator: Juan Ramirez
Tier: Juan Ramirez

Hook: #10-12 Tiemco 2302
Bead: Coffee Lucent tungsten
Thread: Yellow 70-denier Ultra Thread
Underbody: .020" lead
Tail: Gold goose biots
Abdomen: Amber Nature's Spirit Emergence Dubbing
Rib: Copper Ultra Wire (small)
Shell Back: MFC Gold Silly Skin
Thorax: Amber Nature's Spirit Emergence Dubbing
Legs: Specked brown hen
Wing Case: Computer packaging (from an iMac) colored with dark brown Prismacolor.
Head: Amber Nature's Spirit Emergence Dubbing

Note: Use a $^{5}/_{32}$" bead for sizes 10-12. Wing case is cut with #18 caddis wing cutter.

C.P.S. (Caddis-PMD-Sally)

Originator: Steve Henderson
Tier: Steve Henderson

Hook: #12-18 Tiemco 100
Thread: Cream 70-denier Ultra Thread
Rear Tag: Burnt orange 70-denier Ultra Thread
Abdomen: PMD Superfine
Underwing: Natural dun CDC puff
Hackle: Light dun Whiting Farms rooster, trimmed
Wing: Light or bleached elk hair

Matt's Winter Foam Stone

Originator: Matt Miles
Tier: Matt Miles

Hook: #14-16 Tiemco 2302
Thread: Black 8/0 Uni-Thread
Tail: Black turkey biots
Abdomen: Black Razor Foam (.5mm)
Wing: White Z-Lon or McFlylon
Legs: Black Rainy's round rubber legs (small)

Matt's Yellow Sally

Originator: Matt Miles
Tier: Matt Miles

Hook: #14-16 Tiemco 2302
Thread: Light cahill 8/0 Uni-Thread
Tail: Yellow turkey biots
Abdomen: Yellow Razor Foam (.5mm)
Wing: White Z-Lon or McFlylon
Legs: MFC Centipede Legs (small)

Little Black Stone

Originator: Dick Shinton
Tier: Dick Shinton

Hook: #18-20 Dai-Riki 300
Thread: Black 14/0 Gordon Griffiths
Tail: Black Krystal Flash
Abdomen: Black 14/0 Gordon Griffiths
Wing: Steel blue Wapsi Antron
Hackle: Dark dun rooster

Winter Stonefly Adult

Originator: Dick Shinton
Tier: Dick Shinton

Hook: #18-20 Dai-Riki 300
Thread: Black 14/0 Gordon Griffiths
Wing: Grizzly hackle lacquered
Hackle: Dark dun rooster

Puterbaugh's Foam Stone

Originator: Don Puterbaugh
Tier: Umpqua Feather Merchants

Hook: #12-18 Tiemco 100
Thread: Yellow 8/0 Uni-Thread
Underbody: Yellow 8/0 Uni-Thread
Abdomen: Yellow closed-cell foam (2mm)
Wing: Natural elk
Hackle: Brown and grizzly rooster mixed

Designated Hitter Golden Stone

Originator: David Hill
Tier: Umpqua Feather Merchants

Hook: #6-10 Tiemco 5212
Thread: Yellow 70-denier Ultra Thread
Abdomen: Black foam (2mm), golden yellow Super Brite, brown Sharpie
Underwing: Transpore tape, brown Sharpie
Wing: Natural elk (tied in for bullet head)
Legs: Brown rubber legs (medium)
Thorax: Yellow 70-denier Ultra Thread
Hackle: Brown rooster

Rogue Foam Stone (Golden)

Originator: Jack Schlotter
Tier: Umpqua Feather Merchants

Hook: #8-12 Tiemco 2312
Thread: Yellow Danville Monocord
Abdomen: Yellow closed-cell foam (1/8"), sepia marker
Rib: Yellow Danville Monocord
Underwing: 3M Transpore Tape, sepia marker
Flash: Yellow accent flash
Wing: Natural bull elk
Head: Deer hair dyed golden brown
Legs: Speckled pumpkin Sili Legs
Collar: Beige 6/0 Flymaster

Note: Color variations include black and orange. Coat abdomen, underwing, and head with Flexament.

Clark's Stonefly

Originator: Lee Clark
Tier: Umpqua Feather Merchants

Hook: #6-10 Tiemco 5212
Thread: Orange 6/0 Danville
Abdomen: Gold Mylar, rust and gold Z-Lon
Wing: Coastal deer hair
Hackle: Brown rooster

Flutter Bug Salmonfly (Black)

Originator: Eric Paulson
Tier: Umpqua Feather Merchants

Hook: #6-8 Tiemco 200R
Thread: Fluorescent orange 210-denier Ultra Thread
Abdomen: Black 3/16" Evazote foam
Rib: Fluorescent orange 210-denier Ultra Thread
Wing: Mallard dyed wood duck, cow elk
Head: Black dyed elk
Legs: Smoke/blue flake Sili legs

Note: Color variations include Golden Stone.

Clown Shoe Sally

Originator: Jay Zimmerman
Tier: Umpqua Feather Merchants

Hook: #14-16 Tiemco 2487
Thread: Light cahill 6/0 Uni-Thread
Abdomen: Yellow D-Rib over red (butt) and Light Cahill Uni-Thread
Thorax: Sulphur yellow Superfine
Post: Fluorescent cerise McFly Foam
Wing: Bleached elk
Hackle: White rooster

Corn Fed Sally

Originator: Lance Egan
Tier: Umpqua Feather Merchants

Hook: #14-16 Tiemco 921
Thread: Light cahill 8/0 Uni-Thread
Egg Sac: Fluorescent orange 70-denier Ultra Thread
Abdomen: Yellow Superfine
Rib: Fluorescent orange 70-denier Ultra Thread
Hackle: Pale yellow CDC
Wing: Pale yellow CDC
Overwing: Fluorescent yellow poly yarn

Rubber Leg Stimulator

Originator: Randall Kaufmann
Tier: Dick Shinton

Hook: #10-16 Dai-Riki 280
Thread: Fluorescent orange 70-denier Ultra Thread
Tail: Elk hair
Rear Hackle: Brown Whiting Farms Rooster
Abdomen: Fluorescent yellow Antron and brown Whiting Farms hackle, one size small
Rib: Copper Ultra Wire (small)
Wing: Elk hair
Legs: Black/white MFC Centipede Legs (small)
Thorax: Fluorescent orange Antron
Front Hackle: Whiting Farms grizzly hackle

Stimulator (Yellow)

Originator: Randall Kaufmann
Tier: Umpqua Feather Merchants

Hook: #8-14 Tiemco 200R
Thread: Orange 8/0 Uni-Thread
Tail: Elk hair
Abdomen: Yellow Antron dubbing
Rear Hackle: Brown rooster
Rib: Gold Ultra Wire (extra small)
Wing: Elk hair
Thorax: Light orange Antron dubbing
Front Hackle: Grizzly Whiting Farms rooster

Rubber Legged Crystal Stimulator

Originator: Randall Kaufmann
Tier: Umpqua Feather Merchants

Hook: #8-14 Tiemco 200R
Thread: Orange 6/0 Uni-Thread
Tail: Elk hair
Rear Hackle: Brown Whiting Farms rooster
Abdomen: Peacock herl and red Antron dubbing
Rib: Copper Ultra Wire (extra small)
Underwing: Red Krystal Flash and pearl Flashabou
Wing: Elk hair, one shank length long
Overwing: White calf tail
Legs: Grizzly Spirit River round rubber legs (medium)
Thorax: Pearl Ice Dub
Front Hackle: Grizzly Whiting Farms rooster

Foam Stimulator (Black)

Originator: Mathew Thomas variation of Kaufmann original
Tier: Mathew Thomas

Hook: #10-14 Tiemco 200R
Thread: Red 8/0 Uni-Thread
Tail: Black elk
Rear Hackle: Black Whiting Farms rooster
Abdomen: Black Razor Foam (1.5mm)
Rib: Red Ultra Wire (small)
Wing: Black elk
Front Hackle: Black Whiting Farms rooster

Stimulator (Black)

Originator: Rick Takahashi variation of Randall Kaufmann original
Tier: Rick Takahashi

Hook: #10-16 Tiemco 2302
Thread: Black 8/0 Uni-Thread
Tail: Dark moose body hair
Underbody: Black 8/0 Uni-Thread
Rear Hackle: Black Whiting Farms saddle hackle
Wing: Black deer hair
Thorax: Black Fine and Dry
Front Hackle: Grizzly Whiting Farms saddle hackle

Mini Hot

Originator: Greg Garcia
Tier: Greg Garcia

Hook: #14-20 Tiemco 200R
Thread: Fluorescent yellow 70-denier Ultra Thread
Tag: Red Flashabou
Abdomen: Clear Hareline Micro Tubing over tying thread
Underwing: Sand SLF Prism Dubbing
Wing: Nature's Spirit yearling elk
Thorax: Fluorescent yellow SLF Prism Dubbing
Hackle: Light yellow and cream rooster

Bank Robber

Originator: MFC
Tier: MFC

Hook: #4-10 MFC 7002
Thread: Fluorescent fire orange 8/0 Uni-Thread
Tail: MFC speckled white Centipede Legs
Abdomen: Black and orange craft foam
Wing: Natural cow elk flank
Legs: MFC speckled white Centipede Legs
Thorax: MFC insect orange peacock Phoenix Dubbing
Hackle: Brown rooster

Para Yellow Sally

Originator: Jeff Yamagata
Tier: Solitude Fly Company

Hook: #14-16 Daiichi 1100
Thread: Light olive 6/0 Danville
Egg Sac: Red 6/0 Danville
Tail: Dyed mallard flank
Abdomen: PMD Superfine
Wing: Pale watery dun hen hackle and white Antron
Post: White calf hair
Hackle: Light dun rooster

Slow Water Sally

Originator: Brad Befus
Tier: Brad Befus

Hook: #14-16 Tiemco 2302
Thread: Tan 70-denier Ultra Thread
Egg Sac: Wapsi fluorescent orange Antron Sparkle Dubbing
Tail: Ginger goose biots red/orange dubbing ball
Abdomen: Ginger turkey biot
Wing: Mottled brown Medallion Sheeting
Thorax: Sulfur Superfine
Hackle: Dyed pale yellow grizzly rooster

CHAPTER 5

Caddisflies and Their Imitations

Caddisflies are one of the most abundant and diverse groups of aquatic insects. They are members of the order Trichoptera, which includes nearly 1,400 species in North America. The name Trichoptera is derived from the Greek words *trichos*, meaning hair, and *ptera*, meaning wing; the name refers to the fine, silky hairs that cover the tent wings of the mothlike adult. Caddisflies have staggering populations that outnumber both mayflies and stoneflies combined because they are able to survive in a wide spectrum of aquatic habitats. Anglers will find caddisflies inhabiting everything from tiny ponds to huge reservoirs, small creeks to large rivers, and some species are able to thrive in warmwater environments with lower oxygen levels and small traces of pollution, making them important insects in marginal trout streams.

Caddisflies pass through complete metamorphosis, which means their life cycle consists of four stages of development—egg, larva, pupa, and adult. Caddisflies spend most of their lives as a wormlike larva feeding on the bottom of a stream or lake. Most caddisflies complete a full life cycle in one year, but there are a few species that produce two generations a year, while others require two years to complete all four stages of development.

In order to successfully match a caddis hatch, you'll need to thoroughly understand a caddisfly's life cycle. The biggest

Caddisflies are a prominent food source on Colorado's freestones, tailwaters, and stillwater impoundments. The adults can be identified by their tent-shaped wings, which are covered with fine silky hairs. JAY NICHOLS

Western freestones like the Gunnison River are known for their excellent caddis hatches. These hatches will bring out the serious dry-fly fanatics to enjoy some of the best surface activity of the year. MARK ADAMS

Caddis larvae are effective year-round on both tailwaters and freestone streams. Matthew Thomas fooled this fat Roaring Fork rainbow on a caddis larva during the latter part of February.

differences in appearance, behavior, and habitat preference are most obvious in the larvae. The pupae and adults look similar and tend to present fewer challenges as far as their imitations are concerned.

LARVAE

There are three varieties of caddis larvae that all fly fishers should familiarize themselves with—free-living, net spinners, and case makers. Free-living caddis, or *Rhyacophila*, are commonly referred to as Green Rock Worms. Free-living caddis crawl along the stream bottom and do not build a case. They often become a tasty meal for opportunistic trout because they do not have the camouflage or protection that a case affords.

While most *Rhyacophila* are bright green or even chartreuse, it's important to note that not all Green Rock Worm larvae are green. As odd as it might sound, some Green Rock Worm larvae are found in varying shades of dark olive, tan, or brown. John Barr ties his Uncased Caddis Larva in both green and tan to be prepared for a variety of circumstances. In *Barr Flies*, Barr states, "I tied my first caddis larva in the 1980s after seining the Colorado River. All of the larvae were some shade of green, olive, or tan. Through the years, I have caught a lot of fish on caddis larva imitations. My uncased version represents both the net-spinner and free-living caddis equally well."

Mature *Rhyacophila* larvae range in size from one-half to three-quarters of an inch long. They live exclusively in cool

Steve Parrott's Electric Caddis closely resembles Rhyacophila, *which is commonly referred to as the Green Rock Worm. Dead-drifted caddis larvae will often entice nice fish like this Roaring Fork rainbow to capitalize on a hearty meal.*

rivers and streams and thrive in substrates composed of medium- to large-sized boulders. *Rhyacophila* larvae crawl along the stream bottom, hiding in the cracks and crevices, searching for food. They often prey on small aquatic insects such as mayflies and midge larvae. Because *Rhyacophila* larvae live in swifter currents, they are routinely swept away from the substrate and become frequent victims of catastrophic drift. Dead-drifted Rhycophilidae larvae patterns produce exceptionally well because opportunistic trout are always looking for them, regardless of the time of year.

Most entomologists agree that the net-spinning caddis, or Hydropsychidae, is the caddisfly family most important to the angler. Two genera in particular—*Hydropsyche* (Spotted Sedges) and *Cheumatopsyche* (Little Olive Sedges)—produce the most reliable hatches in the West. According to Rick Hafele in *Nymph-Fishing Rivers and Streams*, "If there is one group of caddisflies you should know and be prepared to imitate, it is the net-spinning caddis. Net-spinning caddis larvae look surprisingly similar to Green Rock Worm larvae. They overlap in both size and color with net-spinners ranging from one-quarter to three-quarters inch long and from bright green to dark brown. They also overlap in shape and habitat."

Net spinners, as their name implies, construct nets out of silk threads on the side or on top of a boulder. Their shelter, or silky net, varies in size from roughly one-half to three-quarters inch in diameter. They strategically place their net facing into the current, which allows it to trap or filter drifting food from the water. Hafele notes: "The numbers of net-spinner caddis larvae can be particularly high in tailwater streams below dams. That's because the zooplankton and phytoplankton that grow in reservoirs get washed downstream, where they provide an excellent food source for net-spinning larvae."

Hafele also concludes that the net spinners' homes can become overpopulated and they often need to look for better feeding areas. "Net-spinning caddis larvae often suffer from overcrowding. This occurs when so many nets get built on the same rock that some nets block the current to others. The larvae with nets blocked by an upstream net get little or no food, so they must leave the area and find a less crowded rock," Hafele says.

This phenomenon is known as *behavioral drift*, whereby the aquatic insects let go of their hold on rocks and other structure and drift in the current until they can reattach themselves in a new location. Behavioral drift occurs most often in the low-light hours of early morning or late evening.

The *Brachycentrus* caddis, or American Grannom, is perhaps the best known, as it constitutes the famed Mother's Day hatch in many watersheds. The *Brachycentrus* caddis is considered the second-most important caddis to imitate because of its widespread populations across the western United States. *Brachycentrus* are case makers, fabricating their homes out of plant fibers and other debris with fine silklike threads. They build four-sided cases that look like small twig's and measure one-half to three-quarters inch in length. The cases vary in color from a dark olive to a dark brown depending on the materials used to build them. The larva inside the case is bright green or chartreuse with a noticeable dark head.

I designed my Mercury Cased Caddis to imitate the *Brachycentrus* larva. The casing is tied from natural hare's mask. I prefer a blend of dubbing that has a lot of guard hairs so I typically mix up my own concoction from a natural hare's mask. The guard hairs trap air and provide a buggy appearance. The larva inside the case is bright green, a distinguishing feature of cased caddis. I tie the worm larva out of chartreuse Ice Dub, and the head is constructed from dubbing from a black hare's mask. The clear, silver-lined bead imitates the gases stored in the thorax prior to emergence. The flash from the bead and the chartreuse Ice Dub produces a lifelike look that becomes a trigger and attracts nearby fish. I also tie a tungsten variation in which I swap the black dubbed head with a black tungsten bead, facing the counter sunk part of the bead towards the clear, silver-lined bead. The tungsten version performs better in faster currents where quick sink rates are critical for success.

Brachycentrus attach themselves to rocks, sticks, and branches for camouflage, leaving one end of the case open so they can stick their heads out and feed. I remember picking up a branch on the South Platte near Deckers and finding the entire stick covered with *Brachycentrus* caddis. I have experienced similar situations on the Eagle, Gunnison, Animas, and Arkansas Rivers, which are known for their dense populations of *Brachycentrus* caddis.

Peak behavioral drift with cased caddis occurs midday, rather than at night or early morning as it does with net-spinning caddis. John Barr has witnessed this firsthand. In *Barr Flies* he states, "Behavioral drift occurs most often in low light (late or early in the day or at night), but can happen midday. The only drift I have seen occurred in the early afternoon on the Colorado River below State Bridge, Colorado. There were thousands of cased caddis drifting downstream just below the surface and the trout fed on them feverishly. Cased caddis are one of the few aquatic insects that will behaviorally drift during the day." While cased caddis appear to be well-protected within their case, think again: trout will eat them case and all.

PUPAE

Towards the end of the larval phase (nine to ten months) caddisflies pupate for about one month. This stage of their life begins when the caddis attach their cases (free-living caddis build a makeshift shelter prior to pupation) to rocks on the bottom of the substrate or cover themselves with fine sand or gravel. During the pupation period, caddisflies are not available to feeding fish, as they remain hidden inside a well-protected case similar to a caterpillar's cocoon. In a state of dormancy, the larva changes into a pupa and begins to look like the adult, with noticeable antennae and wing pads, which are swept back along the sides of the thorax.

The final stage of development is where the caddisfly separates itself from its protective shelter and swims toward the water's surface. Entomologists refer to an emerging caddis as a pharate adult (pharate is derived from the Greek word *pharos*, meaning garment) rather than a pupa, because technically the adult is covered in a pupal sheath, which is a thin protective

Caddis pupae imitations like John Barr's Graphic Caddis are a must-have during the caddis season. The sign that fish are keying on caddis pupae is when suspended fish sweep back and forth in the current, moving several inches to several feet to intercept rising pupae.

covering. As the caddisfly makes its final ascent to the water's surface, the pupal sheath breaks open and the adult flies away from the surface to seek refuge on nearby foliage.

Each variety of caddis larvae undergoes a slightly different pupation with regard to time of year, duration, and habitat preference. It's worth noting the differences to enable you to better match the hatch. *Rhyacophila* crawl between the creases of large rocks and dig into the sand or fine gravel, after which the pupae take four to six weeks to mature. Pupation typically occurs in late April or early May. Fully developed pupae quickly swim to the surface, escaping their pupal sheaths, and fly away to streamside vegetation. Similar to the larvae, the pupae are varying shades of green.

Net spinners pupate in the same riffled habitat that the larvae reside in. Similar to *Rhyacophila*, they cover themselves with sand and gravel prior to pupation. Somewhere between two and four weeks the pupae are mature and ready to emerge. Emergence can occur either in the morning or the afternoon, with swimming pupae drifting long distances before reaching the surface.

Brachycentrus caddis pupate within their larval case. Prior to pupation, the larvae attach themselves to a rock or solid object on the substrate and close the open end of their cases with silk thread. The pupae take three to six weeks to mature. *Brachycentrus* provide excellent early-season caddis hatches, which typically occur mid to late morning or midday in late April or early May. This hatch has been referred to as the "Mother's Day Caddis Hatch" because the heaviest hatches tend to occur around Mother's Day. Sporadic hatches continue all summer long, which provides anglers excellent opportunities to fish both pupae and adults.

ADULTS

Adult caddisflies look similar to moths. Beginning in late April or early May, you'll find them fluttering near or above the water or resting on nearby streamside foliage. At rest, the adult's wings lay straight back over its abdomen and form a tent or inverted V-shape. Caddis adults have long, slender antennae, which are equal to the length of their bodies. The adults range in color from tan to almost black.

The most reliable caddis hatches typically occur on freestone streams like the Animas, Rio Grande, Colorado, Gunnison, Eagle, Roaring Fork, and Arkansas. Freestones like the Animas can be inconsistent and unpredictable at times, however, which can frustrate even the best anglers and guides. "The Animas is a stunning, midsized free-flowing river that tumbles its way through Durango, Colorado, before meandering into New Mexico and merging with the San Juan near Farmington, New Mexico," says Will Blanchard, owner of Animas Valley Anglers. "The Animas is one of the West's

When you see adult caddis flying around, it's hard to go wrong with Al Troth's Elk Hair Caddis in a size 14 or 16. The silhouette of the Elk Hair Caddis closely resembles the tentlike wings of the adult caddis.

best-kept secrets. It is a pocket, pool, and riffle fishery that is known for some monster trout. But the Animas trout can frustrate the most ardent of anglers with its technical and moody nature." The timing and density of the hatches on the freestones will vary greatly depending on the drainage, elevation, time of year, flows, and water temperatures. Anglers will experience caddis hatches on tailwaters too, but as a general rule, they are not as impressive as those found on unregulated trout streams.

Matching a caddis hatch does not hinge on imitating a specific species of the adult because they all look similar. Having the appropriate size and color *is* important however. Trout feed on the adults once they reach the surface and prepare for flight. Because adults hop, skitter, and jump before their wings dry and they leave the water's surface, dead-drifted flies are often ignored while skated imitations create explosive strikes.

After the adults leave the water, they seek protection and mate on streamside foliage. Unlike mayflies, adult caddisflies can live for several weeks because they can drink water and nectar to prevent dehydration. This means you'll frequently see good numbers of caddis buzzing around the stream, but it is important to note that they are not available to the trout again until they return to the water to lay their eggs; this may occur anywhere from several days to several weeks after the adult caddis leave the water and mate.

Female caddis typically return to the water in late afternoon or early evening to deposit their eggs. This presents another opportunity for anglers to imitate the adults. Some species dive underwater and swim to the bottom of the river to deposit their eggs. This can provide an excellent wet-fly fishing opportunity, as it will imitate the females struggling to get to the bottom to lay their eggs and return back to the surface. Other species oviposit their eggs by dipping their abdomen into the water, while some land on the water and deposit their eggs.

CADDISFLY FISHING STRATEGIES

The first caddis hatches of the season occur on freestones, because these streams' water temperatures warm quicker than those of tailwaters. Cooler water temperatures, especially those found below deep bottom-release tailwaters, delay hatches well into the summer. Generally speaking, the best caddis hatches on tailwaters occur between late June and July when the water temperatures reach the 52- to 54-degree mark. Intermittent hatches often last through August, which provides anglers with consistent dry-fly fishing opportunities. In terms of tailwater fishing, caddis hatches can be affected by the reservoir spilling (a full pool, with excess water flowing over the spillway), which causes a dramatic increase in the water temperatures because warm surface water is entering the tailrace. If this occurs, caddis hatches can happen as early as mid-May.

Caddis larvae require no special tactics or techniques other than dredging them close to the substrate where the naturals are found. Caddis larvae do not swim, so their imitations should be dead-drifted with a standard two- or three-fly tandem nymphing rig consisting of a strike indicator and enough split shot or moldable tungsten putty to keep the flies close to the stream bottom.

Opportunistic trout will always be looking for caddis larvae, regardless of the time of year, as they provide a big meal in comparison to tiny midges or mayflies. I can't even begin to tell you how many fish I catch each season on caddis larvae—it's mind-boggling to say the least. I typically use a caddis larva as my attractor and drop a mayfly or midge behind it. My favorite caddis larva imitations include: Barr's Uncased and Cased Caddis Larva, Oliver Edwards' Hydropsyche, Harold Tygart's Hydropsyche, Mercury Cased Caddis, and a Buckskin. I typically stock my fly boxes with a wide range of sizes from 14 to 18.

Unlike larvae, fishing pupae imitations requires more of a sophisticated approach. The greatest challenges you'll face will be keeping your flies in the correct part of the feeding zone and imparting action into your fly to make it look like a natural ascending pupae. Early in the hatch, anglers will be required to fish pupae closer to the stream bottom, as they tend to drift a few yards before they begin their initial ascent towards the surface. As the hatch intensifies, the numbers of pupae drifting in the upper water column changes significantly, so you'll need to adjust your tactics accordingly.

Pupae patterns start to become effective in late April and early May, with the heaviest hatches occurring around Mother's Day. Caddis hatches will continue intermittently through the summer. In some drainages you find sporadic hatches occurring during the autumn season. The best method I've found for fishing caddis pupae is to fish them down and across with a classic wet-fly approach, allowing your flies to swing in front of the feeding trout. Mike Mercer's Swing Nymph has become one of my favorite flies to imitate caddis pupae. According to Mercer, "I designed my Swing Nymph series of wet flies with tungsten beads behind the hackle, as I have been frustrated with patterns that are too light, or too bulky, and lacked realistic features."

Mercer's presentation with a Swing Nymph is almost always down and across. The goal is to achieve a balance between a simple, tight-line arcing swing and a gently dropping effect. If fish are just going nuts on pupating caddis, you can sometimes get away with the former, but if they are being more discerning, it won't be as effective. In those situations, Mercer casts his fly across and slightly upstream, and mends his fly line. At this point, the rod tip will still be high—imagine an outstretched arm using the rod to point to the tops of tall trees on the far bank of the river. Then, as the fly begins its slow swing (slow because of the initial mend that was made) Mercer will follow the drift with the rod, tracking the swing of the fly and slowly dropping the rod tip to extend the drift.

His goal is to create an alternately free-drifting and upwardly rising fly presentation, which is pretty much what the trout are used to seeing from the naturals. Mercer tries to split the difference between simply swinging the fly across the river current and dead drifting it like a nymph. As the fly reaches the end of its swing, the rod tip will have finished its descent to a point where it is only inches above the surface of the water. "The strikes will be completely obvious because you'll feel them," Mercer says. "After you feel the strike, lift the rod tip to set the hook."

Opportunistic trout will rarely refuse the chance to eat a caddis larva. The author prepares to release a beautiful rainbow that he fooled with a Hydropsyche on the Blue River. MARK ADAMS

Many tiers use gold beads or other flashy materials to simulate the trapped gases in the thorax area. The gases in the pupal sheath add buoyancy and assist in the pupa's ascent to the surface. The glasslike reflection from these gases becomes a significant trigger to selective trout, so much so that trout often ignore pupae without reflective properties.

ARKANSAS RIVER CADDIS HATCHES

Greg Felt

The Arkansas River has long been known as a caddis river, recognized in particular for the *Brachycentrus* caddis hatch that transpires in late April and early May. The river is home to approximately fifty different caddis species, with hatches typically spread from late March into October. Improvements in water quality initiated in the mid-1990s have made the river more hospitable to mayflies and stoneflies, enhancing the entomological diversity and easing the trout's reliance on caddis species for their sustenance. Caddis are still a key part of the Arkansas River biota, but they are now part of a much broader mix.

Of the fifty or so species that have been identified, many emerge as part of the larger summertime buffet. As a result, summer fish are often not keyed into them specifically but will take them opportunistically when they become available. This is true of both the emerging pupae and the adults on the surface. I think if there is an exception to this, it would be the response to ovipositing females. Since this egg-laying activity often occurs in the low-light hours, it corresponds well with the time of day when brown trout are feeling less vulnerable and more willing to aggressively work the surface. As a result, skittering adult caddis in the evening hours of summer can provide some of the most exciting surface action of the year. Imitating the size and color of available naturals is fine but not critical—the action probably does more than anything to attract trout.

Arkansas River Caddis Hatches

During the daytime in summer, Arkansas River anglers do well with traditional caddis pupa imitations (basically soft-hackle wet flies) by quartering the cast downstream, letting the flies swing with the current, and then lifting them at the end of the swing. This old-school style of taut-line fishing is very effective in Colorado, probably due to the large variety of caddis throughout the state. Contemporary anglers often take a little time to adapt their hook set to this style of fishing—it is easy to pull it away from the trout! The other common summer-season utilization of caddis is adult bugs as a dropper behind a hopper or attractor dry. I often use this as a searching pattern when working the edges of the river. Puterbaugh's Foam Caddis in black, tan, or olive is a good pattern for this approach. It floats well and is durable. I often trail a Foam Caddis early or late in the day on either side of a Yellow Sally/Pale Morning Dun, or at any time when the fish are producing the telltale splashy rise that means they are feeding on caddis.

Another generalized feeding response to caddis on the Arkansas River would be the consumption of cased caddis, particularly during the winter period when there are not many aquatic insects readily available to the fish. A check of stomach contents on a warm day in December may reveal some non-nutritional bits of debris, the undigested remains of a caddis larva consumed case and all. There are a number of cased caddis patterns but some of the most effective imitations of our prolific *Brachycentrus* are size 14-16 Pheasant Tail Nymphs with their tails cut off.

In terms of specific hatches, there are three that stand out. The first would be the emergence we get in early April. While not prolific, this will keep fish looking up, particularly late in the day after the Blue-Winged Olive mayflies have finished. The second is the *Brachycentrus* hatch discussed in detail below. And the third is the "Fourth of July" emergence, which can be intense but generally happens at the end of the day. As a result, many anglers miss this one entirely or may wonder why the early-morning fishing seems a little slower than they expect. This last hatch can produce tremendous swarms of bugs and an amazing feed right at twilight.

The *Brachycentrus* caddis hatch is tied to time of year (second half of April, first half of May) and water temperature (54 degrees). The caddis need to have matured and gone into pupation for the water temperature to matter—54-degree water will not bring off a hatch in March. Similarly, once the caddis seal themselves in their cases for pupation, there is a time limit as to how long they can last in that state. As a result, there have been situations when a segment of the population has gone into pupation and early-rising cold water has prevented those bugs from hatching. This can create areas of low caddis density that persist for some years while the population reestablishes itself.

One can imagine finding 54-degree peak water temperature in Cañon City earlier than in Salida, and in Salida earlier than in Buena Vista, due to the difference in elevation. The hatch thus follows a progression from downstream to upstream as the river warms in spring. On average, hatching bugs are found in Cañon City around April 15, Coaldale and Cotopaxi around the 25th, and in Salida about the first of May. In years with higher spring flow (400 cfs or more), the larger volume of water warms more slowly and in a more uniform fashion with the result that the hatch progresses in a similarly methodical way. In years of lower flow, one very warm day can warm the water over a larger reach of river with the result that the hatch can jump ten miles or so in a single afternoon.

There is generally a lot of emphasis on the leading edge of the hatch, as the bugs are fewer in number and the fish are more aggressive towards them—what one might call a "seller's market." The tail end of the hatch area can be very productive too, though generally the fish will be a bit more circumspect in their feeding. Where things can be challenging is in the middle of the hatch. At times, the *Brachycentrus* hatch can become a blizzard of bugs, thousands within sight on the river's surface. The fish will be gorging, but with so many bugs it is difficult to attract a fish to one's own fly, much less keep visual track of it on the river.

Because of the close connection between water temperature and this hatch, carrying a thermometer is essential. When fishing through the morning in the known or probable location of the afternoon's emergence, one should watch that water temperature closely. When it moves into the 52-degree range, I suspend a bead-head caddis pupa under an adult caddis in anticipation of the first stage of the hatch. A size 16 olive soft-hackled wet fly is a good imitation, and I swing and lift the rig at the end of each drift to best imitate the rising pupa. When the adults start to emerge, they cause quite a commotion on the surface as they "get their wings" and get off the water. It doesn't take a lot of adults to draw the fish's attention upward—as soon as I can get some fish to hit the adult on my rig I usually remove the pupa and just fish the dry. The exception would be cloudy skies —I always hang an unweighted Blue-Winged Olive emerger behind my caddis in these situations.

The part of the emergence that most people miss is the evening ovipositing phase when the fertilized females come back to the river to lay their eggs. As mentioned above, this can provide some of the most memorable fishing of the day and will last from when the light leaves the water until dark. ■

Don Puterbaugh's Foam Caddis has become one of the most popular patterns for imitating the adult. It's easy to see, floats high in choppy currents, and is extremely durable.

Barr's Graphic Caddis has become one of my favorite caddis pupae imitations. I must admit there have been times when I have fished two of them at a time because they are so effective. The true test came when I was fishing them on the South Platte in Cheesman Canyon and Deckers. South Platte trout gobble them with confidence, so I knew there was something special about this fly. According to John Barr in *Barr Flies*, "The name Graphic Caddis comes from the use of silver holographic Flashabou under the stretch-tubing body. The Flashabou gives the illusion of the silvery air bubble that accompanies a pupa as it ascends in the water column."

Caddis hatches can be frustrating at times for even the best anglers and guides. There are times when the air is filled with caddis adults yet not a single trout is eating them on the surface. Will Blanchard explains: "Caddis storms on the Rio Grande and Animas can be very frustrating. You'll see blizzards of insects and yet not a single trout eating them . . . eating them on the surface that is! Sometimes a fast-swinging pupa is the only way to catch fish. Traditional patterns like the Western Coachman as well as 'new school' flies like the Cadistrophic Pupa and Tabou Caddis Emerger can be deadly on the swing." In situations like this, there are so many caddis pupae in the water column the fish get locked into a selective feeding phase and key only on the pupae. It becomes a losing proposition for a trout to rise to the surface and eat an adult when there are thousands of pupae drifting midcolumn. Blanchard recommends, "When the fish are eating the adults on the surface, it's hard to go wrong with an Elk Hair Caddis or Spotlight Emerger on the Rio Grande or Animas."

Adult caddis provide some of the most exciting dry-fly fishing of the year. There are several imitations to choose from, but probably the best-known and most popular pattern is Puterbaugh's Foam Caddis. Don Puterbaugh developed this pattern back in 1964. His goals were simple: create a fly that was easy to tie and floated well. Puterbaugh uses closed-cell foam on his caddis so the fly floats like a cork. He recommends using 2mm foam for size 14 and 1.5mm foam for size 16-18.

Another objective was to develop a fly that was easy to see. "I'm a firm believer in a wing you can see! That's why I tie this pattern with a light bull elk wing, but not bleached elk, because the hair is too brittle," Puterbaugh explains. "The elk wing also assists in higher floatation."

I am also a big fan of the Elk Hair Caddis invented by Al Troth. It floats well and simulates the fluttering wing of its real-life counterpart. I like to tie my Elk Hair Caddis with full wings and spread them out farther than most tiers. The fanned wing emulates the skittering or hopping that occurs when caddis are trying to leave the water's surface. I have caught plenty of trout with an Elk Hair Caddis on the dead drift, but I find them to be more effective when I skate them. The strikes are typically aggressive when you skitter or skate them. If you get a refusal with a dead-drifted Elk Hair Caddis, try skating it—you'll be pleasantly surprised at how effective that strategy can be.

Charlie Craven also endorses the skittering strategy. In *Charlie Craven's Basic Fly Tying* he states, "I fish the Elk Hair Caddis a few different ways. Dead-drifting them under bank-side vegetation can produce great results. It seems that trout can't resist a bug that is trying to get away, and sometimes skittering the fly really rings the dinner bell."

Craven suggests experimenting with the amount of wing material you use in your Elk Hair Caddis: "Flies intended for calm, flat water over selective fish require less hair than the same-size fly meant for heavy pocket water. For heavier water I use as much hair as I can securely attach to the hook." Craven recommends making sure you clean out all the under-fur and short hairs before stacking the elk.

Craven adds a bit of helpful advice for increasing the durability of your Elk Hair Caddis: simply use a copper rib to secure the hackle in place. "I always use a wire rib on this fly, which adds durability and allows me to wrap the hackle from the front of the hook to the back," Craven says. "Tying the hackle in this manner slightly tapers the length of the hackle fibers from longer at the front to shorter at the back, giving the fly a more realistic attitude on the water. Some tiers use fine monofilament for this ribbing, but the wire holds its shape better and is a bit easier for me to work with."

One of the best opportunities to fish adult caddisflies occurs when the females return to the water to oviposit their eggs. As discussed earlier, some species land on the water's surface and broadcast their eggs, while others dip their abdomens in the water to release their eggs. The dry-fly fishing can be spectacular during this flurry of activity! The best piece of advice I can give you is not to leave the river too early during caddis season because the egg layers return to the water in the late afternoon or early evening.

Many species dive underwater to deposit their eggs on the stream bottom. Shane Stalcup's Bead Diving Caddis is a good option for imitating these caddis that dive or crawl underwater to lay their eggs. Ray Chang of Solitude Fly Company states, "The beauty of this fly is its ability to mimic a deep-diving or ascending egg-laying caddis. Unlike trying to dunk a traditional dry-fly caddis, which may have a limited depth, Stalcup's Diving Caddis can be dead drifted or swung in the current. It is especially effective when it lifts in the water column."

CADDIS PATTERNS

Flashtail Buckskin

Originator: Jeremy Hyatt variation of Ed Marsh Original
Tier: Jeremy Hyatt

Hook: #16-22 Tiemco 100
Thread: Black 8/0 Uni-Thread
Tail: Pearl Krystal Flash
Abdomen: Ultra Chamois

V-Rib Caddis

Originator: Mathew Thomas
Tier: Mathew Thomas

Hook: #16-18 Tiemco 3761
Thread: Black 8/0 Uni-Thread
Underbody: Black 8/0 Uni-Thread
Abdomen: Fluorescent chartreuse V Rib (medium)
Head: Hareline black rabbit dubbing

Starling Nymph

Originator: Mathew Thomas
Tier: Mathew Thomas

Hook: #14-16 Tiemco 5262
Thread: Wine 6/0 Flymaster
Abdomen: Peacock herl
Rib: Red Ultra Wire (extra small)
Collar: Starling

Latex Caddis Larva

Originator: Dick Shinton
Tier: Dick Shinton

Hook: #14-18 Dai-Riki 280
Thread: Cream 70-denier Ultra Thread
Tail: Black Krystal Flash
Abdomen: 1/8 inch strip cut from latex glove
Head: Black Ice Dub

Note: Color variations include, olive, tan, and chartreuse. Use permanent marker to color both sides of latex strip. Match tying thread to abdomen color.

Tungsten Pyrite Caddis

Originator: Dr. Eric Pettine
Tier: Dr. Eric Pettine

Hook: #16-20 Tiemco 2488H
Thread: Black 70-denier Ultra Thread
Abdomen: Gray muskrat
Rib: Lagartun oval tinsel (small) with black hackle clipped
Thorax: Caddis green Prism Dubbing, chartreuse bead, black bead
Legs: Black midge hackle

Zombie Caddis

Originator: John Perizzolo
Tier: John Perizzolo

Hook: #14-18 Tiemco 2487
Bead: Gunmetal glass (small)
Thread: Chartreuse 6/0 Uni-Thread
Underbody: Green glow Flashabou
Abdomen: Gray 1/8" Hareline Scud Back
Thorax: Chartreuse Ice Dub

Metallic Caddis Larva

Originator: Larry Kingrey
Tier: Larry Kingrey

Hook: #14-16 Tiemco 2457
Bead: Gold brass or tungsten
Thread: Black 6/0 Uni-Thread
Abdomen: Olive and chartreuse Ultra Wire (small)
Thorax: Peacock black Ice Dub

Note: Use a 1/8" bead for size 14 and 3/32" for size 16.

Banksia Bug

Originator: Jay Zimmerman
Tier: Umpqua Feather Merchants

Hook: #12-14 Tiemco 200R
Bead: Black tungsten
Thread: Black 6/0 Uni-Thread
Abdomen: Light cahill 6/0 Uni-Thread and olive 6/0 Uni-Thread
Thorax: Hellgrammite SLF Dubbing
Rib: Black Ultra Wire (extra small) and olive Ultra Wire (small)
Collar: Gray ostrich herl
Legs: Gadwall flank fibers

Note: Use a 1/8" bead for sizes 12-14.

Tarheel Caddis Larva

Originator: Josh Stephens
Tier: Dick Shinton

Hook: #14-18 Dai-Riki 060
Bead: Black Canadian Llama tungsten match to hook size
Thread: Brown 70-denier Ultra Thread
Tag: Fluorescent orange 70-denier Ultra Thread
Tail: Olive Wapsi turkey flat
Abdomen: Light Hare 'E Hareline Dubbin
Rib: Copper Ultra Wire (small or extra small)
Collar: Caddis green Hareline Dubbin

Note: Use a 1/8" bead for size 14 and 3/32" for sizes 16-18.

Beadhead Hydropsyche

Originator: Pat Dorsey variation of Harold Tygart's Hydropsyche
Tier: Pat Dorsey

Hook: #14-18 Tiemco 2457
Thread: Black 6/0 Uni-Thread
Bead: Black tungsten
Anal Claws: Peacock Wapsi Lifecyle Dubbing
Abdomen: Olive-brown Wapsi Lifecyle Dubbing
Head: Peacock Wapsi Lifecyle Dubbing

Note: Use a 1/8" bead for size 14 and 3/32" for sizes 16-18.

Beadhead Breadcrust

Originator: Variation of Ed Rolka original
Tier: Pat Dorsey

Hook: #10-18 Tiemco 5262
Bead: Gold brass or tungsten
Thread: Dark brown 6/0 Uni-Thread (8/0 for #18)
Underbody: Brown yarn
Abdomen: Red phase ruffed grouse quill
Collar: Grizzly hen

Note: Use a 5/32" bead for size 10, 1/8" for sizes 12-14, and 3/32" for sizes 16-18.

Buckskin

Originator: Ed Marsh
Tier: Pat Dorsey

Hook: #16-20 Tiemco 100
Thread: Black 8/0 Uni-Thread
Tail: Brown hen hackle
Abdomen: Chamois strip
Head: Black 8/0 Uni-Thread

Mercury Buckskin

Originator: Pat Dorsey variation of Ed Marsh original
Tier: Pat Dorsey

Hook: #16-20 Tiemco 100
Bead: Clear silver lined glass (small)
Thread: Black 8/0 Uni-Thread
Tail: Brown hen hackle
Abdomen: Chamois strip
Collar: Peacock herl

Beadhead Buckskin

Originator: Pat Dorsey variation of Ed Marsh original
Tier: Pat Dorsey

Hook: #16-20 Tiemco 2487
Bead: Brass or tungsten
Thread: Tan 8/0 Uni-Thread
Abdomen: Chamois strip

Note: Use a 3/32" bead for sizes 16-18 and 5/64" for size 20.

Mercury Cased Caddis

Originator: Pat Dorsey
Tier: Pat Dorsey

Hook: #16-18 Tiemco 200R
Bead: Clear silver-lined glass (small)
Thread: Tan 8/0 Uni-Thread
Abdomen: Natural hare's ear dubbing and chartreuse Ice Dub
Thorax: Black hare's ear dubbing

Note: Tungsten version swaps a black tungsten bead for black hare's ear dubbing.

Chartreuse S & D Grub

Originator: Steve Parrott
Tier: Steve Parrott

Hook: #10-14 Tiemco 2499SPBL
Weight: Jan Siman flat lead wire (fine)
Thread: Watery olive 70-denier Ultra Thread
Abdomen: Watery olive 70-denier Ultra Thread
Rib: Black Ultra Wire (small)
Hot Spot: Fluorescent hot pink Datum Glo Brite Floss
Head: Black 70-denier Ultra Thread

Note: Coat fly with Clear Cure Goo Hydro or Sally Hansen's Hard As Nails.

Blue Devil Jig Nymph

Originator: Steve Parrott
Tier: Steve Parrott

Hook: #12-16 Tiemco 403BLJ
Bead: Silver slotted tungsten
Thread: Black 70-denier Ultra Thread
Tail: Natural guinea
Abdomen: Black 70-denier Ultra Thread
Rib: Royal blue Flashabou
Collar: Black Arizona Synthetic Peacock Dubbing

Note: Cover abdomen with Clear Cure Goo Hydro.

Culo Rojo Peacock Soft Hackle

Originator: Steve Parrott
Tier: Steve Parrott

Hook: #12-16 Tiemco 403BLJ
Bead: Copper slotted tungsten
Thread: Black 70-denier Ultra Thread
Tail: Red Aunt Lydia's Sparkle Yarn
Abdomen: Peacock Life Cycle Nymph Dubbing
Rib: Lime Mirror Krystal Flash
Hackle: Partridge feather
Head: Peacock Life Cycle Nymph Dubbing

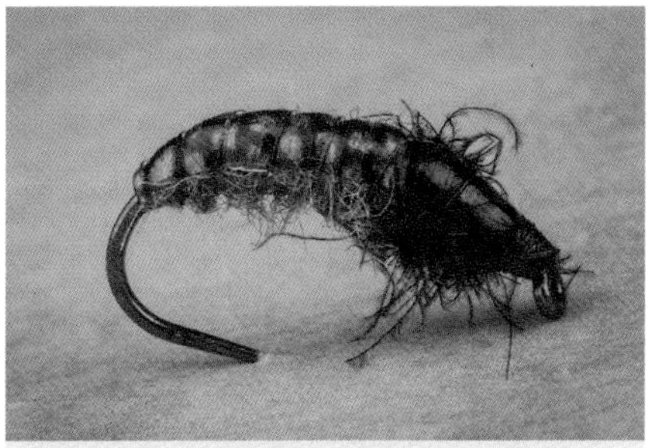

CZN Classic

Originator: Steve Parrott
Tier: Steve Parrott

Hook: #10-14 Umpqua Competition Hook C300BL
Weight: Jan Siman flat lead wire (medium)
Thread: Black 70-denier Ultra Thread
Back Foil: Olive/black Gator Thin Skin. Color head with black permanent marker.
Abdomen: Sow Bug Sow Scud Dubbing
Rib: Gold tinsel (extra small) and .006 mono thread or 6X tippet
Head: Black Metz CDC Dubbing

B.R.O.F. Jig Nymph

Originator: Steve Parrott
Tier: Steve Parrott

Hook: #12-16 Tiemco 403BLJ
Bead: Gold slotted tungsten
Thread: Brown 70-denier Ultra Thread
Tail: Wood duck
Hot Spot: Fluorescent flame Datum Glo Brite Floss (#5)
Abdomen: Light olive 70-denier Ultra Thread and clear Micro Tubing
Collar: Light Arizona Synthetic Dubbing

Note: Use a 5 1/8" bead for sizes 12-14 and 3/32" for sizes 16-18.

Shimmering Soft Hackle Caddis

Originator: Steve Parrott
Tier: Steve Parrott

Hook: #14-16 Tiemco 2499SPBL
Bead: Black slotted tungsten
Thread: Olive brown 70-denier Ultra Thread
Tail: Gold Aunt Lydia's Sparkle Yarn
Abdomen: Caddis green Superfine
Rib: Lime green/pearl Krystal Flash
Collar: India hen back or ruffed grouse feathers
Head: Chocolate brown Hareline Dubbin

Note: Use a 1/8" bead for size 14 and 3/32" for size 16.

Tag Your It

Originator: Steve Parrott
Tier: Steve Parrott

Hook: #14-16 Umpqua Competition C260BL
Bead: Gold tungsten
Thread: Black 70-denier Ultra Thread
Tail: Hot pink Mini Marabou
Abdomen: Olive Mercer's Buggy Nymph Dubbing
Rib: Pearl 1/100 Micro Flashabou
Thorax: Brown stone Kaufmann SLF Dubbing

Note: Use a 1/8" bead for size 14 and 3/32" for size 16.

Tungsten Electric Caddis

Originator: Steve Parrott
Tier: Steve Parrott

Hook: #8-14 Umpqua Competition C300BL
Bead: Black tungsten
Thread: Black 70-denier Ultra Thread
Shell Back: Light brown Magic Shrimp Foil Pearl Strips
Abdomen: Tan Life Cycle Nymph Dubbing
Rib: Pearl Mirror Crystal Flash and .006" mono thread or 6X tippet
Head: Black SLF Spikey Squirrel Dubbing

Note: Use a 5/32" bead for sizes 8-10 and 1/8" for sizes 12-14.

Brown Euro Jig

Originator: Steve Parrott
Tier: Steve Parrott

Hook: #12-16 Tiemco 403BLJ or Hanak H400BL
Bead: Copper slotted tungsten
Thread: Brown 70-denier Ultra Thread
Tail: Wood duck fibers
Abdomen: Brown Micro Tubing
Flash: Opal 1/100 Micro Flashabou wrapped around hook shank
Collar: Canadian brown Arizona Simi-Seal

Note: Use a 1/8" bead for sizes 12-14 and 3/32" for size 16.

Flash Euro Jig

Originator: Steve Parrott
Tier: Steve Parrott

Hook: #12-16 Tiemco 403BLJ or Hanak H400BL
Bead: Black slotted tungsten
Weight: Jan Siman heavy flat lead wire
Thread: Olive 70-denier Ultra Thread
Tail: Wood duck fibers
Abdomen: Tying thread and pearl 1/100 Micro Flashabou
Rib: Black Ultra Wire (small)
Collar: Olive Mercer's Buggy Nymph Dubbing

Note: Use a 1/8" bead for sizes 12-14 and 3/32" for size 16.

Tungsten Leggy Grub

Originator: Steve Parrott
Tier: Steve Parrott

Hook: #10-14 Umpqua Competition C300BL
Bead: Brown tungsten
Thread: Shell pink 70-denier Ultra Thread
Abdomen: Fluorescent shell pink Antron
Rib: Copper brown Ultra Wire
Back: Clear Cure Goo Hydro, colored with brown Sharpie

Note: Use a 5/32" bead for size 10 and 1/8" for sizes 12-14.

Bank Saver

Originator: Steve Parrott
Tier: Steve Parrott

Hook: #14-16 Umpqua Competition C200BL
Bead: Black tungsten
Thread: Black 70-denier Ultra Thread
Tail: Pheasant tail fibers
Abdomen: Rainbow Sow Scud Dubbing
Backstrap: Pheasant tail fibers
Rib: Red Ultra Wire (small)
Hot Spot: Fluorescent hot pink Super Bright Dubbing
Flashback: Opal Mirage Tinsel (medium)
Thorax: Brown angora goat dubbing

Pink S & D Grub

Originator: Steve Parrott
Tier: Steve Parrott

Hook: #10-14 Umpqua Competition C300BL or Hanak H300BL
Weight: Jan Siman flat lead wire (medium)
Thread: Black 70-denier Ultra Thread
Abdomen: Soft pink Uni Stretch Floss
Rib: Black Ultra Wire (small)
Hot Spot: Fluorescent hot pink Datum Glo Brite Floss (#2)
Head: Black 70-denier Ultra Thread

Note: Coat fly with Clear Cure Goo Hydro or Sally Hansen's Hard As Nails.

Electric Caddis

Originator: Steve Parrott
Tier: Steve Parrott

Hook: #10-14 Umpqua Competition C300BL or Hanak H300BL
Thread: Black 70-denier Ultra Thread
Shell Back: Light green Jan Siman Magic Shrimp Foil Pearl Strip
Abdomen: Bright green Life Cycle Nymph Dubbing
Rib: Lime green Mirror Krystal Flash and .006" mono thread or 6X tippet
Head: Black SLF Spikey Squirrel Dubbing

Devil Jig Nymph (Green)

Originator: Steve Parrott
Tier: Steve Parrott

Hook: #12-16 Tiemco 403BLJ or Hanak H400BL
Bead: Copper slotted tungsten
Thread: Brown 70-denier Ultra Thread
Tail: Brown hen hackle
Abdomen: Brown 70-denier Ultra Thread
Rib: Green Flashabou
Collar: Hare's ear Arizona Synthetic Peacock Dubbing

Note: Cover abdomen with Clear Cure Goo Hydro. Use a 1/8" bead for sizes 12-14 and 3/32" for size 16.

Devil Jig Nymph (Gold)

Originator: Steve Parrott
Tier: Steve Parrott

Hook: #12-16 Tiemco 403BLJ or Hanak H400BL
Bead: Gold slotted tungsten
Thread: Brown 70-denier Ultra Thread
Tail: Dark dun hen hackle
Abdomen: Olive 70-denier Ultra Thread
Rib: Gold Flashabou
Collar: Bronze Arizona Synthetic Peacock Dubbing

Note: Cover abdomen with Clear Cure Goo Hydro. Use a 1/8" bead for sizes 12-14 and 3/32" for size 16.

Lighting Bug

Originator: Joe Johnson
Tier: Joe Johnson

Hook: #14-18 Tiemco 2499SPBL
Bead: Gold brass or tungsten
Weight: .020" lead wire
Thread: Fire orange 8/0 Uni Thread
Abdomen: Chartreuse Hareline Flat Diamond Braid
Shell Back: Brown Hareline Flashback
Rib: Black Ultra Wire (small)
Thorax: Bronze Arizona Synthetic Peacock Dubbing

Note: Put on more dubbing than you'll think you'll need and tease it out with a bodkin. Use a 1/8" bead for size 14 and 3/32" for sizes 16-18.

Wee Woolly Caddis

Originator: Joe Johnson
Tier: Joe Johnson

Hook: #12-16 Umpqua C200BL
Bead: Black tungsten
Weight: .020" lead wire
Thread: Chartreuse 70-denier Ultra Thread
Abdomen: Dark brown Wee Wool
Collar: Chartreuse 70-denier Ultra Thread

J's Caddis Pupa

Originator: J Core
Tier: J Core

Hook: #14-18 Dai-Riki 135
Bead: Black tungsten
Thread: Olive 8/0 Uni-Thread
Abdomen: Clear D-Rib
Thorax: Peacock Ice Dub
Wing: Pearl Krystal Flash and pheasant tail fibers (two fibers each)

Note: Use a 1/8" bead for size 14 and 3/32" for sizes 16-18.

Tak's Go 2 Caddis

Originator: Rick Takahashi
Tier: Rick Takahashi

Hook: #14-16 Dai-Riki 060
Bead: Brass or tungsten
Thread: Black 94-denier Lagartun
Tail: Brown hen hackle
Abdomen: Chartreuse Diamond Midge Braid
Wing Post: White poly yarn
Hackle: Brown midge saddle hackle
Collar: Peacock Ice Dub

Note: Use a 1/8" bead for size 14 and 3/32" for size 16.

Caddistrophic Pupa

Originator: Charlie Craven
Tier: Charlie Craven

Hook: #14-18 Tiemco 2487
Bead: Black tungsten
Thread: Olive dun 8/0 Uni-Thread
Rib: Chartreuse Ultra Wire (Brassie)
Shell Back: Brown Super Floss
Abdomen: Pale olive Haretron Dubbing
Wing Buds: Butt ends of Super Floss shell back
Collar: Natural dun CDC
Antennae: Shrimp colored Fluoro Fibre, barred with Sharpie
Head: Peacock SLF Prism Dubbing

Note: Use a 1/8" bead for sizes 14 and 3/32" for sizes 16-18.

Z-Wing Caddis

Originator: Mike Mercer
Tier: Umpqua Feather Merchants

Hook: #14-18 Tiemco 2457
Bead: Copper, brass, or tungsten
Thread: Olive 8/0 Uni-Thread
Abdomen: Mercer's caddis green Select Buggy Nymph Dubbing
Wing Case: Golden brown turkey tail
Rib: Chartreuse Monocord
Wings: Medium dun Z-Lon
Collar: Mercer's caddis green Select Buggy Nymph Dubbing
Head: Peacock herl

Nitro Caddis Pupa (Olive)

Originator: Andrij Horodysky
Tier: Umpqua Feather Merchants

Hook: #12-18 Tiemco 2488H
Bead: Black brass or tungsten
Thread: Brown 14/0 Gordon Griffiths
Abdomen: Olive Pearl Core Braid (medium)
Thorax: Olive Ice Dub
Wing Pads: Gray brown Thin Skin
Legs: Hungarian partridge fibers
Antennae: Mallard flank
Head: Olive brown Ice Dub

Note: Tan is also effective.

Graphic Caddis (Olive)

Originator: John Barr
Tier: Umpqua Feather Merchants

Hook: #14-18 Tiemco 2499SPBL
Thread: Olive 6/0 Danville 6/0
Abdomen: Olive Stretch Tube
Tag: Holographic Silver Flashabou
Legs: Partridge body feather
Head: Natural gray ostrich

Note: Tan is also effective.

RK Emerger

Originator: Mike Kruise
Tier: Mike Kruise

Hook: #14-20 Tiemco 2487
Bead: Black brass or tungsten
Thread: Watery olive 70-denier Ultra Thread
Abdomen: Green Sulky Metallic Thread
Rib: Chartreuse Ultra Wire (small)
Thorax: Caddis green Hareline Dubbin
Wing: UV White Saap's Float Vis
Legs: Motor Oil Sulky Metallic Thread

Note: Use a 1/8" bead for size14, 3/32" for sizes 16-18 and 5/64" for sizes 20-22.

Tabou Caddis Emerger (Tan)

Originator: Steve Schweitzer
Tier: Steve Schweitzer

Hook: #14-16 Dai-Riki 280
Thread: Gray brown 70-denier Ultra Thread
Tail: Tip of Whiting Farms chickabou feather
Abdomen: Natural chickabou feather
Rib: Rio 3X monofilament tippet
Wing: Natural dun Whiting Farms Brahma hen back
Thorax: Fuzz from the butt-end of the wing feather

Note: Color variations include brown, olive, straw yellow, and olive.

Olive Caddis Emerger (House Fly)

Originator: Jim Neiberger
Tier: Jim Neiberger

Hook: #14-18 Tiemco 2488
Thread: Black 8/0 Uni-Thread
Tail: Peacock herl
Rib: Chartreuse Ultra Wire (small)
Shell Back: Pearl Flashabou
Abdomen: Olive Ligas Dubbing
Wing: Mylar tinsel (small)
Head: Peacock herl

G. W. Special

Originator: Larry Friedrichs
Tier: Larry Friedrichs

Hook: #14-16 Tiemco UOO2
Bead: Gold brass or tungsten
Thread: Black 8/0 Uni-Thread
Tail: Brown India hen
Abdomen: Mirage Tinsel (medium)
Rib: Chartreuse Ultra Wire (extra small)
Thorax: Peacock herl
Hackle: Brown India hen

Note: Use a 1/8" bead for sizes 12-14 and 3/32" for sizes 16-18 and 5/64" for sizes 20-22.

Punch It Caddis

Originator: Josef Shafer
Tier: Josef Shafer

Hook: #16-20 Tiemco 2487
Abdomen: Tan Montana Fly Wonder Wrap
Rib: Brown Ultra Wire (small)
Wing: Root Beer Krystal Flash and Larva Lace Dry Foam
Thorax: Tan hare's ear dubbing with extra guard hairs

Note: Color variations include caddis green, orange, and chartreuse.

Mo T (More Trout) Nymph

Originator: Dr. Eric Pettine
Tier: Dr. Eric Pettine

Hook: #14-18 Tiemco 2488
Bead: Gold brass or tungsten
Thread: Black 16/0 Tiemco
Tail: Natural goose biot
Abdomen: Green Holo Tinsel
Rib: Chartreuse Ultra Wire (small and extra small)
Thorax: Black ostrich
Legs: Ginger midge hackle
Wing Case: Fly speck tan/black Thin Skin

Note: Use a 1/8" bead for size 14 and 3/32" for sizes 16-18.

The Cow Dung Variant

Originator: Dr. Eric Pettine
Tier: Dr. Eric Pettine

Hook: #14-18 Tiemco 2488
Thread: Olive 70-denier Ultra Thread
Abdomen: Olive 70-denier Ultra Thread
Rib: Red Ultra Wire (small and extra small)
Thorax: Peacock SLF Prism Dubbing behind black tungsten bead
Hackle: Dark brown India hen back

Bubble Caddis Pupa

Originator: Larry Kingrey
Tier: Larry Kingrey

Hook: #14-16 Tiemco 100BL
Thread: Black 6/0 Uni-Thread
Underbody: 50/50 blend, dark olive Hareline Dubbin and olive Ice Dub
Overbody: Olive Antron
Veil: Dark dun CDC
Wing: Dark dun CDC

Beadhead Caddis Pupa

Originator: Larry Kingrey
Tier: Larry Kingrey

Hook: #14-18 Tiemco 5262
Bead: Gold brass or tungsten
Thread: Black 6/0 Uni-Thread
Abdomen: Dubbing mix, 1/3 each olive rabbit, olive Ice Dub, and olive Antron
Thorax: Same as abdomen, but Antron is cut twice as long as hook, and scrubbed out
Hackle: Dark dun hen, tied wet-fly style

Note: Use a 1/8" bead for sizes 14 and 3/32" for sizes 16-18.

Little Brown Bug

Originator: Mike Mercer
Tier: Umpqua Feather Merchants

Hook: #16-18 Tiemco 2488
Bead: Gunmetal glass (small)
Thread: Camel 8/0 Uni-Thread
Abdomen: Red Quill goose biot
Thorax: Pearl Flashabou
Wing Buds: Brown Thin Skin
Legs: Hungarian partridge fibers
Antennae: Wood duck fibers
Head: Dark brown Mercer's Buggy Nymph Dubbing

Caddis Pluma

Originator: Jin Choi
Tier: Jin Choi

Hook: #14-18 Tiemco 101
Bead: Black tungsten
Thread: Black 8/0 Benecchi
Abdomen: Tan ostrich plume
Thorax: Caddis green Ice Dub
Collar: Brown speckled CDL with chickabou
Head: Black hare's ear dubbing

Royal Gorgeous Caddis

Originator: Juan Ramirez
Tier: Juan Ramirez

Hook: #12-18 Tiemco 2499 SPBL
Bead: Black tungsten or brass
Thread: Black 8/0 MFC
Abdomen: Olive and chartreuse Ultra Wire
Thorax: Olive MFC Generation X Dubbing mixed with olive Ice Dub.

Note: Use a 7/64" bead for size 14 and 3/32" for size 16-18. For size 14, use large Ultra Wire; for size 16-18, use medium. For the thorax, use a heavy amount of dubbing, pick fibers out with dubbing brush or bodkin, then sweep back and clip to body length.

Gigabyte Caddis

Originator: Juan Ramirez
Tier: Juan Ramirez

Hook: #14-18 Tiemco 2488
Bead: Black tungsten or brass
Thread: Black 8/0 MFC
Abdomen: MFC caddis green Wabbit Dubbing
Over Veil: Gray Antron Glo Yarn
Wings: Brown hen neck (3 turns)
Antennae: MFC brown Lucent Wing Fibers
Thorax: Peacock herl

Note: Use a 7/64" bead for size 14 and 3/32" for size 16-18.

Matt's Hi-Viz Caddis

Originator: Matt Miles
Tier: Matt Miles

Hook: #10-16 Tiemco 100
Thread: Brown 8/0 Uni-Thread
Abdomen: Black Razor Foam (.5mm)
Wing: Brown Razor Foam (.5mm)
Post: Cerise McFlylon
Hackle: Whiting Farms brown rooster

Tak's 12 O'Clock Caddis

Originator: Rick Takahashi
Tier: Rick Takahashi

Hook: #14-16 Daiichi 1180
Thread: Hopper Yellow 70-denier Ultra Thread
Underbody: Hopper Yellow 70-denier Ultra Thread
Abdomen: Tan foam (2mm)
Wing: Natural deer hair
Legs: Olive MFC Speckled Sexy-Floss

Tak's Split Winged Caddis

Originator: Variation of Craig Mathews' X-Caddis
Tier: Rick Takahashi

Hook: #14-18 Tiemco 2303 or Dai-Riki 280
Thread: Olive 8/0 Uni-Thread
Tail: Amber Antron fibers (tied sparse)
Abdomen: Caddis green Superfine
Wing: Natural deer hair with center section trimmed out

Caddis Variant

Originator: Chuck Stranahan
Tier: Umpqua Feather Merchants

Hook: #14-18 Tiemco 921
Thread: Rust brown 8/0 Uni-Thread
Abdomen: Rust Antron Dubbing or Antron
Rib: Rust brown 8/0 Uni-Thread
Underwing: Natural deer hair
Overwing: White calf body hair
Hackle: Grizzly dyed ginger saddle, oversized

Parachute Hi-Viz Caddis

Originator: Greg Blessing
Tier: Greg Blessing

Hook: #16-18 Tiemco 100
Thread: Dark brown 70-denier Ultra Thread
Abdomen: Tan closed-cell foam
Rib: Dark brown 70-denier Ultra Thread
Wing: Nature's Spirit bleached elk (Bull #49)
Post: Orange foam (2mm)
Hackle: Variant Whiting Farms saddle

PFD Caddis

Originator: Mathew Thomas
Tier: Mathew Thomas

Hook: #14-18 Tiemco 100
Thread: Tan 8/0 Uni-Thread
Wing: Elk
Post: White Wapsi foam block
Hackle: Brown and grizzly Whiting Farms rooster

The Best Elk Hair Caddis

Originator: Mathew Thomas
Tier: Mathew Thomas

Hook: #16-18 Tiemco 3761
Thread: Light cahill 8/0 Uni-Thread
Wing: Elk
Hackle: Dun and grizzly Whiting Farms rooster

Note: Color variations include brown hackle with a black thread head.

Missing Link (Olive)

Originator: Mike Mercer
Tier: Umpqua Feather Merchants

Hook: #15-19 Tiemco 102Y
Thread: Olive 8/0 Uni-Thread
Abdomen: Olive 8/0 Uni-Thread
Rib: Pearl Flashabou coated with Softex
Thorax: Brown UV Ice Dub
Hackle: Medium dun rooster
Down Wing: Dun Z-Lon
Upright Wing: Natural cow elk

Note: Color variations include yellow, red, Green Drake, and caddis.

Pearl and Elk Caddis

Originator: Dennis Potter
Tier: Umpqua Feather Merchants

Hook: #12-18 Tiemco 100
Thread: White GSP
Abdomen: Opal Mirage Tinsel
Rib: White GSP
Hackle: Light dun rooster
Wing: Light elk

E/C Caddis

Originator: Ralph Cutter
Tier: Umpqua Feather Merchants

Hook: #14-18 Tiemco 9300
Thread: Brown 6/0 Danville
Tail: Ginger Z-Lon
Abdomen: Caddis green, Cinnamon Superfine
Wing: Natural cow elk
Hackle: Grizzly rooster

Simple Spent Caddis

Originator: Unknown
Tier: Duane Redford

Hook: #16-18 Tiemco 100
Thread: Black 6/0 Uni-Thread
Abdomen: Tan rabbit fur
Wing: White Antron
Thorax: Peacock herl

Black Foam Caddis

Originator: Larry Kingrey
Tier: Larry Kingrey

Hook: #14-16 Tiemco 100
Thread: Rusty dun 6/0 Uni-Thread
Abdomen: Black foam (2mm)
Hackle: Grizzly dyed dark olive
Wing: Dark cow elk

Clown Shoe Caddis

Originator: Jay Zimmerman
Tier: Umpqua Feather Merchants

Hook: #14-18 Tiemco 2487
Thread: Black 6/0 Uni-Thread
Abdomen: Light olive D-Rib over olive 6/0 Uni-Thread
Thorax: Black Superfine
Post: Fluorescent cerise McFly Foam
Wing: Dyed dun deer hair
Hackle: Dun rooster

Note: Brown is another effective color.

Corn Fed Caddis

Originator: Lance Egan
Tier: Umpqua Feather Merchants

Hook: #14-16 Tiemco 921
Thread: Tan 8/0 Uni-Thread
Tail: Tan Antron or Z-Lon
Abdomen: Tan Superfine
Wing: Natural dun CDC
Overwing: White over gray poly yarn
Hackle: Natural dun CDC

Note: Olive is also effective.

Diving CDC and Elk

Originator: Hans Weilenmann
Tier: Umpqua Feather Merchants

Hook: #12-18 Tiemco 2499SPBL
Bead: Black tungsten
Thread: Brown 6/0 Uni-Thread
Abdomen: Natural dun CDC feather
Underwing: Natural dun CDC feather
Wing: Mule deer
Thorax: Natural hare's ear dubbing

Note: Use a $^{1}/_{8}$" bead for sizes 12-14 and $^{3}/_{32}$" for sizes 16-18.

Lime Trude

Originator: Variation of
Alfred Trude's original pattern
Tier: Dick Shinton

Hook: #14-18 Tiemco 5263
Thread: Fluorescent green 70-denier Ultra Thread
Tail: Golden pheasant neck fibers
Abdomen: Fluorescent green Antron
Wing: White UV Saap's Float Vis
Hackle: Whiting Farms brown rooster

CDC Fluff Beast

Originator: Chris Johnson
Tier: Chris Johnson

Hook: #10-16 Tiemco 100
Thread: White 50-denier GSP
Abdomen: Spun Marc Petitjean CDC feathers, trimmed flush on bottom (2 bright yellow, 2 yellow, and 1 tan)
Wing: Elk hair stacked
Thorax: Spun Marc Petitjean CDC feathers, trimmed flush on bottom (1 Bistre, 2 yellow, and 1 tan)
Legs: Brown round rubber (small)

Puterbaugh's Caddis

Originator: Don Puterbaugh
Tier: Pat Dorsey

Hook: #14-18 Tiemco 100
Thread: Black 8/0 Uni-Thread
Abdomen: Black closed-cell foam (2mm)
Wing: Natural elk
Hackle: Brown rooster

Slow Water Caddis

Originator: Umpqua Feather Merchants
Tier: Umpqua Feather Merchants

Hook: #14-18 Tiemco 100
Thread: Rusty brown 8/0 Uni-Thread
Abdomen: Brown Superfine
Wing: Brown hen
Hackle: Brown rooster, trimmed on bottom
Head: Rusty brown 8/0 Uni-Thread

Hot Wing Elk Hair Caddis

Originator: Variation of Al Troth original
Tier: Umpqua Feather Merchants

Hook: #14-18 Tiemco 100
Thread: Tan 8/0 Uni-Thread
Abdomen: Tan Superfine
Hackle: Brown rooster
Wing: Elk hair
Indicator: Fluorescent orange McFlylon

Mother's Day Caddis

Originator: Greg Garcia
Tier: Greg Garcia

Hook: #14-18 Tiemco 100SPBL
Bead: Silver lined caddis green plastic (extra small)
Thread: Black 70-denier Ultra Thread
Abdomen: Black Superfine
Underwing: Red (2 strands) and pearl (4 strands) Krystal Flash
Wing: Nature's Spirit bleached yearling elk
Hackle: Brown rooster

Caddis Emerger

Originator: Greg Garcia
Tier: Greg Garcia

Hook: #13-19 Tiemco 212TR
Thread: Tan 8/0 Uni-Thread
Tag: Olive dyed over pearl Flashabou
Abdomen: Olive dyed over pearl Flashabou and tan 8/0 Uni-Thread
Underwing: Cinnamon Caddis EP Trigger Point Fiber
Wing: Bleached elk hock
Post: White EP Trigger Point Fiber
Thorax: Tan Superfine
Hackle: Brown rooster

Bead Diving Caddis (Tan)

Originator: Shane Stalcup
Tier: Solitude Fly Company

Hook: #14-18 Tiemco 2302
Bead: Copper or brass
Thread: Tan 8/0 Uni-Thread
Abdomen: Tan turkey biot
Underwing: Tan Z-Lon
Wing: Tan Medallion Sheeting
Antennae: Tan Betts' Tailing Fibers
Legs: Partridge
Thorax: Tan Superfine

Note: Olive is also effective. You can use another good color. Use a 1/8" bead for size 14 and 3/32" for sizes 16-18.

Micro Caddis

Originator: Jerry Freeman
Tier: Aaron Carithers

Hook: #20-22 Tiemco 101
Thread: Black 8/0 Uni-Thread
Abdomen: Peacock herl
Tail: Grizzly hackle fibers
Wing: Coastal deer hair
Hackle: Grizzly rooster

CHAPTER 6

Other Important Trout Foods and Their Imitations: Aquatic Worms, Scuds, Mysis *Shrimp, and Eggs*

In addition to midges, mayflies, stoneflies, and caddisflies, Colorado anglers will need to familiarize themselves with other important trout foods like aquatic worms and freshwater crustaceans such as scuds and *Mysis* shrimp. While aquatic worms, scuds, and *Mysis* shrimp don't produce epic hatches like the previously mentioned aquatic insects, they do play an vital role in the trout's diet and the angler's fly selection during certain times of the year. Egg imitations have a time and place too and will no doubt become important under the right conditions. Let's take a closer look at each one of these significant food organisms.

AQUATIC WORMS

Aquatic worms, commonly referred to as annelids, look similar to their terrestrial cousin the common earthworm. Their importance to both the angler and trout cannot be underestimated because huge populations of aquatic worms are present in just about every imaginable aquatic habitat from small ponds to large streams.

Aquatic worms thrive in streams with substrates composed of silt, sand, and fine gravel. Fertile weed-rich tailwaters tend to produce the densest biomass of aquatic worms, but don't let that fool you—many freestone streams like the Gunnison River also contain heavy concentrations of aquatic worms.

Aquatic worms vary in color from tan to reddish brown to orangish brown. Most aquatic worms you'll encounter through seine or stomach samples range between one and two inches long. Artificials are tied in a wide variety of colors—tan, earthworm brown, red, pink, and orange. The earth-tone colors tend to produce best in clear water and the brighter colors are most effective during spring runoff when the water is high and roily or after a rainshower that temporarily discolors the water. Red, pink, and orange are also effective in the spring and fall when the fish are in the pre-spawn mode and are willing to attack anything that is brightly colored.

Over the past fifty years, the most commonly used aquatic worm imitation has been the fabled San Juan Worm, which was invented by Paul Pacheco of Shiprock, New Mexico, in the mid-1960s. One of Pacheco's closest friends was Abe Chavez, the original owner of Abe's Fly Shop in Navajo Dam, New Mexico. On one of his regular visits to the fly shop, Pacheco suggested that Chavez stock red Domino Nymphs (invented by Hank Roberts during the 1960s) in his fly shop because Pacheco had been catching a bunch of large rainbows on them. Pacheco was aware that his success with this pattern was probably due to the Domino Nymph imitating the abundant reddish-brown aquatic worms that thrived in the San Juan

Egg-midge combos are an effective strategy during the winter months when there are no obvious hatches. This Colorado River rainbow gobbled up a Hot Tail Flash Egg near the small community of Parshall. MARK ADAMS

River's substrate below Navajo Dam. After seining the river and closely analyzing the natural aquatic worms, Pacheco decided to tie something that was much more realistic.

In its embryonic form, Pacheco tied the San Juan Worm with red thread or floss wrapped around an English bait hook, and then ribbed it with gold wire for segmentation. Many anglers referred to this pattern as a "candy cane" or "hard worm." Some anglers wrapped red Micro Tubing around an English bait hook to achieve the same results. This latter version did not require gold wire for segmentation, as the wound tubing produced a beautiful ribbed effect. This pattern is still a popular fly decades later on the North Platte River at Gray Reef (below Alcova Dam) but the English bait hook has been swapped for a large scud hook. Local anglers and guides refer to this pattern as a "rock worm" and typically fish it off a Pine Squirrel Leech during the spring.

The Pig Sticker, another popular aquatic worm imitation, is a variation of the original hard worm. It is tied on a Gamakatsu C12U in size 6-8. You may opt to wrap the hook shank with .015-gauge lead to increase the sink rate. The body is composed of 140-denier Ultra Thread wound around the hook shank and then covered with a heavy coat of Sally Hansen's Hard As Nails. Effective colors include brown, tan, red, pink, and orange.

The next transition led to today's most popular version in which fly tiers lash a two-inch piece of Ultra Chenille to a hook. A cigarette lighter or candle flame is used to taper the ends of the chenille to give the worm a realistic look. To save time, you can burn the ends of several pre-cut pieces of Ultra Chenille prior to securing them to the hook.

Innovative fly tiers have since incorporated a wide spectrum of new fly-tying materials into the San Juan Worm's design—chamois strips, Flexi Floss, Pearl Core Braid, and wire. Jim Cannon's Worm is one of the most realistic aquatic worm imitations I've come across. Cannon uses dyed chamois strips (brown, tan, and red) and secures them to a Tiemco 2499SPBL. "A good worm imitation starts with an excellent hook!" Cannon advises. "Perfect for holding aggressive fish, this hook is 2X heavy and 2X short with a 3X-wide gape. Forged-bronze construction with a curved shank, this hook is strong and allows anglers to dredge this pattern, bouncing it along the bottom. It won't open up when you're snagged or fighting a large fish. The extra-wide gap allows the hook to penetrate and hold. Since the hook is barbless you do not have to worry about pinching down the barb and it is easy to get out of the fish's mouth."

Unlike many aquatic worm imitations, which are secured to the hook shank in two or more locations, Cannon attaches

Aquatic worm imitations are effective on both tailwaters and freestone streams, especially during higher flows when the naturals get swept away in the current. Jim Cannon persuaded this Gunnison River brown trout to eat one of his Cannon's Worm imitations during the initial phases of spring runoff.

Aquatic worm imitations are effective on tailwaters where flow fluctuations are a common occurrence. The San Juan Worm is one of Jeremy Hyatt's go-to patterns on the South Platte below Deckers where river levels are adjusted on a daily basis to meet downstream irrigation and urban demand.

the chamois strip in one spot, which allows for a more realistic, lifelike movement that Cannon believes triggers more strikes. "I tie the chamois strip in at the one-third point of the hook shank with orange 3/0 thread," Cannon says. "This allows more of the chamois strip to move freely in the current. Orange Scud Back is wrapped over the connection to simulate the sex ring. If you are using the natural color, it will darken up in water."

Another advantage to Cannon's Worm is its durability. Without a doubt, it will outlast most other aquatic worm imitations. "Chamois is very durable when cut into strips," Cannon adds. "After it absorbs water, it increases in size. Chamois is a tanned lambskin and has the texture, appearance, and feel of a real worm when in the water."

AQUATIC WORM FISHING STRATEGIES

Aquatic worm imitations are most effective during higher flow regimes when the naturals get washed loose from the substrate. During the initial phases of spring runoff, it's not uncommon to find trout stuffed with aquatic worms—so much so, they literally have them hanging out of their mouths. "The South Platte River near Deckers has a very strong population of aquatic worms," says Jeremy Hyatt, co-owner of Flies & Lies fly shop. "I am a big fan of fishing aquatic worm imitations in

Bright pink San Juan Worms can save the day during spring runoff when the river is typically high and off-colored. Pink San Juan Worms are also a good option when river levels rise below a tailrace. MARK ADAMS

the spring when water levels rise. During May and June worm imitations are a must-have in the Deckers area." Under these conditions, fishing two worm imitations is never out of the realm of possibility. I vary my colors based on the clarity of the water. "Red San Juan Worms are my go-to when the water is high and off-color," Hyatt adds. "I also fish flesh and bright pink during these times in an attempt to make the fly more visible. As a rule, as the water clears up I will go back to a tan color to closely match the natural worm."

Conversely, aquatic worm imitations are not as effective during receding or low flows when there is an absence of naturals drifting in the current. When the flows are receding but still above their normal historic levels, I typically fish with a Micro San Juan Worm. I tie my Micro San Juan Worms with a smaller chenille (small instead of standard) and use a smaller hook, typically a size 16 or 18.

Heavy afternoon rain showers, however, can wash terrestrial worms into the river, again causing a feeding frenzy on worm imitations. "After big rainstorm on the Gunnison River, the fish are really keyed in on earthworms," says Jason Booth. Booth also notes that terrestrial worms are continuously washed into the Gunnison River from ranchers irrigating their hayfields. "The upper Gunnison River system flows from Almont to Blue Mesa Reservoir. Along the way ranchers have headgates that divert water into their hayfields to irrigate their pastureland; then the water comes back into the Gunnison River with large concentrations of earthworms in it. The ranchers are constantly flooding different fields so worms are an important food source." As far as worm imitations are concerned, a worm is a worm—any of the previously mentioned imitations will fool trout keying on either aquatic or terrestrial worms.

Jeremy Hyatt also believes aquatic worm patterns are a good option during the autumn months when the fish are looking to eat large, protein-filled meals before the onset of winter and the brown trout spawning. Hyatt chooses the color and size of his worm imitations based on the prevailing conditions, most often fishing a brown, red, or tan pattern. Red seems to trigger aggression strikes in spawning brown trout.

Most anglers fish their worm imitations with a 9-foot 4X leader and trail their droppers with 5X fluorocarbon tippet. Trout keying on worm imitations are typically not leader-shy, so it is in your best interest to fish with the largest tippet possible to avoid any potential risk of a breakoff.

Many fly fishers opt to use aquatic worm imitations as their attractor in their two- or three-fly tandem nymphing rigs because they feel it draws attention to their lower fly or flies. A typical rig might consist of a San Juan Worm dropped with midge larvae trailed with a *Baetis* nymph. Most anglers match the hatch with dropper patterns that will imitate the current hatches. For instance, if there is a dense midge hatch in progress, I would recommend dropping a midge larva trailed by a midge pupa. At midday, if Blue-Winged Olives are present, I would switch my flies to a couple *Baetis* nymphs, and so on. "I carry a full assortment of aquatic worms including different sizes and colors," Booth says. "I like using them as an attractor in my two-fly nymphing rigs. My dropper fly is selected according to what's hatching that day."

Some anglers prefer to fish their aquatic worm imitations as their point fly because they feel they drift more naturally in the current. Typically the flies farthest from the weight behave more naturally compared to the flies closest to the weight. The tippet size, weight, and distance between the weight can affect the way the flies behave in the current. For instance, 4X tippet is more rigid than 5X tippet, which can have an adverse effect on your drift. Most anglers would agree that you'll get more strikes on the droppers as opposed to the attractor because the tippet is smaller in diameter, which allows the flies to drift naturally in the current. Aquatic worm imitations should be fished dead drift, allowing them to look helpless in the current.

Bob Dye prefers to fish his aquatic worm imitations as the point fly because he feels he gets more strikes when the worm imitations are farthest from the weight. "I move my worm imitations around in my tandem rigs, but more times than not, I find myself fishing them in the point-fly position," Dye says. "It is my belief that they behave more naturally—wiggling, twisting, and turning more freely—the farther they are away from the weight."

SCUDS

Scuds are freshwater crustaceans that provide a high-protein food source to trout in both lakes and streams. Scuds are members of the Amphipoda order and do not have as complicated a life cycle as other aquatic insects; they begin their lives as small scuds and die as large scuds, which greatly simplifies your fly selection. Two genera are of interest to Colorado fly fishers: *Gammarus* and *Hyalella*. The *Gammarus* scuds are the larger of the two varieties, with specimens ranging between 10mm and 25mm. The *Hyalella* scuds are smaller, between 3mm and 5mm. I recommend that you fill your fly boxes with size 10-18 scud imitations to cover both genera and their various stages of development.

Stillwater advocates like Richard Pilatzke understand the importance of carrying a thorough selection of scuds in your fly boxes. "Scuds are of importance to the stillwater angler

Scuds are abundant in Colorado's lakes and streams. Having a thorough selection of scud imitations in sizes 12 to 18 is important. JAY NICHOLS

Pat Dorsey prepares to net a Cheesman Canyon rainbow that he caught on a scud imitation. Anglers who frequent tailwaters should carry a thorough assortment of scuds in orange, olive, and tan in size 12-18. MARK ADAMS

because they are a year-round food source," Pilatzke explains. "They are not dependent on timed hatches, so they are especially significant in the shoulder seasons (spring and fall). Scuds thrive in weedy, alkaline lakes. These lakes are also the most productive lakes for fish growth. We are fortunate in Colorado to have world-class stillwaters like Antero, Spinney, and Delaney Buttes Lakes and many others. When the conditions are right, I tend to fish a size 10 *Gammarus* imitation in Colorado stillwaters a large percentage of the time."

In rivers and streams, scuds prefer shallow water, slow- to moderate-paced currents, stable water temperatures, and substrates composed of heavy aquatic vegetation. Some of the largest populations of scuds are found in Colorado's deep bottom-release tailwaters, where they are often responsible for fat and healthy fast-growing trout. Tailwater junkies will need to make sure their fly boxes are stuffed with *Gammarus* scuds in size 12-18 before they head to their favorite tailrace.

Scuds have a shrimplike appearance with a flattened head, two pairs of antennae, a segmented body, a shell back, and a tail. Scuds are excellent swimmers. They use their legs to propel themselves forward through dense stands of aquatic vegetation and use their tails to push themselves backwards in the event danger threatens. Scuds are sensitive to bright light, therefore they are most active during the morning and evening hours or during overcast conditions. Scuds flatten their bodies when they are swimming and curl up when they are knocked loose from weed beds drifting in the current. Anglers should carry scud imitations on both standard hooks (straight shanks) as well as scud hooks (curved shanks) to imitate each behavior as needed.

Your scud selection should consist of a variety of colors—gray-olive, olive, tan, and orange. My seine samples lead me to believe that most scuds in moving water are some shade of olive. Occasionally you'll find a tan scud in your seine, which suggests the scud you are looking at has recently molted, shedding its old exoskeleton for a newer, shinier one.

Scuds turn orange quickly after they die. I was reminded of this one afternoon when I sat down on the river's edge to eat my lunch. While I was sitting on the streambank I noticed an olive scud on my gravel cuff turning orange right before my eyes. I was amazed by how quickly the scud perished and turned orange.

I have never collected an orange scud in my seine, but my occasional stomach samples reveal a different story. I traditionally get a mixture of orange and olive scuds in the samples. The only drawback is that it's not clear whether the trout ate a dead (orange) scud or an olive scud that turned orange inside the trout's belly. In all likelihood, most orange scuds that you'll encounter are a result of a flow reduction from the dam, which leaves scuds stranded. They eventually die and

Tailwater trout find it hard to resist a scud. Scud imitations are especially effective during the low-light hours or during flow fluctuations when the naturals get knocked loose from weed beds. LANDON MAYER

turn orange. When the flow rises again to meet downstream irrigation and urban day-to-day demand, the dead scuds are swept into the current and the fish key on them. This occurs on many of Colorado's tailwaters where regular flow fluctuations occur.

I have had my best results with orange scuds in Cheesman Canyon during the high-water season. I'm convinced part of this has something to do with the rainbows spawning in May and June. Despite what many anglers believe, Cheesman Canyon rainbows spawn well into the latter part of June. This is due to the cold water temperatures, which delay the rainbows' spawning instincts. In many cases, I believe trout are eating orange scuds as eggs rather than as dead scuds. Anglers frequently fish a scud as an attractor and drop a mayfly or midge behind it. Concentrate your efforts in the faster slots and seams behind the spawning flats where eggs are drifting downstream.

SCUD FISHING STRATEGIES

Scud tactics and techniques vary greatly depending on the angler and fishery. In moving water, some of the best scud fishing occurs during higher flows, or periods of extreme variation. For instance, in the South Platte's Cheesman Canyon, rising water during the initial phases of spring runoff flushes many of the larger food organisms—scuds, aquatic worms, crane flies, and stoneflies—loose from the canyon's substrate and weed beds. When fish key on scuds during higher flow regimes, it can lead to some of the best nymph fishing of the year.

Stillwater enthusiasts will find excellent scud fishing during most of the year. "Spinney and Antero Reservoirs are two perfect examples where scuds play an important role in a trout's diet," says Josef Shafer, a stillwater guide for the Blue Quill Angler. "Spinney and Antero are shallow reservoirs in comparison to many other Colorado reservoirs. This shallow water creates dense beds of aquatic vegetation, loaded with aquatic insects and scuds. I have actually watched trout punch the weed beds with their snouts, swim through the vegetation, then come back and grab the scuds that have been knocked loose."

A swimming scud will straighten out its body, whereas a drifting scud that has been knocked loose from a weed bed will curl up. It's extremely important that you choose a scud imitation that matches the presentation you have in mind. Stillwater anglers will need to select a scud pattern that correctly imitates the correct profile or silhouette of a swimming scud. Rich Pilatzke notes, "Stillwater scuds should be tied on a straight-shank hook, not a curved scud hook. In stillwaters, scuds are swimming in an elongated, stretched-out position, unlike in moving water, where scuds curl up when dislodged into the moving current."

Many stillwater anglers opt to fish their scud imitations with a floating line under a strike indicator suspended over weed beds. They routinely impart action into the fly with a hand twist or short strips to mimic the lifelike movement of the natural. Another option would be to fish your scuds with a long leader (12 to 15 feet terminating in 3X or 4X) and no strike indicator, and incorporating a similar retrieve. Some anglers have had good results with intermediate sinking lines and slowly retrieving their scud with intermittent pauses. Experiment by varying the speed of your retrieve and find out what works best.

"In the spring when ice comes off our Colorado stillwaters is a good time to hit the banks," Shafer advises. "The water warms quickly closest to the shore and the vegetation starts to grow. The trout will move towards the shallows to get oxygen and food in the vegetation. When I'm searching for places to fish, I typically look for areas that have a 2- to 5-foot flat with a deep drop-off. Trout cruise these flats looking for food after a long winter and scuds are what they are after in many cases."

When the water begins to warm up, the trout head for deeper water. Anglers will have to adjust their tactics accordingly to catch fish. According to Shafer, "Once the water warms trout move back out toward the deeper parts of the lakes. This is when I hop in my float tube and kick out to the weed beds. When you find the weed beds, you'll find the fish. The weed beds hold the food and scuds are plentiful in these areas. When the wind comes up and you can't stay in a boat, I fish the windward side of the lakes or in the mud lines that are created by the waves turning up the bottom in the shallow areas. The windward side of the lake is a good option because a lot of scuds get dislodged from vegetation and get pushed toward the bank."

If you're using scud imitations in rivers you'll typically dead drift them with a conventional two- or three-fly tandem nymphing rig. My colleagues and I typically use a 9-foot tapered leader terminating in 4X. I have not found scud-feeders to be leader shy or sensitive to heavier tippets. I typically use my scud as an attractor and drop a midge or mayfly

Anglers will find excellent scud fishing on stillwater impoundments like Antero Reservoir. Trout cruise along the weed beds looking for scuds, which presents anglers with the perfect opportunity to fish scud imitations. I typically tie my scuds on curved hooks; a Tiemco 2457 is generally my hook of choice. LANDON MAYER

imitation off of it. I choose my droppers based on any evident hatches. For instance, if a midge hatch is occurring, I'll typically fish with either a midge larva or pupa. If I see Blue-Winged Olives or Pale Morning Duns hatching, I will use the appropriate nymph to match the hatch, and so on. I recommend using 5X fluorocarbon tippet for your droppers.

As previously discussed, scuds are light sensitive, so they are naturally more active during the low-light hours. This phenomenon is often referred to as behavioral drift, which is when aquatic insects drift in greater numbers than usual. If these food organisms are actively moving, the odds go up they will get knocked loose from the weed beds and get swept away in the current.

Scud imitations are most effective during higher flows, such as spring runoff, or below tailraces where flow variations occur on a regular basis to meet downstream irrigation demand. The South Platte below the Spinney, Elevenmile, or Cheesman dams is a notable example. "In May and June, spring runoff can provide exceptional scud fishing from the higher flows," says Greg Blessing, head guide for Angler's Covey in Colorado Springs. "I fish a lot of scuds when the Denver Water Board kicks up the flow in the spring in Elevenmile Canyon. I typically fish with olive, olive-gray, or orange scuds in size 14-20. Scuds are a great lead fly in a multi-fly nymphing rig."

I have found similar conditions to exist in Cheesman Canyon. I believe May and June are two of the best months to fish scuds in the three-mile section below Cheesman Dam. "I consider any time the water level rises to be a good time to fish with a scud imitation because it knocks natural scuds loose from the vegetation," says longtime South Platte River guide Randy Smith. Smith's nickname has been "Scudmo" for decades. He has fooled more trout in Cheesman Canyon on scuds than any other angler I can think of.

Landon Mayer agrees that some of the best nymph fishing in the spring and summer takes place below Spinney Dam in the Charlie Meyers State Wildlife Area (the "Dream Stream") with scuds. "Like midges, scuds are also an extremely important as a year-round food source on the Dream Stream. I use scuds throughout the course of a year, but they are especially effective when water levels increase during spring runoff or during flow fluctuations from Spinney Dam," Mayer says. "These crustaceans become available to the trout in a couple of ways: by being flushed from Spinney Reservoir into the river, or being swept off the vegetation along the river's bottom to feeding fish."

MYSIS SHRIMP

If you have lived in Colorado for any length of time, you've probably heard anglers talking about *Mysis* shrimp. More

Some of the best scud fishing of the year occurs in May and June along the South Platte corridor. Craig Davis caught this South Platte beauty on a scud imitation after a midday flow increase below Cheesman Reservoir. MARK ADAMS

importantly, you have probably seen pictures or heard stories about the trophy trout that were caught with *Mysis* imitations on the Frying Pan, Taylor, and Blue Rivers. It shouldn't come as any surprise that you'll need a thorough assortment of *Mysis* shrimp if you plan on fishing one of these renowned tailwaters.

Mysis shrimp, or opossum shrimp, are indigenous to Russia, Scandinavia, and parts of Canada. Initially *Mysis* shrimp were planted in British Columbia's Kootenay Lake as an experiment to see if they would affect the growth rates of Kokanee salmon. They did: the salmon's growth rates increased dramatically. This prompted other game and fish agencies in 1949 to introduce *Mysis* shrimp into other stillwater fisheries that support Kokanee salmon. In the early 1970s the Colorado Division of Wildlife (CDOW), now Colorado Parks and Wildlife, began stocking *Mysis* shrimp in Dillon, Taylor Park, and Ruedi Reservoirs in an effort to fatten up the Kokanee salmon that resided in the shallow bays, coves, and inlets of these manmade impoundments.

Early on, it was unclear as to whether the Kokanee salmon were actually benefiting from the introduction of the *Mysis* shrimp. It appeared that CDOW's strategy was backfiring due to the *Mysis* shrimp being omnivorous filter feeders, feeding heavily on zooplankton—an important food source for juvenile trout and small Kokanee salmon.

Will Sands' Mysis is a must-have if you fish the tailrace below Ruedi Reservoir. This chunky rainbow could not resist it. MARK ADAMS

Will Sands sight-fishes to a Frying Pan rainbow with one of his Mysis *shrimp imitations. A Sands' Mysis is always a good option as an attractor in your tandem nymphing rigs when you're fishing the Frying Pan.* MARK ADAMS

As time went on, the CDOW encountered other setbacks, including the discovery that *Mysis* shrimp are light-sensitive and thrive in water temperatures that are 57 degrees or lower. This meant that as the shallow-water areas warmed the *Mysis* shrimp migrated to deeper water during the day to seek cooler temperatures. The *Mysis* shrimp would return to the shallow water when the temperatures cooled down at night. As it turned out, the Kokanee salmon had exactly the opposite migratory pattern, which did not allow them to benefit from the stocking of the *Mysis* shrimp.

What the Colorado Division of Wildlife did not account for was the impact that the *Mysis* shrimp would have on the trout in the tailraces below the reservoirs. These tailwaters have never been the same—huge, resident trophy trout now reside below these dams. According to Will Sands, manager of Taylor Creek Fly Shop in Basalt, "The greatest concentrations of *Mysis* shrimp exit the dam during higher flows because there is greater suction near the dam face. While many anglers tend to shy away from higher flows that are commonly associated with spring runoff, it can provide some of the best fishing of the year on the Taylor, Frying Pan, and Blue Rivers."

Several years ago, during the height of spring runoff, I used a stomach pump on a 14-inch brown on the Blue River near Silverthorne; the tube was filled with *Mysis* shrimp. There was not a single midge larva, pupa, or mayfly nymph in the stomach contents—it was 100 percent *Mysis* shrimp. That was an eye-opening experience! It taught me that fish can be very selective at times, and furthermore, it punctuated the importance of having a thorough fly selection to match a wide variety of food organisms.

MYSIS SHRIMP FISHING STRATEGIES

Living *Mysis* shrimp are transparent within the reservoir but die quickly after they enter the tailrace below. Close to the dam you'll want to dead drift living (i.e. clear) *Mysis* shrimp imitations, but as you move away from the dam or go downstream, the *Mysis* shrimp die and change color. Dead *Mysis* shrimp are opaque, so you'll need to carry a white imitation too. "Anglers need to carry two varieties of *Mysis* shrimp in their fly boxes: a translucent imitation to mimic live shrimp and an opaque pattern to mimic the dead ones," says Landon Mayer. My stomach pump samples lead me to believe that *Mysis*-fed trout eat both transparent and opaque imitations. Savvy anglers will choose their imitations based on their proximity to the dam, or use one opaque and one white imitation to cover all scenarios.

Most anglers dead-drift their *Mysis* shrimp patterns with a traditional two- or three-fly tandem nymphing rig. Many guides, including myself, use *Mysis* shrimp imitations as an attractor, then drop either a midge or mayfly nymph below

Clay Anselmo caught this Taylor River brown on a Mysis *shrimp imitation during the latter part of May. The heaviest concentrations of* Mysis *shrimp exit the dam during higher flow regimes.*

them. Fly selection changes with the season and any obvious hatches. As with other food sources, if you see midges hatching, you should drop a midge larva or midge pupa off your *Mysis* shrimp. If you see mayflies or caddis hatching, fish with the appropriate flies to match the hatch. One advantage to fishing with *Mysis* shrimp imitations is they are easy to see under the water. "You can see the white *Mysis*, which aids in knowing where your droppers are in relation to the fish you are stalking," says Sands.

Weight adjustments and indicator depth are critical to success. Closely observe where the fish are holding in the water column and make adjustments accordingly. Sands offers this great tip: "Once the *Mysis* shrimp get flushed from the dam, they try to swim toward the surface because they do not like moving water. At times the trout really key on *Mysis* shrimp near the surface of the water and I will grease a poly *Mysis* shrimp or drop my Epoxy Mysis shrimp off a traditional dry fly and fish it like a dry-and-dropper rig."

EGG IMITATIONS

Colorado anglers should carry a thorough selection of egg patterns to prepare themselves for the shoulder seasons. During the spring months (February through April), rainbow, cuttbow, cutthroat, and Kamloops rainbow trout spawn, depositing their eggs in bowl-like depressions called redds. Eggs routinely get swept out of these spawning areas and become an important food source for opportunistic trout.

A similar spawning season occurs during the fall (late September through November) with brook, brown, and rainbow trout, Kokanee salmon, and mountain whitefish. While most rainbows spawn during the spring, there has been an increasing number of fall-spawning rainbows in the last decade, so don't be surprised if you encounter a few of them.

Observant anglers will notice that each gamefish deposits a slightly different-sized and colored egg. I tie a variety of egg patterns with McFly Foam to prepare myself for a variety of situations. The most productive colors include apricot, McCheese, golden, and chartreuse. Apricot and golden work well for brook and brown trout, Kokanee salmon, and most species of rainbow. Kamloops rainbows deposit a chartreuse-colored egg, so you'll need to adjust accordingly when fishing that species. Whitefish spawn between October and November and their egg imitations can be deadly when the fish broadcast their eggs on gravel bars and shallow riffles. Whitefish eggs are cream-colored and smaller than trout eggs, requiring another adjustment.

I also tie the Nuclear Egg in a wide variety of colors, including apricot, orange, pink, and chartreuse. I first learned about the Nuclear Egg from Roger Bittell, a colleague of mine at the Blue Quill Angler. "I have fooled more trout with a

This massive Yampa River cuttbow was fooled by Mark Adams with one of Steve Henderson's size 12 chartreuse egg patterns. Don't be afraid to think outside the box from time to time—you might be surprised with the outcome.

Nuclear Egg than any other egg pattern in my box. I can't imagine fishing or guiding in Colorado without a fly box stuffed with them," Bittell says.

The Nuclear Egg has an interesting history. While guiding for steelhead on Michigan's Betsie River, Walt Grau, an Orvis-Endorsed Guide from the Pere Marquette Lodge, kept noticing colored yarn clippings on the snow near the river's edge. Grau discovered the source of these clippings when he one day stumbled upon a "steelheader" who was adding yarn to spawn that was already on a snelled hook. The angler was using a monofilament loop on the snelled hook (inserting the yarn into the mono-loop and then closing it tightly) and catching several steelhead.

Anglers soon discovered that the steelhead would bite just on yarn, and steelhead enthusiasts found that by using one color of yarn for the nucleus and another for the outer membrane, or "halo," they could produce a realistic single-egg imitation. Grau took this concept to the tying vise and the Nuclear Egg was born. The Nuclear Egg was then introduced to Colorado angler Bob Kennedy—a Michigan native and close friend of Grau's—who sent two dozen to his close friend Roger Bittell, who is credited with popularizing the Nuclear Egg in the Rocky Mountain region.

It is my belief that most fly tiers tie their egg imitations too big—if you closely inspect trout eggs, they are much smaller than you might think. I typically tie my egg patterns on a size 18 scud hook (Tiemco 2457 or 2487) and keep them between one-eighth and three-sixteenths inch in diameter. I also tie micro eggs on size 20 and 22 scud hooks, which can be important when trying to imitate whitefish eggs.

Of course, opinions vary greatly depending on the angler or guide you talk to. Steve Henderson, owner of Henderson Fly Fishing in Steamboat Springs, often fishes with big eggs. "I typically fish my egg patterns in large sizes (size 12) as I feel the color is the main reason the fish grab them," Henderson says. "The bigger egg patterns give the fish a larger silhouette to look at. I typically use a chartreuse or pink color when the skies are overcast. In the winter, when it's snowing, chartreuse has worked the best. Orange and Oregon cheese fish better on sunny days."

Henderson's strategy obviously works well. On a recent trip to the Yampa River, my fishing buddy Mark Adams fooled one of the biggest trout of his life on one of Henderson's egg patterns. Henderson spotted a massive fish sitting underneath an overhanging willow. "I must have made fifty or more casts into that run," Adams says. "Steve Henderson had tied on every combination of popular patterns for the area. When he handed me a thumbnail-sized chartreuse egg, I raised an eyebrow and looked at him. With a look of confidence, he simply said, "Fish it." First cast the massive fish crushed it; the strike indicator disappeared like it was never coming back. Two monstrous runs, one upriver then back down, and she was in the net." The fish was an impressive 9-pound, 27 $^{1}/_{2}$-inch cuttbow, one of the most impressive trout I've seen in Colorado.

EGG PATTERN FISHING STRATEGIES

First and foremost, do not fish to trout on redds. Fishing to spawning fish is unethical and has a negative impact on the natural recruitment of our precious gamefish. If you are new to the sport of fly fishing, have someone educate you on what a redd looks like. Redds are spawning beds, little bowl-like depressions in the substrate that are typically lighter in color than the surrounding streambed. During the shoulder seasons, if you see fish in shallow water, it's safe to assume they are spawning and you should leave them alone. Please watch your step in shallow riffles, as you can easily step on redds and damage them without realizing it.

As you might imagine, egg patterns are most effective in riffled water below spawning flats. Egg-midge or egg-*Baetis* nymph combos are excellent tandem rigs between the latter part of February through April, and then again from late September until the middle part of November. Most anglers typically fish their egg patterns with a 9-foot, 4X leader because trout feeding on eggs are not leader-shy. The strikes are typically aggressive so you'll want use the heaviest tippet you can get away with. I routinely fish a three-fly tandem rig (an egg and two droppers), spacing my flies 6 to 8 inches apart, tying each dropper off the bend of the hook. I use 5X fluorocarbon tippet for my droppers. It is a good idea to keep your strike indicator adjusted to one and a half to two times the depth of the current you are fishing.

Anglers who think outside the box will find that egg patterns work well during other times of the year too. Egg-midge combos can be effective during the winter months when fishing traditionally starts to slow and the fish become lethargic. I have found egg imitations to be excellent attractors, which aids in drawing attention to your smaller midge imitations. Egg imitations can be especially effective when there are no evident hatches. "I use egg patterns in the winter when there is no obvious hatch, when I need to entice the fish into biting," Henderson says. "Opportunistic trout are always on the lookout for eggs and will rarely pass on the opportunity to eat one, especially when there are no bugs hatching. I can remember guiding on numerous occasions when switching to an egg pattern during the winter months saved the day."

Chartreuse eggs fish well during the high-water season, when you'll find off-colored water and tough fishing conditions. There have been days where I thought catching fish would be impossible because of the poor water quality, but to my surprise a chartreuse egg managed to somehow fool a few fish. I'll routinely drop a chartreuse Nuclear Egg off a pink San Juan Worm or Chamois Leech when the water is stained. I cannot even begin to tell you how many fish I have fooled with a chartreuse Nuclear Egg in Cheesman Canyon when the Denver Water Board raised the flow and the water turned murky.

OTHER PATTERNS

San Juan Worm (Red)

Originator: Steve Henderson variation of Paul Pacheco original
Tier: Steve Henderson

Hook: #12 Dai-Riki 135
Thread: Red 140-denier Ultra Thread
Abdomen: Red Ultra Chenille (standard)
Rib: Red Ultra Wire (Brassie)

Note: Effective color variations include fluorescent pink, wine, and earthworm brown.

Two-Tone San Juan Worm

Originator: Greg Blessing
Tier: Greg Blessing

Hook: #10-14 Dai-Riki 270
Thread: Brown and orange 140-denier Ultra Thread
Abdomen: Tan and maroon standard chenille

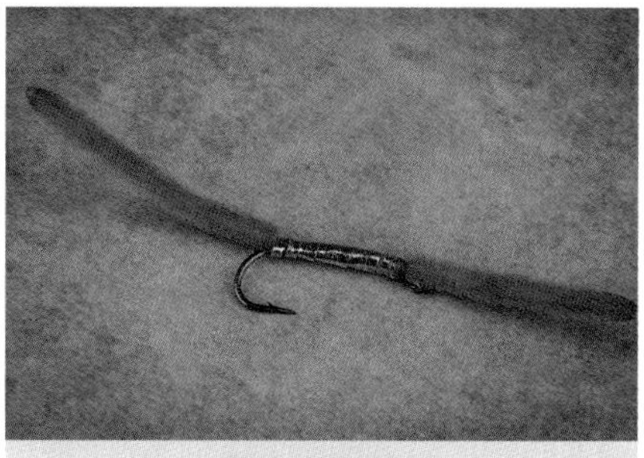

Flash Worm

Originator: Jeremy Hyatt
Tier: Jeremy Hyatt

Hook: #14 Tiemco 3761
Thread: Orange 6/0 Uni-Thread
Abdomen: Hareline earthworm brown chenille
Flash: Pearl Mylar tinsel (medium)

Red San Juan Worm

Originator: Mathew Thomas
Tier: Mathew Thomas

Hook: #14 Tiemco 2488H
Thread: Red 8/0 Uni-Thread
Abdomen: Red Ultra Chenille (medium)

Note: Taper end with cigarette lighter.

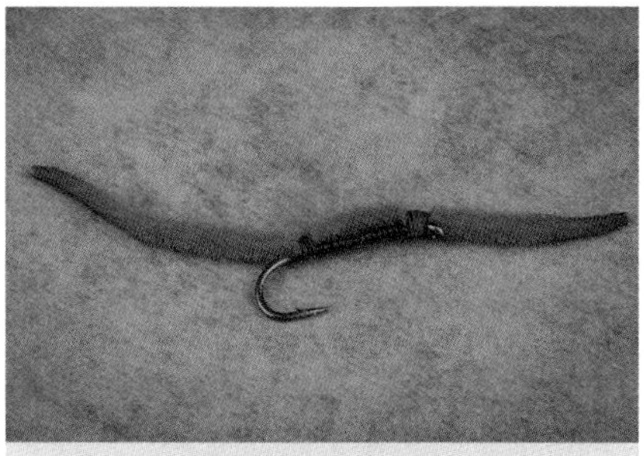

San Juan Worm

Originator: Variation of Paul Pacheco original
Tier: Tom Whitley

Hook: #14-18 Tiemco 5262
Thread: Brown Coats and Clark
Abdomen: Earthworm brown Ultra Chenille (standard)
Thorax: Fluorescent orange 6/0 Uni-Thread

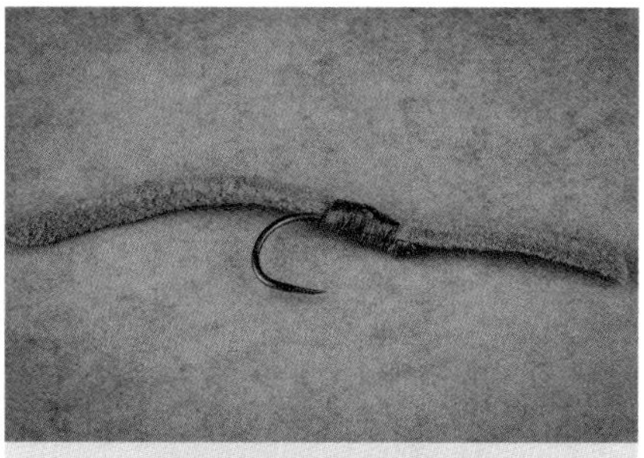

Cannon's Worm (Tan)

Originator: Jim Cannon
Tier: Jim Cannon

Hook: #14-16 Tiemco 2499SPBL
Thread: 3/0 orange Monocord
Abdomen: Chamois strip dyed earthworm brown
Thorax: Orange Scud Back (1/8")

Note: Color variations include red, tan, tan and red, brown and red.

Pig Sticker

Originator: Unknown
Tier: Chris Wells

Hook: #8-14 Mustad 37160
Body: Red 6/0 Uni-Thread
Band: Pink 6/0 Uni-Thread

Note: Color variations include brown and pink.

Kleistodon Worm

Originator: Jon Kleis
Tier: Jon Kleis

Hook: #12-14 Mustad 37160
Thread: Red 70-denier Ultra Thread
Thorax: Fluorescent pink 70-denier Ultra Thread
Body: Red Hareline Ice Stretch
Top Coat: Clear Cure Goo (thick)

McFly Foam Egg (Golden)

Originator: Unknown, variation of Glo Bug
Tier: Steve Henderson

Hook: #12-18 Tiemco 2488H
Thread: White 100-denier Ultra Thread Gel Spun
Abdomen: Orange McFly Foam

Note: Effective color variations include chartreuse, Oregon cheese, pink, and apricot.

Nuclear Egg

Originator: Walt Grau
Tier: Roger Bittell

Hook: #14-18 Dai-Riki 135 or Tiemco 2457
Thread: Orange 6/0 Danville
Nucleus: Dark orange McFly Foam
Halo: Candy Cane Glo Bug Yarn

Note: Egg or white Glo Bug Yarn will also work for the halo.

Two-Tone Gray and Tan Ray Charles

Originator: Greg Blessing
Tier: Greg Blessing

Hook: #16-18 Dai-Riki 60
Thread: Red 70-denier Ultra Thread
Abdomen: 1 gray and 1 tan Dan Bailey ostrich herl
Rib: Red Ultra Wire (small)
Backstrap: Flat pearl tinsel (large)
Hackle: Dark dun Whiting Hebert Miner

Rainbow Scud

Originator: Jeremy Hyatt
Tier: Jeremy Hyatt

Hook: #10-16 Tiemco 2457
Thread: Orange 6/0 MFC
Weight: .010" lead wire
Tail: Tan mallard flank
Shell Back: Tan Thin Skin
Abdomen: Rainbow Sow Scud Dubbing
Rib: 3X mono tippet

Stillwater Scud

Originator: Richard Pilatzke
Tier: Richard Pilatzke

Hook: #12-14 Dai-Riki 070
Thread: Olive 6/0 Uni-Thread
Tail: Mallard flank fibers
Rib: Silver Ultra Wire (Brassie)
Underbody: Two lengths of olive knitting wool, tied to hook shank and light olive UV Ice Dub wrapped over the wool
Overbody: Metallic twist ribbon, flattened and cut into a strip
Legs: Pick out the dubbing with a 22-caliber bore brush

Orange Scud (Orange)

Originator: Herman deGala
Tier: Herman deGala

Hook: #18-12 Tiemco 3761 #12
Thread: Trico 17/0 Uni-Thread
Antennae: Medium Coq de Leon
Eyes: 17# burnt mono
Underbody: Clear V-Rib (large)
Abdomen: Nymph Skin or $^{1}/_{8}$" latex strip from surgical glove
Legs: Amber ostrich herl

Note: Color abdomen with an AD chrome orange marker. Prior to whip-finishing, color the thread with the same marker to match body color. Olive is also effective.

Hot Spot Sow Bug (Gray)

Originator: Herman deGala
Tier: Herman deGala

Hook: #18-12 Tiemco 3761
Thread: Trico 17/0 Uni-Thread
Antennae: Medium Coq de Leon
Eyes: 17# burnt mono
Underbody: Lead substitute, smashed (large)
Abdomen: Nymph Skin or $^{1}/_{8}$" latex strip from surgical glove
Legs: Gray ostrich herl

Note: Color the abdomen with an AD cool gray marker. Prior to whip-finishing, color the thread with the same marker to match body color.

Scud

Originator: Josef Shafer
Tier: Josef Shafer

Hook: #16-18 Tiemco 100SPBL
Thread: Clear 4mm Uni-Mono (fine)
Shell Back: Olive black Thin Skin
Rib: 3X mono
Body: Olive brown Sow Scud Dubbing
Hot Spot: Bighorn orange Sow Scud Dubbing and hot orange UV Ice Dub (50/50 mix)
Eyes: Black Sharpie

Hunchback UV Scud

Originator: Michael McLellan
Tier: Umpqua Feather Merchants

Hook: #14-16 Tiemco 2457
Thread: Olive 70-denier Ultra Thread
Underbody: Lead tape cut to shape
Shell Back: Clear Scud Back ($^{1}/_{8}$")
Rib: Smoke mono thread (.006")
Abdomen: Olive UV Ice Dub
Hot Spot: Hot pink UV Ice Dub

Note: Color variations include tan and orange.

Smitty's Scud (Orange)

Originator: Randy Smith
Tier: Randy Smith

Hook: #10-18 Tiemco 2457 or 2487
Thread: Orange 6/0 Danville
Tail: Orange saddle fibers
Rib: 5X tippet
Shell Back: Ziploc bag strip
Abdomen: Orange Ligas Dubbing

Note: Pull legs down with a needle or gun brush. Trim to desired length. Color variations include tan and olive.

UV Scud (Orange)

Originator: Pat Dorsey
Tier: Pat Dorsey

Hook: #10-18 Tiemco 2457 or 2487
Thread: Orange 6/0 Danville
Tail: Orange Antron
Rib: 5X tippet
Shell Back: Ziploc bag strip
Abdomen: Shrimp pink UV Ice Dub
Antennae: Orange Antron

Note: Pull legs down with a needle or gun brush. Trim to desired length. Color variations include olive, dark olive, tan, and pink.

Scud (Tan)

Originator: Brian Kelso
Tier: Brian Kelso

Hook: #14-18 Hanak H300BL
Thread: Tan 70-denier Ultra Thread
Antennae: Natural Cul de Canard
Rib: Monofilament
Shell: Ziploc plastic bag
Dubbing: Red Squirrel Nymph Thorax Whitlock's SLF Dubbing
Hot Spot: Fluorescent hot pink Ice Dub
Legs/Collar: Natural CDC

Note: Pull dubbing fibers with dubbing brush to create legs. Color variations include orange and olive.

Chewy Scud

Originator: Steve Schweitzer
Tier: Steve Schweitzer

Hook: #12-18 Daiichi 1120
Weight: .010" or .015" lead wire
Thread: Gray 8/0 Uni-Thread
Body: UV olive Chewee Skin
Rib: 5X monofilament
Legs: Gray ostrich herl
Eye: Black Sharpie marker

Matt's Mysis

Originator: Matt Miles
Tier: Matt Miles

Hook: #16-20 Tiemco 200R
Thread: White 8/0 Uni-Thread
Tail: White Z-Lon or McFlylon
Abdomen: Pearl glass Spirit River glass beads (extra small)
Eyes: Burnt monofilament
Thorax: White ostrich herl

Mysis Shrimp

Originator: Mathew Thomas
Tier: Mathew Thomas

Hook: #18-20 Tiemco 3761
Thread: White 70-denier Ultra Thread
Tail: Translucent Spirit River Spectra Flash Mylar Motion
Abdomen: White Pearl Spirit River Magic Minnow Body
Legs: White Pearl Spirit River Magic Minnow Body
Shell Back: Translucent Spirit River Spectra Flash Mylar Motion
Antennae: Translucent Spirit River Spectra Flash Mylar Motion

Note: Coat antennae, shell back, and tail with five-minute epoxy.

Mysis Shrimp

Originator: Herman deGala
Tier: Herman deGala

Hook: #18-20 Tiemco 2487
Thread: Trico 17/0 Uni-Thread
Antennae/Tail: Medium Coq de Leon
Abdomen: Hareline Clear Tubing (medium), threaded with medium Coq de Leon and UV Knot Sense
Legs: White Fluoro Fibre
Eyes: 17# burnt mono
Hot Spot: Red Sharpie or red tinsel

Note: Color thread with an AD permanent marker to match body color.

Laney's Mysis

Originator: Josef Shafer
Tier: Josef Shafer

Hook: #14-22 Tiemco 200R
Thread: Clear 4mm Uni-Mono (fine)
Abdomen: Pearl Flashabou
Eyes: Black Wapsi round rubber legs (medium)
Head: Bright white Wapsi Antron and orange Super Hair
Shell: 5-minute epoxy or Loon UV Clear Fly Finish

Mayer's Mysis

Originator: Landon Mayer
Tier: Umpqua Feather Merchants

Hook: #16-20 200R
Thread: 8/0 White Uni-Thread
Abdomen: Large Mylar tinsel
Eyes: Black rubber legs (medium)
Antennae: White Wiggly Hackle
Head: Mylar tinsel
Legs: White ostrich plume

McFlylon Mysis

Originator: Pat Dorsey variation of Randy Smith's Mysis
Tier: Pat Dorsey

Hook: #16-20 Tiemco 100
Thread: White 6/0 Danville
Tail: White McFlylon
Abdomen: White ostrich herl
Shell Back: White McFlylon
Eyes: Black Hareline Micro Tubing

BTS Mysis

Originator: Rob Kolanda
Tier: Solitude Fly Company

Hook: #16-22 Daiichi 1120
Thread: 2 lb. monofilament
Tail: White Super Hair
Abdomen: Pearl UV Ice Dub
Eyes: Black Midge Tubing
Antennae: White Super Hair

Note: Cover top of abdomen with clear hot glue.

Sands' Mysis

Originator: Will Sands
Tier: Umpqua Feather Merchants

Hook: #16-20 Tiemco 200R
Thread: Uni Mono
Underbody: Uni Mono
Abdomen: 5-minute Z-poxy
Eyes: Burnt 20 pound fluorocarbon (color ends with black Sharpie)
Antennae: White CDC cut short with wood duck shank extending over top
Feelers: White Z-Lon tied directly under eyes

Kleis' Mysis

Originator: Jon Kleis
Tier: Jon Kleis

Hook: #12-18 Tiemco 2487
Thread: White 14/0 Sheer
Antennae: White Widow's Web
Eyes: Purple round rubber legs (fine)
Thorax: White ostrich herl
Shell Back: Lagartun French Mini Flat Braid
Abdomen: Glow in the dark Flashabou
Rib: Silver Lagartun wire (extra small)
Tail: Lagartun French Mini Flat Braid

Note: Cover shell back with Clear Cure Goo (thick).

CHAPTER 7

Terrestrials and Their Imitations

Land-dwelling insects, or terrestrials—ants, beetles, hoppers, cicadas, and crickets—are also an important part of a well-rounded Colorado fly selection. Many anglers underestimate the importance of terrestrials because they are not present in the same concentrations as aquatic insects. In many cases, terrestrials become an important food organism, so fly fishers need to remain open-minded and pay close attention when they are present on the water.

Trout have become conditioned to look for terrestrials. Opportunistic trout will rarely refuse a grasshopper, cicada, beetle, or ant, even during selective feeding phases when they might be keying on midges or mayflies. "I look forward each year with great anticipation for the opportunities of fishing large terrestrial patterns," says Rick Takahashi. "I love to see a trout eagerly rise to the surface to take a grasshopper or to sip a diminutive ant in the surface film. Terrestrial patterns such as grasshoppers, beetles, ants, crickets, and other land-borne insects represent a larger meal or 'more bang for the buck' than the usual fare; the trout gains a greater reward for the energy spent."

Large terrestrials like Tak's Hoppers and Chernobyl Ant–type patterns are must-haves in your fly collection. They can be fished as a single dry fly or used for dry-and-dropper rigs.

Joe Johnson understands the importance of having a fly box filled with terrestrial imitations. Terrestrials will provide reliable surface activity near grassy banks and underneath overhanging bushes and trees.

Seasoned anglers know that terrestrial imitations produce reliable surface activity during the summer and autumn months along the edges of the stream, especially near grassy banks, underneath deadfalls, and below overhanging bushes and trees. Terrestrials can be found on the water any time during the day from midmorning to late evening, which increases the odds of trout eating them.

Terrestrials are an important part of a stillwater angler's fly selection too, as gusty upslope winds routinely blow these land-based critters into the water and produce a sizeable meal for opportunistic bank cruisers. "If I had one fly to fish anywhere on Colorado's lakes, it would be a black beetle," Rich Pilatzke says. "I have caught more fish in Colorado on my Colorado Crystal Beetle than any other fly. A Colorado Crystal Beetle is always the first dry fly out of my fly box."

Pilatzke believes that a beetle serves as a crossover imitation for a wide array of food organisms, including snails, any number of winged terrestrials such as wasps and houseflies, water boatmen, or aquatic beetles. Pilatzke also notes, "Terrestrials are extremely important on high-altitude lakes in Colorado because they do not contain *Callibaetis* mayflies, damselflies, dragonflies, and scuds. Terrestrial insects make up a large proportion of the food items eaten by trout in these waters from midsummer to early fall."

I learned the importance of ants and their imitations when I was ten years old from my uncle Jim Cantrall. His favorite fly was the Swayback Ant, a pattern that was developed by the caretaker of the Swayback Ranch, a private fishing club located a few miles downstream from the town of Deckers. Uncle Jim was a Cheesman Canyon regular and the Swayback Ant was one of his favorite flies during the summer and autumn months. He consistently fooled trout with a Swayback Ant on other rivers too, especially the Arkansas and Roaring Fork.

As a young boy, it didn't take me long to figure out why ants were so effective. On just about any lake or stream, I noticed ants crawling on the ground or on nearby foliage. When you really look for them, it's an eye-opening experience; the numbers of ants crawling around can be mind-boggling. Try walking through a dense stand of willows or trees during the summer months, and you'll see exactly what I'm talking about. You'll find ants crawling all over your shirt by the time you reach the river.

Unlike many anglers who learn to tie a Gold-Ribbed Hare's Ear or a San Juan Worm as their first fly, my uncle taught me how to tie the Swayback Ant. It had a simple thread-body construction, consisting of a black abdomen, a red thorax, and a red head. The legs were composed of three turns of brown rooster between the thorax and the head. I tied dozens of them and my dad and I fished them hard on lakes and streams throughout Colorado.

My dad has been fishing Uncle Jim's Swayback Ant for years as one of his go-to flies during the summer months in the Gunnison Valley. I can vividly remember my dad hooking and landing a 25-inch brown trout on the Gunnison River at the Lost Canyon Resort with one of Uncle Jim's Swayback Ants. My dad fishes the Swayback Ant as a wet fly, down and across, and allows the fly to swing in the current. Most of the strikes occur on the swing, when his fly gently lifts towards the river's surface. My dad has fooled fish after fish on the Swayback Ant. Tie some up—you'll be pleasantly surprised with how well they perform!

Black ants are also an important part of your terrestrial fly selection. My stomach pump samples prove that trout eat a considerable amount of black ants during the summer months. I have fooled countless trout on the lower Blue River and other freestone streams with drowned black ant imitations. I tie them similar to the Swayback Ant, but in smaller sizes (18-20) with a black abdomen, black thorax, and black head. Similar to the Swayback Ant, I use a brown rooster hackle to simulate the legs. I drown my black ant imitations with a conventional nymphing rig, typically fishing them mid-column. Fishing drowned ants has been a guide secret for years.

Hopper fishing in July and August can be some of the most exciting dry-fly fishing of the summer season. Hopper imitations are especially effective on windy days when the naturals get blown into the river.

Small meandering meadow streams are prime areas to fish with grasshopper imitations. South Park's Tarryall Creek, the Middle and South Forks of the South Platte, Four Mile Creek, and Charlie Meyers State Wildlife Area are excellent hopper streams. According to Landon Mayer, "Hoppers on the Dream Stream [Charlie Meyers State Wildlife Area] can be a very exciting topwater bite if you time it correctly. Prime season is from July through late September, with August being the best month."

The terrestrial fishing on noted freestones like the Colorado, Gunnison, Roaring Fork, Arkansas, and Colorado is not shabby either. Greg Felt says that "Many segments of the Arkansas River have a rich riparian belt that is home to hoppers, beetles, ants, etc. A check of stomach contents from a sample of fish in July and August will show that some fish make quite a bit out of this food source and others do not. Most often I would tie those results to location of fish. So that would be the fishery answer. The fishing answer would be a lot more emphatic. Trout, and especially brown trout, are opportunists and will take anything that is plausible and presented correctly. As a result, ArkAnglers guides do a lot of dry and dry-dropper fishing during those months. We aren't casting to rising fish. We are fishing the structure or to parked fish that we have sighted and then bringing them up."

The Gunnison Gorge is known for its reliable hopper fishing from mid-July through late August. "Historically hopper fishing in the Gunnison Gorge starts around the second week in July and ends near the second half of August," says Ben Olson. "At the beginning and end of the hopper season we tend to fish a dropper but when it is in full swing all you need is a single fly. Much like the Salmonfly hatch your fly needs to be close to the banks. My ideal conditions for hopper fishing are gusty days. Anytime a hopper jumps on a windy day he gets swept into the river. My go-to patterns are size 6-10 Yeager's Tantrum (red, tan, or green), Schroeder's Hopper (olive or tan), and the Charlie Boy Hopper (green and tan)."

Any trout stream surrounded by dense forestland becomes a good candidate for fishing a beetle imitation. It's hard to go wrong with a size 16 foam beetle, especially in shallow riffles underneath pine trees and overhanging bushes, as trout are opportunistically looking for beetles during the summer and autumn months. Unlike grasshoppers, beetles are poor swimmers. They should be presented on the dead drift instead of being twitched or skated like many other terrestrials. It is not uncommon for beetles to get swept underwater, especially in the faster reaches of a stream, so nymphing a drowned beetle is another option.

TERRESTRIAL FISHING STRATEGIES

Most anglers fish their terrestrial imitations with a 9-foot leader terminating in 3X or 4X tippet. As a general rule, trout and other Colorado gamefish are not leader-sensitive when it comes to fishing terrestrials; therefore, anglers should use the largest tippet they can get away with and still get strikes. Occasionally you'll get an aggressive strike, so it's to your advantage to use heavier tippet to avoid any potential risk of a breakoff.

While most trout fooled with terrestrials are near the streambank or underneath bushes and trees, don't rule out fishing a grasshopper, beetle, or ant in the middle of the stream from time to time. Terrestrials have wings; therefore, they may be found anywhere in the stream. It is entirely possible to encounter hatchlike conditions in which swarms of terrestrials arrive on the water's surface at the same time. Beetle, ant, hopper, cricket, or cicada infestations, heavy wind, ranchers haying their pastures (thus forcing hoppers and other terrestrials to migrate to other areas)—all can produce large concentrations of terrestrials heavy enough at times to create a feeding frenzy.

The carpenter ant, *Camponotus pennsylvanicus*, produces epic dry-fly fishing during the summer on the San Juan River. Aaron Carithers, Durango-based guide and owner of Anasazi Angler, states, "The black carpenter ant is about three-quarters of an inch long and winged. The first hard rain of the early summer, typically the last week of June to the third week of July, triggers the mating cycle, which brings the swarmers out of the colony where they couple and many of them fall into the water, where they trigger a surface-feeding frenzy. The fish eat nearly every bug with little hesitation. This can occur a few times with each proceeding rain event with fewer ants falling each time. An angler can fish nearly any big black dry-fly pattern. I fish a size 8 or 10 black Stimulator with a white tuft of hair tied on top of the black wing."

Terrestrials also tend to fish well during non-hatch periods, when aquatic insects are inactive. "As the complex hatches of summer die off, the trout are still in the mood to look up and will usually not shy away from a big meal," says Landon Mayer. Strikes can vary between explosive, splashy rises to slow, confident riseforms. Most of the time, however, trout take terrestrials slow and with confidence. Trout have become accustomed to terrestrials being helpless and generally do not take them aggressively. The slow, confident riseform presents the greatest challenge because anglers often set the hook too early, resulting in a missed opportunity. "I always warn my clients about the slow rise," says Josh Cranson, head guide for Black Canyon Anglers. "Sometimes the fish will put his nose right under the fly and drift with it a bit before slowly eating it, or sometimes giving it a bump and then turning away and then coming back for the take. It's important to let the fish eat your fly and turn its head down before setting the hook."

Greg Felt offers some tips for fishing terrestrials during high summer flows: "With the swift and turbulent water that

Opportunistic trout will rarely refuse the chance to eat a grasshopper. Some of my favorite hopper imitations include: Joe's Hopper, Dave's Hopper, Madam X, Schroeder's Hopper, Charlie Boy Hopper, and Stalcup's Hopper.

Josh Cranson fooled this Gunnison River brown trout with a Charlie Boy Hopper. Guides like Cranson prefer using foam hoppers because they are extremely durable and float better than hopper imitations tied with fur and feathers.

characterizes much of the Arkansas, there is a real emphasis on lead dries that are visible and buoyant—hence, a reliance on patterns like Parachute Madam Xs, foam hoppers, Parachute Hoppers, and Stimulators. That swift and turbulent summer flow also pushes a lot of browns out to the edges which is why a single large dry will take a lot of fish that are not otherwise rising—they are in shallow water and will move on whatever comes into their window. This is attractor fishing that preys on a fish's gullibility and greed." Anglers can also try a tandem-rig approach: "The other terrestrial approach is to trail representations of the smaller classes of bugs—the beetles and ants—and fish them behind something a little bigger and more visible. For this, small unadorned ants are my favorite. Guests have to learn to take a field view of the water rather than focusing on a single spot (like a Thingamabobber) and watch for subtle movement, but I have seen a lot of really nice fish taken in the midday heat off a slightly submerged ant fished downstream toward structure from a boat. They see the ant first and just gently take it."

With modern synthetic fly-tying materials (such as foam bodies, rubber legs, and McFly Foam), one can easily be led to believe that not all hopper imitations are created equal. For instance, some hoppers are more durable than others, some float better than others, some are easier to see, and so on. Foam patterns seem to be the guide's preference these days, as they are extremely durable and simply float better. In the Gunnison Gorge, Josh Cranson prefers to fish with foam patterns like the Charlie Boy Hopper, Amy's Ant, the B/C Hopper, and Yeager's Tantrum. "These foam patterns float a lot longer, if not all day," Cranson says. "With Class 2 and 3 rapids to deal with while rowing my clients, the more maintenance-free fly patterns there are the better for me."

Landon Mayer agrees: "I prefer 'low riders,' foam-body flies that do not rely on hackle or other materials to achieve a quality float on the surface. They are visually easy to see and produce a realistic silhouette to the trout below. It's hard to go wrong with Charlie Boy Hopper, Fat Albert, or an Amy's Ant on the Dream Stream."

Slapping your foam hopper on the water is often an effective strategy. Grasshoppers are bulky and heavy, and when they fall to the water the "splat" on the surface draws the attention of opportunistic trout. If the trout are not showing any interest in your terrestrial pattern, try twitching it. I have found this to be especially effective with hopper imitations. Trout will oftentimes refuse dead-drifted offerings until you impart action into them by skating or skittering them and mimicking the lifelike movement of a natural hopper. Skated or skittered flies can produce aggressive strikes when the trout feel their food is trying to escape them. "The key to hopper fishing in the Gunnison Gorge is a half-inch twitch," Ben

Olson says. "Once the fish get stung a few times you will not get them to eat without a twitch."

Greg Felt agrees. "We've come to realize that at the appropriate times of year on the Arkansas River, hopper imitations are observed by the fish on nearly every drift," Felt says. "We can't see the fish but they are watching the fly. They may be skeptical, like it's too good to be true, and they may have been stung by a few big attractors already that season. However, we've found that a little bit of motion—not a strip, just a twitch—will appeal to the predatory instinct in a way that the dead-drifted fly will not."

"South Park is known for its heavy winds, especially at the Dream Stream, where wind gusts up to 10 to 20 miles an hour are not uncommon," Mayer says. "While most anglers try to put the wind at their back for protection, when delivering hoppers you want to face the wind and cast to the bank where the gusts are blowing into the river. This is where the natural grasshoppers will land on the edge, making it an easy meal. The other benefit of drifting on the gusty bank is that the high grass will offer some protection for a more natural drift."

Hopper-dropper combinations (dry-and-dropper rigs) have become popular in recent years. John Barr popularized the hopper-copper-dropper combo a few years back. In *Barr Flies* he states, "When there are no rising trout, fishing a Copper John behind a B/C Hopper is one of my favorite approaches spring through fall. The Copper John sinks rapidly and is an effective pattern on its own. You can also add a third fly to this rig, dropped off the bend of the Copper John, that imitates the prevailing natural such as a *Baetis* or PMD nymph or emerger."

This is a versatile rig wherein the hopper becomes the strike indicator, allowing anglers to fish one or two nymphs below it. Dry-and-dropper rigs cater to fly fishers who like to fish skinny water where traditional nymphing rigs tend to spook trout or get hung up. They are especially effective for guides who regularly fish from drift boats or inflatable rafts because they can fish a variety of water. For instance, anglers can pound the banks, fish shallow riffles, and drift their flies over midchannel shelves, all with the same rig. It's a no-brainer rig, requiring very little maintenance, which is important for guides steering watercraft. Guides can fine-tune the sink rate of the droppers by adding additional tippet or by using either brass or tungsten beads (tungsten sinks quicker) or heavily weighted nymphs to get the flies drifting mid-column.

Stillwater enthusiasts can opt to fish terrestrials from the bank, personal watercraft, or powerboats. Motorized boats offer a distinct advantage because anglers can change locations quickly and can get off the water if the wind picks up abruptly. Rich Pilatzke fishes his terrestrials with a 9-foot, 5-weight rod: "I tend to fish my terrestrials, especially the larger ones, on a 2X tippet. I generally use an 8- to 10-foot leader and don't give the fly much motion. I will typically give my fly a little twitch just after it lands and then let it sit stationary. If I do not get any strikes, I twitch the fly and repeat the process as needed."

Sight-fishing to suspended trout is an effective method for targeting fish with terrestrials. Your odds go up dramatically if your flies are in front of trout. Once again, if the fish do not take your fly, twitch it in order to draw attention to your fly. If you opt to fish blind, cover the water methodically. Fish all the likely spots, including the downwind shoreline, the banks, and underneath trees and bushes.

TERRESTRIALS

Black Ant

Originator: Steve Henderson
Tier: Steve Henderson

Hook: #16-18 Tiemco 100
Thread: Black 8/0 Uni-Thread
Abdomen: Black Superfine
Hackle: Brown Whiting Farms rooster saddle
Wing: Medium dun Z-Lon
Legs: Black Krystal Flash
Thorax: Black Krystal Flash
Head: Black Superfine

Chernobyl Ant

Originator: Mark Forslund
Tier: Steve Henderson

Hook: #6-10 Tiemco 5263
Thread: Black 140-denier Ultra Thread
Underbody: Grizzle saddle palmered over black hare's mask dubbing
Overbody: Black foam (2mm), two layers
Legs: Grizzly round rubber
Indicators: Yellow and orange foam (2mm)

Tak's Foam Carpenter Ant

Originator: Rick Takahashi
Tier: Rick Takahashi

Hook: #10-16 Tiemco 2302
Thread: Black 8/0 Uni-Thread
Body: Black foam (2mm)
Hackle: Brown Whiting Farms saddle hackle
Wing: Clear Medallion Sheeting
Legs: Black round rubber (medium)

Amy's Ant

Originator: Jack Dennis
Tier: Umpqua Feather Merchants

Hook: #4-12 Tiemco 5263
Thread: Brown 6/0 Uni-Thread
Underbody: Tan foam
Overbody: Brown foam
Legs: Brown rubber (medium)
Hackle: Brown rooster
Abdomen: Olive Krystal Chenille
Underwing: Rainbow Krystal Flash
Wing: Light elk hair
Thorax: Arizona Peacock Dubbing

Paintbrush ICU Ant

Originator: Richard Pilatzke
Tier: Richard Pilatzke

Hook: #12 Fenwick barbless
Thread: Black 6/0 Uni-Thread
Body: 1/8" Evasote foam cut into a strip and formed into 3 segments
Legs: 2 nylon paintbrush bristles, glued with liquid Krazy Glue
Indicator: Yellow Evasote 1/8" foam

Note: Apply a drop of liquid Krazy Glue to the base of the indicator to increase durability.

Snake River Chernobyl Ant

Originator: Mark Forslund and Alan Woolley
Tier: Richard Pilatzke

Hook: #8-10 Dai-Riki 730
Thread: Fire orange 6/0 Uni-Thread to match body color
Underbody: Orange craft foam (2mm)
Overbody: Black craft foam (2mm)
Legs: Black round rubber (medium)
Indicator: Yellow craft foam (2mm)

Note: Change the underbody colors to imitate golden stoneflies, hoppers, crickets, and cicadas.

Cupboard Ant

Originator: Mike Kruise
Tier: Mike Kruise

Hook: #18 Tiemco 100
Thread: Black 70-denier Ultra Thread
Abdomen: Black shelf and drawer liner
Legs: Grizzly Whiting Farms rooster

The Bloody Ant

Originator: Dr. Eric Pettine
Tier: Dr. Eric Pettine

Hook: #18-20 Tiemco 101
Thread: Black 16/0 Tiemco
Back Hackle: Black midge hackle
Abdomen: Rusty orange Hare 'E Ice Dub
Thorax: Red Holo Tinsel
Head: Blood black Hare 'E Ice Dub
Front Hackle: Black midge hackle

Los Alamos Ant

Originator: Harrison Steeves
Tier: Dick Shinton

Hook: #12-16 Dai-Riki 280
Thread: Fluorescent orange 70-denier Ultra Thread
Tail: Orange/black Hareline striped rubber legs (medium)
Underbody: Peacock herl
Abdomen: Tan closed-cell foam (2mm)
Overbody: Yellow closed-cell foam (2mm)

Flip Flop Ant

Originator: Harrison Steeves variation
Tier: Dick Shinton

Hook: #14-18 Tiemco 100
Thread: Black 70-denier Ultra Thread
Tail: Pearl Krystal Flash
Underbody: Black 70-denier Ultra Thread
Abdomen/Head: Black Wapsi foam cylinder ($^{1}/_{8}$")
Hackle: Black Whiting Farms rooster

Carl's Foam Ant

Originator: Carl "Boomer" Stout
Tier: Umpqua Feather Merchants

Hook: #12-18 Tiemco 101
Thread: Black 6/0 Uni-Thread
Underbody: Peacock herl
Overbody: Black craft foam
Wing: Medium dun hen hackle tips
Legs: Black round rubber legs (small)
Indicator: Orange EVAZOTE foam tied with orange thread and colored with a black Sharpie on the bottom

AC's Ant Thrax

Originator: Aaron Carithers
Tier: Aaron Carithers

Hook: #10-12 Tiemco 200R
Thread: Black 6/0 Uni-Thread
Underbody: Peacock herl and grizzly rooster
Abdomen: Black craft foam (2mm)
Underwing: Brown Krystal Flash and dark gray Antron
Wing: Coastal deer hair
Legs: Black medium rubber legs
Collar: Grizzly rooster
Head: Gray foam

Tak's San Juan Ant

Originator: Rick Takahashi
Tier: Rick Takahashi

Hook: #10-16 Tiemco 2302
Thread: Black 8/0 Uni-Thread
Body: Black foam (2mm)
Wing: Bleached elk
Legs: MFC speckled black and brown legs

Tak's SJ Ant

Originator: Rick Takahashi
Tier: Rick Takahashi

Hook: #10-16 Tiemco 9300
Thread: Black 8/0 Uni-Thread
Underbody: Black foam (2mm)
Abdomen: Black foam (2mm)
Wing: Deer hair
Legs: Medium round rubber
Head: Black foam (2mm)

Chernobyl Black Ant

Originator: Rick Takahashi variation of Mark Forslund original
Tier: Rick Takahashi

Hook: #10-16 Tiemco 2302
Thread: Black 8/0 Uni-Thread
Underbody: Dun Whiting Farms Midge Saddle Hackle
Abdomen: Black foam
Legs: Black round rubber legs (medium)
Indicator: Yellow foam (2mm)

John's Black Ant

Originator: Alan Woolley
Tier: Rick Takahashi

Hook: #10-16 Tiemco 9300
Thread: Black 8/0 Uni-Thread
Underbody: Black 8/0 Uni-Thread
Abdomen: Black Evazote
Indicator: Red foam (1mm)
Legs: Black round rubber (medium)

Woolley's Chernobyl Ant

Originator: Alan Woolley
Tier: Rick Takahashi

Hook: #10-16 Tiemco 9300
Thread: Black 8/0 Uni-Thread
Underbody: Black 8/0 Uni-Thread
Abdomen: Black Evazote
Indicator: White foam (1mm)
Legs: Black round rubber (medium)

Tak's Winged Black Ant

Originator: Rick Takahashi
Tier: Rick Takahashi

Hook: #10-16 Tiemco 2302
Thread: Black 8/0 Uni-Thread
Underbody: Black 8/0 Uni-Thread
Abdomen: Black foam (2mm)
Wings: White Antron
Indicator: Red foam (1mm)
Legs: Black round rubber (medium)

B 3 Bomber

Originator: Bubba Smith
Tier: Bubba Smith

Hook: #8-16 Tiemco 5212
Thread: Black 6/0 Uni-Thread
Underbody: Peacock herl
Abdomen: Black craft foam (2mm)
Thorax: Peacock herl
Wing: White poly yarn
Hackle: Brown Whiting Farms rooster
Legs: MFC red/black Centipede Legs (medium)

Note: Color variations include brown and tan.

San Juan River Ant

Originator: Bubba Smith
Tier: Bubba Smith

Hook: #10-14 Tiemco 5212
Thread: Black 6/0 Uni-Thread
Underbody: Black 6/0 Uni-Thread
Abdomen: Black craft foam (2mm)
Wing: White poly yarn
Hackle: Brown Whiting Farms rooster
Legs: MFC white/black Centipede Legs (medium)

Black Foam Ant

Originator: Bubba Smith
Tier: Bubba Smith

Hook: #10-14 Tiemco 5212
Thread: Black 6/0 Uni-Thread
Underbody: Black 6/0 Uni-Thread
Abdomen: Black craft foam (2mm)
Wing: White poly yarn
Hackle: Brown Whiting Farms rooster

Psycho Ant

Originator: Bubba Smith
Tier: Bubba Smith

Hook: #6-10 Orvis 1225
Thread: Black 6/0 Uni-Thread
Underbody: Purple peacock herl
Abdomen: Black craft foam (2mm)
Underwing: UV pearl Krystal Flash
Wing: White poly yarn
Legs: MFC white/black and orange/black Centipede Legs (small)
Hackle: Brown Whiting Farms rooster

Swayback Ant

Originator: Unknown
Tier: Pat Dorsey

Hook: #14-18 Tiemco 5262
Thread: Black 6/0 Uni-Thread
Abdomen: Black sewing thread
Thorax: Black sewing thread
Hackle: Brown rooster
Head: Black sewing thread

Note: Color variations include red head/thorax with black abdomen.

Parachute Hopper

Originator: Ed Shroeder
Tier: Umpqua Feather Merchants

Hook: #8-14 Tiemco 5212
Thread: Tan 140-denier Ultra Thread
Abdomen: Tan Antron dubbing
Rib: Rust brown 140-denier Ultra Thread
Wing: Turkey tail
Legs: Pheasant tail fibers, knotted
Post: White calf tail
Hackle: Grizzly Whiting Farms rooster
Thorax: Tan Antron dubbing

Takahopper

Originator: Variation of Ed Shenk's Letort Hopper
Tier: Rick Takahashi

Hook: #14-16 Tiemco 2303 or Dai-Riki 280
Thread: Yellow 3/0 Monocord
Abdomen: Golden yellow Fly Rite Dubbing
Underwing: MFC Wing Material
Overwing: Natural deer hair
Head: Natural deer hair, clipped

Tak's Hapa Hopper

Originator: Rick Takahashi
Tier: Rick Takahashi

Hook: #8-12 Tiemco 5263
Thread: Hopper Yellow 70-denier Ultra Thread
Abdomen: Natural round rubber leg
Rib: Brown Whiting Farms Midge Saddle
Underwing: Amber Blue Ribbon Z-Lon yarn
Legs: Natural round rubber legs, colored with black and red Sharpie
Head/Wing Cover: Tan foam (2mm)
Indicator: Fluorescent orange acrylic paint

Chubby Chernobyl

Originator: Idylwilde Flies
Tier: Idylwilde Flies

Hook: #4-16 Tiemco 5263 or Dai-Riki 710
Thread: Tan 140-denier Ultra Thread
Tail: Yellow Krystal Flash
Underbody: Tan Thin Fly Foam added for buoyancy (size 10 and larger)
Abdomen: Tan SLF Prism Dubbing
Overbody: Tan foam (2mm)
Wing: White McFlylon
Legs: Brown Sili Legs

Parachute Madam X

Originator: Doug Swisher
Tier: Idylwilde Flies

Hook: #12-18 Tiemco 100 or Dai-Riki 305
Thread: Black 70-denier Ultra Thread
Tail: Natural elk
Underbody: Natural elk wrapped to mid shank
Abdomen: Peacock herl and brown rooster
Rib: Copper Ultra Wire (extra small)
Wing: Natural elk
Post: White McFlylon
Hackle: Brown rooster

Fo-low Rider (Yellow)

Originator: Cody Scott
Tier: Cody Scott

Hook: #14-16 Tiemco 200R or Dai-Riki 270
Thread: Black 8/0 Uni-Thread
Abdomen: Yellow 2mm Fly Foam
Underwing: Rainbow pearl Krystal Flash
Wing: Tan Fly Foam (2mm)
Thorax: Black Superfine
Legs: Wapsi Brown barred round rubber legs
Indicator: White Fly Foam (2mm)

Note: Wing cut with River Road Creations Hopper Wing Cutter. Color variations include green and tan.

Foamex

Originator: Richard Pilatzke
Tier: Richard Pilatzke

Hook: #8-10 Dai-Riki 070
Thread: Yellow 6/0 Uni-Thread
Tail: Orange deer hair
Underbody: Yellow craft foam (2mm)
Overbody: Whitetail deer
Legs: Yellow/black MFC Centipede Legs

Hoppin John (Yellow/Tan)

Originator: Richard Pilatzke
Tier: Richard Pilatzke

Hook: #8-10 Dai-Riki 730
Thread: Chartreuse 6/0 Uni-Thread to match body color
Underbody: Yellow craft foam (2mm)
Overbody: Tan craft foam (2mm)
Rear Legs: Tan craft foam (2mm)
Legs: Tan/black MFC Centipede Legs
Indicator: Orange craft foam (2mm) tied over the legs

Note: Thread is wrapped along shank and covered with liquid Krazy Glue prior to tying down the underbody. Underbody and overbody are cut with Beavertail RRC cutter; rear legs cut with RRC small hopper leg cutter. Color variations include black/brown (cricket imitation) or tan/yellow, green/yellow, brown/yellow (hopper imitations).

Madonna's Bloomers

Originator: Richard Pilatzke
Tier: Richard Pilatzke

Hook: #8-10 Dai-Riki 730
Thread: Fire orange 6/0 Uni-Thread
Tail: Tan marabou fibers
Underbody: Yellow craft foam (2mm)
Overbody: Red craft foam (2mm)
Legs: Wapsi Orange round rubber
Indicator: Yellow craft foam (2mm)

Note: Apply liquid Krazy Glue to the base of the indicator for durability.

Mormon John

Originator: Richard Pilatzke
Tier: Richard Pilatzke

Hook: #6-8 Dai-Riki 700
Thread: Black 6/0 Uni-Thread
Underbody: Brown craft foam (2mm)
Overbody: Black craft foam (2mm
Rear Legs: Black craft foam (2mm
Front Legs: Black Rainy's round rubber legs (medium)
Indicator: 2mm strip of yellow craft foam

Note: Underbody and overbody are cut with medium RRC Beavertail cutter; rear legs cut with medium RRC hopper leg cutter. Apply liquid Krazy Glue to the base of the indicator for durability.

Charlie Boy Hopper (Tan)

Originator: Charlie Craven
Tier: Charlie Craven

Hook: #8-12 Tiemco 100
Thread: Tan 3/0 Monocord
Body: Thin Fly Foam (2mm)
Legs: Round rubber (medium)
Wing: Natural deer hair
Eye: Black Sharpie

Note: Color variations include yellow and olive.

Baby Boy Hopper

Originator: Charlie Craven
Tier: Charlie Craven

Hook: #12-16 Tiemco 2499SPBL
Thread: Olive 14/0 Gordon Griffiths
Body: Chartreuse Thin Fly Foam
Legs: Lime green round rubber (medium)
Wing: Natural deer hock
Eye: Black Sharpie

Note: Color variations include tan and yellow.

Cricket Hopper

Originator: Charlie Craven
Tier: Charlie Craven

Hook: 12-16 Tiemco 2499SPBL
Thread: Black 14/0 Gordon Griffiths
Body: Black Thin Fly Foam
Legs: Black round rubber (medium)
Wing: Natural deer hock

Dickster Hopper (Tan)

Originator: Dick Shinton
Tier: Dick Shinton

Hook: #10-16 Tiemco 5212
Thread: Orange 6/0 Uni-Thread
Abdomen: Wapsi closed-cell foam cylinder
Underwing: Pearl Wapsi Wing N' Flash
Wing: Elk hair
Legs: Copper brown MFC Speckled Sexi-Legs

Note: Color variations include yellow and olive. Drill the foam cylinder with Laughing Grizzly Foam Drills.

Papa Ape

Originator: Larry Kingrey
Tier: Larry Kingrey

Hook: #8-10 Daichi 1750
Thread: Black 6/0 Uni-Thread
Tail: Cow elk
Abdomen: Wrightway Sports red, yellow, red laminated foam strip (3mm)
Wing: Cow elk
Post: Orange foam cylinder
Thorax: Peacock Cactus Chenille (midge)
Hackle: Grizzly rooster

Sweetgrass Hopper

Originator: Doug McKnight
Tier: Umpqua Feather Merchants

Hook: #8-12 Tiemco 5262
Thread: Yellow 140-denier Ultra Thread
Abdomen: Cream Fly Foam (2mm)
Legs: Tan and black barred rubber
Underwing: Tan Razor Foam (1mm)
Wing: Tan Neer Hair
Wing Case: Tan Razor Foam (1mm)
Eyes: Black permanent marker

Note: Color rear legs with a red permanent marker.

Thunder Thighs Hopper

Originator: Eric Paramore
Tier: Umpqua Feather Merchants

Hook: #8-14 Tiemco 5262
Thread: Tan 140-denier Ultra Thread
Body: Tan and brown Fly Foam (2mm)
Wing: White poly yarn
Indicator: Orange Fly Foam (2mm)
Thorax: Tan Buggy Nymph Dubbing
Legs: Tan Fly Foam (2mm) and tan Span Flex (upper half colored with brown Sharpie)
Eyes: Black Fly Foam (2mm)

Note: Yellow is also effective.

Fat Albert (Tan)

Originator: Brent Taylor
Tier: MFC

Hook: #4-10 Tiemco 5262
Thread: Chartreuse 140-denier Ultra Thread
Abdomen: Tan and brown craft foam (2mm)
Underwing: Pearl Flashabou
Wing: White McFly Foam
Legs: Olive Centipede Legs (small)

Note: Color variations include black, orange, and yellow. Hi-viz variations can be tied by using pink or chartreuse McFlylon.

Dave's Hopper

Originator: Dave Whitlock
Tier: Umpqua Feather Merchants

Hook: #12-18 Tiemco 5263
Thread: Tan 6/0 Uni-Thread
Tail: Red saddle hackle
Abdomen: Yellow wool yarn
Hackle: Brown saddle hackle, trimmed
Wing: Mottled turkey
Legs: Pheasant tail fibers, knotted at joint
Head/Collar: Spun natural deer hair

Hopper Juan

Originator: Juan Ramirez
Tier: Juan Ramirez

Hook: #8-12 Tiemco 3769
Thread: Tan 140-denier Ultra Thread
Abdomen: Tan and brown foam (2mm) with River Road Creations (Chernobyl taper cutter)
Underwing: MFC Mottled Web Wing Material River Road Creations (Stonefly Wing Cutter)
Legs: MFC speckled tan Rubber Legs
Flash: MFC pearl Krystal Flash (midge)
Wing: Select cow elk hair
Indicator: MFC hot pink Gator Hair

Note: Apply Krazy Glue to secure body to hook shank on all segments and on top of foam bullethead. Color variations include chartreuse/olive, black/orange, and yellow/tan.

Hollywood Hopper

Originator: Juan Ramirez
Tier: Juan Ramirez

Hook: #8 MFC 7022
Thread: Sand 8/0 MFC
Abdomen: Tan/peach foam (2mm)
Wing: Brown foam (1.5mm)
Legs: Tan MFC barred rubber legs. Rear legs colored with red permanent marker
Indicator: Pink foam (1.5mm)
Eyes: Brown on olive Hoppize (3.5mm)

Note: Body formed from foam (2mm), two sheets glued together with 3M Super 77, then folded and glued together again to form an 8mm piece with a rounded edge. Cut a strip 1/4" wide. Body length is 26mm long. Foam is placed on top of hook and glued to hook shank with Krazy Glue. Color variations include tan/tan, pink/tan, purple/black, and olive/tan. Cut the indicator with a small Chernobyl cutter; cut the wing with MFC Stonefly Wing Cutter (#8).

Stalcup's Hopper

Originator: Shane Stalcup
Tier: Umpqua Feather Merchants

Hook: #12-22 Tiemco 5263
Thread: Tan 6/0 Uni-Thread
Abdomen: Tan Fly Foam (2mm)
Wing: Hopper tan Medallion Sheeting
Thorax: Tan foam (2mm)
Back Legs: Clear tubing, serrated with hemostats with red ostrich herl inserted. Knot tubing at leg joint.
Front Legs: Tan rubber legs (medium)
Head/Collar: Deer hair
Indicator: Orange Fly Foam (2mm)

Keeler Bug

Originator: Jin Choi
Tier: Jin Choi

Hook: #8-12 Tiemco 200R
Thread: Fluorescent green 140-denier Ultra Thread
Abdomen: Peacock herl and grizzly hackle
Underwing: Black foam (2mm) with yellow foam cylinder (3/16")
Wing: Black Krystal Flash and bleached elk hair
Legs: Yellow barred black Sili Legs
Hackle: Black rooster

Cartoon Hopper

Originator: Bubba Smith
Tier: Bubba Smith

Hook: #8-10 Orvis 1225
Thread: Tan 6/0 Uni-Thread
Underbody: Purple peacock herl
Abdomen: Tan and brown craft foam (2mm)
Underwing: UV pearl Krystal Flash
Wing: White and orange poly yarn
Legs: MFC tan/black Centipede Legs (small)
Thorax: Peacock Ice Dub
Hackle: Brown Whiting Farms rooster
Eyes: Plastic eyes from a craft store

Back Swimmer

Originator: Richard Pilatzke
Tier: Richard Pilatzke

Hook: #14 Dai-Riki 305
Thread: Black 6/0 Uni-Thread
Tail: Pearl Krystal Flash (three strands)
Underbody: Pearl/black Hareline Speckled Chenille
Overbody: Self-adhesive craft foam (2mm) with metallic rainbow Staedler hot foil pen refill applied and the Mylar backing peeled off
Legs: Black goose biots

Heavy Metal Beetle (Green)

Originator: Richard Pilatzke
Tier: Richard Pilatzke

Hook: #10-14 Dai-Riki 305
Thread: Black 6/0 Uni-Thread
Underbody: Lime/black Hareline Speckled Chenille
Legs: Black Crystal Flash, 3 strands
Back: Black adhesive foam (2mm) with Staedler Green Hot Foil Pen Refill applied to the surface and the Mylar covering removed
Indicator: Yellow Evasote foam (1/8") (liquid Krazy Glue applied to the indicator will increase durability)

Note: Color variations include blue, red, and oil slick back colors with appropriate color-coordinated underbody material to match the back.

Water Boatman (Black)

Originator: Richard Pilatzke
Tier: Richard Pilatzke

Hook: #10-14 Dai-Riki 305
Thread: Black 6/0 Uni-Thread
Tail: Pearl Krystal Flash (three strands)
Overbody: Black craft foam (2mm) cut into strip
Underbody: Silver tinsel chenille
Legs: Black goose biots

Note: Color variations include tan, brown, and olive.

Beetle

Originator: Tom Whitley
Tier: Tom Whitley

Hook: #14-18 Tiemco 2487
Thread: Black Coats and Clark
Underbody: Black Ice Dub
Abdomen: Black foam (2mm)
Post: Orange foam (2mm)

Hub's Gold Bow Tie Beetle

Originator: Jerry Hubka
Tier: Jerry Hubka

Hook: #14 Tiemco 2302
Thread: Black 70-denier Ultra Thread
Underbody: Red dyed peacock herl
Overbody: Northern Lights Wapsi Loco Foam (2mm)
Wings: Gold Spirit River Crystal Splash
Legs: Black Hareline Flex Floss
Shell Back: Northern Lights Wapsi Loco Foam (2mm)
Antennae: Black Krystal Flash
Indicator: Yellow 2mm craft foam
Adhesive: Zap-a-Gap and Clear Cure Goo Hydro

Note: Shell back is cut with River Road Creations #16 Beetle Body cutter. Color variations include pearl, black, and blue.

Adult Dragon Fly (Red)

Originator: Richard Pilatzke
Tier: Richard Pilatzke

Hook: #8 Dai-Riki 730
Thread: 6/0 Uni-Thread to match body color
Eyes: Plastic bead chain (5mm)
Underbody: Estaz to match body color
Wings: White twisted poly (macrame yarn) brushed out and barred with a black Sharpie
Abdomen: Craft foam (2mm) cut with a River Road Creations large damsel/dragon cutter and segmented with a black Sharpie

Note: Color variations include blue, green, and brown.

Neon Blue Adult Damsel

Originator: Richard Pilatzke
Tier: Richard Pilatzke

Hook: #12 Dai-Riki 730
Thread: Light blue 6/0 Uni-Thread
Eyes: Black plastic bead chain
Underbody: Sky blue twisted poly (macrame yarn)
Wings: White twisted poly yarn brushed out and barred with a Sharpie
Abdomen: Damsel blue craft foam (2mm) cut with a River Road Creations damsel body cutter and marked with a Sharpie to give body segmentation

Double Dragon

Originator: Richard Pilatzke
Tier: Richard Pilatzke

Hook: #10 Dai-Riki 700
Thread: Camel 6/0 Uni-Thread
Eyes: Black plastic bead chain (3mm), 2 pairs
Underbodies: Root beer Ice Chenille
Wings: White twisted poly, barred with a black Sharpie
Abdomens: Rust craft foam (2mm), cut out with a medium River Road Creations damsel/dragon cutter and marked with a Sharpie

Flash Damsel Nymph

Originator: Richard Pilatzke
Tier: Richard Pilatzke

Hook: #10-12 Dai-Riki 270
Thread: Olive 6/0 Uni-Thread
Tail: Olive marabou
Rib: Gold Ultra Wire (extra small)
Underbody: Olive knitting yarn
Eyes: Burnt 50-pound mono
Abdomen: Olive Superfine
Thorax: Olive Superfine
Wing Case: Metallic Twist Ribbon
Throat/Legs: Olive aftershaft fibers from saddle hackle

Hula Damsel

Originator: Herman deGala
Tier: Herman deGala

Hook: #16-18 Tiemco 2499
Bead: Gold brass or tungsten
Thread: Trico 17/0 Uni-Thread
Tail/Gills: Olive ostrich herl
Abdomen: Flymen Fishing Company Articulated Wiggle-Tail Shank with medium olive-brown D-Rib and olive ostrich herl
Joint: 3X fluorocarbon tippet
Wing Case: Olive brown Medallion Sheeting
Legs: CDC and light olive UV Ice Dub
Eyes: 50# burnt mono

Note: Color thread with an AD permanent marker to match body color. Use a $^{3}/_{32}$" bead for sizes 16-18.

CHAPTER 8

Attractors

Many anglers interpret the word *attractor* differently. Some think of an attractor as a large, brightly colored dry fly, while others think of it as the lead fly in a tandem nymphing rig. Still others argue that streamers are attractors because their main goal is to produce a reactionary strike.

The good news is that all of these interpretations are correct. Attractors—whether they're a dry fly, nymph, or streamer—are all designed to attract opportunistic trout. In many cases attractors do not represent a particular food item, but instead a variety of food organisms. For instance, a trout may eat a Stimulator because it thinks it is a caddis, Yellow Sally, or a grasshopper. Another example is John Barr's Meat Whistle—it can imitate a variety of baitfish, leeches, or crawfish depending on the retrieve. In other cases, an egg pattern or a San Juan Worm is an imitative pattern that routinely fools trout, but it also has a dual role of attracting fish to the dropper fly (or flies) in a tandem nymphing rig.

ATTRACTOR DRY FLIES

After staring at a strike indicator all season long, most anglers and guides welcome the opportunity to cast attractor dry flies during the latter part of the season. Like many of my

Mark Adams fights a powerful Gunnison River rainbow that he fooled with a size 12 Parachute Adams. Freestones like the Gunnison River are known for their superb attractor dry-fly fishing in July and August.

Fishing attractor dry flies becomes an effective strategy as soon as spring runoff subsides. Guides like Chris Wells look forward to fishing with attractors because opportunistic trout will rise and eat dry flies when there is no evident hatch.

colleagues, I consider attractor fishing a refreshing break from the day-in, day-out grind of nymph fishing. Attractor dry flies start to become a good option during the post-runoff period (late June) and continue to be effective through the autumn months.

"Fishing a size 12 or 14 attractor dry fly is wonderful fun. Fishing any dry fly is so incredibly visual that many fly anglers, me included, would never fish a nymph or streamer when trout can be caught on a dry fly, even if it means fewer fish caught," Dr. Eric Pettine says. "Best of all is having trout rise to a large dry fly. Seeing a big old trout rise out the depth and suck in a dry fly is almost a religious experience to most anglers. Yet few fly fishers seem aware that large attractor patterns can still catch a lot of trout when there is no hatch. Fishing an attractor dry fly is almost a lost art. Yet it is still an effective way to fish for trout, especially on our freestone waters in Colorado, once the trout are 'looking up.' My two favorites are a size 12 Rio Grande King and a Royal Wulff."

Attractor dry-fly fishing is effective for several reasons. First off, anglers can fish to less-pressured trout that hold in shallow water—those spots the average angler either overlooks or cannot fish because his nymphing rig either spooks trout or gets hung up on aquatic vegetation or on the substrate. Trout in these areas tend to be less suspicious of overhead threats and will typically feed with confidence on dry flies. Anglers who fish with attractors can probe a variety of water with one simple rig.

Trout feeding on attractors eat opportunistically, which simplifies your fly selection and eliminates the need to match a specific hatch. Attractor dry flies imitate a wide array of food organisms from mayflies to terrestrials and everything in between. As far as the trout is concerned, it looks like food so they eat it. "As a wild brown trout fishery situated in a relatively steep gradient and therefore subject to a swift current velocity, the Arkansas River can be something of a 'seller's market' when it comes to presentation," Greg Felt says. "Many of these browns are conditioned to be opportunistic and impulsive, living a life where they do not have time or inclination to inspect everything that they eat." You'll need the approximate right size, shape, and color, but your success usually does not hinge on choosing only one fly.

Attractors' size also benefits anglers. You can quickly tie your fly on without magnification aids, and you're fishing a fly that is extremely visible at all times, which increases your odds of hooking and landing more trout. There is nothing more frustrating than an inability to see a small dry fly on the water, which of course ultimately affects your productivity. In all likelihood, if you cannot see your fly, you're going to miss most of your strikes. Many attractors are brightly colored, incorporating calf hair wings and posts into their design, or they have high-visiblity posts or indicators made out of McFlylon, which makes them easier to see in harsh light, foam lines, or choppy currents.

And finally, your hookup-to-landing ratio is generally much better with larger flies. You tend to lose considerably more trout on smaller dry flies, especially size 18 and smaller. If you are consistently losing fish, you might want to increase the size of your attractor and see if that makes a difference.

In a *Fly Talk* blog post titled "Tip: Spread Out Your Cast When Fishing Attractor Dry Flies (*Field and Stream*)," my longtime friend and Colorado-based angler Kirk Deeter states, "I've learned that there is a subtle difference between fishing with dry flies when you are matching a hatch, and fishing with attractor dry flies. With imitations of natural bugs, you want to mix in with the real things, and pinpoint your casts in very precise spots like on the current seams and bubble lines where the hatch is concentrated. With attractors, you want to space things out a bit, not only to cover more water, but also to keep the fish guessing." So you'll want to use different attractor patterns to trigger an opportunistic feeding response.

Fishing an attractor is a good tactic when the trout have been accustomed to feeding on the surface. For instance, Amy's Ant is effective for a few days to several weeks after a stonefly emergence. The same holds true with caddisfly hatches: I have found Puterbaugh's Foam Caddis to fish well for up to a month after the hatch.

Attractors also fish well during non-hatch periods when there is a noticeable shortfall of aquatic insects, forcing the trout to feed opportunistically. This is especially true during the dog days of August when the water gets warm, trout become finicky and sluggish, and hatches are sporadic. "The fish hit these flies purely as a reaction to something that looks too good to let pass by," Deeter says. Beetles, grasshoppers, and ants routinely fill an important void between the summer hatches of PMDs and Green Drakes and the autumn hatches of Blue-Winged Olives. As we discussed earlier, opportunistic trout will rarely refuse the chance to grab a hearty meal if the opportunity presents itself.

Size 12-18 Royal Wulffs, H&L Variants, Limeades, Renegades, Para Wulffs, Humpies, Stimulators, and Parachute Adams are some of my favorite attractors. Trout consistently rise to these patterns in riffled currents, glassy pools, runs, tailouts, and pocket water after the high-water season subsides. Many of the hard-to-get-to spots that were eliminated by spring runoff now become prime areas to target with attractors.

I grew up fishing attractors like the H&L Variant, Orange Asher, and Renegade on the Gunnison watershed. By the latter part of July and continuing through August, nymphing was rarely a consideration on the Taylor, East, and Gunnison

This brown trout fell for a size 12 Limeade on the Taylor River. Opportunistic trout will rarely refuse the chance to eat large dry flies, especially during the summer season when Green Drakes are present.

Joe Johnson methodically covers the water with an attractor dry fly on the Fall River in Rocky Mountain National Park. Showing your dry fly to as many fish as possible is one of the key ingredients for success when you are targeting opportunistic feeders.

Rivers. Toss in the smaller streams that the area is known for, such as Brush, Cement, Slate, Tomichi, and Cocheptopa Creeks, and the dry-fly fishing experience was generally nothing short of excellent. My dad fooled fish after fish on Renegades. I could hardly tie them fast enough for him. It seemed like the more beat up they got, the better they worked.

ATTRACTOR DRY-FLY FISHING STRATEGIES

I recommend fishing your attractor dry flies on the dead drift with a 9-foot leader terminating with 3X to 5X tippet. Once again, try to use the largest tippet you can get away with and still get strikes. If you are getting refusals, consider decreasing the size of your tippet or the size of your fly. In most cases, this will take care of any problems that arise with refusals so long as you are getting a good dead drift. In a few cases, imparting action or skittering or twitching your attractors can be an effective strategy, especially with grasshopper imitations.

The most effective strategy when fishing attractor dry flies is to methodically cover the water, showing your fly to as many fish as possible. "Ideally, you want your fly to just 'appear' and the fish to suddenly see it and decide to eat it," Deeter says. "If the fish sees something slowly sweeping back and forth in the near distance, chugging its way downstream like it's on a pendulum, that's not going to work." Don't pound the same piece of water over and over again. Your best chance to fool a fish with an attractor is on your first drift through any given area. Keep moving and covering new water at all times.

According to Greg Felt, "It is not always evident what fish are eating, if anything particular, or even what type of water they are occupying. An attractor pattern can then be a good way to search the river, covering a fair bit of water, different depths, speeds, structure, and drifts, and offering the fish something plausible. If that works, then trailing more imitative patterns behind it may help an angler stay engaged and tuned in while figuring out if there is something more specific that the fish are actually eating."

Attractors can be fished upstream, downstream, up and across, or down and across. I vary my presentation based on the water type and delivery that I am looking for. For instance, in pocket water I typically fish my attractors upstream, working the water systematically, fishing all the likely spots in which you would expect to find trout. I recommend hopscotching from one pocket to another, starting with the closest pocket, then wading into that pocket after you have fished it. Repeat this process as you move upriver. With this approach, you're only standing in the fast water when you are navigating between pockets, which allows you to take full advantage of the current break provided from the boulder above.

In the softer currents, like those found along the river's edge, a reach mend will help you achieve a drag-free float.

The reach mend is typically used in conjunction with a down-and-across delivery, which allows the fly to end up above your fly line. As the fly floats downriver, the first thing that comes into the trout's window of vision is the fly—not the tippet, leader, or fly line, which can easily put the fish down.

ATTRACTOR NYMPHS AND STREAMERS

Many anglers opt to use an attractor in their nymphing rigs to draw attention to their dropper flies. As a general rule, an attractor nymph is typically larger than the dropper fly (or flies), and in many cases, it is flashy or brightly colored. It's good practice to change your attractor with the season or as the conditions change. For instance, during the winter months, I might use a flashy midge or micro-egg pattern as my attractor. Egg patterns are a no-brainer during the shoulder seasons when the trout are spawning and the fish are keying on eggs. As previously discussed, egg-midge or egg-*Baetis* nymph combinations are one of my go-to rigs in March and April and then again in September and October.

In May when caddis hatches are prevalent I often fish with a caddis larva or pupa as my attractor; June is an excellent month to use a stonefly nymph as an attractor, and so on. A bright pink worm or chamois leech is a good attractor in dirty water. I think you get my point—attractor nymphs can be an effective strategy if you're willing to put some thought into your fly selection.

Greg Felt has an interesting interpretation with regard to attractors: "The word attractor brings two different concepts to mind: 1) flies that are not clear-cut imitations of any particular insect, or even order of insects, and 2) flies that are physically manipulated on the water to literally attract a fish's attention," Felt says. "Certainly both interpretations are of utility on the Arkansas River. A good example of the former would be the Pheasant Tail Nymph. On the Arkansas, size 10-12 Pheasant Tails could be taken as stonefly nymphs; a size 14-16 could be a cased caddis or caddis pupa; an 18-20 would be a mayfly nymph. It's not an exact representation of any of them, but it's close enough to work well during much of the season. A lot of our 'meat-and-potatoes' nymphs work that way—the Hare's Ear, Copper John, Prince Nymph, and Pheasant Tail families of flies."

Imparting action into a fly, such as by allowing a caddis pupa to swing in the current, skittering a hopper, or stripping a streamer, will generally entice a fish to strike your fly. "Streamers would be the obvious example of flies that are manipulated to attract a fish's attention. Yes, they represent baitfish, but the only significant forage fish we really have on the Arkansas are baby trout (there are few suckers, dace, or sculpins). Some of the streamers we use could represent a fingerling brown but most do not. Rather it is the action that attracts the fish. I think of a resting brown trout like a big dog lying on the sidewalk. If you walk slowly and calmly around him he won't even get up. But if you run past him, he may chase you. That's how it is with streamers here and the reason we strip them and impart a lot of action. We're not asking the trout to inspect it—we are appealing to his predatory instincts at a level that he can't control."

Attractor nymphs do not require any special tactics or techniques. Follow the same guidelines we discussed earlier for fishing nymphs. Vary your tippet size based on the current conditions, clarity of the water, size of the fly and fish. Make adjustments as necessary. Your dropper selection should match the prevailing hatches; in other words, if there are midges or Blue-Winged Olives present, fish the appropriate imitations.

Attractor nymphs help draw attention to your dropper flies, as they are typically larger and brighter in color than your dropper. Steve Henderson's San Juan Worm box allows him to be prepared for a variety of conditions.

ATTRACTOR PATTERNS

Bunny Sculpin

Originator: Steve Henderson
Tier: Steve Henderson

Hook: #4-6 Tiemco 777SP
Thread: White 140-denier Ultra Thread
Eyes: $^{3}/_{16}$" black brass dumbbell
Belly: Flesh Hareline bunny strip
Back: Barred olive Hareline bunny strip
Lateral Line: Black Krystal Flash, five strands
Pectoral Fins: Red Sparkle Braid and barred sand Hareline bunny strip

Mohair Bugger (Olive/White)

Originator: Steve Henderson
Tier: Steve Henderson

Hook: #4-8 Tiemco 5623
Weight: .035" lead
Thread: Dark brown 140-denier Ultra Thread
Tail: Yellow over ginger marabou
Body: Hare's ear dubbing
Hackle: Grizzly Whiting Farms pro grade dry-fly cape
Rib: Copper Ultra Wire (Brassie)

Note: Effective color variations include brown/orange.

Zonker (White)

Originator: Dan Byford
Tier: Umpqua Feather Merchants

Hook: #4-6 Tiemco 5253
Thread: White 140-denier Ultra Thread
Weight: .025" lead
Belly: Pearl Mylar tubing (medium)
Wing: White Hareline bunny strip
Eye: Yellow paint with black pupil

Note: Effective color variations include natural and black.

Kelley's Pond Special

Originator: John Keefover
Tier: John Keefover

Hook: #6-8 Tiemco 5262
Thread: White 6/0 Uni-Thread
Underbody: .010" lead wire
Tail: White rabbit
Abdomen: UV pearl Frizzle Chenille
Overwing: White Hareline barred rabbit strip
Head: Black 6/0 Uni-Thread

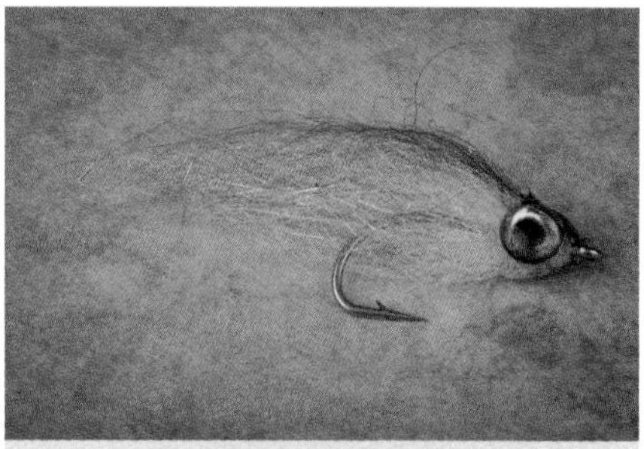

Tak's Mini Minnow

Originator: Rick Takahashi
Tier: Rick Takahashi

Hook: #8 Tiemco 811S (800S)
Thread: White 140-denier Ultra Thread
Abdomen: Senyo's White Laser Dub
Dorsal: Hareline Custom Blend Dragon Olive Dub
Eyes: Metz $^{1}/_{8}$" molded eyes
Head: Tack Free Clear Cure Goo

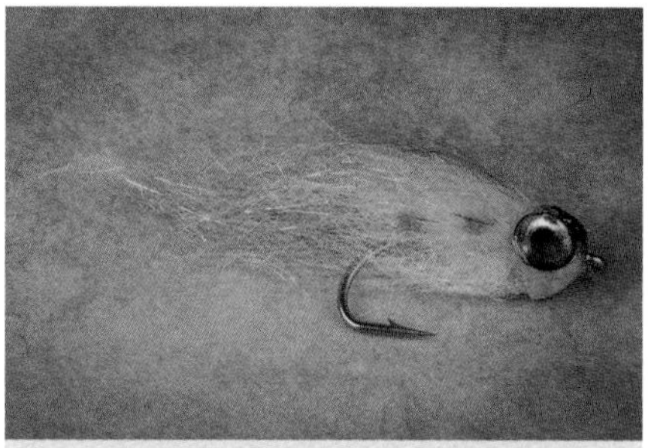

Tak's Rainbow Mini Minnow

Originator: Rick Takahashi
Tier: Rick Takahashi

Hook: #8 Tiemco 811S (800S)
Thread: White 140-denier Ultra Thread
Abdomen: Senyo's White Laser Dub
Dorsal: Hareline Custom Blend Dragon Olive Dub
Lateral Line: Senyo's Pink Laser Dub
Eyes: Metz $^{1}/_{8}$" molded eyes
Head: Tack Free Clear Cure Goo

Note: Make several parr marks along the pink lateral line with light blue permanent marker.

Tak's White Ghost Streamer

Originator: Rick Takahashi
Tier: Rick Takahashi

Hook: #4-10 Daiichi 1750
Thread: White 70-denier Ultra Thread
Cone: Silver or black MFC with eyes
Tail: White marabou
Flash: Pearl Krystal Flash
Abdomen: Pearl Estaz (medium)
Hackle: White schlappen
Topping: Mallard
Wing: Natural deer hair
Collar: Pearl Ice Dub

Note: Use large cone for sizes 4-6 and medium for sizes 8-10.

Equalizer

Originator: Eric Atha
Tier: Eric Atha

Hook: #8-10 Tiemco 8089
Thread: Chartreuse 3/0 Uni-Thread
Cone: Copper (medium)
Underbody: Chartreuse MFC UV Frog's Hair Dubbing
Abdomen: Chartreuse Hareline extra-select marabou
Flash: Pearl Spirit River Mylar Motion (12 strands)
Thorax: Chartreuse MFC UV Frog's Hair Dubbing

Stanley Steamer

Originator: Jim Stanley
Tier: Eric Atha

Hook: #6-8 Tiemco 5263
Bead: Gold tungsten
Thread: Black 6/0 Uni-Thread
Tail: Peacock sword (12 strands)
Abdomen: Peacock herl
Wing: Peacock herl (blue feathers from eye)
Beard: Natural mallard flank

Note: Use a 3/16" bead for size 6 and 5/32" for size 8.

Platte River Dirty Hippy

Originator: Charlie Craven
Tier: Charlie Craven

Hook: #4-8 Tiemco 5263
Weight: .030" lead wire
Thread: Yellow 3/0 Monocord
Cone: Copper tungsten or brass
Flash: Copper, gold, and pearl Flashabou
Wing: Brown and yellow marabou
Collar: Orange Arctic fox faced with brown Arctic fox
Eyes: 3-D Holographic Gold

Note: Cone guidelines: Large for sizes 4-6 and medium for sizes 8-10.

Double Gonga (Black)

Originator: Charlie Craven
Tier: Charlie Craven

Thread: Black 3/0 Monocord
Back Hook: #4 Tiemco 5262
Tail: Black marabou
Hackle: Black saddle hackle or schlappen
Body: Peacock black Ice Dub
Connection: 50# Fire Line, with four green 6/0 glass beads
Front Hook: #4 Tiemco 5262
Eyes: Lead eyes (medium), painted green with black pupil
Tail: Black marabou
Hackle: Black saddle hackle or schlappen
Body: Peacock black Ice Dub
Legs: Green and black Chrome Sili Legs
Collar: Black Polar Fiber
Head: Black Polar Fiber

Note: To form the head, spin the Polar Fibre in a dubbing loop and trim to shape. Color variations include olive, rust, tan/yellow.

Thin Mint

Originator: Unknown
Tier: Umpqua Feather Merchants

Hook: 6-10 Tiemco 5263
Bead: Gold tungsten
Thread: Black 6/0 Uni-Thread
Tail: Black, olive, and brown marabou
Abdomen: .020" lead wire and peacock herl
Rib: Pearl tinsel, gold Ultra Wire (small)
Hackle: Brown rooster

Note: Use a 3/16" bead for size 6, 5/32" for sizes 8-10.

Olive Slump Buster (Olive)

Originator: John Barr
Tier: Umpqua Feather Merchants

Hook: #4-10 Tiemco 5263
Thread: Olive 70-denier Ultra Thread
Cone: Gold tungsten
Abdomen: Peacock Sparkle Braid
Rib: Chartreuse Ultra Wire (Brassie)
Wing: Olive pine squirrel
Collar: Olive pine squirrel

Note: Color variations include rust, black, and natural. Cone guidelines: Large for sizes 4-6 and medium for sizes 8-10.

Ella's Beast

Originator: Josef Shafer
Tier: Josef Shafer

Hook: #8-10 Tiemco 5263
Bead: Orange tungsten (3.5mm)
Thread: Olive 70-denier Ultra Thread
Tail: Olive/brown marabou
Abdomen: Olive brown Orvis Scud Dubbing, Hareline olive brown UV Polar Chenille

Egg Butt Blue Trout

Originator: Dr. Eric Pettine
Tier: Dr. Eric Pettine

Hook: #6-10 Tiemco 5263
Stinger Hook: Gamakatsu #02308
Thread: Black 70-denier Ultra Thread
Egg: Deep red McFly Foam
Tail: Black guinea hackle
Abdomen: Blue Holographic Flash
Underwing: Blue squirrel tail
Wing: Blue Holographic Flash, blue and black ostrich herl
Head: Black zonkered squirrel

Note: Attach stinger with .015" Beadalon Wire.

Zombie Daddy

Originator: John Perizzolo
Tier: John Perizzolo

Hook: #8-10 Umpqua C400BL
Bead: Nickel tungsten (4mm)
Thread: Chartreuse 6/0 Uni-Thread
Tail: Glow in the dark green Flashabou
Abdomen: Rusty brown and dark olive strung marabou blood quills
Thorax: Chartreuse Ice Dub
Collar: Color tying thread black with a Sharpie

Pop's Bugger (Copper)

Originator: Mark Miller
Tier: Umpqua Feather Merchants

Hook: #6-12 Tiemco 5263
Bead: Gold brass
Thread: Rusty brown 6/0 Uni-Thread
Tail: Olive and brown marabou with UV copper Krystal Flash
Abdomen: Brown/dark olive Speckled Chenille
Hackle: Olive Palmer Chenille (small)

Note: Color variations include black, olive, purple, olive/black, copper/olive, and black/chartreuse. Use a 3/16" bead for size 6, 5/32" for sizes 8-10, and 1/8" for size 12.

Conehead Wool Sculpin (Black)

Originator: Mike Lawson
Tier: Umpqua Feather Merchants

Hook: #4-6 Tiemco 5263
Thread: Black 6/0 Uni-Thread
Cone: Black or gold
Tail: Rabbit fur strip over black Krystal Flash
Abdomen: Black rabbit
Gills: Red wool
Pectoral fins: Black hen
Head: Black spun wool, clipped to shape

Note: Other effective colors are tan and olive. Use large cones for sizes 4-6.

Meat Whistle (Crawdad)

Originator: John Barr
Tier: Umpqua Feather Merchants

Hook: #3/0-1/0 Gamakatsu 90-degree jig hook
Thread: Rusty brown 140-denier Ultra Thread
Cone: Copper (extra large)
Rib: Copper brown Ultra Wire (Brassie)
Abdomen: Copper Diamond Braid
Wing: Rust rabbit strip
Legs: Pumpkin barred Sili Legs
Flash: Copper Flashabou
Collar: Brown marabou

Note: Color variations include black, white, olive, and ginger.

Sculpzilla

Originator: Solitude Fly Company
Tier: Solitude Fly Company

Main Hook: #1/0 Tiemco 811S
Cone: Black Spirit River 3/8" Cross Eyed Cone
Eyes: Red 3D Eyes
Trailing Hook: #4 Gamakatsu Octopus
Connection: 20-pound Dacron
Thread: Black Monocord
Abdomen: White Ice Dub
Wing: Black rabbit strip
Gills: Red guinea body feather
Skirt: Black marabou
Collar: Black chickabou

Note: Cut the 811S off at the bend once the fly is complete.

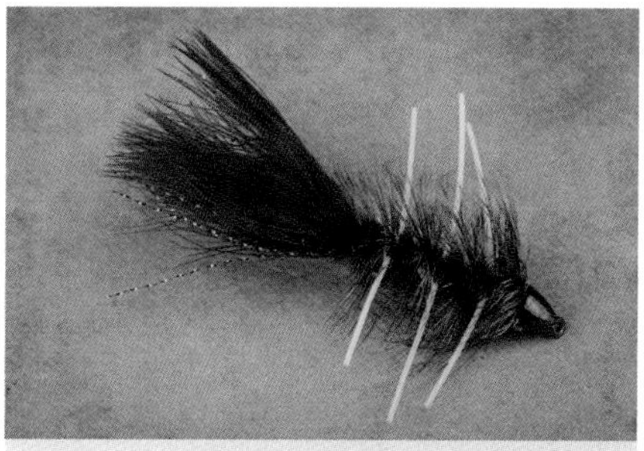

Autumn Splendor

Originator: Tim Heng
Tier: Umpqua Feather Merchants

Hook: #4-10 Tiemco 5263
Cone: Copper
Weight: .030" lead wire
Thread: Brown 6/0 Uni-Thread
Tail: Brown marabou with copper Krystal Flash
Abdomen: Brown Chenille (medium)
Rib: Copper Ultra Wire (small)
Hackle: Orange and olive dyed grizzly
Legs: Yellow round rubber legs

Crystal Bugger (Olive)

Originator: Variation of Raymond Blessing original
Tier: Umpqua Feather Merchants

Hook: #4-10 Tiemco 5263
Bead: Gold brass or tungsten
Weight: .020" lead wire
Thread: Olive 6/0 Uni-Thread
Tail: Olive marabou with olive Krystal Flash
Abdomen: Olive pearl Chenille (medium)
Hackle: Olive saddle hackle

Note: Use a 3/16" bead for sizes 4-6 and 5/32" for sizes 8-10. Color variations include black and brown.

Tungsten Streamer Nymph

Originator: Brian Kelso
Tier: Brian Kelso

Hook: #10-12 Tiemco 3761SPBL
Bead: Black tungsten
Thread: Black 140-denier Ultra Thread
Tail: Black Mini Marabou
Abdomen: UTC Ice Blue Tinsel (Large)
Thorax: Black Micro Polar Chenille
Collar: Black CDC coated with thinned head cement

Note: Color variations include olive. Use a 5/32" bead for size 10 and 1/8" for sizes 12.

Minkie Variant

Originator: Brian Kelso
Tier: Brian Kelso

Hook: #8-12 Umpqua C900BL
Thread: Black 140-denier Ultra Thread
Tail: Fluorescent chartreuse Mini Marabou
Abdomen: Black Micro Polar Chenille
Underwing: Silver Krystal Flash
Wing: Black Pine Squirrel Zonker strip
Collar: #12 fluorescent chartreuse Datum Glo-Brite Floss, varnished

Note: Colors variations include red marabou and #3 fluorescent red Datum Glo-Brite Floss for collar.

Black Bunny Buster (Black)

Originator: Chris Wells
Tier: Chris Wells

Hook: #6-10 Tiemco 9395
Weight: .025" lead wire
Eyes: Silver barbell lead eyes
Flash: Pearl Krystal Flash
Tail/Body: Black bunny strip

Note: Color variations include olive and rust.

Bellyache Minnow

Originator: Rob Kolanda
Tier: Solitude Fly Company

Hook: #1/0-4 Gamakatsu SC15
Weight: Tungsten fly hump
Thread: Tan 6/0 Danville
Tail: Black barred over gold variant rabbit hide
Abdomen: Pearl Ice Dub (use dubbing loop and brush out)
Thorax: Rusty brown Ice Dub (use dubbing loop and brush out)
Gills: SLF fiery blood red dubbing
Eyes: 3D Eyes #948 coated with epoxy

Lunch Money (Tan)

Originator: Matt Bennett
Tier: Matt Bennett

Hook: #2-6 Gamakatsu B10S
Eye: Gold painted lead (extra small, small for #2)
Thread: Olive 140-denier Ultra Thread
Tail/Collar: Hareline gold variant black barred rabbit strip
Legs: Olive Barred Nymph Sili Legs
Head: Dark tan, tan, and sculpin olive Senyo's Laser Dub

Note: Color variations include olive, shad, rust, sculpin, easter bunny, fire tiger, and chartreuse.

Secret Weapon

Originator: Tyler Befus
Tier: Tyler Befus

Hook: #10-12 Tiemco 100SPBL
Bead: Brass or tungsten
Thread: Olive 70-denier Ultra Thread
Tail: Chartreuse grizzly marabou
Abdomen: Chartreuse grizzly marabou wrapped
Rib: Copper Ultra Wire (small)
Wing: Chartreuse grizzly marabou
Legs: Chartreuse barred Sili Legs
Thorax: Chartreuse Ice Dub

Note: Use a 5/32" bead for size 10 and 1/8" for sizes 12-14.

Squirrely Minnow

Originator: Brad Befus
Tier: Brad Befus

Hook: #8-10 Tiemco 9395
Thread: Olive brown 140-denier Ultra Thread
Cone: Brass or tungsten
Body: Cream Soda Sparkle Leech Dubbing
Wing: Natural pine squirrel
Legs: Pumpkin Sili Legs
Collar: Grizzly dyed hen saddle (one olive and one brown)

Note: Use a medium cone for sizes 8-10.

Spun Bunny Muddler

Originator: Steve Schweitzer
Tier: Steve Schweitzer

Hook: #6-12 Tiemco 5263
Thread: Tan 6/0 Uni-Thread
Tail: Natural rabbit fur
Abdomen: Golden brown Ice Dub
Underwing: Pearl Holographic Mylar Motion
Wing: Lemon wood duck or dyed mallard flank
Head: Spun bunny fur

Note: Head is formed from spun bunny fur, in a dubbing loop. Cut half of the spun fur down to form the head, leaving the other half to flow back over the body.

Pine Squirrel Leech (Gray)

Originator: Seth Kapust
Tier: Bob Dye

Hook: #8-14 Tiemco 200R
Thread: Gray 8/0 Uni-Thread
Tail: Natural Hareline Micro Pine Squirrel Strip
Abdomen: Natural Hareline Micro Pine Squirrel Strip
Head: Fluorescent orange 8/0 Uni-Thread

Note: Effective color variations include brown, rust, and black.

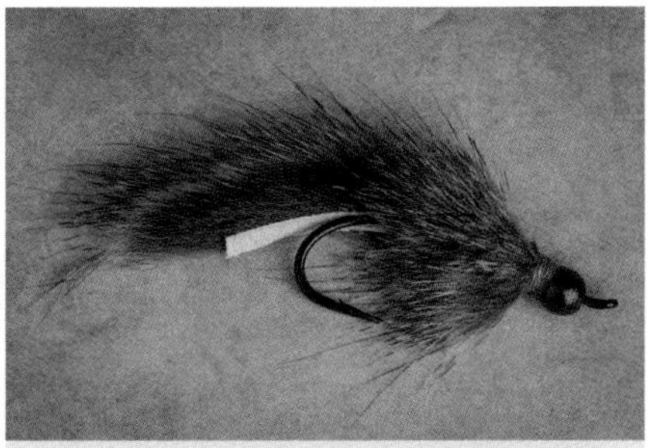

J's Egg Sucking Pine Squirrel Leech

Originator: J Core
Tier: J Core

Hook: #8-10 Dai-Riki 899
Bead: Red tungsten
Thread: Fluorescent fire orange 140-denier Ultra Thread
Abdomen: Natural pine squirrel strip

Note: Use a 5/32" bead for sizes 8-10.

Lead Headed Leech

Originator: Cody Scott
Tier: Cody Scott

Hook: #8-12 Fly Tying Specialties European Competition Streamer Hook
Weight: Gold dumbbell eyes (small)
Thread: Black 3/0 Danville Waxed Monocord
Tail: Natural pine squirrel strip
Underbody: Orange standard Ultra Chenille
Thorax: Pearl Flashabou covered with Clear Cure Goo Hydro
Collar: Natural pine squirrel strip

Beadhead Squirrel Leech (Olive)

Originator: Charlie Craven
Tier: Charlie Craven

Hook: #12 Tiemco 2488H
Bead: Gold tungsten
Thread: Olive 6/0 Uni-Thread
Flash: Single strand Mottled Gold Flashabou
Tail: Olive squirrel strip
Collar: Olive squirrel fur, spun in a dubbing loop

Note: Use a 1/8" bead for size 12 color variations include black and rust.

Mini Leech (Black)

Originator: Landon Mayer
Tier: Umpqua Feather Merchants

Hook: #16-18 Tiemco 2488H
Thread: Black 8/0 Uni-Thread
Abdomen: Black Krystal Flash
Body: Black Micro Pine Squirrel
Thorax: Black ostrich herl

Note: Color variations include brown and gray.

Articulated Leech (Black)

Originator: Umpqua Feather Merchants
Tier: Umpqua Feather Merchants

Front and Rear Hooks: #2-8 Tiemco 7999
Eyes: Bead chain
Thread: Black 6/0 Uni-Thread
Back Abdomen: Black marabou
Lateral Line: Black Accent Flash
Front Abdomen: Black marabou

Note: Connect Tiemco 7999 behind another 7999 hook w/twisted stainless steel wire. Color variations include olive and rust.

Goat Leech (Black)

Originator: Umpqua Feather Merchants
Tier: Umpqua Feather Merchants

Hook: #8-10 Tiemco 5262
Thread: Black 140-denier Ultra Thread
Underbody: .020" lead wire
Tail: Black marabou with red Krystal Flash
Abdomen: Dubbing loop with black African goat combined with red and black Angel Hair

Note: Color variations include brown, olive, claret, and gray.

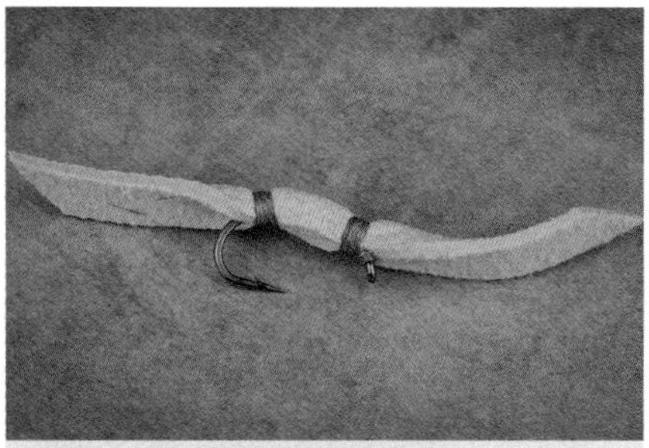

Chamois Leech

Originator: Variation of Paul Pacheco San Juan Worm
Tier: Pat Dorsey

Hook: #10-12 Tiemco 2457
Thread: Tan 6/0 Uni-Thread
Abdomen: Chamois strip

Chamois Leech

Originator: Dick Shinton
Tier: Dick Shinton

Hook: #12-14 Tiemco 200R
Thread: Red 70-denier Ultra Thread
Underbody: Peacock herl
Abdomen: Buckskin strip, 1/8" wide

CHAPTER 9

Presentation: Mastering Nymph, Dry-Fly, and Streamer Tactics

A good presentation is ultimately the underlying factor for success on any body of water. Presentation is an accumulation of skills that include understanding entomology, choosing the appropriate fly, reading the water, wading, and executing the proper techniques to catch fish under a wide range of conditions. The goal of a good presentation is to deliver your artificial flies (nymphs, dry flies, wet flies, or streamers) in a manner in which they look and behave like the naturals in the water you're fishing.

The ultimate goal in fly fishing is becoming a well-rounded angler. Being able to execute a wide variety of fly-fishing disciplines—fishing nymphs, dry flies, wet flies (soft hackles), and streamers—will no doubt add to the enjoyment and productivity of your angling experience. There are many schools of thought with regard to equipment and terminal tackle options, so you'll have to study them carefully and experiment with them yourself before you come to any conclusions. Hopefully some of my thoughts and the comments from the professional guides will help you gain a better understanding of the products that are available.

NYMPH FISHING

Entomologists believe that somewhere between 80 and 90 percent of a trout's diet occurs subsurface, which emphasizes the importance of nymph fishing. The word nymph has several meanings and can be interpreted differently depending on how it is used. As a noun, it can mean the premature aquatic stage of an insect that passes through incomplete metamorphosis. This would include those aquatic insects with three stages of development: egg, nymph, and adult.

The immature stage of an insect that passes through complete metamorphosis is referred to as a larva. These insects have four phases in their life cycle: egg, larva, pupa, and adult. While not technically correct, anglers use the word nymph as a general term that refers to any fly that is fished subsurface. In Nymph-Fishing Rivers and Streams, Rick Hafele writes, "Because the word nymph has multiple meanings, it is easy to get confused. Just remember that nymph and larva both refer to the immature stage of insects and the nymph patterns are designed to imitate them." As a verb, nymph is the act of fishing flies below the surface of the water, which can further complicate things.

A skilled nymph fisherman will have the upper hand over a dry-fly purist because most of an aquatic insect's life is spent in the water. For instance, a mayfly spends 364 days of its life as a nymph and one day as an adult. The only reason a mayfly leaves the water is to mate. Many other aquatic insects have similar life cycles. Most professional guides, including myself, nymph-fish most of the time because it is the most effective strategy for ensuring their paying clients catch fish.

During my extensive travels throughout Colorado I was exposed to a variety of new tactics. I think anglers in general get stagnant in their thought processes and rarely experiment with new methods and techniques. I must admit I am a creature of habit myself, but this project has reminded me of the importance of thinking outside the box.

It's refreshing to learn a new wrinkle or two about nymphing rigs or to explore new strategies and techniques with dry flies and streamers. While a large part of your success as a fly fisher will hinge on your becoming a proficient nymph fisherman, don't get trapped in a rut and overlook dry-fly fishing and streamer fishing. Catching a fish on a dry fly is one of the most rewarding experiences in fly fishing. When conditions are right, streamer fishing can produce some of the biggest trout of the season.

NYMPHING STRATEGIES

Most anglers use a 7 ½- to 9-foot tapered monofilament leader for their nymphing rigs. To prolong the life of your leader and maintain its original length and taper, it is a good idea to attach an additional piece of tippet, 12 to 18 inches long, to the terminating end. This methodology ensures that as you change or replace flies, you are not chewing up an expensive leader, but rather cutting into the tippet material that is much more economical to replace. For pennies on the dollar, you can repair leaders as opposed to continuously replacing them.

Steve Henderson prefers fluorocarbon leaders: "I use flourocarbon leaders because they are less visible to the trout and they sink faster than nylon." Henderson believes he catches more fish with fluorocarbon leaders and feels the additional cost is well worth the investment. Most guides I know do not use fluorocarbon leaders, however.

Entomologists believe that 80 to 90 percent of a trout's diet occurs below the surface of the water. That's why nymph fishing is the most productive method of catching fish. MARK ADAMS

GUIDE PREPARATION

I find it interesting to watch how different guides prepare for their day. Some guides are more casual in their approach, while others have a well-executed game plan. Some guides rig their rods on the stream while others have their rods pre-rigged in their trucks or use rod vaults to store their assembled rods. Guides that use inflatable rafts or drift boats can easily keep multiple rods rigged, which becomes a distinct advantage over carrying a single rod. Walk-and-wade guides that hike in and out of rugged canyons and other rigorous terrain do not have the luxury of carrying pre-rigged rods because they are at a much higher risk of breaking them. Unfortunately, I have to rig my rods on location every day as most of my guided trips take place in Cheesman Canyon.

Steve Henderson makes it a point to arrive to the river equipped with multiple rods rigged with dry flies, nymphs, and streamers. During the winter, Henderson attaches several pre-rigged rods to a snowmobile before he transports his customers to the stream. During the winter months, a snowmobile is the best way to reach several sections of the Yampa (below Stagecoach or above Catamount, for example) because there is typically several feet of snow lying on the ground, which does not allow for easy foot access.

Once Henderson reaches the stream, he typically starts out by either fishing dry flies (if there are obvious hatches) or dry-and-dropper rigs. Then he breaks out the nymphing rig. After he has thoroughly fished an area with the previously mentioned rigs, he then fishes the same water with a streamer. Carrying multiple rods saves him valuable time because he does not have to re-rig rods if he decides to change tactics. During the summer and autumn months, Henderson hand-carries multiple rods to the stream with the same goals in mind.

Jason Booth has a similar philosophy that he executes from his drift boat. The Gunnison River that he fishes has a mixture of prime trout habitat, from shallow riffles to deep runs, beautiful pocket water, midchannel shelves, and undercut banks. Booth keeps several rods rigged in his drift boat at all times. He generally has two nymphing rigs, one with smaller offerings (midges and mayflies), and one with larger flies (stoneflies, caddis, drake nymphs, aquatic worms, etc.), as well as a dry-fly rod, a dry-and-dropper setup, and one stiff-action rod equipped with a streamer. "The Gunnison River gets a lot of fishing pressure. I have to be smarter than the other anglers and guides that fish this stream to get my clients on fish," explains Booth. "I have to remain open-minded and be methodical all day. The multiple rod system keeps my customers fishing, [and] there is very little downtime, if any, due to broken rigs or changing flies. If my client breaks off a rig, I simply hand them another rod and they're back to fishing." Having fished with Booth numerous times, I can tell you this is a distinct advantage over carrying only one rod.

Booth typically nymphs the deeper runs, starting out with larger food organisms like a size 8-10 Pat's Rubber Legs or a size 14 San Juan Worm. After he catches a few fish, he will then fish the same run with some smaller flies such as a size 18 Red Two-Bit Hooker, a size 18-20 Copper John, or a size 20 Mercury Flashback RS 2. Then he moves to another stretch. "I do not pound a hole—I catch a few fish and move on. That's good etiquette, and it allows everyone to catch a few fish in each hole," Booth says. "That's important, especially for float fishermen and other guides." Booth takes a similar approach when he fishes midchannel shelves or gravel bars. He will typically start with a dry-and-dropper rig, then he will nymph the same water using a similar approach as he took in deeper water. ■

Steve Henderson (right) is one of the top guides in Colorado. He increases his odds of catching more fish by carrying multiple rods rigged with nymphs, dries, and streamers. This strategy allows him to be prepared for a variety of situations and keeps his paying customers happy. MARK ADAMS

Colorado-based guide Aaron Carithers uses a micro yarn strike indicator to detect subtle strikes on the San Juan River's soft, glassy currents.

The vast majority of guides I fished with use monofilament leaders in conjunction with fluorocarbon tippet. Across the board, guides believe fluorocarbon tippet fools more trout than monofilament. Furthermore, fluorocarbon gives you the advantage of fishing thicker tippet diameters without compromise. For instance, I would typically fish 5X fluorocarbon tippet instead of 6X monofilament. This results in fewer broken tippets and lost fish and allows you to maximize your down-time by not having to re-rig as often.

Chris Wells, owner of Mile High Angler, has a different opinion, as he prefers monofilament over fluorocarbon tippet: "I prefer monofilament for several reasons. One, monofilament's breaking strength and knot strength is better. It stretches, allowing more room for angler error. Two, it is more supple, allowing for more movement of the fly, which creates a better presentation. Three, fluorocarbon sinks and if you have to switch to drys quickly, the fluorocarbon will actually cause your fly to sink. Four, monofilament is less expensive. It's less than half the cost of fluorocarbon. And finally, because it works! I catch plenty of fish using monofilament."

Most guides put their split shot or split shot/moldable tungsten putty above the knot that joins their tippet and leader together. Placing the weight above the knot reduces the chances of the weight coming off or sliding down the leader toward the first fly. The spacing between the weight and the lead fly (attractor) varies from guide to guide. As a general rule, most guides leave between 10 and 16 inches between their weight and the first fly. I generally space my first fly about 12 to 14 inches from the weight.

The next decision is whether or not you want to fish one, two, or three flies in your nymphing rig. Although anglers have been experimenting with multiple-fly rigs for centuries, they did not become the norm until the mid-1980s. Now it's rare not to see an angler fishing with a two- or three-fly rig. There are two schools of thought with regard to how anglers rig their flies. Some anglers prefer connecting their flies eye-to-eye, while other favor dropping their second (or third) fly off the bend of the upper fly.

My colleague Bob Dye prefers to fish with three-fly rigs. "I like to use a three-fly nymphing rig for several reasons," explains Dye. "First and foremost, I can simply cover more water. Another reason is that I like to fish a lot of emerger patterns and this enables me to tie a third fly on. Lastly, I enjoy coming up with new patterns, which allows me to field-test them in the point-fly (third fly) position without sacrificing any results with my catch rate.

Dye's spacing between nymphs varies depending on the season: "I space my flies between 10 to 12 inches when the water is cold (mid-30s to mid-40s) and 12 to 15 inches when the water is optimum temperature (high 40s to low 60s).

Bob Dye is one of the most proficient nymph fisherman in Colorado. He typically fishes with a three-fly rig, which increases his odds of catching fish.

Keeping the flies closer together when the trout are sluggish and unwilling to move greater distances can be a tremendous advantage."

Henderson has a unique nymphing rig, as he spaces his flies farther apart than most guides. Henderson believes that the spacing of his flies is an integral part of his success because he feels his flies drift better when tied farther apart. "The increased distance between my flies allows the flies to drift better in the current," Henderson says. "They are not restricted by heavy weight, thus they drift naturally mid-column and look realistic to the trout."

The length of nymphing rigs varies from angler to angler. Most often this decision is based on how deep the water is they are fishing. Dye sets up his nymphing rig so that he can fish water that is anywhere from 3 feet to 12 feet deep. Dye starts his nymphing rig with a 9-foot, 4X leader and places a yarn strike indicator 4 or 5 feet down from the fly line. On the terminating end of his leader, Dye adds an additional 3 feet of 4X or 5X tippet material, onto which he'll tie on his first fly. He typically ties on some sort of attractor, such as an egg pattern or flashy midge, as his lead fly. Off the bend of the lead fly he allows 10 to 15 inches before attaching his second fly. He repeats this process for the third fly.

The length of Dye's leader provides him with a long monofilament butt section between the fly line and the yarn strike indicator. "This is a distinct advantage to fishing a long leader," Dye says. "The longer butt section tends to line less fish [spook fish by the fly line hitting the water], which ultimately means catching more fish."

STRIKE INDICATORS

There are many options to choose from in regard to strike indicators. The most popular strike indicators are Thingamabobbers, Fish Pimps, Lightning Strike Indicators, Skip's Turn-On Strike Indicators, Frog Hair Indicators, and the Rubber O-Ring Poly Yarn Strike Indicator. Each strike indicator has its share of tradeoffs and compromises; you'll need to pick the one that works best for you. Carefully weigh the pros and cons of each strike indicator before you come to any conclusions.

I personally believe that yarn is the best strike indicator available. A yarn indicator offers ease of adjustment and detects subtle strikes better than any other product on the market. Several years ago, my colleague Dan Wright and I began experimenting with a variety of craft cords, trying to find the ultimate strike indicator. The idea was spurred by a recent fishing trip to the San Juan River below Navajo Dam. We noticed that most of the guides were using a tuft of yarn for their strike indicator. Neither Wright nor I had ever been exposed to yarn strike indicators before, but we immediately recognized how sensitive they were.

Many guides and anglers believe that yarn strike indicators are the best option because they land on the water softly, adjust easily, and detect subtle strikes. As a general rule, most guides keep the strike indicator adjusted to twice the depth of the water from the weight, unless there is an unusual circumstance that requires a shorter distance (such as suspended fish just below the surface of the water). MARK ADAMS

Wright ultimately found the material that I use today. It met all the criteria we were looking for: it was easy to see, it floated well, and it was extremely sensitive to subtle strikes. Early on we used a girth hitch to attach the yarn to our leader. This was satisfactory, but it had some limitations in terms of adjustment. Furthermore, it crinkled the leader when you changed the depth, which in time hampered or outright ruined the leader. A couple years later Clay Anselmo, one of the senior guides at Blue Quill Angler, showed me a slick way to use an orthodontist's rubber band to attach the yarn to the leader. This allowed for quick and easy adjustment of the yarn without damaging the leader.

"My favorite strike indicator, hands-down, is yarn with an orthodontist's rubber band," Wells says. "The yarn supports a lot more weight than most indicators, which allows me to fish big fast water, like I encounter when I guide on the Williams Fork and North Fork of the South Platte. Yarn is extremely sensitive, which allows me to pick up on the most subtle strikes. I use a natural color, tan or beige, which I feel spooks fewer fish. Yarn strike indicators are easy to adjust—the orthodontist's rubber band allows me to slide the indicator up and down the leader quickly without damaging the leader."

Bob Dye builds his own strike indicators by combing out a 12-inch section of tan three-ply craft cord. He applies a bead of Aquel floatant down the yarn's length and brushes the floatant into the yarn. He then cuts the frizzed-out yarn into one-and-a-half-inch pieces, and then stores them in a Ziploc bag until he gets to the stream. He puts an orthodontist's rubber band around each premade indicator, which saves him from having to dig through his pack in search of one.

Aaron Carithers uses a micro yarn strike indicator on the San Juan River to assist him in fooling some of the most selective midge feeders in the West. "The San Juan River consists of short riffles and runs followed by long intermediate to slow tailouts. Due to the silt load created by the lack of current in these areas, they offer prime midge habitat where trout will lazily feed on midge pupae, emergers and adults," Carithers explains. "When fishing subsurface to these midging fish I prefer to use a 'micro' yarn indicator because the angler is able to turn over the nymph rig more efficiently and it gives the angler the advantage when it comes to detecting subtle strikes. Subsurface midge fishing can be effective in water depths from a few inches to several feet; typically very little weight is needed to get the fly to the fish. A small indicator, consisting of only three to four strands of well-separated Antron yarn dressed with floatant and trimmed down to about the size of a dime will easily support a lightweight nymphing rig. Slow to intermediate current, very small flies (size 22 to

26), and slow-moving fish that are unwilling to go more than a few inches to intercept your offering can all lead to nearly imperceptible grabs. Due to the small size and lack of significant mass the 'micro' indicator will register the strike more readily and lead to more 'positive' hookup."

Carithers says that he fishes a bigger yarn strike indicator on the Animas and Rio Grande Rivers, where the strikes are more aggressive and more weight is required in your nymphing rigs. Don't be afraid to experiment a bit and be willing to change your tactics as needed.

Steve Henderson's favorite strike indicator is the Frog Hair Single-Use Indicator. All indicators have pros and cons but Henderson believes this indicator proves its versatility through its ease of use on the water. He advises to not let the "single use" label fool you. "For castability I have not found a better strike indicator," Henderson says. "It is less affected by wind than other indicators and it roll-casts exceptionally well. These strike indicators also resist getting tangled better than most. Fishing at the proper depth is extremely important and this indicator can easily and infinitely be adjusted by sliding the indicator up or down the leader." As a general rule Henderson keeps his strike indicator adjusted to one and a half to two times the depth of the water. Inadvertent slipping rarely occurs with this indicator unless it is positioned on the smaller-diameter leader sections. He says, "This indicator is also maintenance-free: it require no floatants and will not freeze with water and sink like other styles of indicators." Henderson tackles the single-use problem by leaving the rods rigged and storing them in his truck. With this approach, Henderson has indicators that provide more than thirty days of use.

"The properties of a strike indicator are important to me, especially on most sections of the Yampa River [where] I find myself doing less high-stick nymphing and more long-line nymphing," Henderson says. "I may lose the yarn's sensitivity, but I gain the ability to cast farther, especially in the wind."

Landon Mayer, like the vast majority of guides I know, uses Thingamabobbers for his nymphing rigs: "I like the low maintenance and versatility of the Thingamabobber compared to other strike indicators. I can rely on the consistent buoyancy day in and out." Mayer keeps an array of Thingamabobbers handy: "I carry three sizes with me at all times: large, medium, and small. Large for stillwaters and big rivers where I can fish heavily weighted flies below them without sinking the strike indicator. It will stay afloat in heavy stillwater winds or turbulent river currents. Medium is my most common size for the tailwaters that I fish. This size is big enough to suspend most nymph rigs and remain out of the trout's view. Another nice feature compared to another indicators, like yarn, is the ease of casting with less resistance, as they cut through wind easier. Small is my go-to size for low water and the winter months when trout are very wary."

San Juan River trout feed heavily on midge pupae. Aaron Carithers fooled this beautiful San Juan River rainbow with a size 24 midge pupa suspended below a micro yarn strike indicator.

Float guides such as Josh Cranson like Thingamabobbers because they are maintenance-free. They float high in choppy currents and cast easily from inflatable rafts, especially when it is windy.

The Thingamabobber is available in several colors—red, yellow, orange, chartreuse, black, white, clear, and glow-in-the-dark. Some colors are easier to see in foam lines or other high-glare situations, so pick one that best suits your needs. "The color I use the most is clear or glow-in-the-dark. From below the water's surface the Thingamabobber is translucent." Mayer says. "The trick is preventing any contrast against the sky and not allowing trout to know a big object like an indicator is actually within their view. While white looks like foam from above the water's surface, it appears darker from below. The clear Thingamabobber allows the color and light to travel through the plastic, preventing the trout from detecting it. The only disadvantage in using a Thingamabobber is they can leave a kink in your leader. You can overcome this simply by stretching the leader above or below where the indicator is placed."

Yarn advocates believe Thingamabobbers are "all or nothing"—in other words, you will not detect subtle strikes with them, as they don't twist and turn, quiver, twitch, or create small a dimple when you get a subtle strike. This can be especially important in slower currents, where many of your strikes will go unnoticed with a Thingamabobber. Additionally, Thingamabobbers hit the water much harder than yarn, which can spook trout if you are not careful. Personally, I believe what you gain in casting ease you lose in sensitivity, which in the long run can cost you fish.

John Perizzolo, a guide for Breckenridge Outfitters, uses two Thingamabobbers in his nymphing rigs. "On larger, stained rivers, streams with more gradient, or in the wind, I use a double Thingamabobber rig," Perizzolo says. "I attach a small Thingamabobber closer to the fly line, and a medium Thingamabobber four to six inches below that. If you draw a line through the two indicators, that will tell your where your flies are. This aids in getting a good drift, especially when you are guiding out of a drift boat. Sometimes you'll see a small change in the drift speed between the two. If the larger indicator slows down first, that is a sure sign of a subtle hit."

The final extreme is guides who fish without a strike indicator, like Will Sands at Taylor Creek Fly Shop. "I have noticed that hard-pressured fish can be a bit sensitive to strike indicators and even feel some fish get a bit edgy to split shot (especially on the Taylor River) and during these times I believe a more minimal approach can be more successful," Sands says. Fishing without a strike indicator can be especially effective in low-water situations. "When I fish on my own, and I can cast to specific fish that I can watch eat my fly, I often forgo an indicator," Sands adds. He admits that he often uses strike indicators when he guides unless the customer requests otherwise, which is a rare occurrence.

WEIGHT

Having the appropriate weight in your nymphing rig can make or break your success on just about any given day. There's truth to that old cliché that the difference between a good fisherman and a great one is one split. Many factors can influence the amount of weight you'll need to get your flies drifting in the correct part of the water column. For instance, you'll need to consider the depth and speed of the water, as well as where the fish are holding. If there is a sporadic hatch, the fish will more than likely be holding tight to the bottom. Under these conditions, you will need more weight to get your flies down to the fish. If there is a dense midge or mayfly hatch, the fish will more than likely be holding in the upper part of the water column, feeding on suspended midge pupae or emerging mayfly nymphs. When these conditions exist, you'll need to fish with less weight and keep your flies mid-column or slightly above.

There are several weight options to choose from, including twist-ons, split shot (lead or tin), and moldable putty alternatives. My travels throughout Colorado revealed that about two thirds of the guides I fished with used split shot rather than moldable tungsten putty alternatives.

I was surprised with this finding, as I personally believe using moldable weights greatly increases your productivity as a nymph fisherman. The advantage to using moldable weight in your nymphing rig is in the ease of adjustment. My favorite is JP's Nymphing Mud (formerly called Mojo Mud), because it allows me to make frequent changes with my weight, keeping my flies in the correct part of the water column based on the current hatches. Another advantage is that tungsten is heavier than lead, which assists in achieving a quicker sink rate.

John Perizzolo owns Sweetwater Labs, the manufacturer of JP's Nymphing Mud. He says, "Using moldable putty allows you to 'fine-tune' your weight to a degree not possible with split shot. Often you will add a small amount and suddenly start catching fish. As you move through a run, you can make the small adjustments needed for varying currents and depth, taking it off and putting it back on easily. As an added bonus, if you get hung up, usually it will deform or come off without losing your flies."

John Perizzolo and I share a similar philosophy in regard to weight in our nymphing rigs. We begin by placing a size 4 or size 6 split shot on the knot that joins our leader and tippet. In many cases, especially in shallow riffles or when fishing transitional zones like midchannel shelves and gravel bars, a

John Perizzolo's moldable tungsten putty (JP's Nymphing Mud) allows him to make quick and easy adjustments with his weight for a wide range of current speeds and depths. He believes it's one of the key ingredients for successful nymphing. MARK ADAMS

small split shot is sufficient to keep your flies at the proper depth. As the need for weight increases with changing depths or current speeds or the location of the fish, we simply add weight. Anglers can make small adjustments quickly without fumbling split and dropping them in the water. As you age, split shot becomes more challenging to work with (i.e., seeing the split), so this factor in itself is a huge advantage to JP's Nymphing Mud.

Steve Henderson uses a Tungsten Beadhead Hare's Ear as his lead (attractor) fly. "The heavy tungsten bead is my main source of weight for my nymphing rig. I like to fish my nymphs mid-column and rarely dredge my flies near the substrate when I'm nymphing," Henderson says. "I'm looking for actively feeding trout that are suspended in the water column. I tend to cast my flies several feet above the feeding fish, which give my flies plenty of time to sink." If Henderson feels his flies are not getting down into the fish's feeding zone, he'll add a split shot 14 inches above his lead fly.

Bob Dye uses split shot to get his flies into the proper feeding zone. "I've never been a big fan of soft weight [putty alternatives] for adjusting my weight. I like long natural drifts that only a split shot will allow. Soft weight tends to be too heavy for this system and the flies don't drift naturally in the current. There is a time and place for moldable putty (when you have to get your flies down quick), but most of the time I use split shot."

Like many guides, Dye carries the Super Doux assortment, which contains split shot in sizes 0, 2, 4, and 6. He micromanages his nymphing rig until he occasionally taps the stream bottom. "Most importantly, I watch the speed of the yarn strike indicator in relationship to the speed of the water," Dye says. "If the strike indicator is floating about the same speed as the bubbles, then I know I have my weight adjusted correctly."

DRY-FLY FISHING

Many anglers consider dry-fly fishing to be the epitome of our sport. Dry-fly enthusiasts typically possess the skills most essential for fly-fishing success—delicate, yet precise, casting and a flawless presentation. Many anglers like my longtime friend Monroe Coleman have become dry-fly purists. For years Monroe has taken a "dry or die" approach to fly fishing.

It's no secret that most of a trout's diet occurs subsurface. Day in and day out, the odds are you'll be more successful with nymphs compared to dry flies. Tell that to Coleman and he'll tell you that every fish he catches on a dry fly counts for ten fish to every one caught on a nymph. I think you get my point—dry-fly fishermen are often a unique breed, and in many cases they are set in their ways.

I try to not make it a point to limit my success by being stubborn. My goal as an angler is to be diversified, and I fish with a variety of tactics and techniques as the need arises. For instance, during the non-hatch periods, I'll fish with nymphs. When I detect a hatch, I'll begin fishing with emergers. Once the fish commit to feeding on the surface, I'll fish with dry flies. This approach to fly fishing just makes sense! Now, don't get me wrong—I would prefer to catch my fish on dry flies, but in many cases, dry-fly fishing is not always the most effective strategy.

If a hatch becomes evident, you'll want to be prepared for a variety of situations, however. Don't limit your success by

Catching a trout on a dry fly is one of the most rewarding parts of fly fishing. This Spinney Mountain Ranch cuttbow was fooled with a Puterbaugh's Caddis during an afternoon caddis hatch.

An upstream delivery helps reduce the possibility of spooking a rising trout because you're casting from the trout's blind spot.
MARK ADAMS

coming to the river unprepared! Make sure your dry-fly boxes have a variety of midge adults, clusters, and trailing shuck imitations. You'll also need mayfly duns, cripples, and spinners to imitate Blue-Winged Olives, Pale Morning Duns, Green Drakes, Gray Drakes, Red Quills, and Tricos.

Carry plenty of caddisfly adults and adult stonefly imitations to cover Golden Stoneflies, Salmonflies, Yellow Sallies, and Winter Stoneflies. And of course, do not forget about terrestrials, which can make or break your success on any given day in the summer or autumn. Make sure your dry-fly selection includes a wide variety of sizes; once again, don't hinder your success by carrying a limited fly selection. Carry at least six of each pattern so you don't run out of flies when you need them.

DRY-FLY STRATEGIES

A 9- to 12-foot tapered leader will suffice for most of your dry-fly needs in Colorado. The diameter of the terminating end will vary greatly depending on the size of your fly, the water you're fishing, the size of the fish, and finally, how selective the fish are. In most cases, a 9-foot, 5X leader is the most versatile. It allows anglers to be successful under a wide range of conditions, in most cases by simply making an adjustment or two by adding the appropriate-sized tippet to lengthen the leader.

I would recommend following these simple guidelines. When I'm fishing a large attractor (such as size 8-10 Amy's Ants or size 12-14 Royal Wulffs), I'll typically fish with a 9-foot, 3X or 4X leader, then add 18 to 24 inches of 4X or 5X tippet. If I'm fishing smaller flies (size 16-18 Pale Morning Duns), especially when I'm trying to match a particular hatch, I'll use 18 to 24 inches of finer tippet (5X to 6X) because a little more finesse will be involved. Swinging to the far extreme, if I'm fishing with size 20 and below (size 20 Sparkle Dun or size 22 CDC Trico Compara-dun), I'll use 7X tippet to increase my odds of fooling more trout. In all cases, I use monofilament tippet because it floats better and is more supple than fluorocarbon.

FLOATANTS

I use a combination of paste floatants and dry-fly crystals to keep my flies floating on the surface. I traditionally begin by applying Aquel floatant to my dry flies with the exception of CDC or snowshoe rabbit patterns. For those patterns you'll need to use Frog's Fanny or Shimazaki Dry Shake, as paste floats will ruin them.

I carry all three of the above-referenced varieties of floatants because, in my opinion, each one has a time and place. After my dry fly becomes waterlogged or it gets slimed up from a fish eating it, I reapply either Frog's Fanny or Shimazaki Dry Shake. I am especially fond of the Frog's Fanny on my smaller dry flies (size 18 and smaller) because the handy applicator brush allows me to rub the powder into the

The approach is an important part of successful dry-fly fishing. Landon Mayer crawled on his hands and knees and kept his profile low before casting to a rising fish on the opposing bank. MARK ADAMS

hackle and wings. I feel like I have better control with the applicator brush and can apply a generous amount of the desiccant to the underside of my fly keep it floating high on the water's surface. I also like to rub a fair amount on the topside, because it turns the fly white, which helps me see my fly on the water.

For larger dry flies, attractors, grasshoppers, and other foam-bodied terrestrials, my preference is the Shimazaki Dry Shake. Simply open up the lid, place your fly in the plastic container, and shake it several times. Pull your fly out and you're ready to fish again. After several applications of Shimazaki Dry Shake or Frog's Fanny, I'll reapply the Aquel paste floatant and dress my fly with either Frog's Fanny or Shimazaki Dry Shake as needed.

THE APPROACH

There are several factors you must consider before moving into the proper casting position. Will your presentation involve casting upstream, up and across, down and across, or downstream? Furthermore, will you need any type of slack-line cast (reach mend or S-cast) to offset any conflicting currents that might result in drag? Is there a high-glare situation that might require you to fish in a particular area in order to see your fly? Is there adequate room for your backcast? Is there sufficient room for line management? Where will you land the fish after you hook it? You should have answers to all these questions prior to making your first cast.

The primary goal when fishing with a dry fly is to get as close to the rising fish as possible without spooking them. I know this sounds completely obvious, but trust me, it is tougher than it seems. This often means crawling on your hands and knees and keeping a low profile until you get to the desired casting location. Expert dry-fly anglers like Ed Engle agree with this philosophy. "Get as close to a rising trout as you can without spooking it. The less fly line you have on the water the less chance there is of something going wrong," Engle advises. "Make your first presentation your best presentation. I'd rather make one good presentation than fifteen not-so-good presentations. Take an extra minute to figure out the best approach and casting position and then make your cast count."

Matt Miles is one of the finest dry-fly anglers I've ever had the pleasure to fish with. Miles' cast is effortless and his delivery is as delicate and precise as anyone in the business. I have learned a wealth of knowledge about dry-fly fishing from just watching him. His biggest tip for success is making sure you have an accurate delivery. "The biggest problem I encounter is anglers casting their flies too far upstream in relationship to the fish they want to catch," Miles says. "Casting five or ten feet above your target, then having to mend, usually pulls the fly out of the trout's feeding lane, causing drag. My preference is to land the fly a foot or two above the rising fish, which alleviates the mend and reduces the chances of moving the fly out of the fish's feeding window. You only need a foot of drag-free drift to fool a trout, so keep your cast short and precise."

UPSTREAM DELIVERY

An upstream delivery involves an angler standing broadside to the current, casting his or her flies into the oncoming current. It is important to note that not all upstream deliveries are upriver. Reverse currents, also known as back eddies, are an example of an oncoming current that might be flowing downstream or sideways (relative to the main river channel) in either a clockwise or counterclockwise rotation.

An upstream delivery greatly reduces the chances of spooking fish because you are casting from the trout's blind spot. Excessive false casting over rising fish will tend to put them down or spook them, as surface feeders are extremely sensitive to overhead threats. To eliminate this problem, keep your false casting to a minimum, and false cast to the side of the rising trout.

Another advantage to an upstream delivery is drag is much easier to control because your fly line and leader are running parallel with the oncoming current. Fly fishers will need to strip the fly line from underneath their casting-hand index finger as the flies drift toward them. This will alleviate poor line management, which may result in a poor drift or bad hook set. If you change your angle of attack to fishing up and across, conflicting currents will force you to mend your fly to offset drag.

The greatest benefit to an upstream delivery is a downstream hook set. A downstream hook set impales the fly back into the trout's jaw, which more times than not guarantees a good hookup. One of the biggest problems faced by dry-fly anglers is setting the hook prematurely. Dry-fly fishing requires patience; you must allow the fish to come up and eat your fly and dip its head below the surface before you gently lift the rod tip. I cannot even begin to tell you how many times I have set the hook too early or broke the tippet because I set the hook too hard. It happens all the time, so don't worry—you're not alone.

DOWNSTREAM DELIVERY

Downstream deliveries, as their name implies, involve an angler casting flies down and across, or downstream, to a rising fish. In many cases, you'll need a slack-line cast (reach mend, S-cast, parachute cast) to offset any conflicting currents that may result in drag. In almost all scenarios, a little slack will be your friend with these types of deliveries.

If given the choice, I'll incorporate a downstream presentation with dry flies most of the time. A downstream delivery is effective because the first thing the fish sees is your fly—not the tippet, leader, or fly line—which in many cases may result in a refusal or spooking the trout. "When possible, I present the fly down and across to rising fish," Miles says. "Trout that see a lot fishing pressure can be leader-shy. So show them the fly first and not the leader. A down-and-across cast with a reach mend will usually not drag as quickly as casting straight across the current."

Be careful with your approach, however, because the fish are facing into the current and are easily spooked by movement, sloppy casting, or aggressive wading. Wear drab-colored clothing, keep your profile low, and move carefully and quietly.

Matt Miles fooled this Williams Fork brown trout on a Mathews' Sparkle Dun with a down-and-across delivery with a reach mend during an autumn Blue-Winged Olive hatch.

An up-and-across delivery allows an angler to methodically cover the water. This can be especially advantageous on larger freestones and tailwaters like the Colorado and Williams Fork Rivers where anglers like Matt Miles fish a lot of dry flies.

One of the biggest challenges with a downstream delivery is getting a good hook set. Unlike the upstream presentation, you're pulling the fly away from the trout's jaw, which naturally decreases your odds of a good hookup. Once again, be patient; allow the fish to dip below the surface before you set the hook. If possible, use a sidearm or sweeping motion to gently set the hook. If you set the hook straight upstream, chances are good you will miss the fish.

UP-AND-ACROSS DELIVERY

The advantage to an up-and-across delivery is you can cover twice the water as compared to the two previously mentioned methods. I typically use the up-and-across method when fishing with attractors because it allows me to methodically cover the water, showing my fly to as many fish as possible. This method requires impeccable line-handling skills, as you will be required to mend the fly line to offset drag.

The up-and-across presentation is nothing more than a combination of the two previously mentioned tactics. The first part of the drift is an upstream delivery and the second part of the drift is a downstream delivery. Don't be afraid to skate or skitter your flies on the downstream segment of your delivery, as this can trigger an aggressive strike. Experiment with your tactics; dead drift your flies in conjunction with imparting action into them from time to time. Follow the guidelines above for setting the hook.

DRY-AND-DROPPER RIGS

Dry-and-dropper rigs are an effective strategy for fishing dry flies and nymphs at the same time. With this concept, your dry fly becomes a strike indicator trailed by one or two nymphs. Dry-and-dropper rigs allow anglers to fish shallow-water areas where conventional nymphing rigs will typically get hung up, snagged, or have a tendency to spook trout.

Many anglers, including myself, carry multiple rods in order to be prepared for a variety of situations. Dry-and-dropper rigs allow anglers to fish the skinny water (shallow water, less than two feet deep) that many fly fishers tend to overlook. Targeting less-pressured trout in unlikely spots has always been an effective strategy of mine.

Dry-and-dropper strategies vary depending on the season. During the winter, I will fish with a heavily hackled Hi-Viz Griffith's Gnat (adding three to five turns of additional hackle to support a dropper) and drop a Tungsten Black Beauty or Poison Tung off it. The distance between my dry fly and dropper can be anywhere between 12 and 24 inches depending on the conditions. That decision is based on the feeding activity of the trout and their position in the water column. Refer to the midge chapter for further details.

During the spring, summer, or autumn months, I use a similar strategy, choosing a dry fly that matches the prevailing hatches. For instance, if caddisflies are hatching, I would use an Elk Hair Caddis or Puterbaugh's Foam Caddis as my dry fly, and drop a caddis pupa like Mercer's Swing Nymph below it. This combo has proven itself to be effective in late April and early May. Once again, the spacing between my dry fly and dropper varies depending on the depth of the water and where the trout are holding in the water column.

Another example would be fishing a Yellow Stimulator dropped with a Mitchell's Tungsten Split Case PMD during the months of June and July. This rig would imitate adult Yellow Sallies and Pale Morning Dun nymphs, two of the prevalent hatches occurring during the midsummer months. If you put some thought into dry-and-dropper rigs, you'll find they can be an effective strategy for fooling selective trout.

You can control your sink rates by either shortening or lengthening your tippet, or fishing glass, brass, or tungsten beads or weighted flies. In slower currents and glassy pools, lighter flies are preferred; in faster riffles and pocket water, I would recommend using heavily weighted flies, flies with either brass or tungsten beads, or a combination of both.

Another effective strategy is to fish with two dry flies or a dry fly and an emerger or spinner dropper in a two-fly tandem rig. I must admit, I find myself fishing with two dry flies a large percentage of the time. Certainly there are some trade-offs and compromises associated with this approach, but in most cases I believe it is beneficial to fish with two flies. You increase your odds of catching more fish with the additional fly. I typically use a standard hackled fly as my lead fly and drop a parachute, no-hackle, or Compara-dun for my second fly. This provides two different silhouettes for the fish to scrutinize, especially when they become extremely selective during the height of a hatch. Oftentimes I'll trail a small Parachute Adams, size 24 or 26, behind the fly that I believe will be most effective in matching the hatch. In many cases, the trout will eat the smaller offering. The one downfall to fishing with two flies is in some cases you'll get micro-drag that might lead to a refusal.

Ed Engle offers a helpful bit of advice for reducing micro drag when fishing tandem rigs:

> *If you think you're getting good drag-free drifts and believe your selection of fly imitations is good, but you're not hooking up or you're getting refusal rises, the odds are that your presentation is a victim of micro-drag. To correct the problem, try shortening the length of the tippet material between the two flies. The shorter length tends to keep both flies in the feeding lane where the trout is rising, which reduces micro-drag.*
>
> *If that fails try fishing just the emerger or spent spinner. Use a tiny bit of strike putty on the knot between your leader and tippet, approximately 18 to 30 inches from the fly. The strike putty causes very little drag and will help you key in on the area where your emerger or spent spinner is. If you see a rise or bulge on the surface in that area, gently set the hook.*

STREAMER FISHING

Fishing with streamers is a fun and exciting way of hunting for large fish. Oftentimes you're looking for that "one fish"—the biggest, nastiest, most aggressive trout in the river or lake. Make no mistake about it, streamer fishing is hard work—

Dry-and-dropper rigs allow you to fish a dry fly and nymph at the same time. This Arkansas River brown trout took the PMX trailed by Charlie Craven's red Two-Bit Hooker.

casting a stiff 6- or 7-weight rod and stripping flies all day can be exhausting. Trust me, you'll earn every fish you catch with streamers, but in most cases, the rewards are worth the effort!

Big fish tend to be opportunistic feeders and are more willing to chase larger food items like minnows, sculpins, daces, baby trout, leeches, and crawfish. Once a fish reaches 16 inches in length, it begins to supplement its daily diet of miniscule mayflies and midges with forage items. Large trout quickly learn to become efficient with their feed patterns—they have figured out that it takes dozens of midges (larvae and pupae) or mayfly nymphs to equal one baby trout or minnow. In many cases, a trout can eat one forage item and be good for several hours, which reduces the fish's workload and the likelihood of being attacked by predators.

The shoulder seasons can produce some of the most exciting streamer fishing of the year, as migratory pre-spawn fish become targets for streamers. My favorite time to fish streamers is during the autumn months, especially on the Gunnison, the Colorado, and Williams Fork. Several rivers throughout Colorado provide similar experiences, especially if they have a robust population of brown trout or a nearby lake or reservoir.

Autumn is generally the best time of the year to catch big brown trout. By the latter part of September, wary and crafty brown trout begin moving from deeper water and other heavily structured areas into shallow water as they search for areas to spawn. Large brown trout also migrate from stillwater impoundments into feeder streams and other tributaries with the same goals in mind. Steamer fishing near the inlets of these lakes can be especially productive this time of year.

One of my favorite streamer patterns is Tim Heng's Autumn Splendor. I have fooled numerous trout during the autumn season with Heng's concoction. "Over twenty-five years ago I had a client in my drift boat floating down the Roaring Fork. It was a real slow day and we had tried almost everything in my fly box with little or no success when my client said that he had a bass fly that he had a lot of success with back home," Heng explains. "It was a monstrosity of a fly, probably a 2/0 or 3/0 hook, with big doll eyes. Since we weren't catching anything with my flies, I thought what the heck, let's try it. To my surprise, we really started moving fish. I don't think we actually caught anything on it, but the fish were chasing, looking, and pretty much doing everything but eating it. So I went home and took a similar color scheme and style, and scaled it down to trout size. I fished it for a while and caught a bunch of fish. Then I put yellow rubber legs on it, and it worked even better. That same year in October I had a different customer in my boat, once again floating the Roaring Fork, and this new fly was hammering fish. I said to my customer, what do you think I should name this fly? He said 'the Autumn Splendor,' and that's what it became." Heng's Autumn Splendor has evolved over the years. When he first tied it, he weighted it with lead wire near the head to give

Don't rule out fishing with streamers during the winter. Steve Henderson fooled this Yampa rainbow by swinging a streamer through a classic winter run. MARK ADAMS

Autumn is an excellent time to fish with streamers. This Colorado River brown trout inhaled Tim Heng's Autumn Splendor about an hour before dark.

it a jigging action. Several months later, he added a bead head, and eventually a cone head. Many fly tiers now tie the Autumn Splendor with dumbbell eyes.

Brown trout become vulnerable during the fall because their spawning behaviors override their normal instincts to hide around structure and feed during the low-light hours. Brown trout that have been hiding for several months become fair game for two to three weeks. Take advantage of this opportunity while you can because your window is short and sweet. Rainbow trout provide similar experiences during the spring months. The tactics and techniques required to fool them are comparable.

STREAMER STRATEGIES

Streamer tactics vary greatly depending on the angler and what they want to accomplish. Some anglers prefer fishing a single streamer while others choose to fish with tandem rigs. In either case, the most common method is the strip-and-swing technique, which is achieved by casting your streamer at a 45-degree angle downstream and allowing the fly to swing in the current while imparting action into it by stripping the fly line under your index finger. Vary your retrieve and never rule out experimentation. Sometimes a slow strip will trigger a strike while other times a faster retrieve works better for inducing an explosive take because trout think their prey is trying to escape them.

Steve Henderson is an accomplished streamer fisherman. "I fish streamers often, as we have a large population of sculpins and dace in the Yampa River. Our trout are often eager to take a larger offering," Henderson says. "I fish streamers generally on a downstream swing from one side of the bank swinging to the angler's side. This is a very active method to cover a lot of water and is a good way to find fish. I find that trout will take a streamer any time of the year. In the winter, you need to fish the streamer very close to the bottom with a slow swing. Generally this means you are fishing the slow deep holes on the river. In the summer and fall months your streamer takes can occur anywhere but particularly in the faster riffles and along depth changes in the streambed."

There are two schools of thought when fishing streamers. You can fish blind and cover the water methodically or you can cast your flies to specific lies and allow them to swing into the desired structure or in front of fish. You can control depth by using sinking-tip lines, by adding slack into the line, by mending, or even by tightening the line and forcing the fly to swing and rise in the current. You can add a split shot to the leader, which will further assist in depth control. Some anglers place the split shot snug on the eye of the hook while others place the weight 6 inches from the fly. Each method will provide a slightly different action. Once again, be willing to think outside the box from time to time and experiment.

Chris Wells is another die-hard streamer fanatic. "When I fish streamers I let the fish and the river tell me how to present the flies. I usually prefer to fish streamer patterns in faster water because the fish have to decide quickly whether or not to attack them," Wells says. "My streamer rigs begin with an old leader cut back to 4 feet. I attach 18 inches of 16- to 20-pound monofilament tippet to the leader. The size varies depending conditions (size of the fish, clarity, etc). On the end of the tippet, I tie on my first fly, the biggest and heaviest streamer, with

Chris Wells chases down a Williams Fork brown that hammered one of his streamers. Wells prefers fishing streamers in faster water where the fish have to decide quickly whether or not to grab his offering. The strikes are generally explosive in fast water.

a clinch knot. Then I then attach an 18-inch piece of 16- to 20-pound tippet to the bend of the hook, and tie on my second streamer using a nonslip mono loop."

Wells prefers fishing his two-fly streamer rigs with the traditional down-and-across presentation. Once the streamer hits the water, he begins to strip the fly quickly. As the fly begins to swing, he slows down his retrieve. Wells recommends mending the line during the swing, which adds a little slack and allows the streamer to sink lower in the water column. When a trout grabs your streamer the line will tighten abruptly. There will be no doubt you've had a strike. Once you feel the line go taut use a strip set or lift the rod tip to set the hook. "A strip set is the best way to set the hook with a streamer. If the fish short-strikes and you keep stripping, the fly is still in front of the fish," Wells says. "If you set the hook with the lift of the rod and the fish misses, the fly travels a great distance and is no longer in front of the fish. Strip set, and once you come tight, just lift the rod tip and play the fish to the net."

Dead-drifting a streamer is another effective tactic. This method works well in faster riffles and pocket water and is especially effective on point bars and midchannel shelves. Fish sitting in transitional areas will attack a streamer when they drift over a drop-off. A high-stick approach works best when you're dead-drifting streamers because you can control the depth with the butt end of your leader, simply moving your arm up and down to achieve the proper depth.

Brown trout can be voracious feeders on the Williams Fork River. One of Chris Wells' favorite streamers is a Clouser Minnow.

CHAPTER 10

Colorado Stillwater Summary

Richard Pilatzke

Colorado is blessed with an abundance of stillwater fisheries. There are thousands of lakes for Coloradans to choose from, but the most productive bodies are weedy, alkaline lakes that are generally located between approximately 7,900 and 8,900 feet in elevation. These lakes are food factories—they contain an abundance of organisms that can allow for trout growth rates of one inch a month during the prime season. These lakes almost all contain damselflies, dragonflies, *Callibaetis* mayflies, chironomids, leeches, scuds, water boatmen, backswimmers, and also a variety of terrestrials. These prey items offer very similar seasonal opportunities for taking very large trout.

STILLWATER EQUIPMENT

Equipment for stillwater fisheries is similar to that used on rivers, with some notable exceptions. I prefer to use a 10-foot, 5-weight rod for much of my stillwater fishing, especially for dry-fly and indicator fishing. A 6- or 7-weight rod will work

Spinney Mountain Reservoir is one of Colorado's premier stillwater fisheries. JAY NICHOLS

Your stillwater fly selection should include Callibaetis *mayflies, chironomids, leeches, scuds, water boatmen, backswimmers, terrestrials, dragonflies, and damselflies. This Antero Reservoir rainbow was fooled with a damselfly nymph.* JAY NICHOLS

better in windy conditions. I use an 8- or 9-foot rod for subsurface fishing with a clear intermediate sinking line. I always carry two basic fly lines for stillwaters: a weight-forward floating line and a clear intermediate sinking line.

Leaders for drys are typically eight to ten feet long and taper to a 2X to 4X tippet. Leaders for the clear intermediate sinking line are three to four feet long and taper to a 0X to 3X tippet. I use fluorocarbon tippet for subsurface flies and for droppers and indicator fishing. For dry flies, I use monofilament tippets. I prefer boot-foot waders for lakes, mainly because they work so well with fins in a pontoon boat or float tube.

A personal flotation device should always be worn or carried. A good landing net is also a must for the stillwater angler. It should be good sized—I have seen too many people come to a lake and find the fish are too big for their net. The stillwater angler should always use sunscreen and wear a hat that provides protection from the sun and covers the ears (to protect from both sun and errant casts). Especially in the shoulder seasons (spring and fall), anglers should dress for the weather, with warm clothing, glacier gloves for the hands, and especially good wool socks to protect from hypothermia.

EARLY SEASON: ICE-OFF TO TURNOVER

This early season is one of my favorite times of year to fish Colorado lakes. I like to catch the lakes just as the winter icepack is melting off. The time for ice-off will vary with the altitude of the lakes and with the depth of the snow and ice. I have seen lakes in South Park thaw as early as March and as late as early May. This period is what I call "Glacier Glove time." Your guides can ice quickly and you may have to clear them as you fish, but the fishing can be very rewarding.

Fish at this time of year have been confined under the ice for many long months and can really be receptive to properly presented flies. The aquatic food sources at this time are limited and dictate what flies are effective. For the first few weeks of open water, oxygenated water is concentrated in the upper levels of a lake. The fish will be in this oxygenated water near the shore and will feed actively here.

Some of my favorite patterns at this time are leech imitations, scuds, and dragonfly nymphs. Leeches are present year-round in the lakes, but at this time they are more important because the vegetation hasn't regenerated and the leeches are more visible. Leech imitations can be fished on a clear intermediate sinking line or even suspended under an indicator.

Dragonfly nymphs are active at this time and the larger instars, which will hatch later in the season, are important food items for the fish. I often will fish a size 4 dragonfly nymph to imitate the larger nymphs.

Scuds are active immediately after ice-off and are sought eagerly by trout because they represent an easy target. I fish my stillwater scud (tied on a straight-shank nymph hook) under an indicator.

Another good food source at this time are fathead minnows (*Pimephales promelas*). These small minnows are present in many of Colorado's lakes and are actually stocked in many stillwaters as a food source for the fish. I imitate the fathead minnows with a size 10 bead-head Woolly Bugger in gold or silver. I like to fish it from the shore and draw it up the slope break toward the shoreline.

Water boatmen and chironomids are also on the menu at this time and can be successfully fished in the shallows. I generally like to fish from shore at this time of year and often don't even bring my pontoon boat. Don't hesitate to throw a dry fly if you see surface activity. I have caught fish on my Colorado Crystal Beetle when the ice was still heavy on the lakes. I caught some aquatic beetle activity in March in a lake in South Park and the beetle pattern imitated the olive-colored beetles very well.

LATE EARLY SEASON TO TURNOVER

This period usually runs from turnover to mid-to-late May. During this time certain aquatic organisms are preparing to hatch and others are just adjusting to the warmer water conditions. I especially like to fish water boatman imitations at this time.

Water boatmen overwinter under the ice and are full-size adults at this time. They will mate and lay eggs in early June and then die. From June onward, only small, immature individuals are present until the fall, when they once again become a significant food source for the fish. Water boatmen inhabit the shallows of the lake because they breathe air and must periodically return to the surface to get a bubble of air. Fly patterns imitating water boatmen often incorporate flash materials to imitate the air bubble. Backswimmers generally have two generations in a season. They hatch from eggs early in the year and reach adult size in midseason. They lay eggs at this time and the nymphs will reach full size in late fall. They generally can live in deeper water than water boatmen but are important food items midseason and late in the year.

I always will fish my Colorado Crystal Beetle at this time and I feel that it is successful because it can imitate a number of different aquatic food organisms. It can look like a water boatman, a backswimmer, a snail, an aquatic beetle, or any variety of terrestrial insects.

Another aquatic food source that is active at this time is dragonfly nymphs. Dragonfly nymphs generally live from three to five years and at full size can be three to four inches long. They are a major food source for fish near the time when they migrate from the depths of a lake to near shore. This is usually in late spring, but there are some species that emerge later in summer or early fall. They will swim up to the shore and crawl out of the water to hatch into adults. Very few people see this emergence, as most dragonflies emerge at night to avoid bird predation.

I have caught the major dragonfly migration to the shoreline in South Park only a few times, but the fishing can be outstanding. The fish will locate along the shelf break at that time and be looking for the olive to brownish-olive nymphs swimming toward the shore. The strikes on your dragonfly nymph imitations can be savage and the fish will readily strike right next to the shore. Having a large fish on a very short line can be challenging. I generally fish my dragonfly imitations on a clear intermediate sinking line and have a 0X tippet. You want to stand on the shore and retrieve your dragonfly nymph imitation right to your boot tops.

Starting about the third week in May, I will fish dragonfly adults, either as single flies or in mated pairs. The dragonflies have usually emerged at this time and fish have seen a few of them on the water, either as cripples or while laying eggs. The mated pairs will fly over the water and will touch the water surface repeatedly, laying eggs each time they touch. You can often see fish swipe at the dragonflies when they lay their eggs. This can occur all summer and into early fall.

At this time of year, large chironomids are also generally present in most lakes. A size 12 chironomid is not unusual at this time and chironomid imitations are often fished suspended under an indicator or as a dropper behind a dry fly. The indicator can be polypropylene yarn or any number of commercial indicators.

I successfully fish a size 12 Chironomid Bomber pattern as a dropper behind a size 4 Colorado Crystal Beetle at this time of year. The chironomids typically rise slowly to the surface to hatch and the fish will cruise near the surface and try to intercept them on their rise. The trout often will be seen making head and tail rises when the chironomids are hatching, and they will pick off the chironomid pupae as they hang under the surface of the water. Bloodworm imitations (red chironomids) are a good choice at this time of year and red on any chironomid pattern is always a good idea.

SUMMERTIME: MAJOR HATCHES

What I consider the two major stillwater hatches occur from late May to early July, again depending on altitude and time of ice-off. These hatches are the *Callibaetis* mayfly and the damsels. One of the nicest things about this time of year is that lake hatches are at their peak when rivers in Colorado are usually in full runoff mode. This gives fly fishers an alternative to the fast-moving rivers, and many hit the lakes at this time.

Callibaetis mayflies spend winter under the ice. They are fairly good-sized nymphs early in the year, and the first generation will hatch in late May or early June. The *Callibaetis* life cycle is about six weeks from egg to egg-laying adult. They will have two to three generations in a season, so you will see this mayfly emerge from late May to early September. Each succeeding generation will be smaller than the last; *Callibaetis* in May are a size 14 or 12 and in September will be a size 18. The most prolific hatches usually occur in the first and second generations, while the last hatch can be very sparse.

The *Callibaetis* typically emerge from about 10 a.m. to 11 a.m. and the hatch can continue for several hours. I have fished *Callibaetis* hatches in driving sleet and snow in June. In colder, cloudy weather, the duns sit on the water a little longer than normal and the dry-fly fishing is better. On typical warm summer days, the *Callibaetis* nymphs rise to the surface, split their nymphal cases, and fly away in less than a minute. My favorite *Callibaetis* emerger imitation is the Callibaetis Quigley Cripple, which imitates the dun emerging from its

The Callibaetis *hatch occurs in late May or early June on stillwaters. For many stillwater enthusiasts, the* Callibaetis *emergence is the highlight of the entire lake-fishing season.* JAY NICHOLS

nymphal shuck. This pattern was originated by Bob Quigley to imitate PMD (Pale Morning Dun) mayflies on Hat Creek in California. He quickly adapted the pattern to imitate any emerging mayfly by varying the size and body/wing colors. This is generally the only *Callibaetis* pattern that I use to imitate the duns and spinners of this mayfly. I will often fish a Callibaetis Quigley Cripple during the hatch with a *Callibaetis* nymph dropper.

A very good strategy for fishing the summer *Callibaetis* hatch is to fish a *Callibaetis* nymph suspended under an indicator prior to the hatch. I take my pontoon boat over the weed beds that *Callibaetis* inhabit and let the fly line with indicator trail behind me. I will kick several times with my fins and then stop, letting the nymph sink slowly. This motion will make the nymph rise and fall over the weed bed. This mimics the natural motion of a *Callibaetis* nymph prior to emergence. A *Callibaetis* nymph will get an air bubble under its thorax, rise toward the surface, and then swim back down into the water column. It will do this several times before the air bubble gets too large and it must rise to the surface to emerge. The fish will be looking for these rising and falling nymphs prior to a *Callibaetis* hatch.

The second major hatch of the summer is the damsel hatch. This generally occurs around the first week of July, again depending on elevation and winter snowpack. What is great about the timing of this hatch is that it occurs when rivers are usually in runoff. I like to fish damsel adults and damsel tenerals (freshly emerged damsels) at this time. Tenerals are yellowish olive in color when they emerge from their nymphal shucks and must dry their wings and harden their bodies before taking flight. They often end up being blown into the water near the shoreline and fish will line up near shoreline vegetation looking for tenerals in the water. I fish a damsel adult with a damsel nymph dropper at this time.

I also fish mated pairs of damsels, which occur in blue-tan pairs and blue-blue pairs. Prior to the major damsel emergences, it can be very exciting fishing a damsel nymph from the shore. The damsels swim toward the shore and will crawl up near shore vegetation to emerge. Fish will line up facing outward from the shore and watch for swimming damsels coming in to emerge. I like to fish the damsel nymphs on a clear intermediate sinking line with a 3X tippet. The strikes are usually quite deliberate and hard.

An important thing to remember when fishing any dry fly on lakes is that you must never "line" a rising or cruising fish. With as many bird predators as we have in Colorado, any overhead shadow will immediately send fish down and greatly reduce your chances to hook up. False-cast your fly at right angles to the direction you want to place it and then lay out your cast without a false cast in that direction.

The midsummer period is also a great time to fish terrestrial patterns. These can be ants, beetles, bees, crickets, hopper imitations, or even large Chernobyl Ant variations. I have often caught my largest trout of the year on ant patterns such as my ICU Paintbrush Ant. Falls of flying ants can occur any time past June and when they do, all the fish in a lake will be feeding on ants. The surface of the lake literally boils with rises at this time. I have only caught a fall of flying ants a few times, but it is memorable.

Terrestrials are also a great go-to fly for high mountain lakes. These lakes often do not have the damsel and *Callibaetis* hatches of lower-elevation lakes, but they do have a lot of flying terrestrials and also what Gary LaFontaine terms "terrestrial rain." Mountain areas have violent updrafts that draw small insects upward in the air. These insects settle out as "terrestrial rain," often in late afternoon and early evening when winds die down. A great strategy for high mountain lakes is to fish a lake at daylight, as the terrestrials have fallen overnight in the dark and fish will cruise the lake at first light and pick up those insects.

LATE SUMMER

Toward the end of summer, the *Callibaetis* hatches get thinner, most damsels are already hatched, and terrestrials are in full swing. A good combination at this time is a beetle with a *Callibaetis* nymph dropper. Water boatmen are getting to full size and will be present in numbers, and the beetle provides a close imitation of a water boatman. The *Callibaetis* nymphs of the last generation are hatched and growing.

Immature damsel nymphs are often found in trout's stomach contents at this time, so it pays to tie and fish small damsel nymph imitations. Adult dragonflies will be actively laying eggs and offer a great opportunity to take some big fish. There will be adult damsels present and on the trout's menu up until the first frost.

Adult dragonflies are more hardy and can survive several frosts before dying off. I have caught trout on adult dragonflies as late as mid-October at elevations over 9,000 feet. I like to fish large terrestrials like Chernobyl Ants at this time, when they can attract some of the bigger fish.

EARLY FALL TO TURNOVER

The major hatches are over by this time, although if you are fortunate, you may see a water boatmen flight. Water boatmen have wings and can take off in flights to colonize new waters. I have only witnessed this once in twenty-plus years of fishing lakes, but such occurrences are feeding frenzies for the fish. I like to fish a water boatman as a dropper behind a beetle or even behind another water boatman.

Terrestrials are still a good option at this time right into mid-October. Chironomids will become a staple but they will be smaller than in the spring. They can be effectively fished

Stillwater experts like John Perizzolo know the importance of carrying a thorough selection of chironomids. This Spinney Mountain Reservoir rainbow was fooled with his Zombie Bomber Pupa.

under an indicator, as a dropper on a dry fly, or on a clear intermediate sinking line. Leeches, minnow imitations, dragonfly nymphs, scuds, *Callibaetis* nymphs, and small damsel nymphs are good subsurface patterns in this period, especially after the lakes turn over and the weed growth dies down.

TURNOVER TO ICE-ON

This time is a favorite of mine. Like the early season, it is cold. Your guides can ice up very easily and you need to dress for the weather. The fish will be feeding in preparation for the upcoming winter, so a well-presented fly will often be taken readily. After turnover, the weed growth dies down and subsurface flies can be fished without catching a lot of weeds. The fish are also very often close to the shallows, so it is easy to fish from the shore. I like to fish things like leeches, dragonfly nymphs, small damsel nymphs, and minnow patterns before the ice locks up the lakes—some very big fish can be taken at this time.

At this time I will especially target fish that prey on the fathead minnows. It is not unusual to have trout follow right to your boot tops and take a minnow imitation right at your feet. I usually fish minnow imitations on a clear intermediate sinking line with 0X tippet—the fish are not leader-shy when targeting minnows. Leech patterns fished on a clear intermediate sinking line are also a favorite of mine. Some of the "fish any time" patterns like scuds, Beadhead Princes, chironomids, and small *Callibaetis* nymphs can also be very productive. Lakes will generally ice over anywhere from late October to mid-November, depending on weather.

CONTRIBUTORS

Captain Chris Wells

Captain Chris Wells (303-324-1854) is the owner of Mile High Angler (milehighangler.com) and Tailing Charters (tailingcharters.com). He is also the fly-fishing ranch manager of The Meadows, a two-mile stretch of private water on the North Fork of the South Platte.

A native of Colorado, Wells started fly fishing around the age of five with his father, Dr. Gray Wells. Together they spent countless hours fishing the Colorado and South Platte Rivers. Wells started guiding for trout while attending college at Metropolitan State University in Denver where he earned degrees in Communications and Business Management. Wells has been a full-time guide for the past fifteen years.

Captain Wells is a certified U.S. Coast Guard captain and guides the Lower Florida Keys for tarpon, bonefish, and permit in the winter and spring. He guides for trout in Colorado during the summer and fall.

Captain Matt Thomas

Captain Matt Thomas (970-481-9086, Riplips.com) grew up with a fly rod in his hand. Tying flies and catching fish has been his passion from the beginning. Becoming a guide was a natural progression. With a start at the Blue Quill Angler in Evergreen, Colorado, in 1994, his experience quickly grew into what it is today.

Thomas has a consistent, growing business on Colorado's Western Slope, where he guides anglers on the Roaring Fork and Colorado Rivers. In 2004, Captain Thomas embarked on a new era of his guide career. After earning a captain's license through the US Coast Guard, he began guiding for Florida's giant migratory tarpon in the spring and Louisiana's monster redfish in the late fall.

In 2005 Captain Thomas was invited to be an individual Orvis-Endorsed Guide and to date remains the only individually endorsed guide in the state of Colorado.

Bob Dye

Bob Dye (303-674-4700) is a Colorado native with two passions in life: his family and fly fishing. Dye spends over 175 days a year on the water guiding for the Blue Quill Angler (bluequillangler.com) in Evergreen, Colorado; he spends most of his time on the Colorado River, consistently fooling hard-fished, wild brown trout. Dye has been guiding for twelve years, spending five years in Wyoming and seven in Colorado. He is a Simms Ambassador.

Dye grew up fishing the Colorado River with his father, Bob Dye. His knowledge of the Colorado River is unparalleled; he has fished the river and its feeder streams extensively, from the headwaters in Rocky Mountain National Park downstream to Silt. In addition to the Colorado River, Dye guides Troublesome Creek, Williams Fork, the Blue River, and the Cheesman Canyon, Deckers, and Dream Stream portions of the South Platte. Dye is the author of *Seasons of the Colorado*, published by Headwater Books in 2016.

Will Sands

Will Sands' (970-927-4374) passion for fly fishing and tying flies was instilled at an early age by his mother and father. He began fooling landlocked salmon on his own ties at the age of twelve. After drifting west to work as a backcountry ranger with the United States Forest Service, Sands discovered the bountiful waters of the Roaring Fork Valley. Shortly afterwards, he shifted careers toward the fly-fishing industry.

Sands has worked at Taylor Creek Fly Shop (taylorcreek.com) since 1999, guiding, managing the shop, and plying the rivers of the West. Sands is a fly designer for Umpqua Feather Merchants, and his Sands' Mysis is a popular fly on the Frying Pan for targeting the huge, *Mysis*-fed trout that reside below Ruedi Reservoir. Saltwater fishing and wingshooting excursions fill his free time. Sands resides in Basalt, Colorado, minutes away from some of the state's best fishing.

MARK ADAMS

Steve Henderson

Steve Henderson (970-846-4719, hendersonflyfishing.com) was born in Long Beach, California. His family moved to Big Bear Lake, California, when he was three years old and remained there until he was fourteen. Henderson spent much of these years wandering the lakes and small streams fishing for rainbows and brookies with his older brother. Henderson moved to Virginia when he was fifteen. There he was introduced to smallmouth bass fishing on the James River, Henderson spent many days on the James rock-hopping for smallmouth bass.

Henderson moved to Colorado in 1992 and started guiding in 1994. He now owns Henderson Fly Fishing in Steamboat Springs, where he has access to both public and private water in the Steamboat Valley.

Jason Booth

Jason Booth (970-901-9489) is one of the most respected and well-rounded anglers in Colorado's Gunnison Valley. Booth's passion for fly-fishing is unparalleled, and his addiction to catching selective trout will become obvious the first time you meet him. From the complexities of catching trout on nymphs, to a wide range of dry-fly applications and streamer tactics, Booth teach clients the nuances of catching trout on the fabled Gunnison River.

Booth is a co-owner of Gunnison River Guides (gunnisonriverguides.com), a fly-fishing guide service that caters to all levels and abilities. Booth and his partner Joel Aslanian have a combined thirty years guiding experience in the Gunnison Valley. When Booth is not guiding clients or fishing on his days off, he can be found hiking the backcountry in search of elk and deer. Booth and his wife Sherry live in a log home along the Gunnison River.

MARK ADAMS

Aaron Carithers

Aaron Carithers (970-759-0809, sanjuanguides.com) is a Colorado native whose family goes back five generations on the Front Range. Carithers' grandfather Arthur Ohanian introduced him to fly fishing at age seven, when he started fishing the Little Michigan in North Park before moving on to the Big Thompson, Poudre, and St. Vrain.

After attending Fort Lewis College in Durango, Carithers worked for Jerry Freeman's Anasazi Angler Guide Service for five seasons, guiding mostly on the San Juan River, and then spent six seasons guiding on the San Juan, the Piedra, the Animas, the Rio Grande, the Dolores, and Lime and Cascade Creeks for Duranglers. In 1998 Carithers purchased Anasazi Angler.

During Carithers' twenty-three years as a fly-fishing guide, outfitter, and business owner, he has had the good fortune to fish throughout the western United States, the Gulf Coast of Florida and Texas, the Yucatan, Belize, and the Bay Islands of Honduras. Carithers is currently the vice president of the San Juan River Guides Association.

STEVE SCHWEITZER

Mike Kruise

Mike Kruise (303-772-9110) is a Colorado native who grew up in the Longmont–Lyons area. Kruise began tying flies and fly fishing as an young boy. Kruise and his longtime friend Scott Bley opened the Laughing Grizzly Fly Shop (laughinggrizzlyflyshop.net) in Longmont in 2007. In addition to running the store's day-to-day operations, Kruise guides clients on the St. Vrain, the North Fork of the South Platte, the North Platte, Red Feather Lakes, and many Rocky Mountain National Park streams such as the Upper Poudre and the Colorado.

The Laughing Grizzly is a full-service and guide shop that offers the best names in fly-fishing products, and instruction in all facets of fly fishing. It has one of the largest fly-tying departments in Northern Colorado. Mike is a popular tying clinic presenter, and teaches all types of fly casting. Mike has guided on the San Juan and the North Platte. Mike is the coauthor a book, *A Fly Fishing Guide to Colorado's Indian Peaks Wilderness Area*, with Steve Schweitzer.

MIKE KRUISE

Dick Shinton

Dick Shinton (303-772-9110) was a human resources executive with Colorado Front Range technology companies for more than thirty years, during which he consulted with a variety of clients in human resources and organizational development. Shinton has also served on the boards of directors of several nonprofit organizations.

After retirement, Shinton became a guide for Estes Anglers in Estes Park. In 2007, Shinton joined the newly opened Laughing Grizzly Fly Shop (laughinggrizzlyflyshop.net) in Longmont, working in the shop and as a guide. His "office" is Rocky Mountain National Park, where he introduces his guide clients to the joys of fishing for wild trout in small streams. As a fly-tying clinic leader, Shinto specializes in simple fly patterns that catch fish. He is the Youth Education Chair of the Board of the St Vrain Anglers Chapter of Trout Unlimited, teaches a Kids Learn to Fly Fish program, and has been on the staff of the Colorado Trout Unlimited Youth River Conservation and Fly Fishing Camp since 2008.

BEN OLSON

Ben Olson

Ben Olson (970-835-5050) was born in Denver but grew up in Iowa. Olson brings this Midwest hospitality to Black Canyon Anglers (blackcanyon anglers.com), where he is a guide and a director. Olson strives to make every client feel at home when they visit Black Canyon Angler's lodge. Olson has been guiding on the Gunnison River since 2005. In addition to guiding, he has owned his own fly shop, taught hundreds classes on fly fishing, entomology, and fly tying, and served as president of the local Trout Unlimited Chapter. He enjoys angling in both fresh and salt water. A strong boatman, Olson explores multiday float trips all over the country in his spare time.

Olson took over the helm of Black Canyon Anglers in 2010. He is driven to provide the best customer service in the industry, extending a family-felt welcome to each client that walks through the door.

Josh Cranson

Josh Cranson (970-835-5050) is a Colorado native who has been fly fishing since childhood. He grew up on a farm along the banks of the North Fork of the Gunnison. During his youth he spent much of his time exploring the rivers and creeks in the West Elk Wilderness and the Black Canyon.

In 2001 he began guiding multiday wilderness float trips through the Black Canyon and within five years he became head guide for Black Canyon Anglers (blackcanyonanglers.com). Josh is known for his flawless moves in the rapids, efficiency in camp, humble personality, and world-famous cooking. He prides himself on making sure clients experience the best quality trip he can provide. When Josh is not on the water you will find him guiding elk hunts in the Ragged Wilderness, helping out on the family farm, or hanging out with his wife Cris and their two Labradors in an off-grid, solar-powered home they built from the ground up.

Greg Felt

Greg Felt (719-539-4223) is co-owner and guide service manager of ArkAnglers (arkanglers.com), based on the banks of the Arkansas River in Salida, Colorado, and with a second fly shop in Buena Vista. As time allows, he does float-fish guiding, a continuous pursuit of Greg's since 1985. Greg has developed a reputation for comprehensive and comprehendible fishing reports and presentations; he receives daily reports from his staff of eighteen guides and the many retail customers who frequent ArkAnglers, and he studies weather, flow, and snowpack data, gathering insight from his long involvement in the water management community. He combines this input with his own direct experience on the river. He is the best source for accurate and timely information about the Arkansas River fishery.

Felt started out as a regular kid, but once a fly rod was placed in his hand during his tenth summer he became a committed fly fisherman. A nearly fatal inner tube trip the next year made a lifelong whitewater enthusiast out of him. Thirty years into these as a vocation, he voices few regrets.

MARK ADAMS

Greg Blessing

Greg Blessing (719-337-5084, troutblessing.com) started fishing at the age of four with his grandpa Clark in the Adirondacks in upstate New York. Blessing's grandpa bought him a Hank Roberts fly-tying kit and fly rod for Christmas in 1966. This was a beginning to a lifetime enjoyment of fly fishing.

Blessing has been guiding for over twenty-five years. He is the head guide at Angler's Covey fly shop in Colorado Springs, Colorado. His expertise includes access to public and private waterways with his specialty being fooling the super-selective trout that reside in the South Platte River at Elevenmile Canyon.

Blessing has held a Montana Guide License for seventeen years, and frequently guides the Big Horn River out of Fort Smith, Montana. Blessing is a FFF Certified Casting Instructor and a fly designer for the Orvis Company. Blessing's patterns are available in fly shops throughout the United States or directly from the Orvis Company.

JAY NICHOLS

Landon Mayer

With over two decades of experience, Landon Mayer (719-210-0619, landonmayer.com) is fueled by an addiction to pursuing large trout with small flies and lightweight fly-fishing equipment. Mayer shares his techniques and on-river knowledge with fellow anglers and has developed innovative strategies for sighting, hooking, and landing selective trout. He shares these tips and secrets in his books *Colorado's Best Fly Fishing*, *Sight Fishing for Trout*, and *How to Catch the Biggest Trout of Your Life*, in addition to two DVDs: *Landing the Trout of Your Life* and *Weapons of Bass Production*, both of which also feature John Barr.

Mayer is a contributing writer for *Fly Fisherman* and *High Country Angler* magazines. His contributions also have been featured in *Fly Rod and Reel*, *American Angler*, *Southwest Fly Fishing*, *Field and Stream*, and *Fish and Fly* magazines.

Mayer is a royalty fly designer for Umpqua Feather Merchants. He has been guiding in Colorado on the South Platte River for the last seventeen years, and one full season on the Naknek River in Alaska. He resides with his wife, Michelle, and their four children in Florissant, Colorado.

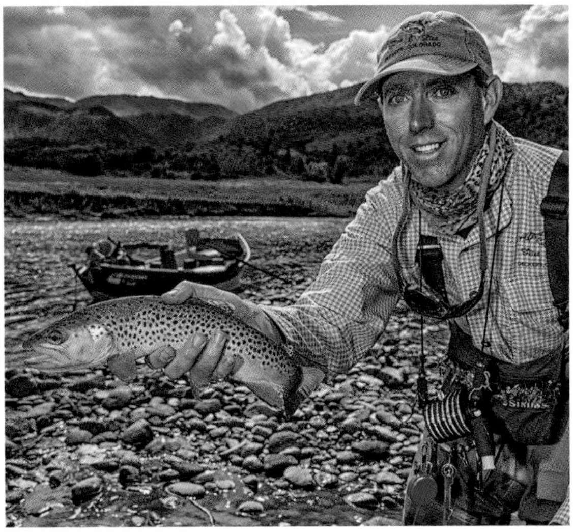

MARK ADAMS

Jeremy Hyatt

Jeremy Hyatt (303-647-2237, flies-n-lies.com) is a professional angler and guide with over fifteen years of experience. His home water is the South Platte River near the town of Deckers, Colorado. Hyatt is a native of Evergreen, Colorado. Hyatt has been fly fishing in Colorado since his early youth. The passion that he developed for the sport, coupled with his love of and respect for the outdoors, drove him to turn what most people consider a hobby into a lifestyle.

Hyatt was fortunate to have fantastic fly-fishing mentors such as Kirk Deeter and Tom Whitley. He has honed the information and guidance he received from them into a finely tuned fly-fishing approach. Hyatt enjoys passing on his knowledge of entomology, proper fly presentation through drift mechanics, and casting fundamentals.

Now the owner of Flies & Lies on the South Platte River near Deckers, Hyatt spends most of his time on the river with clients, developing new fly patterns, or in the fly shop helping customers with specific river information, equipment, rigging questions, and fly selection. Hyatt resides in Bailey, Colorado with his wife, Danielle, and his daughter Dalilah.

CHRIS PETTINE

Dr. Eric Pettine

Dr. Eric Pettine (970-218-0525, eapfish@comcast.net) has been fly fishing for more than sixty-five years, tying flies for fifty-four years, and guiding since 1961. For seven years, Dr. Pettine was on the Chevy Truck Pro Team of outdoor personalities doing print ads and producing fly-fishing videos. They were some of the first outdoor videos produced.

Dr. Pettine has done fly-fishing presentations and tying demos for International Sportsmen's Expositions, Trout Unlimited, and Federation of Fly Fishers clubs for more than thirty years. Dr. Pettine has written numerous articles in fly-fishing magazines and is the author of the *North Platte River Journal*. Dr. Pettine is a fly designer for Umpqua Feather Merchants in Louisville, Colorado. He also has written a biweekly column for the *Coloradoan* newspaper in Fort Collins for five years.

Dr. Pettine has hosted trips to Norlakes Lodges in British Columbia and to Cinco Rios Lodge in Chile among others. Dr. Pettine and his wife reside in Windsor, Colorado.

Richard Pilatzke

Richard Pilatzke (370-979-8425, rhpiscator@aol.com) has lived in Colorado for over thirty years. Pilatzke has been fly-tying and fly-fishing for over thirty-four years, and for the last twenty years he has specialized in tying flies for and fishing the high mountain lakes of Colorado. He especially likes fishing damselfly and dragonfly hatches and terrestrials.

Pilatzke does fly-tying demonstrations at national and international expos and conferences and at clinics in many Denver-area fly shops and TU and FFF chapters. Pilatzke's flies have been exhibited at the Boulder Art Museum and the Prichard Art Museum in Idaho Falls. Pilatzke's fly patterns have been featured in books by Gary LaFontaine, Pat Dorsey, Marty Bartholomew, and Jim Schollmeyer and also in *Southwest Fly Fishing*.

Pilatzke is a member of Cutthroat Chapter of Trout Unlimited in Littleton and has been a member of the Board of Directors for over twenty years. Pilatzke is a life member of both Trout Unlimited and the Federation of Fly Fishers. He lives in Littleton, Colorado, with his wife, Cheryl, and border collie mix, Bella.

BOB DYE

John Perizzolo

John Perizzolo (303-674-4700) was born and raised in Colorado and he has guided throughout the state on the South Platte, the Blue, the Colorado, Williams Fork, and the Arkansas, as well as on many of Colorado's stillwaters.

Perizzolo has been guiding for twelve years and is a senior guide at the Blue Quill Angler (bluequillangler.com) in Evergreen, Colorado. His specialty is float trips on the Colorado River from Pumphouse to Radium, and powerboat stillwater guided trips on Spinney Mountain and Antero Reservoirs. Perizzolo also guides timberline lakes for cutthroats.

During the winter months, Perizzolo is a bird-hunting guide, both upland and waterfowl, over a five-state area. Perizzolo used to breed, train, and field trial Labrador retrievers; though he no longer trains or competes professionally, he still trains, hunts, and guides with three labs of his own. Recently Perizzolo started Sweetwater Saddlery (sweetwatersaddlery.com) and stays busy making custom holsters for handguns, as well as other leather products like the HemoHolster for fly fisherman. Perizzolo and his wife, Denise, reside near Bailey, Colorado.

WILL BLANCHARD

Will Blanchard

Will Blanchard (970-259-0484, will@gottrout.com) was raised on the small brook trout creeks of Virginia's Shenandoah Valley. He was lured to Durango, Colorado, in 1989 by the mountains and streams of the West. Blanchard's passion for fly fishing and the outdoors eventually led him to make a career in the fly-fishing industry.

Blanchard is one of the head guides and owner of Durango-based guide service Animas Valley Anglers. He can be found fishing and guiding throughout the region well over 200 days each year. He started guiding in 1992 and brings a tremendous amount of knowledge and expertise and a positive, enjoyable attitude to every guide trip. Float or wade, Blanchard is comfortable on any body of water, in pursuit of any species of fish—Rio Grande browns, picky San Juan rainbows, Babine steelhead, or anything in between.

When he is not guiding, booking trips, or documenting the fly-fishing experience through the lens of his camera, he can be found playing hockey, splitting firewood, and chasing around his toddler.

Matt Miles

Matt Miles (434-238-2720, mattmilesflyfishing.com) grew up in Lynchburg, Virginia, and started fly fishing as a young boy. In 1996, after graduating from high school, Miles moved to Colorado to chase his dream of becoming a fly-fishing guide. While in Colorado, Miles met Pat Dorsey on the Williams Fork River and they became immediate friends. Miles started guiding with Blue Quill Angler in Evergreen, Colorado, in 1997, where he guided customers on the South Platte and its North Fork and Arkansas, Blue, Colorado, and Williams Fork Rivers.

Miles' specialty has always been the Colorado and Williams Fork Rivers near Parshall, Colorado. In 2003, Miles moved back to Virginia to start a family and open up his own outfitting business. Miles is an innovative fly tier and is a fly designer for Umpqua Feather Merchants in Louisville, Colorado. When Miles is not guiding clients, he spends his spare time with his wife, Tara, and son, Brody.

LANDON MAYER

Devan Ence

Devan Ence (208-270-4674, devanence@gmail.com) is an accomplished fly tier and fly designer with Solitude Fly Company. Two of his most popular patterns are the Tungsten Salvation Nymph and the Bruised Baetis Nymph. Ence is also a member of the Daiichi Pro Staff. Throughout his fishing career he has spent a tremendous amount of time at the vise as a commercial tier. Ence is passionate about photography and filming anything that has to do with the outdoors.

Ence managed and guided full-time for the Estes Angler in Estes Park, Colorado, before moving to southwest Colorado where he guided full-time and managed Conejos River Anglers for seven years. Currently Ence is the assistant manager at Henry's Fork Anglers.

When Ence is not on the water guiding or at the vise tying flies, he is spending time with his beautiful wife Jasmine and their son Emmett. Jasmine is passionate about fly fishing and the family travels the country pursuing anything that will eat a fly.

Mark Adams

Mark Adams (810-516-6623, m.5280@hotmail.com) was raised in the flatlands of southern Michigan, where he developed a passion for fishing at an early age, tying all manner of fuzzy bugs to fling at the sunfish and largemouths of the area's numerous farm ponds. A special uncle kindled within Mark an interest in fly fishing, starting a 40-plus-year love affair with the sport. Immediately upon getting a car, Adams' first trip was to the Wanigas Fly Rod Company, the fly shop of TU founder Art Neumann in nearby Saginaw. With a car and a fly rod the rivers of northern Michigan became his pursuit, the sunfish and largemouths replaced by brown trout, rainbows, and brookies. College and professional school at the University of Michigan stymied his angling opportunities for many years, but upon graduation and the establishment of a practice in Flint, Michigan, the gates to the north and the fabled Au Sable River opened once more.

In 2006 a professional relocation to Denver provided Mark with a dream come true—direct access to the fabled trout water of the West. Here he marries his passions of photography and angling as he pursues his loves from Montana to New Mexico. He still returns yearly to the fabled Au Sable and her Hex hatch. His photography credits include several fly fishing books and *Fly Fisherman Magazine* contributions.

Additional contributors

Ed Engle, Joe Shafer, Robert Younghanz, Jim Cannon, Kirk Deeter, Tim Heng, John Barr, Ray Chang, Rick Takahashi, Randy Gorby, Greg Garcia, Mike Mercer, Joe Mitchell, J Core, Craig Mathews, Pat Bennett, Larry Kingrey, Randy Smith, and Roger Bittell.

REFERENCES

Arbona, Fred, Jr. *Mayflies, the Angler, and the Trout*. New York: Lyons and Burford, 1989.

Barr, John. *Barr Flies: How to Tie and Fish the Copper John, the Barr Emerger, and Dozens of Other Patterns, Variations, and Rigs*. Mechanicsburg, PA: Stackpole Books, 2007.

Borger, Gary A. *Presentation*. Harrisburg, PA: Tomorrow River Press, 1995.

Craven, Charlie. *Charlie Craven's Basic Fly Tying: Modern Techniques for Flies That Catch Fish*. Mechanicsburg, PA: Stackpole Books, 2008.

———. *Charlie's Fly Box: Signature Flies for Fresh and Salt Water*. Mechanicsburg, PA: Stackpole Books, 2010.

Dorsey, Pat. *A Fly Fisher's Guide to the South Platte River*. Boulder, CO: Pruett, 2005.

———. *Fly Fishing Tailwaters: Tactics and Patterns for Year-Round Waters*. Mechanicsburg, PA: Stackpole Books, 2010.

———. *Tying & Fishing Tailwater Flies: 500 Step-by-Step Photos for 24 Proven Patterns*. Mechanicsburg, PA: Stackpole Books / Headwater Books, 2011.

Engle, Ed. *Fishing Small Flies*. Mechanicsburg, PA: Stackpole Books, 2005.

———. *Fly Fishing the Tailwaters*. Harrisburg, PA: Stackpole Books, 1991.

Hafele, Rick. *Nymph-Fishing Rivers & Streams: A Biologist's View of Taking Trout Below the Surface*. Mechanicsburg, PA: Stackpole Books, 2006.

Hafele, Rick, and Scott Roederer. *An Angler's Guide to Aquatic Insects and Their Imitations*. Boulder, CO: Johnson, 1987.

Harrop, Réne. *Trout Hunter: The Way of an Angler*. Boulder, CO: Pruett, 2003.

Lawson, Mike. *Spring Creeks*. Mechanicsburg, PA: Stackpole Books, 2003.

Marinaro, Vincent C. *In the Ring of the Rise*. New York: Crown, 1976.

Miller, Bob. *Tricos: A Practical Guide to Fishing and Tying Tricorythode Imitations and Related Patterns*. Allentown, PA: Rod Crafters Press, 1997.

Nichols, Jay. *Tying Dry Flies: How to Tie and Fish Must-Have Trout Patterns*. Mechanicsburg, PA: Stackpole Books, 2009.

Pobst, Dick. *Trout Stream Insects: An Orvis Streamside Guide*. New York: Lyons and Burford, 1990.

Takahashi, Rick, and Jerry Hubka. *Modern Midges: Tying & Fishing the World's Most Effective Patterns*. Mechanicsburg, PA: Stackpole Books, 2009.

INDEX